Burn:

Burns the Radical

Poetry and Politics in
Late Eighteenth-Century Scotland

Liam McIlvanney

TUCKWELL PRESS

First published in Great Britain in 2002 by
Tuckwell Press Ltd, The Mill House
Phantassie, East Linton
East Lothian, Scotland

Reprinted in 2003

ISBN 1 86232 177 9

The publishers acknowledge subsidy from the
Scottish Arts Council towards the publication of this volume

British Library Cataloguing-in-Publication Data
A catalogue record is available on request from
the British Library

Typeset by Antony Gray
Printed and bound by Bell and Bain Ltd, Glasgow

For Valerie

Contents

Acknowledgements

My thanks are due to the University of Aberdeen and to the Arts and Humanities Research Board for periods of research leave that enabled me to finish this book. I would also like to thank the Atlanta Burns Club for helping to finance a research trip to the Thomas Cooper Library at the University of South Carolina in 1996. Of the many scholars who have provided assistance and encouragement over the course of this project, Bernard O'Donoghue, Kenneth Simpson and Andrew Noble deserve my warmest thanks. For perceptive comments on individual chapters, I am very grateful to George Watson, Hamish Mathison, Fiona Stafford, Tom Paulin, John Tuckwell, Alistair Rennie, Donald Wesling, Gerry Carruthers, and Siobhán McIlvanney. In preparing this book, I have also benefited from many hours of stimulating discussion with students on my Burns course at the University of Aberdeen, and my sincere thanks are due to them.

Parts of this work first appeared, in slightly different form, in the following places: ' "Why should na poor folk mowe?": An Example of Folk Humour in Burns', in *Scottish Literary Journal*, 23 (1996), 43–53; ' "Sacred Freedom": Presbyterian Radicalism and the Politics of Robert Burns', in *Love and Liberty: Robert Burns, A Bicentenary Celebration*, ed. by Kenneth Simpson (East Linton, 1997), pp. 168–82; and 'Robert Burns and the Ulster Scots Literary Revival of the 1790s', in *Bullán: An Irish Studies Journal*, 4.2 (Winter 1999 / Spring 2000), 125–43. I am grateful to the respective editors for permission to reproduce this material.

I would also like to record my gratitude to the staff of the following libraries: the Bodleian Library; the Oxford University English Faculty Library; Glasgow University Library; the Mitchell Library, Glasgow; Aberdeen University Library; the Thomas Cooper Library at the University of South Carolina; the Linen Hall Library, Belfast; the National Library of Scotland; and the Dick Institute, Kilmarnock.

My greatest debts, finally, are personal ones. I owe a great deal to the inspiration and encouragement of my late mother, Moira, and to the love and support of my wife, Valerie, and my son, Andrew.

Abbreviations

Kinsley   *The Poems and Songs of Robert Burns*, ed. by James Kinsley, 3 vols (Oxford: Clarendon Press, 1968)

Note: The Letter K followed by a number, in parenthesis after the title of a poem, refers to the numbering system employed by Kinsley, and not to page numbers.

Note 2: While following Kinsley's texts, I have supplied the missing letters in proper names and place-names, where Burns disguised these with asterisks.

Letters   *The Letters of Robert Burns*, ed. by J. De Lancey Ferguson, 2nd edn, rev. by G. Ross Roy, 2 vols (Oxford: Clarendon Press, 1985)

Introduction

On 1st July, 1999, the first Scottish Parliament in almost three hundred years opened its doors on Edinburgh's Mound. It was a day of rather vacuous festivity, one of those ceremonial occasions at which, protractedly, under the languid gaze of the television cameras, not a great deal happens. There were fanfares and processions, sedate flag-waving crowds, some speeches and recitations. In time, however, the day did find its focus, the iconic moment that would define the event. It came, with the new parliamentarians assembled in the chamber, and the invited guests seated in the gallery, when the folksinger Sheena Wellington sang a song by Robert Burns: 'Is there for honest Poverty', better known as 'A Man's a Man for a' that'. She sang unaccompanied, her strong voice gathering resonance in the hushed chamber. And the Queen, the Duke of Edinburgh and the Prince of Wales sat in respectful silence, listening to lines about rank being merely 'the guinea's stamp', about 'yon birkie ca'd, a lord', about the 'tinsel show' of wealth and privilege. The MSPs joined in on the final verse, with its prayer for universal brotherhood: 'That Man to Man the warld o'er, / Shall brothers be for a' that'.

The song was a fitting overture to the work of a new parliament, a reminder of high ideals and aspirations before the workaday business of debates and committees and political compromise. But the occasion also marked a watershed in the public celebration of Scotland's 'National Bard'. For much of the nineteenth and twentieth centuries, the Burns invoked at public, ceremonial occasions was an anodyne icon of rural virtue and domestic piety. For a nation traumatised by industrialisation, the rise of the cities, and mass emigration, Burns came to symbolise the vanished certainties of an increasingly mythologised rural past. Throughout the nineteenth century, the key text for Burns Night orators and literary sermonisers was not 'A Man's a Man for a' that', but – inevitably – 'The Cotter's Saturday Night', held up as a documentary image of the 'true' Scotland that was on the way out.[1] Editors and biographers colluded in promulgating this 'largely sentimental and apolitical vision of Burns'.[2] The radical bard of the democratic revolution, with his rumbustious 'heresies in Church and State',[3] had been transformed into the earnest hymner of

---

1 Andrew Nash, 'The Cotter's Kailyard', in *Robert Burns and Cultural Authority*, ed. by Robert Crawford (Edinburgh, 1997), pp. 180–197.
2 Richard J. Finlay, 'The Burns Cult and Scottish Identity in the Nineteenth and Twentieth Centuries', in *Love and Liberty: Robert Burns, A Bicentenary Celebration*, ed. by Kenneth Simpson (East Linton, 1997), pp. 69–78 (p. 75).
3 'Fragment – Epistle from Esopus to Maria' (K, 486).

peasant virtue, the poet laureate of family values. Writing in the 1940s, Edwin Muir summarised the process neatly by observing that 'Holy Willie, after being the poet's butt, has now become the keeper of his memory'.[4]

It may be that, with the rendition of 'A Man's a Man' at the opening of the new Scottish parliament, Holy Willie has been relieved of his post. The mythologised Burns of the Victorian bardolaters has been all but laid aside, in both popular and academic approaches to the poet. And if it is no longer the case that Burns's 'worshippers are ashamed of the best part of his nature and his work',[5] as De Lancey Ferguson complained in 1939, then the credit must go to the many scholars and critics who, over the past six decades, have restored Burns to his intellectual and cultural contexts by attending to the full range and complexity of his poetic production. De Lancey Fergusson holds a distinguished place on this roster, alongside critics like Franklyn Bliss Snyder, David Daiches, James Kinsley, John C. Weston, Carol McGuirk, Raymond Bentman, Kenneth Simpson and Robert Crawford.

As far as our understanding of Burns's politics is concerned, mention must be made of J. R. Campbell's incisive and unjustly neglected little pamphlet, *Burns the Democrat* (1945), which, in the course of forty pages, neatly expounds the poet's dissident views. However, perhaps most significant here – as in so many aspects of Burns criticism – has been the work of Thomas Crawford. Crawford's 1960 study brings a new sophistication to the treatment of Burns's politics. Focusing shrewdly on Burns's technique of 'vernacular raillery', Crawford provides brilliant close readings of poems in which 'the American Revolution and the Enlightenment, agrarian crisis and class conflict' are inescapable points of reference. His discussion of the concept of 'liberty' in the poet's work is a critical *tour de force*. Later scholars have built on Crawford's foundations, and indeed his influence can still be detected in some of the important work of the past five or six years, when interest in Burns's politics has burgeoned. In 1996, Patrick Scott Hogg sparked an intense and often intemperate debate when he announced his discovery of 'lost' radical poems by Burns, retrieved from the files of opposition newspapers. Around the same time, a lively new collection of essays, edited by Robert Crawford, explored Burns's resistance to various forms of 'cultural authority'. More recently, we have seen Jeffrey Skoblow's virtuoso study of Burns's dissident poetics and, most important of all, a major new edition of the poems, which specifically aims to reconstitute Burns as a major figure in the 'radical British literary culture which emerged with the loss of America'.[6]

4 Edwin Muir, 'Burns and Holy Willie', in *Edwin Muir: Uncollected Scottish Criticism*, ed. by Andrew Noble (London, 1982), p. 190.
5 J. De Lancey Ferguson, *Pride and Passion: Robert Burns 1759–1796* (New York, 1939), p. 308.
6 J. R. Campbell, *Burns the Democrat* (Glasgow, 1945); Thomas Crawford, *Burns: A Study of the Poems and Songs* (1960; repr. Edinburgh, 1994), pp. 147–92, 236–56; Patrick Scott Hogg, *Robert Burns: The Lost Poems* (Glasgow, 1997); *The Canongate*

Such work has enlarged our awareness of Burns's radical writings. There remain, however, certain powerful obstacles to a proper appreciation of Burns's political poetry. The first of these is the persistent conception of Burns's satires as lightweight occasional poems. This view originates with the brief 'Character Sketch' of Burns written by his friend Maria Riddell, which appeared in the *Dumfries Journal* shortly after the poet's death:

> The keenness of satire was, I am at a loss whether to say his forte or his foible; for though nature had endowed him with a portion of the most pointed excellence in that dangerous talent, he suffered it too often to be the vehicle of personal and sometimes unfounded animosities . . . [T]he darts of ridicule were frequently directed as the caprice of the instant suggested, or the altercations of parties and of persons happened to kindle the restlessness of his spirit into interest or aversion.[7]

Everything in Riddell's account is calculated to dispel the notion that Burns's political satires were motivated by anything more coherent than a momentary access of spleen or an impetuous sally of wit. '[H]is wit . . . had always the start of his judgement', Riddell asserts, and trusts that 'much allowance will be made by a candid mind for the splenetic warmth of a spirit whom "distress had spited with the world," and which . . . continually experienced the curbs imposed by the waywardness of his fortune'.[8] The note of condescension here is palpable. Burns's satires are to be treated with indulgence, as the regrettable excesses of a lower-class poet whose natural animosity was often inflamed by pique. We are not far here from the peevish Burns who, according to his brother Gilbert, betrayed a 'particular jealousy of people who were richer than himself, or who had more consequence in life'.[9]

Riddell's treatment of the satires as a kind of proletarian safety-valve, a way for the poet to let off steam, is echoed by later critics, including those who look to celebrate – rather than excuse – Burns's satirical output. In an influential essay, John C. Weston argues that, for Burns, satire is 'simply an instrument of self-therapy, revenge, and protection . . . He seems always to have composed satire under the immediate emotion of resentment'.[10] Donald Low, too, contends that the 'basis of a good deal of Burns's satiric writing is personal'.[11] The point is not that

---

Burns: The Complete Poems and Songs of Robert Burns, ed. by Andrew Noble and Patrick Scott Hogg (Edinburgh, 2001); *Robert Burns and Cultural Authority* (*op. cit.*); Jeffrey Skoblow, *Dooble Tongue: Scots, Burns, Contradiction* (Newark, NJ, 2001).

7 *Robert Burns: The Critical Heritage*, ed. by Donald A. Low (London, 1974), p. 103.

8 *The Critical Heritage*, p. 103.

9 Gilbert Burns's memoir of his brother, originally composed as a letter to Mrs Dunlop in 1797, is reproduced in Alan Bold, *A Burns Companion* (London, 1991), pp. 418–28 (p. 425).

10 John C. Weston, 'Robert Burns's Satire', in *The Art of Robert Burns*, ed. by R. D. S. Jack and Andrew Noble (London, 1982), pp. 36–58 (pp. 45, 46).

11 Donald A. Low, *Robert Burns* (Edinburgh, 1986), p. 61.

these views are necessarily wrong. Burns doubtless did at times compose under the spur of indignation, and he did employ his satire to settle personal scores: the factor in 'The Twa Dogs', for instance, is drawn from the life. But the problem with this type of approach is that it once more obscures the intellectual sophistication of Burns's work. It tends to suggest that his satires are fuelled *only* by 'class anger',[12] and not by a principled and coherent critique of the British political system. The image of an intemperate, capricious, splenetic Burns assists those critics who prefer to trivialise and disparage Burns's political intelligence – it creates the kind of situation in which W. P. Ker can fatuously remark of Burns that 'His Scottish politics are determined by Scotch drink'.[13]

Criticism of Burns's radical poetry is further hampered by the notion of Burns's political 'confusion'. Since Ramsay of Ochtertyre described Burns's principles as 'abundantly motley'[14] – Burns being both passionate Jacobite and radical Whig – commentators have tended to dismiss his politics as hopelessly muddled and inconsistent.[15] From this diagnosis of political confusion, it is a short step to the trite proposition that Burns is all things to all men – Edwin Muir's 'Protean figure' whom 'we can all shape ... to our own liking', a judgement echoed recently in Don Paterson's reference to Burns's 'furious shapeshifting'.[16] Again, there is a degree of truth in these characterisations. Burns is writing poetry, not political philosophy, and as such is not aiming for strict consistency or logical coherence. Nevertheless, Burns's politics *are* more coherent than either Ramsay or Muir suggests. Like other radicals of the period, he drew on a wide variety of intellectual traditions and discourses, but there are (as I hope to show) common threads and motifs which run from the early satires through to the late political songs. There is also – it is important to note – no necessary contradiction between Burns's radicalism and his Jacobitism. By the later eighteenth century, Jacobitism as a cause was dead, its anti-Hanoverian rhetoric taken up by the radical Whigs.[17] It would, moreover, be foolish to assume that Burns is equally committed to each of the political idioms he articulates. As Tom Paulin has pertinently observed:

> The choice of a political subject entails no necessary or complete commitment
> to an ideology – Burns, for example, was a radical republican but he nevertheless

12 Weston, p. 41.
13 'The Politics of Burns', in *Collected Essays of W. P. Ker*, ed. by Charles Whibley, 2 vols (London, 1925), I, 138.
14 John Ramsay of Ochtertyre, *Scotland and Scotsmen in the Eighteenth Century*, ed. by Alexander Allardyce, 2 vols (Edinburgh, 1888), II, 554.
15 See, for instance, Ian McIntyre, *Dirt & Deity: A Life of Robert Burns* (London, 1995), p. 123.
16 Edwin Muir, 'The Burns Myth', in *New Judgements: Robert Burns*, ed. by William Montgomerie (Glasgow, 1947), pp. 5–12 (p. 6); *Robert Burns: Poems selected by Don Paterson* (London, 2001), vii.
17 De Lancey Ferguson, *Pride and Passion*, p. 287. On the alliance between Jacobitism and radical Whiggism, see also Fintan O' Toole, *A Traitor's Kiss: The Life of Richard Brinsley Sheridan* (London, 1997), pp. 31–2.

based 'Charlie He's My Darling' on popular Jacobite songs about the Young Pretender. He could combine a dedicated egalitarianism with a pride in the House of Stuart that was both personal and national.[18]

Burns would not be the last Scot to cherish the House of Stuart as a symbol of national pride, while holding no brief for monarchical absolutism.

If Burns's Jacobitism does not adequately define his politics, then neither does his Jacobinism. Since Thomas De Quincey, in his essay on 'A Liverpool Coterie', entered his 'protestation on behalf of Burns's jacobinism',[19] Burn criticism has been dogged by the lazy assumption that the political songs and satires are best understood as a response to the French Revolution. Overwhelmingly, critics have viewed Burns's politics, not merely as part of a democratic historical moment whose climactic expression was the Revolution of 1789, but as somehow defined and even constituted by that event. In his essay on Burns's 'Life, Genius, Achievement' in the centenary edition of the poems, W. E. Henley set the tone for modern commentators by noting Burns's 'rather noisy sympathy with the leading ideas of the French Revolution'. Subsequent critics have followed this lead, including Hector Macpherson, who sees Burns as 'the incarnation of the new [Revolutionary] spirit'; Christina Keith, who avers that 'Liberty, Equality and Fraternity are the keynotes of all Burns's social thought'; Howard Brogan, who refers to the poet's 'revolutionary idealism'; and W. J. Murray, who finds that the poet's political ideals 'were, broadly speaking, the ideals of the French Revolution'. John Strawhorn even argues that it was the outbreak of the French Revolution that *initiated* Burns's engagement with politics: 'Only then . . . did he begin to concern himself seriously with political matters'.[20]

The present study pursues a rather different approach to Burns's political poetry. When we consider that much of Burns's best political work was written three or more years prior to the fall of the Bastille, it is easy to appreciate Marilyn Butler's recent contention that critics have 'overstated the links of Burns with the French Revolution'.[21] The French Revolution *is* important for Burns's later work (and forms a constant point of reference in Part 5 of this book), but it is hardly the alpha and omega of Burns's political consciousness. The fact that Burns's support for

18 Tom Paulin, 'Political Verse', in *Writing to the Moment: Selected Critical Essays, 1980–1996* (London, 1996), p. 101.
19 *The Critical Heritage*, p. 431.
20 *The Poetry of Robert Burns*, ed. by W. E. Henley and T. F. Henderson, 4 vols (London, 1896), IV, 335; Hector Macpherson, *A Century of Intellectual Development* (Edinburgh, 1907), pp. 182–83; Christina Keith, *The Russet Coat: A Critical Study of Burns' Poetry and of its Background* (London, 1956), p. 186; Howard O. Brogan, 'Satirist Burns and Lord Byron', *Costerus*, 4 (1972), 29–47 (pp. 42–3); W. J. Murray, 'Poetry and Politics: Burns and Revolution', in *Studies in the Eighteenth Century IV*, ed. by R. F. Brissenden and J. C. Eade (Canberra, 1979), pp. 57–82 (p. 59); John Strawhorn, *The Scotland of Robert Burns* (Darvel, 1995), p. 118.
21 Review of Ian McIntyre, *Dirt & Deity*, *London Review of Books*, 8 February 1996, p. 9.

the Revolution was somewhat belated – it dates from 1792 – and not altogether solid, suggests that the popular image of 'Burns the Jacobin' is impressionistic at best. Commentators habitually quote Cockburn's account of the Revolution's impact on Scotland ('Everything rung, and was connected, with the Revolution in France . . . '), but few record his scepticism regarding the existence of genuine Scottish Jacobins – 'we had wonderfully few proper Jacobins'.[22] 'French principles', it must be remembered, were not simply swallowed whole by British radicals, but were absorbed into indigenous traditions of radical discourse. Too often in Burns criticism, a vague gesture towards the 'ideals of the Revolution' has concealed a failure to engage with the structure of political debate in Burns's Britain.

In 1897, however, an alternative approach to Burns's political work had been outlined – ironically, by a critic whose explicit concern was with the literary effects of the French Revolution. In *The French Revolution and English Literature*, Edward Dowden argued that the 'French' ideals to which Burns responds in the 1790s were ones with which, as a Scots Presbyterian, he was already familiar: 'by the fact that he belonged to the democratic Presbyterian Church and sympathized with the party of spiritual revolt, Burns was fitted to be a spokesman of the passions of the time'.[23] Now, while Dowden's remark has been fleetingly endorsed – notably by A. B. Jamieson and Alan Bold – it has never been taken up as the basis of a sustained analysis of Burns's politics.[24] This is unfortunate, for, with this remark, Dowden suggests how we might move beyond the superficial image of a 'Jacobin' Burns and begin to explore the historical provenance of his political ideas and idioms. As the work of John Brims has made clear, late eighteenth-century Scottish radicals were heavily indebted to the political inheritance of Scottish Presbyterianism. They drew their inspiration and their idiom from the seventeenth-century Covenanters.[25] Scottish radicals did not separate their grievances into discrete categories of civil and religious; rather, they saw themselves facing an integrated 'system of ecclesiastico-political tyranny, sometimes designated as Toryism, which stood in diametrical opposition to the principles of Presbyterianism'.[26]

It was not only in Lowland Scotland but throughout the late eighteenth-century British Atlantic world that radicalism was informed by religion. Following the work of several influential historians, the key research on popular radicalism has focused on the nexus between radical politics and Dissenting/Presbyterian religion.[27] This

22 Henry Cockburn, *Memorials of His Time* (Edinburgh, 1856), pp. 80–82.

23 Edward Dowden, *The French Revolution and English Literature* (London, 1897), p. 146.

24 A. B. Jamieson, *Burns and Religion* (Cambridge, 1931), p. 114; Alan Bold, *A Burns Companion* (London, 1991), p. 94.

25 John Brims, 'The Covenanting Tradition and Scottish Radicalism in the 1790s', in *Covenant, Charter, and Party: Traditions of Revolt and Protest in Modern Scottish History*, ed. by Terry Brotherstone (Aberdeen, 1989), pp. 50–62.

26 John D. Brims, 'The Scottish Democratic Movement in the Age of the French Revolution' (unpublished doctoral thesis, University of Edinburgh, 1983), p. 128.

27 See J. G. A. Pocock, *The Machiavellian Moment: Florentine Political Thought and the Atlantic Republican Tradition* (Princeton, 1975); J. C. D. Clark, *The Language of Liberty*

historical scholarship has in turn facilitated reassessments of major Romantic authors. The past few years have seen several important studies in which the politics of leading Romantic writers – Blake, Keats, Hazlitt – have been reinterpreted in the light of Dissenting radical culture.[28] Robert Burns is another major author of the period whose work demands to be reassessed in this way. It remains unfortunate that Burns's run-ins with the kirk have obscured the extent to which his own political philosophy is grounded in his religious inheritance. His politics are shaped by two complementary strands of Presbyterian thought: on the one hand, the New Light, with its subjection of all forms of authority to the tribunal of the individual reason; on the other, the traditional contractarian political theory long associated with Presbyterianism. These influences are evident in Burns's repeated avowal of 'revolution principles', in his support for the American Revolution, and, above all, in his satirical attacks on political corruption. The whole framework of assumption on which Burns's political satires rest recalls the contractarian principles of Presbyterian thought: that authority ascends from below; that government is a contract, and political power a trust; and that even the humblest members of society are competent to censure their governors. That Burns deplored certain aspects of Calvinism – its harsh soteriology, its emphasis on faith over works – should not blind us to his sincere identification with the Presbyterian political inheritance:

> THE Solemn League and Covenant
> Now brings a smile, now brings a tear.
> But sacred Freedom, too, was theirs;
> If thou 'rt a slave, indulge thy sneer.[29]

It is the premise of this book, then, that Burns is a more sophisticated and complex poet than his critics have tended to suggest, and that there is more to his political writings than either lower-class spleen or fashionable French extremism. Burns's *technical* sophistication is widely accepted, and in what follows I pay due attention to Burns's manipulation of idiom and register, his artful treatment of personae, his handling of metre and stanza, and his often innovative approach to generic convention. But I also wish to acknowledge the poet's intellectual reach, the range of radical discourses on which he draws, his creative engagement with political and religious ideas. If Burns's letters display a 'polemical and dialectical skill based on a

1660–1832: Political Discourse and Social Dynamics in the Anglo-American World (Cambridge, 1994); A. T. Q. Stewart, *A Deeper Silence: The Hidden Origins of the United Irishmen* (London, 1993); Ian McBride, *Scripture Politics: Ulster Presbyterians and Irish Radicalism in the Late Eighteenth Century* (Oxford, 1998); E. W. McFarland, *Ireland and Scotland in the Age of Revolution: Planting the Green Bough* (Edinburgh, 1994).

28 See E. P. Thompson, *Witness Against the Beast: William Blake and the Moral Law* (Cambridge, 1993); Nicholas Roe, *John Keats and the Culture of Dissent* (Oxford, 1997); Tom Paulin, *The Day-Star of Liberty: William Hazlitt's Radical Style* (London, 1998).

29 'The Solemn League and Covenant' (K, 512).

wholly coherent grasp of the key intellectual issues of his age',[30] then so too do his poems.

Three of the chapters in *Burns the Radical* address the intellectual context of Burns's political writings. Chapter 1 outlines the radical political discourses to which Burns was exposed, including Calvinist resistance theory, the 'revolution principles' of the British Real Whigs, the political theory of the Scottish Enlightenment and the general European idiom of civic humanism. The second chapter considers Burns's political education, primarily through a consideration of the influence of Burns's Whiggish tutor, John Murdoch, but looking also at Burns's wider reading and his participation in local book clubs and debating societies. Chapter 5 explores the influence of liberal 'New Light' ideas – both political and religious – on Burns: following a brief account of the genesis and development of New Light Presbyterianism, this chapter traces Burns's connections with the 'candid, lib'ral band' of Ayrshire New Lights, and also discusses the reading matter which shaped Burns's New Light ideas.

'Almost everything that Burns ever wrote was political,' writes Thomas Crawford, 'in the broadest sense of the word.'[31] My own definition of Burns's 'political poetry' is a catholic one, and the chapters devoted to close readings of Burns's work encompass not only the political satires of the 1780s (discussed in Chapter 3) and the revolutionary lyrics of the post-1789 period (discussed in Chapter 8), but also the group of verse epistles Burns wrote to fellow Ayrshire dissidents in 1785/86 (Chapter 4), the large body of anticlerical satire (Chapter 6), and the often subversive erotic poems – what one critic has termed Burns's 'political bawdry' (Chapter 7).[32] In addition, I am also concerned with how contemporaries responded to Burns's political verse, and Chapter 9 examines Burns's contemporary status as a 'poet of liberty' by assessing his connections with a group of radical Ulster poets attached to the United Irishmen's newspaper, the Belfast *Northern Star*.

Mention has already been made of the recent controversy over proposed new additions to the Burns canon, and it may be useful to say something here concerning my own approach to the 'lost poems'. In 1961, the American scholar Lucyle Werkmeister suggested that a detailed trawl through the files of the opposition newspapers of the 1790s might throw up previously undiscovered radical poems by Burns.[33] More than thirty years later, and apparently without knowing Werkmeister's work, Patrick Scott Hogg undertook this task, reading through the London *Morning Chronicle*, the *Edinburgh Gazetteer* and other papers. As a result of these researches, Scott Hogg retrieved fifteen radical poems which he then presented as lost works by Burns in his *Robert Burns: The Lost Poems* (1997).

---

30 *The Canongate Burns*, xxiv.
31 *Burns*, p. 238.
32 Robert Burns, *Selected Poems*, ed. by Carol McGuirk (Harmondsworth, 1993), p. 277.
33 Lucyle Werkmeister, 'Some Account of Robert Burns and the London Newspapers, with special reference to the Spurious *Star* (1789)', *Bulletin of the New York Public Library*, 65 (1961), 483–504 (p. 504).

Ten of these poems are included in *The Canongate Burns*, edited by Scott Hogg and Andrew Noble.[34]

In retrieving this material, Scott Hogg has performed an invaluable service to Burns studies. Undoubtedly, his original haul of fifteen poems was rather ampler than was strictly warranted by the evidence. There were also certain flawed premises to his supporting argument, perhaps the most significant of which was his assumption that, of all the poets active in the period 1793–96, only Burns could have composed the poems in question.[35] It has since been proved that at least two of Scott Hogg's Burns attributions are the work of the radical Catholic priest, Alexander Geddes,[36] and there are numerous other radical poets – Scottish, English and Irish – who must be contenders for authorship of the other 'lost poems'. It has to be said, too, that many of the recovered poems neither stand up well as works of art nor throw much new light on Burns's politics. However, there are exceptions, and some of the new poems are not only exceptional but bear the stamp of Burns. To my mind, Scott Hogg and Andrew Noble have made a compelling case for regarding at least three of the 'lost poems' – 'The Dagger', and the two 'Ghost of Bruce' poems[37] – as works of Burns, and they are treated as such in this study.

In a work entitled *Burns the Radical*, a preliminary definition of terms is perhaps required, particularly given the recent scholarly controversy surrounding the labelling of eighteenth-century political doctrines. 'Radical' and 'radicalism' are such familiar terms of intellectual and political history, and so prevalent in analyses of British society in the later years of the eighteenth century, that their use here may seem unexceptionable. As applied to late eighteenth-century Britain, 'radicalism' commonly denotes both the practical agitation for political reform that emerged in the wake of the American Revolution, and the intellectual resources of the reform movement – for instance, the contractarian and Real Whig ideas primarily associated with Dissenting and Presbyterian denominations. Beyond this usage, 'radical' and 'radicalism' have been applied both to later and earlier movements of a dissident or (in modern parlance) 'left-wing' tendency, including the reform movement of the 1820s, the republicans and Levellers of the Civil War period, the English Whigs of the 1680s and the Protestant Reformers of the sixteenth century ('the radical Reformation', 'Calvinist radicalism').[38]

---

34 *The Canongate Burns*, xcvii.
35 *The Lost Poems*, pp. 61, 63, 67–8.
36 Gerard Carruthers, 'A Note on Poems Newly Attributed to Burns', *Burns Chronicle* (December, 1998), 26–8; 'Alexander Geddes and the Burns "Lost Poems" Controversy', *Studies in Scottish Literature*, 31 (1999), 81–5.
37 *The Canongate Burns*, pp. 456–72.
38 Raymond Williams, *Keywords: A Vocabulary of Culture and Society*, 2nd edn (London, 1983), pp. 251–2; William M. Lamont, 'The Puritan revolution: a historiographical essay', in *The Varieties of British Political Thought, 1500–1800*, ed. by J. G. A. Pocock and others (Cambridge, 1993), pp. 119–43; Howard Nenner, 'The later Stuart age', in *The Varieties of British Political Thought, 1500–1800*, pp. 180–208; Quentin Skinner, *The Foundations of Modern Political Thought*, 2 vols (Cambridge, 1978), II, 75, 225.

Though the usage is well established, one distinguished student of the eighteenth century has recently objected to these terms as 'anachronistic'. J. C. D. Clark argues that, as coinages of the early nineteenth century, 'radical' and 'radicalism' are best avoided in discussions of the pre-1800 Britain.[39] It seems to me that Clark is being needlessly fastidious here. As Clark himself acknowledges, the phrase 'radical reform' was current from the early 1780s 'in the context of demands for parliamentary reform',[40] and so there is no great violence in extending the usage to encompass the nouns 'radical' and 'radicalism'. More pertinently, however, it is not clear that there exists a viable alternative term to cover the phenomenon in question. As a 'useful' alternative to radicalism, Clark suggests 'Jacobinism', a term which applies only to the 1790s and unfortunately obscures the reformers' debts to indigenous British traditions of protest. Nor, if we are to avoid calling Burns a 'radical', are the contemporary alternatives particularly useful. 'Democrat' is too narrowly focused; 'leveller' too pejorative; 'patriot' and 'friend to liberty' too vague and ambiguous; 'reformer' too programmatic; 'republican' misleading. We are in the situation in which the phenomenon we seek to describe is most aptly rendered by a (marginal) anachronism. In any case, Clark's central objection to the term 'radicalism' is that, carrying connotations of secularity, it obscures the importance of denominational rivalry in the eighteenth century.[41] However, the currency – in the present study as in the literature generally – of formulations like 'Dissenting radicalism' or 'Presbyterian radicalism' rather obviates this problem. Finally, the fact that radicalism, as something of a portmanteau word,[42] has a variety of applications, makes it more – not less – useful in a study of this kind, which is not narrowly focused on Burns's political allegiances, but addresses his general nonconformity and contentiousness, the comprehensive dissidence of a man who could boast: 'I set as little by kings, lords, clergy, critics, &c. as all these respectable Gentry do by my Bardship' (*Letters*, I, 108). So, J. C. D. Clark notwithstanding, *Burns the Radical* it is.

In his introduction to *The Canongate Burns*, Andrew Noble reiterates the familiar plea of Burns's recent critics. Let us stop treating Burns as *sui generis*, a maverick, marginal figure, and let us recognise his centrality to the cultural life of his time, and in particular to the culture of British literary radicalism:

> Burns is not to be understood as some sort of barely rational political oddity. With Blake, he is a central poet of a long established revolutionary vision. Consciously or otherwise, the vast bulk of Burns criticism has detached him from his proper intellectual, cultural and political contexts so that, an isolated figure, his politics can be seen as subjective, whimsical, even eccentric.[43]

39 J. C. D. Clark, *English Society 1660–1832: Religion, Ideology and Politics during the Ancien Regime*, 2nd edn (Cambridge, 2000), pp. 5–10.
40 *English Society*, p. 8.
41 *Language of Liberty*, p. 143, n7.
42 Clark, *English Society*, p. 6.
43 *The Canongate Burns*, xxiv.

It is the aim of this study to restore Burns to his proper contexts, to recover the traditions of radical thought and practice which Burns interrogated, adapted and engaged with in his writings. The book does not purport to offer a definitive reading of Burns's political poetry; nor is its title designed to challenge or invalidate other important dimensions of his artistic personality – 'Burns the Sentimentalist', say, or 'Burns the Lyricist'. Rather, my aim is to show how important politics are to the poet's artistic achievement and to begin to restore this 'neglected master'[44] to his rightful position, as one of the great political poets of his own – or any – age.

---

44 Jerome McGann describes Burns thus on the dustjacket of Skoblow's *Dooble Tongue*.

PART ONE

INHERITANCE

CHAPTER ONE

'First Principles in Religion and Politics': Discourses of Radicalism in Late Eighteenth-Century Scotland

In December 1792, in the lull before Pitt's government launched a ferocious clampdown on domestic 'Jacobins', the Society of the Friends of the People in Scotland held its first General Convention in Edinburgh. Neither the high-sounding resolutions nor the well-turned orations could quell the note of foreboding that underlay the proceedings. Rightly apprehensive about provoking a nervous government, the Friends of the People trod carefully. A sedulously moderate Convention saw them denouncing all 'riot and tumult' and declaring their attachment to 'the established constitution of Great Britain on its genuinely acknowledged principles'.[1] Though many of the radicals favoured universal manhood suffrage, their published demands referred coyly to 'an Equal Representation of the People'.[2] The circumspection of the reformers was evident when one headstrong delegate, the advocate Thomas Muir, produced an Address to the Convention from the Society of United Irishmen in Dublin, and began to read:

> We take the Liberty of addressing you in the Spirit of Civic Union, in the Fellowship of a just and common Cause. We greatly rejoice that the Spirit of freedom moves over the Face of Scotland; that Light seems to break from the Chaos of her internal Government; and that a Country so respectable for her Attainments in Science, in Arts, and in Arms, for Men of literary Eminence, for the Intelligence and Morality of her People, now acts from a Conviction of a Union between Virtue, Letters, and Liberty, and now rises to a Distinction; not by a calm, contented, secret Wish for a reform in parliament, but by openly, actively, and urgently *willing* it, with the Unity and Energy of an embodied Nation. We rejoice that you do not consider yourselves as merged and melted down into another Country, but that in this great national Question you are still Scotland – the Land where Buchanan wrote, and Fletcher spoke, and Wallace fought.[3]

---

1 Henry W. Meikle, *Scotland and the French Revolution* (Glasgow, 1912), pp. 247–8.
2 *Caledonian Mercury*, 28 July 1792.
3 Reproduced in McFarland, *Ireland and Scotland*, p. 248.

The millenarian enthusiasm of this Address, its Jacobin swagger, unsettled the nervous Scots, and many delegates felt that the Irish had indeed taken a liberty in sending such unguarded greetings. Flattering references to Caledonian achievements in science and literature did not sway the Convention: after some debate, the delegates declined to answer the Address and Muir agreed to withdraw the document.

Though the Irish Address, as it was known, was prudently smothered by its recipients, it remains a significant document of late eighteenth-century British radicalism. For one thing, it points to the eclectic nature of that radical culture. Here was a group of Irish reformers confidently invoking the icons of Scottish libertarian politics: George Buchanan, the political theorist of the Scottish Reformation; Andrew Fletcher, the statesman and opponent of the 1707 Union; and William Wallace, the guerrilla fighter of the Wars of Independence. When we learn that the principal author of the Address was one William Drennan, the transnational context becomes even clearer. An Ulster Presbyterian, educated at Edinburgh University, brought up on the classics of English Whig political theory and now leading the Dublin United Irishmen, Drennan embodies the pan-British nature of late eighteenth-century radical culture. Radicals in different parts of the British Isles had their own lineage of radical thought and action (and this chapter will focus predominantly on Scottish thinkers and writers), but they drew with catholic relish on the intellectual resources of other areas.

The Irish Address is also significant in its attempt to establish a pantheon of libertarian heroes. As Andrew Noble points out, 'looking to the past for virtuous political models and heroic embodiment of these models'[4] was a standard practice of late eighteenth-century radicals. In this instance, the United Irishmen are addressing a Scottish convention, so their choice of models is exclusively Scottish. However, at that very convention, the Scots reformers invoked Magna Carta and the liberties of the English constitution in the days of King Alfred, as well as the 'Scotch freedom' of the native constitutional tradition.[5] This breadth of reference is entirely typical. In its ideological make-up, eighteenth-century radicalism was a mélange of discourses, which included Whig constitutionalism, Calvinist resistance theory, civic humanism, 'Country' ideology, natural law, classical republicanism, 'New Light' Presbyterianism, Protestant millenarianism, Jacobinism, and even (after 1760) Jacobitism. As John Dinwiddy observes, radicals moved between these various discourses 'without any great regard for logical consistency'.[6] British reformers were perfectly ready to combine what might seem to modern scholars incompatible discourses: for instance, they 'often managed to proclaim the glories of the ancient constitution and the traditional rights of Englishmen, while

4 *The Canongate Burns*, xxx.
5 Meikle, p. 251.
6 J. R. Dinwiddy, *Radicalism and Reform in Britain, 1780–1850*, ed. by H. T. Dickinson (London, 1992), p. 169.

simultaneously advocating future progress on the basis of abstract, rational principles'.[7]

In this chapter I discuss some of the discourses – and some of the specific texts – on which late eighteenth-century reformers drew, and to which Robert Burns in particular was exposed. My concern is not with the practical programme of the radical reformers (extension of the franchise, shorter parliaments, equal constituencies, payment of MPs, the secret ballot and so forth), but with the political languages that shaped radical thought and action. Of these discourses, three in particular coloured radical politics in lowland Scotland: the contractarianism associated with the Presbyterian tradition (sometimes known as 'Calvinist resistance theory'); the 'Country' ideology of the Real Whigs; and the political theory of the Scottish Enlightenment (particularly in its Glaswegian manifestation). To these might be added the influence of New Light Presbyterianism, with its potentially inflammatory insistence on the Protestant right of private judgement, which will be discussed at length in Chapter 5. While these discourses do not constitute a rigorously coherent or integrated tradition, they remain, as we shall see, cognate registers of the language of liberty in late eighteenth-century Scotland.

Calvinism and the Right to Resist: The Political Theory of the Scottish Reformation

In 1788, on the centenary of the Glorious Revolution, a statue of George Buchanan was erected in Scotland. In describing Scotland as 'the land where Buchanan wrote', the United Irishmen were shrewdly invoking the tutelary genius of Scottish political radicalism. Polymath, celebrated Latinist, and unblinking defender of regicide, George Buchanan was a talismanic figure for Scottish radicals in the eighteenth century. In the wake of the French Revolution, James Anderson's radical magazine, *The Bee* (1791–94), ran a series of articles on Buchanan, in the course of which he was hailed as a 'herald of civil and religious liberty' and an advocate of the 'rights of man'.[8] *Vindiciae Gallicae* (1791), James Mackintosh's riposte to Burke, identified Buchanan as the still unsurpassed theorist of 'popular politics, and the maxims of a free government'.[9] David Steuart Erskine, the radical Earl of Buchan, described Buchanan in 1792 as 'the father of whiggery as a system in Britain, if not in Europe; the Lord Bacon or Newton of political science and sentiment'.[10] Buchanan is also approvingly quoted by radical Scottish journalists like 'Timothy Thunderproof' (James Thomson Callender).[11] What this indicates is the readiness with which late

---

7 H. T. Dickinson, 'Radicals and Reformers in the Age of Wilkes and Wyvill', in *British Politics and Society from Walpole to Pitt, 1742–1789*, ed. by Jeremy Black (Basingstoke: Macmillan, 1990), pp. 123–46 (p. 128).

8 *The Bee*, 5 (1791), 232.

9 *The Miscellaneous Works of Sir James Mackintosh*, 3 vols (London, 1846), III, 137.

10 David Steuart Erskine, *Essays on the Lives and Writings of Fletcher of Saltoun and the Poet Thomson* (London, 1792), p. xxii.

11 *The Bee*, 8 (1792), 233.

eighteenth-century reformers traced their creed to the political theorist of the Scottish Reformation and to the political legacy of Scottish Presbyterianism. The tradition of Presbyterian radicalism was an important intellectual resource for eighteenth-century reformers.

The association of Presbyterianism with political radicalism reflects the pattern of development of the Calvinist Reformation. Whereas Lutheranism and Anglicanism tended to develop through the sponsorship of princes, and so remained politically quiescent and deferential to the civil power, Calvinism developed in open conflict with hostile Catholic courts in Scotland as in France, and produced more radical theories of resistance.[12] Repudiating the right of the king to intervene in matters of spiritual moment, Calvinism stood for limited government in an age of monarchical absolutism. Moreover, Calvinism drew its support from social classes – merchants, artisans, peasants – which were excluded from existing power structures. It gave these groups a share in ecclesiastical power by adopting a partially democratic system of government by church courts (Presbyterianism). And increasingly, given its hostile relationship with the crown, Scottish Calvinism asserted not only the religious but also the civil and political competence of the people, their right to resist bad government.

The theory of justified resistance was developed by Presbyterian thinkers in a series of polemical works, often written in times of armed rebellion: George Buchanan's *De jure regni apud Scotos* (1579), written after the deposition of Mary; Samuel Rutherford's *Lex Rex: The Law and the Prince* (1644), written during the Presbyterian resistance to Charles I; and Alexander Shields's *A Hind Let Loose* (1687), written during the later Covenanting struggles. In these seminal works, the right to resist is put forward as part of a contractarian theory of government, in which sovereignty is seen to be vested in the people as a whole. The seminal exposition of this theory, the *ur*-text of Scottish Calvinist radicalism, is George Buchanan's *De jure regni apud Scotos*.

Buchanan's immediate purpose in the *De jure* is to vindicate the Scots' deposition of Mary Stuart in 1567, an act which had alarmed and horrified the rulers of Europe. In attempting to exonerate the Scots, Buchanan adopts two main strategies. On the one hand, he appeals to historical precedent, citing the various Scottish rulers who have been justly deposed, and claiming the right to resist tyrants as an accepted feature of Scottish constitutional tradition.[13] More importantly, however, Buchanan undertakes a more general theoretical discussion of political society, in which he attempts to deduce the scope and limits of legitimate authority and to determine the distinction between kingship and tyranny.

---

12 Lutheran thinkers might sanction the resistance of territorial princes to an imperial overlord, as in the case of the Schmalkaldic League's resistance to Emperor Charles V, but they balked at confirming the right of the people as a whole to resist their prince.

13 George Buchanan, *The Art and Science of Government among the Scots, Being George Buchanan's 'De Jure Regni Apud Scotos'*, ed. and trans. by Duncan H. MacNeill (Glasgow, 1964), p. 83 (hereafter 'Buchanan').

Buchanan begins his political discussion by advancing an emphatically social anthropology. Man is an inherently gregarious animal, drawn to associate with his fellows not merely from motives of expediency, but from a natural instinct to socialise:

> There is an urge of some kind in nature which is implanted not only in human beings, but also in the more domesticated animals, in such a way that even if the attractions of expediency are lacking, they nevertheless gladly associate with their fellow-creatures.

Society is man's state of nature, the arena in which he fulfils his natural need to associate. This is evident not only from nature but from scripture: 'we should love the Lord our God and our neighbours as ourselves'.[14] Society is not merely a natural but a sacred phenomenon; people associate from a 'spiritual urge' which comes from 'divine inspiration'.

For Buchanan, then, society is a good in itself. The political arrangements which men agree to establish in order to regulate society must therefore be geared to the good of that society as a whole. The role of government is to nurture and preserve society, and the ruler must be a physician to his people, promoting their health and welfare: 'kings have been appointed not in their own interest, but for the benefit of the people'.[15] It is when a king forgets his position as a servant to the public, and seeks instead his own aggrandisement, that his legitimacy ends and he becomes a tyrant. In such a case, the people have the right to act – either directly or through their representatives – to depose their monarch and install a new one. In so doing, they are restoring the health of the state, redeeming the body politic from corruption.[16]

Buchanan's theory draws on the important biblical concept of a contract or covenant between ruler and ruled. There is 'a mutual contract between the king and the people', by which the people are obliged to render obedience to the king so long as he governs in the interest of the commonwealth and allows himself to be bound by law; should he fail to do so, they may freely depose him.[17] In contemporary Protestant political theory, the covenant established at the inauguration of kings was conceived as having two distinct parts. The first part was a covenant between God, the king and the people, by which king and people each undertook to maintain the proper worship of God. The second part was a covenant between the king and the people, to the effect that the people would obey the king so long as he ruled with justice.[18] Buchanan's primary concern in the *De jure* is with the second part of the covenant, that between king and people, by which obedience must be rendered only to the righteous monarch.

14 Buchanan, p. 23.
15 Buchanan, p. 25.
16 Buchanan, pp. 24–26, 35, 83.
17 Buchanan, pp. 25–27, 80–96.
18 *Vindiciae, Contra Tyrannos: or, concerning the legitimate power of a prince over the people, and of the people over a prince* (1579), ed. and trans. by George Garnett (Cambridge, 1994), p. 21.

This contractarian tradition exerted an important influence on later Presbyterian political theorists. The notion of the covenant lies behind Samuel Rutherford's insistence on the consensual character of government; according to Rutherford, political authority proceeds 'from *God* by the mediation of the consent of a Communitie, which resigneth their power to one or moe Rulers'.[19] Similarly, Alexander Shields relies on the second part of the biblical covenant when he argues that 'Government is nothing else but a mutual stipulation between Kings & People'.[20] The same principle informs the Covenanters' Sanquhar Declaration, which announces that Charles II has forfeited his crown through his 'breach of covenant both to God and his Kirk, and . . . by his tyranny and breach of the very *leges regnandi* in matters civil'.[21] Arguments from historical precedent were by no means laid aside by Presbyterian thinkers; in his *History of the Church of Scotland 1660–1679* (written around 1693 but not published until 1817), James Kirkton justified the use of 'defensive arms' against tyranny as 'the ancient national practice of Scotland'.[22] Nevertheless, it is on natural rather than conventional rights that the Presbyterian thinkers lay the greater emphasis. No matter what the particular form of government or the constitutional traditions of a given society, the fundamental principle of the covenant applies: where the government pursues the good of the whole society, it must be obeyed; but where it frustrates the public welfare, it may be resisted.

As well as the concept of the covenant, Calvinist resistance theorists employed arguments derived from the structure of Presbyterian church government. Civil and religious regimes were habitually analogised in early modern political debate,[23] and Buchanan's conception of the sovereignty of the people and their rights vis-à-vis their monarch is implicitly aligned with a Presbyterian understanding of the priesthood of all believers, of the rights and the competence of the laity vis-à-vis the clergy.[24] For Scottish Presbyterians, the political connotations which their ecclesiological regime carried were largely civic. Presbyterianism was a species of republic or commonwealth – not altogether democratic, to be sure, but embodying the principle that congregations were competent to appoint and to cashier their ministers. Inevitably, Presbyterians conflated Buchananite political with

---

19 Samuel Rutherford, *Lex Rex: The Law and the Prince* (London, 1644), p. 5.

20 Alexander Shields, *A Hind Let Loose* ([n.p.], 1687), p. 35.

21 Gordon Donaldson, *Scottish Historical Documents* (Edinburgh, 1970), p. 241.

22 James Kirton, *A History of the Church of Scotland 1660–1679*, ed. by Ralph Stewart (Lampeter, 1992), p. 49.

23 Mark Goldie, 'The civil religion of James Harrington', in *The Languages of Political Theory in Early Modern Europe*, ed. by Anthony Pagden (Cambridge, 1987), pp. 197–222.

24 At one point during his discussion of tyranny, Buchanan describes the rule of the Pope as 'a despotism the most severe of all that have ever existed' and employs the example of 'the uncontrolled power of the Roman pontiff' to illustrate the danger of confining the privilege of interpreting the laws to one person alone (pp. 44–45).

Presbyterian religious tenets to form that 'Buchananite and covenanting synthesis' which so characterises a particular strain of early-modern Scottish thought.[25]

The Calvinist understanding of ecclesiastical authority – whereby a fully competent lay community delegates a conditional authority to its ministers – underwrites the notion of contractual magistracy, according to which government wields an authority which is not absolute, but conditional on its acting for the good of the public. Where authority – either civil or religious – is not used for the good of all, the people are held to be justified in resuming direct control. Allegiance must be conditional, not absolute:

> [I]n Conscience, we are no more free to Prostitute our Loyalty and Liberty absolutely, in ouning every Professor of the Magistracy; than we are free to Prostitute our Religion and faith implicitely, in ouning every Pretender to the Ministry.[26]

The citizen must scrutinise the actions of his magistrate in the same way that the Presbyterian was accustomed to scrutinise his minister.[27]

As a doctrine of resistance, the innovative feature of Scottish Calvinist political thought, by which it is distinguished from the theories of the Lutherans and conciliarists and even from the French Calvinists, is that the right to resist is ultimately ascribed to the people as a whole, and not confined to the nobility or to inferior magistrates.[28] According to Buchanan, even 'poor and almost unknown men from among the lowest ranks of the people' may legitimately cashier the ruler.[29] It is this radical extension of the right to resist which leads Quentin Skinner to identify Buchanan as a seminal figure in the history of European political thought, being the first modern thinker to enunciate a fully populist theory of resistance 'in a completely unequivocal and consistent form'. Buchanan initiates a tradition of populist resistance theory which carries forward to John Locke's *Two Treatises of Government* (1690), the work which Skinner views as 'the classic text of radical Calvinist politics'.[30]

Presbyterian thinkers and historians, then, were concerned to establish a natural right to resist tyrannical government. It would be erroneous, however, to suggest that Buchanan and his successors were preoccupied solely with the constitutional or

25 Pocock, 'Two kingdoms and three histories? Political thought in British contexts', in *Scots and Britons: Scottish Political Thought and the Union of 1603*, ed. by Roger A. Mason (Cambridge, 1994), pp. 292–312 (p. 301).
26 Shields, p. 269.
27 On the rigour with which the Presbyterian laity, even in the eighteenth century, scrutinised their clergy, see Henry Grey Graham, *The Social Life of Scotland in the Eighteenth Century*, 2nd edn, 2 vols (London, 1900), II, 66–68.
28 Quentin Skinner, *The Foundations of Modern Political Thought*, 2 vols (Cambridge, 1978), II, 210–211, 339.
29 Buchanan, p. 81.
30 Skinner, *Foundations*, II, 239.

jurisprudential concept of political rights. On the contrary, Buchananite political
theory is equally concerned with the essentially civic concept of duty, with the
citizen's political virtue, his obligation to the public. Buchanan's reverence for
society (the 'sacred bond of fellowship'), over and above any material advantages it
affords its members, determines the strongly civic orientation of his philosophy. If
political society is not merely the arena in which each individual pursues his own
material interest, but an expression of the definitively human need to associate, then
it commands our disinterested allegiance. Buchanan, along with later Presbyterian
theorists, can thus argue for the existence, not just of self-interested rights, but of
social duties; not only *ius*, but *virtus*. In the work of seventeenth-century religious
historians like Rutherford and Shields, the Presbyterian ideal of the active layman,
interrogating the scriptures for himself and competent to share in the government
of his church, underwrites the civic ideal of the active citizen, determined to
participate in his country's government, and willing to bear arms in defence of its
liberties.

As David Allan has demonstrated, what we are dealing with in the work of
Buchanan and the later Calvinist historians is a self-consciously republican
discourse: republican, in the sense that the true end of government is taken to be the
good of the public – the 'common wealth', the 'res-publica' – and that the active
citizenship of the people is deemed essential to that end. *Salus populi, suprema lex* is
considered the ground rule of government, and a concern for the public the only
source of legitimate authority. This equation of virtue with public spirit could be
employed to destabilise traditional notions of social leadership: the truly great man
is no longer the prince or the earl; it is the virtuous, public-spirited man of whatever
station who alone is truly noble.[31]

From the perspective of political theory, what is immediately striking about this
Presbyterian political discourse is its close resemblance to that Renaissance civic
humanism about which J. G. A. Pocock has written.[32] Civic humanism denotes a
tradition of early modern political thought which emphasises the values of
participatory citizenship as practised in the republics of classical antiquity. On an
intellectual level, this tradition of thought draws heavily on the ideas of Aristotle as
mediated by the humanist thinkers of the Florentine Renaissance, particularly
Machiavelli and Guicciardini. From a civic humanist perspective, the ideal political
society is an association of free and equal citizens, each of whom actively contributes
to the welfare of the political association or *polis*, both by participating in the
processes of government, and by bearing arms in defence of the state. The
unceasing civic exertions of the citizens, it is argued, combat the processes of decay
to which the state is naturally incident. A Roman ideal of voluntary dedication to the
public good preserves the *polis* from the perils of corruption, which include

31 David Allan, *Virtue, Learning and the Scottish Enlightenment: Ideas of Scholarship in
    Early Modern History* (Edinburgh, 1993), pp. 34–5, 88–9.
32 See Pocock's magisterial survey of civic humanist thought, *The Machiavellian
    Moment*.

'luxurious' consumer indulgence, oppressive standing armies, and arbitrary government. Implicit in the civic ideal is the legitimacy of resisting tyrannical rule.

Rooted in the conditions of the classical city states, the civic ideal was not directly realisable in the context of early-modern Europe. The increased populousness and extent of early-modern states made direct participation in government impossible, while the division of labour and advances in military technology tended to make soldiering a specialised profession rather than a civic duty. Nonetheless, the essential civic premise – that the health of a state depended on the public-spirited activities of its citizens – remained operative for many contemporaries. Civic humanism was in any case, in Pocock's terms, 'a language, not a programme', and it remained a major European political idiom throughout the age of the Enlightenment and beyond.[33] As we have seen, Buchanan approaches politics through a civic framework, in which public virtue confronts corruption. In the *De jure* Buchanan rehearses the standard topoi of civic thought: the public good as the proper object of government; the condemnation of luxury ('riches and voluptuousness'); the praiseworthy example of Spartan temperance and *severitas*; the preference for a citizen militia over a standing army.[34] Buchanan's politics, to a large extent, are the politics of civic humanism.

As commentators have noted, there is, on a variety of counts, a substantial correspondence or affinity between civic humanist and Calvinist discourses. The two discourses coalesce around a critique of human corruption and degeneracy. Both are highly moralistic and censorious, attacking excessive sensual indulgence and 'luxury', and teaching their adherents to strive towards a state of purity and virtue in despite of man's natural depravity and selfishness.[35] Calvinism also shares with the civic tradition a positive attitude towards the mundane, mutable world of political action: in late sixteenth-century Scotland, 'it was the Presbyterians, admirers of Aristotle's *Politics*, who insisted on the dignity of the particulars of political action' against Roman Catholic *contemptus mundi*.[36] The Calvinist ideal of the active Christian – reading the scriptures for himself, vindicating his own position, rejecting priestly authority, and relating to other Christians on terms of equality – has obvious affinities with a participatory political ethic of active citizenship.[37] Finally, the civic humanist opposition to extravagant consumption dovetails with the Calvinist insistence on temperance and restraint: when Andrew

---

33 *The Political Works of James Harrington*, ed. by J. G. A. Pocock (Cambridge, 1977), p. 15.

34 Buchanan, pp. 23, 32–33.

35 Richard B. Sher, *Church and University in the Scottish Enlightenment: The Moderate Literati of Edinburgh* (Edinburgh, 1985), pp. 325–6.

36 David Norbrook, '*Macbeth* and the Politics of Historiography', in *Politics of Discourse: The Literature and History of Seventeenth-Century England*, ed. by Kevin Sharpe and Steven N. Zwicker (Berkeley, 1987), pp. 78–116 (p. 99).

37 Stephen Ozment, *Protestants: The Birth of a Revolution* (London, 1993, first published 1992), p. 20.

Fletcher rails against 'the pursuit of refined and expensive pleasures', he is speaking in the combined accents of Calvinism and civic humanism.[38]

The congruence of Calvinist and civic humanist idioms was not lost on the Calvinists themselves, and from very early on we find the Reformed historians drawing explicitly on humanist values of civic patriotism and active citizenship. Buchanan summarises his entire argument in the *De Jure* with a quotation from Cicero: 'I have sought for nothing in this whole discussion, as you will have observed, other than that Cicero's dictum should be revered and held inviolable: "Let the safety of the people be the supreme law" '.[39] Later, we find the Presbyterian historian Robert Fleming drawing on Juvenalian notions of virtue as the only true nobility, Alexander Shields commending the civic virtue of the classical patriots, and the Covenanters being eulogised as civic humanist heroes, bands of citizen militia defending the nation's liberties against the mercenary troops of a tyrant.[40] Of course, as Allan shows, there were obstacles to the successful integration of Calvinist and humanist discourses – for example, the treatment of free will and historical causality, where Calvinist determinism could conflict with the humanist model of an active *virtu* overcoming *Fortuna*. Nevertheless, there was sufficient common ground to create among early modern Scots Presbyterians an integrated – or at least a composite – political discourse which has been tentatively labelled 'Presbyterian humanism' or 'Calvinist humanism'.[41]

The Balanced Constitution: Real Whigs and Commonwealthmen

It is important to appreciate that this Presbyterian political discourse was not confined to a few Scottish extremists. On the contrary, it soon spread to become a central component of a wider British dissenting culture. In *Writing the English Republic* (1999), David Norbrook shows how a Scotland whose 'people had arguably internalized the discourses of classical republicanism more than the English' provided intellectual stimulus to English republican culture in the mid-seventeenth century, George Buchanan in particular proving inspirational to Republican polemicists like Milton, Nedham and John Hall.[42] Perhaps more significantly, the arguments of the Scottish resistance theorists were also taken up during the constitutional crises of the late seventeenth century. The contractarian ideas of the

38 Andrew Fletcher of Saltoun, *A Discourse of Government with relation to Militias*, in
    Selected Political Writings and Speeches, ed. by David Daiches (Edinburgh, 1979),
    pp. 1–26 (p. 5).
39 Buchanan, p. 42.
40 Allan, pp. 80–98.
41 Arthur Williamson, *Scottish National Consciousness in the Age of James VI: The
    Apocalypse, the Union, and the Shaping of Scotland's Public Culture* (Edinburgh, 1979),
    p. 87; Allan, p. 109.
42 David Norbrook, *Writing the English Republic: Poetry, Rhetoric and Politics 1627–
    1660* (Cambridge, 1999), pp. 93–94, 150, 205–6, 219.

Scottish theorists found eloquent expression in Locke's *Two Treatises of Government* (1690) and in countless Whig resistance tracts of the years around 1690. A radical Buchananite or Lockean version of 'revolution principles' was disseminated in various Whig tracts, notably the enormously popular *Political aphorisms* (1690), and the Revolution period also witnessed reprintings of Buchanan's *De jure* (in 1680 and 1698) and the *Vindiciae, contra Tyrannos*.[43] In this way, the contractarian political theory of the Presbyterians – often conjoined to the highly compatible idiom of European civic humanism – became part of the currency of political debate throughout the British Isles.[44] Above all, it influenced the 'Real Whigs' and 'Commonwealthmen' as discussed by Caroline Robbins in her seminal study of political radicalism, *The Eighteenth-Century Commonwealthman*.[45]

Who were these 'Real Whigs'? Tracing their descent from the radical Whiggism current during the Exclusion Crisis, they adopted the designation 'Real' or 'True' Whigs to distinguish themselves from the ruling Whig regime which governed almost continuously between 1714 and 1760, and which is usually referred to as the 'Whig supremacy' or the 'Whig oligarchy'.[46] In the eyes of the dissenting Real Whigs, these governing Whigs had departed from the original principles of Whiggism as established in the later seventeenth century. They had shown themselves to be shamefully neglectful of the subject's liberties, allowing the crown to manipulate and corrupt the representative part of the constitution through the dispensation of patronage. Against this apostasy, the Real Whigs aimed 'to refurbish traditional Whig principles'.[47]

The Real Whigs were not an organised party, but a loose grouping of like-minded thinkers, writers and politicians scattered throughout the British Isles. Their ranks included Robert Molesworth, Andrew Fletcher, Francis Hutcheson and William Molyneux, as well as imaginative writers like Addison, Thomson, Akenside, and Fielding. Typically educated at Glasgow University or the English dissenting academies, the Real Whigs promoted the liberal doctrines taught at those institutions. They advocated a right of resistance to tyrannical government. They praised the free states of the classical world – Athens, Carthage, Sparta and republican Rome – and championed citizen militias over standing armies. They stood for religious toleration (unlike the Presbyterians discussed in the previous

---

43 Richard Ashcraft and M. M. Goldsmith, 'Locke, Revolution Principles, and the Formation of Whig Ideology', *Historical Journal*, 26 (1983), 773–800.
44 Lois G. Schwoerer, 'The right to resist: Whig resistance theory, 1688 to 1694', in *Political Discourse in Early Modern Britain*, ed. by Nicholas Phillipson and Quentin Skinner (Cambridge, 1993), pp. 232–252.
45 Caroline Robbins, *The Eighteenth-Century Commonwealthman: Studies in the Transmission, Development and Circumstance of English Liberal Thought from the Restoration of Charles II until the War with the Thirteen Colonies* (Cambridge, MA, 1959).
46 Mark Goldie, 'The Roots of True Whiggism 1688–1694', *History of Political Thought*, 1 (1980), 195–236.
47 Goldie, 'True Whiggism', p. 196.

section) and freedom of enquiry, placing great emphasis on education as a key tool in the training of politically active, literate citizens. They proposed a federal constitution for the British Isles. Above all, they attacked ministerial influence, the corruption of the legislature by government patronage.[48]

Among the most influential Real Whig writers were John Trenchard and Thomas Gordon, authors of a series of political essays which appeared in the early 1720s and were collected as the *Independent Whig* and *Cato's Letters*. Throughout these works, the conduct of the government is scrutinised with a jealous eye. The Independent Whig

> . . . claims a Right of examining all publick Measures and, if they deserve it, of censuring them. As he never saw much Power possessed without some Abuse, he takes upon him to watch those that have it; and to acquit or expose them according as they apply it to the good of their country, or their own crooked Purposes.[49]

This right of private judgement, and ultimately of resistance, is the cornerstone of the Glorious Revolution: 'Upon this principle of People's judging for themselves and resisting lawless force, stands our late happy *Revolution*'.[50] Given this commitment to the right of resistance, it is no surprise to learn that Buchanan's *De Jure* was a 'favourite work' with eighteenth-century Real Whigs, including Thomas Hollis, and William Pitt, Lord Chatham.[51]

They may have upheld the right to resist, but the Real Whigs were far from being democrats. The principle that only those with property should possess the franchise was not one that the Real Whigs challenged. Nevertheless, they did advocate an extension of the franchise to make Parliament more representative, and they campaigned vigorously against placemen in Parliament and ministerial corruption of the legislature. In a letter written during the elections of 1734, William Talbot offered the following definition of the Real Whig ethos:

> The principles of a Real Whig, in my sense of the term are these, that government is an original compact between the governors and the governed, instituted for the good of the whole community; that in a limited monarchy, or more properly legal commonwealth, the majesty is in the people and tho' the person on the throne is superior to any individual, he is the servant of the nation; – that the only title to the crown is the election of the people; that the laws are equally obligatory to the Prince and the people; that as the constitution of England is formed of three legislative branches, the balance between each must be preserved, to prevent the destruction of the whole; – that elections ought to be free, the elected independent; – that a Parliamentary influence by

48 Robbins, pp. 3–21.
49 *A Collection of Tracts* (1751), quoted in Robbins, p. 1
50 *Cato's Letters*, 3rd edn (London, 1733), II, no. 59, 225, quoted in Robbins, p. 123.
51 Robbins, p. 265.

places and pensions is inconsistent with the interest of the public; and that a Minister who endeavours to govern by corruption, is guilty of the vilest attempt to subvert the constitution.[52]

In this passage we can chart the developing trajectory of Real Whig thought. While Talbot begins with the principle of government as a contract (and the implied existence of a right to resist), he ends by emphasising the need to maintain the balance of the constitution by combating the undue influence of ministerial patronage.

Talbot's emphasis is significant. For eighteenth-century Real Whigs, the practical application of 'revolution principles' had less to do with armed resistance to tyranny than with preserving the balance of the constitution and the independence of the House of Commons. The concept of the balanced constitution is perhaps the key motif of eighteenth-century Whiggism. Liberty is to be maintained by a constitution properly balanced among its constituent parts. The power of the crown requires to be limited by a truly representative and independent legislature. In many ways, this discourse was an expression of anti-court sentiment, an attack on modern centralisation and that burgeoning bureaucracy which had augmented the power of the executive in such a way that the governmental contract was in danger of breaking down. Particularly in England, Real Whigs tended to identify the governmental contract with the actual English constitution. The principles of this constitutional discourse are propounded by Pocock as follows:

> There exists an ancient constitution in England, which consists in a balance or equilibrium between the various organs of government, and within this balance the function of Parliament is to supervise the executive. But the executive possesses means of distracting Parliament from its proper function; it seduces members by the offer of places and pensions, by retaining them to follow ministers and ministers' rivals, by persuading them to support measures – standing armies, national debts, excise schemes – whereby the activities of administration grow beyond Parliament's control. These means of subversion are known collectively as corruption, and if ever Parliament or those who elect them – for corruption may occur at this point too – should be wholly corrupt, then there will be an end of independence and liberty. The remedy for corruption is to expel placemen, to ensure that members of Parliament become in no way entangled in the pursuit of power or the exercise of administration, and to see to it that parliaments are frequently elected by uncorrupted voters.[53]

Even in the 1790s, many radicals viewed reform as a process, not of innovation, but restoration: the aim was to restore the constitution to its original purity. Often, this was taken to mean recovering the rights enjoyed by Englishmen under the 'free and

---

52 William Talbot, letter to Thomas Rundle, quoted in Robbins, p. 283.
53 J. G. A. Pocock, *Politics, Language and Time: Essays on Political Thought and History* (London, 1972), p. 125.

popular' constitution of King Alfred, prior to the Norman Conquest, when every free man had the right to vote and parliaments were annual.[54] Of course, the Real Whig position did not always entail reference to the historical precedent of an ancient constitution. There were those who regarded the governmental contract as a principle of natural law, who were prepared, in Mark Goldie's phrase, to 'cut the Gordian knot with an account of natural rights', to appeal *tout court* to the concept of the covenant.[55]

As Robbins and Norbrook emphasise, Scottish Presbyterian ideas had been central to the development of Irish and English Real Whig thought. And these ideas came back to refertilise Scottish thought when the work of English and Irish Real Whig thinkers – Molesworth, Harrington and others – became widely disseminated and admired in Scotland. A crucial figure in this process was the Real Whig theorist, member of the Molesworth circle and 'father' of the Scottish Enlightenment, Francis Hutcheson.

Participatory Citizenship and the Virtues of Small States: The Political Theory of the Scottish Enlightenment

Throughout the eighteenth century, the University of Glasgow drew around 16 per cent of its students from the Protestant Dissenters of Ireland. The 'Scoto-Hiberni', as the matriculation roll termed them, formed a distinctive sub-section of the student body.[56] However, by far the most significant figure among the Glasgow 'Scoto-Hiberni' was a member of the teaching staff. An Ulsterman of Ayrshire stock, Francis Hutcheson held the Moral Philosophy chair at Glasgow University (where he had himself been a student) between 1730 and his death in 1746. The influence he exerted was profound, both philosophically (he was the teacher of Adam Smith), religiously (along with his protégé Leechman, he helped to liberalise the clergy of the south-west) and, above all, politically. Hutcheson was instrumental in creating the culture of liberal politics for which the University was to become famous. He did this partly by importing and disseminating the contractarian ideas of Irish Real Whig thinkers like Molesworth and Molyneux. A charismatic and compelling presence in the classroom, Hutcheson helped to create among the student body an abiding enthusiasm for the Real Whig canon. His own enthusiasm for parliamentary reform (he advocated an extension of the franchise and more frequent elections) informed the lectures on jurisprudence and government which – unusually for the time – he delivered in English, not Latin.[57] His students recalled

54 Dinwiddy, p. 177; Meikle, p. 251.
55 Goldie, 'True Whiggism', p. 210.
56 I. M. Bishop, 'The Education of Ulster Students at Glasgow University during the Eighteenth Century' (unpublished master's thesis, The Queen's University of Belfast, 1987).
57 William Robert Scott, *Francis Hutcheson: His Life, Teaching and Position in the History of Philosophy* (Cambridge, 1900), p. 63.

him as a passionate and eloquent promoter of Real Whig values, a man who inspired his hearers with 'an esteem for Liberty and a contempt for tyranny and tyrants'.[58] And it was while at Glasgow that Hutcheson committed his own contractarian political ideas to paper.

For Hutcheson, government must be conducted in accordance not merely with positive law but with God's law or the law of nature. This means, primarily, that government must be directed towards the good of society as a whole. Like Buchanan, Hutcheson has a strong sense of society as man's natural, God-given state, to which he is drawn not merely by interest but by impulse. In A *Short Introduction to Moral Philosophy* (1747), Hutcheson argues that

> a friendly society with others, and a mutual intercourse of offices, and the joint aids of many, are absolutely necessary not only to the pleasure and convenience of human life, but even to the preservation of it; which is so obvious that we need not reason upon it. Whatever appears necessary for preserving an amicable society among men must necessarily be enjoined by the law of nature.[59]

The end of government, then, is the welfare of the society as a whole. This being so, no government is legitimate which does not govern by the consent of the governed.[60] In A *System of Moral Philosophy* (1755), Hutcheson appeals to the familiar Presbyterian notion of government as a contract or covenant involving

> a mutual agreement or contract between the governors . . . and the people, the former obliging themselves to a faithful administration of the powers vested in them for the common interest, and the latter obliging themselves to obedience.[61]

When the governors fail to fulfil their side of the bargain, then the people have undoubted 'rights of resistance'.[62] Crucially, Hutcheson's 'whole-hearted endorsement of the right of resistance'[63] extended not merely to individuals but to colonies in relation to the mother country. He upheld the right of colonies to secede when colonial subjection proved burdensome and oppressive: 'Large numbers of men cannot be bound to sacrifice their own and their posterity's liberty and happiness, to the ambitious views of their mother-country . . .'.[64] It was statements such as these that made Hutcheson's works such a favoured resource of the American colonists during the War of Independence.

---

58 *The Defects of an University Education* (London, 1772), p. 9, quoted in Scott, p. 76.
59 Francis Hutcheson, *Philosophical Writings*, ed. by R. S. Downie (London, 1994), p. 162.
60 *Philosophical Writings*, p. 157.
61 Hutcheson, *A System of Moral Philosophy*, 2 vols (London, 1755), II, 227.
62 *System*, II, 279.
63 Robbins, p. 188.
64 *Philosophical Writings*, p. 196.

The writings of Hutcheson testify to the continuing acceptability of Presbyterian political theory even in polite, latitudinarian circles. It is often argued that their denomination's radical heritage proved an embarrassment to eighteenth-century Presbyterians, keen to demonstrate their Hanoverian loyalty.[65] However, the Glorious Revolution had itself been interpreted by many as a vindication of Buchananite principles, and 'polite' Presbyterians did not hesitate to affirm the traditional Presbyterian right of resistance. Francis Hutcheson was not alone in this respect. Thomas Reid gave an annual sanction to Buchananite resistance theory in his Glasgow lectures on pneumatology.[66] In his series of lectures on moral philosophy, John Witherspoon averred that, where the government is exercised in a tyrannical manner, then 'the subjects may certainly . . . resist and overthrow it'.[67] In *The Theory of Moral Sentiments* (1759), Adam Smith argues that '[a]ll constitutions of government . . . are valued only in proportion as they tend to promote the happiness of those who live under them. This is their sole use and end'; when the constitution fails to promote that end, then a patriot may legitimately indulge the 'daring, but often dangerous spirit of innovation' and seek to alter the constitution.[68] Even the terminally douce William Robertson was prepared to advance 'a modest theory of resistance appropriate to the political culture of modern Britain'.[69]

Indeed, the Buchananite tradition of contractarian political thought – with its strong civic overtones – provides a major point of continuity between Reformation Scotland and the age of the Enlightenment. As Dugald Stewart observed, Buchanan's political philosophy bears 'in its general spirit, a closer resemblance to the political philosophy of the eighteenth century, than any composition which had previously appeared'.[70] In the works of Enlightenment writers like Hutcheson, Ferguson, Smith, Witherspoon, Reid, Stewart and Millar, we encounter a familiar nexus of 'Calvinist humanist' ideas and values: a republican concern for the general good; an opposition to luxury and 'effeminacy'; an ideal of active civic participation, together with a constitutionalist belief in limited government and the ultimate right to resist. And again, as with Buchanan, this civic ethos is founded on a decisively social view of man: Dugald Stewart cites Buchanan as an authority for his

65 See, for instance, Colin Kidd, *Subverting Scotland's Past: Scottish Whig Historians and the Creation of an Anglo-British Identity, 1689–c.1830* (Cambridge, 1993).
66 J. C. Stewart-Robertson, '*Sancte Socrates*: Scottish Reflections on Obedience and Resistance', in *Man and Nature: Proceedings of the Canadian Society for Eighteenth-Century Studies*, ed. by Roger L. Emerson and others (London, Ontario, 1982), pp. 65–79 (p. 68).
67 *The Works of Dugald Stewart*, 7 vols (Cambridge, 1829), VII, 103.
68 Adam Smith, *The Theory of Moral Sentiments*, ed. by D. D. Raphael and A. L. Macfie (Oxford, 1976), pp. 185, 231–2.
69 Kidd, pp. 197–98.
70 Dugald Stewart, *Dissertation, exhibiting a General View of the Progress of Metaphysical, Ethical, and Political Philosophy, since the Revival of Letters in Europe*, in *Works*, VI, 57.

assertion that 'we are led by a natural and instinctive desire to associate with our species'.[71]

Nevertheless, despite these points of continuity, we must be wary of glib and unhistorical comparisons. Political discourses are implicated in particular social contexts, and the society of Smith and Ferguson was significantly different from that of Buchanan or even of Andrew Fletcher. Accordingly, the civic tradition does not appear unchanged or unchallenged in the works of the Scottish Enlightenment. John Robertson and Nicholas Phillipson have shown how, in the work of Hume and Smith, the civic paradigm (to use Pocock's phrase) is supplemented by a liberal paradigm, to meet the changed environment of modern commercial society. Certain traditional civic principles – that commercial wealth is incompatible with virtue, that citizenship requires ownership of land – are modified by the insights of liberal political economy: commerce could benefit the public through increased revenue, while the spread of wealth might permit a broader diffusion of citizenship.[72] With the development of commerce, as both Smith and Millar note, increasing numbers of people are freed from feudal dependence on great proprietors; wage-labourers develop 'notions of liberty and independence', and free and regular government is enabled to flourish.[73]

However, it would be a mistake to conclude that Buchananite civic humanism as a political discourse had become defunct or outmoded in Enlightenment Scotland. For one thing, 'Addisonian politeness', as John Dwyer has shown, supplemented rather than superseded the discourse of Buchananite or Fletcherian civic humanism.[74] Civic humanism remained the prevalent idiom of political discussion in the British Isles throughout the eighteenth century, and was utilised by political actors of various persuasions. Particularly as a polemical register for attacking ministerial influence, the position of placemen, and other components of the 'Whig supremacy', civic humanism was ubiquitous.[75] Being rather a 'reservoir of concepts' than a systematic programme, civic humanism could continue to inform the work of the Enlightenment literati.[76]

---

71 *The Philosophy of the Active and Moral Powers of Man*, in *Works*, V, 19, 26n.

72 John Robertson, 'The Scottish Enlightenment at the limits of the civic tradition', in *Wealth and Virtue: The Shaping of Political Economy in the Scottish Enlightenment*, ed. by Istvan Hont and Michael Ignatieff (Cambridge, 1983), pp. 137–78; Nicholas Phillipson, 'Adam Smith as civic moralist', in *Wealth and Virtue*, pp. 179–202.

73 Adam Smith, *An Inquiry into the Nature and Causes of the Wealth of Nations*, ed. by R. H. Campbell and A. S. Skinner, 2 vols (Oxford, 1976), I, 412; William C. Lehmann, *John Millar of Glasgow 1735–1801: His Life and Thought and his Contributions to Sociological Analysis* (Cambridge, 1960), pp. 289–92.

74 John Dwyer, 'Enlightened Spectators and Classical Moralists: Sympathetic Relations in Eighteenth-Century Scotland', in *Sociability and Society in Eighteenth-Century Scotland*, ed. by John Dwyer and Richard Sher (Edinburgh, 1993), pp. 96–118.

75 M. M. Goldsmith, 'Liberty, luxury and the pursuit of happiness', in *The Languages of Political Theory in Early-Modern Europe*, pp. 225–51 (pp. 232–35).

76 Robertson, 'The Scottish Enlightenment at the limits of the civic tradition', p. 140.

And continue it did. For, if modern commercial society had challenged the civic tradition, it is equally true that, for many Enlightenment writers, the civic tradition constituted a powerful challenge to the values and mores of modern commercial society. If commercial society created the *material* conditions for widespread citizenship, it tended to destroy the *moral* conditions of citizenship. Both Ferguson and Smith agree that, in a commercial society, government must act not only to protect the lives and property of its citizens, but also to nurture and develop the public spirit of those citizens whose mental and moral faculties are impaired by the division of labour.[77] Ferguson's *Essay*, in particular, is haunted by the erosion of public spirit in modern centralised states:

> If national institutions, calculated for the preservation of liberty, instead of calling upon the citizen to act for himself, and to maintain his rights, should give a security, requiring, on his part, no personal attention of effort; this seeming perfection of government might weaken the bands of society . . . [78]

Many eighteenth-century Presbyterians, nurtured in a tradition of active armed resistance to Stuart tyranny and Jacobite rebellions, found it difficult to remain content with a government which asked nothing more of its citizens than docile obedience. Anxiety over the waning of public spirit in modern commercial societies was evident in the (unsuccessful) campaigns for a Scots militia which many of the literati undertook in 1759–62 and 1775–83.[79] Alarm at the decline of public spirit was only heightened by the burgeoning radius of British imperial dominion. As Linda Colley argues, an increased fear of corruption, and of contamination by 'Asiatic luxury', accompanied the sudden massive expansion of Britain's Empire following the Seven Years War.[80] Again, this anxiety is evident in the works of the later Scottish Enlightenment. In the work of Ferguson, the mood of confidence in the harmonious progress of commerce and virtue, the mood one associates with Hume, has given way to a much more pessimistic vision of commercialism's social consequences. In what amounts to an exercise in conjectural history as jeremiad, Ferguson laments the fragmentation of public spirit in modern commercial societies, the 'Corruption incident to Polished Nations'. It is this type of anxiety which explains the tendency of the literati to eulogise the vigorous civic patriotism of more primitive societies – whether the highland society of James Macpherson's Ossian poems, or the classical states admired by Ferguson. When Ferguson praised the ancient Greek republics, it was on the grounds that 'the people were generally

---

77 Adam Ferguson, *An Essay on the History of Civil Society 1767*, ed. by Duncan Forbes (Edinburgh, 1966), pp. 250, 263; Smith, *Wealth of Nations*, II, 781–82.

78 *Essay*, p. 191.

79 For which, see John Robertson, *The Scottish Enlightenment and the Militia Issue* (Edinburgh, 1985).

80 Linda Colley, *Britons: Forging the Nation, 1707–1837* (1992; repr. London, 1994), pp. 101–5.

admitted to a share in the government; and . . . were obliged, by necessity, to bear a part in the defence of their country'.[81]

The superior civic virtue of small, independent polities is a recurrent topos in the works of the later Scottish Enlightenment. As John Dwyer observes, many of these works 'can be read as attempts to counter the ethical contamination emanating from the seat of an increasingly extended and decadent empire'.[82] In *The Wealth of Nations*, Smith argues that Great Britain 'resembles one of those unwholesome bodies in which some of the vital parts are overgrown, and which, upon that account, are liable to many dangerous disorders'.[83] Ferguson is similarly concerned about the threat to national liberty posed by the enlargement of national territory:

> In proportion as territory is extended, its parts lose their relative importance to the whole. Its inhabitants cease to perceive their connection with the state, and are seldom united in the execution of any national, or even of any factious, designs. Distance from the seats of administration, and indifference to the persons who contend for preferment, teach the majority to consider themselves as the subjects of a sovereignty, not as the members of a political body.[84]

Territorial enlargement leads to the alienation not only of individuals but of the peripheral areas and regions of a polity – the 'parts' become indifferent to the 'whole'. In such a situation, public vigilance falters, and the abuses of government proceed unchecked. Not very far below the surface of these remarks is the fear that the despotic sway which the British state is exercising over its imperial conquests will encourage high-handed government in the domestic sphere. Of all the circumstances which lead a country to descend into despotism, 'there is none, perhaps, that arrives at this termination, with so sure an aim, as the perpetual enlargement of territory'.[85]

In small polities, however, this descent into despotism is unlikely to occur. Instead of feeling alienated and overawed by a distant seat of government, the members of such communities maintain an intimate scrutiny of their rulers:

> Small communities, however corrupted, are not prepared for despotical government: their members, crouded together, and contiguous to the seats of power, never forget their relation to the public; they pry, with habits of familiarity and freedom, into the pretensions of those who would rule . . . [86]

Ferguson's conviction that it is easier to exercise the right of private judgement in a small state than a large one is shared by John Millar, the dedicated radical who held

81 *Essay*, p. 229.
82 John Dwyer, 'Introduction: A "Peculiar Blessing": Social Converse in Scotland from Hutcheson to Burns', in *Sociability and Society in Eighteenth-Century Scotland*, pp. 1–22 (p. 6).
83 *Wealth of Nations*, II, 604.
84 *Essay*, pp. 271–2.
85 *Essay*, p. 272.
86 *Essay*, p. 271.

the chair of civil law at Glasgow. In small states, argues Millar, where the public forms a cohesive, compact unit, it can mobilise swiftly against the encroachments of government:

> When a state consists only of a small territory, and the bulk of the inhabitants live in one city, they have frequently occasion to converse together, and to communicate their sentiments upon every subject of importance. Their attention therefore is roused by every instance of oppression in the government; and as they easily take the alarm, so they are capable of quickly uniting their forces in order to demand redress of their grievances.

In larger countries, by contrast, the inhabitants are not only less attentive to the actions of their government but are also unlikely to respond with sufficient speed or cohesion to attacks on their liberties:

> In large and extensive nations, the struggles between the sovereign and his people are ... more likely to terminate in favour of despotism. In a wide country, the encroachments of government are frequently over-looked; and, even when the indignation of the people has been roused by flagrant injustice, they find it difficult to combine in uniform and vigorous measures for the defence of their rights.[87]

The difficulties encountered by the Friends of the People in co-ordinating Scottish and English activism in the 1790s – a pan-British Convention held in Edinburgh in October 1793 had to be adjourned pending the late arrival of the English delegates – rather underscores Millar's point. Millar also points to the fact that the sovereign's public revenue will be proportionately greater in a large and populous country, augmenting the influence to be gained through the dispensation of crown patronage.[88]

One important subtext of Millar's remarks on crown patronage was the widespread contemporary view that George III was seeking to extend the influence of the crown in a manner that threatened the balance of the British constitution. The king's determination to have a completely free choice in the appointment of ministers and to enjoy an 'unfettered use of royal prerogatives' led radicals to believe that, in the words of John Dunning's parliamentary motion of 1780, 'the influence of the crown has increased, is increasing, and ought to be diminished'.[89] The 'high-handed' conduct of the dispute with the American colonies merely reinforced the view of George III as an overweening monarch determined to subvert the constitution. Many radicals feared that the court was 'using the colonies as a testing ground for its policy of subverting liberty'.[90]

---

87 Lehmann, pp. 292–3.
88 Lehmann, p. 293.
89 Dickinson, 'Radicals and Reformers', p. 125.
90 H. T. Dickinson, *Liberty and Property: Political Ideology in Eighteenth-Century Britain* (London, 1977), p. 215.

Alarm at 'regal usurpation' and the subversion of the British constitution is a recurrent motif in Millar's writings. In his *Letters of Crito*, originally published in the *Scots Chronicle* between May and September 1796, Millar attacks the war against France as the last throw of a corrupt regime out to save its own skin. The aim of the British government, says Millar, is nothing less than to restore the ancient 'despotism' in France, for the sole purpose of deterring those domestic reformers who are campaigning for the renovation of the British constitution. In the course of his argument, Millar declares his attachment to the British constitution, *on revolution principles*, but he also points to the 'urgent necessity of correcting some very flagrant abuses' which have 'produced a remarkable deviation from its original principles'. In particular, there is a need to make the House of Commons once more a truly representative body, by extending the franchise to a much larger proportion of the nation. This will help to counter the 'prodigious progress of Ministerial influence and corruption'[91] which the growth of government patronage and the extension of royal prerogative have permitted.

Millar founds his political views on the Hutchesonian principle of 'utility'.[92] That the legitimacy of sovereign power depends on its being exercised for the benefit of the society at large, is, for Millar, a self-evident truth:

> If the people should once be led to *think* upon the subject of government, they . . . must immediately see that government is intended, by the wise and good Author of nature, for the benefit of the whole community; and that every power, inconsistent with this great principle, assumed by any person, under whatever title, of prince, king, or emperor, is manifestly unjust and tyrannical.[93]

For Millar, such tyrannical power may properly be resisted. As he indicates in the *Historical View of the English Government* (1787), 'it is the height of absurdity to suppose, that, when an illegal and unwarrantable power is usurped, the people have no right to resist the exercise of it by punishing the usurper'.[94]

The Presbyterian roots of Millar's politics are evident throughout his writings, not least in his ferocious anticlericalism and his sallies against 'priestcraft'. He insists that the freedom to submit the measures of government to the tribunal of one's individual reason is part of the Protestant right of private judgement: 'why may not the inhabitants of this island enjoy the right of private judgement in speculating upon their government?' Like many Presbyterian and Dissenting radicals of the period, he interprets the French Revolution in millenarian terms as heralding the downfall of the popish antichrist:

> The Roman Catholic superstition, that gigantic monster which has drunk so much human blood, that dragon which has long guarded the den of ignorance,

91 John Millar, *Letters of Crito, on the Causes, Objects, and Consequences, of the Present War* (Edinburgh, 1796), p. 103.
92 Lehmann, p. 352.
93 *Letters of Crito*, p. 9.
94 Lehmann, p. 352.

and held more than the half of Europe in the chains of moral and political slavery, seems now to be fast approaching his last agonies.[95]

As his references to Catholicism as the instrument of 'undue influence and corruption' make clear, Millar regards corruption and tyranny in church and state as part of the same malaise.[96] Both Roman Catholic dogma and divine right ideology are species of 'superstition' designed to reduce the public to slavery. What Millar, in the *Historical View*, calls the 'connexion . . . between . . . religious and civil plans of government' is also his reason for celebrating the Whiggish principles of Presbyterians. The limited, conditional authority delegated to the Presbyterian clergy disposes Presbyterians to favour a civil government of limited, conditional monarchy.[97] Moreover, as public servants, the Presbyterian clergy have typically acted as the mouthpiece of the people, speaking out in defence of the liberties of the subject: historically, the Presbyterian ministers 'beheld with jealousy and apprehension the lofty pretensions of the crown, and sounded throughout the kingdom the alarm of regal usurpation'.[98] With this reference to Presbyterianism's radical past, returning us once more to the age of Buchanan and Knox, we perceive again the thread which connects the Reformers of the sixteenth with those of the eighteenth century.

*   *   *

This chapter has discussed some of the key political discourses which shaped radical thought and action in lowland Scotland in the later eighteenth century. There is a sense in which these discourses may be regarded as forming a discursive tradition, connecting George Buchanan and the Reformation theorists to the Real Whigs, the thinkers of the Scottish Enlightenment and the 1790s radicals. This tradition might be characterised in various ways: whether with Caroline Robbins, as a Scottish Real Whig canon (comprising Buchanan, Fletcher, Hutcheson, Smith, Ferguson and Millar); or, with David Allan, as the 'Calvinist and humanist' radical tradition; or, with Christopher Harvie as 'a tradition of Scottish constitutional thought' which constitutes a 'continuum between the Scots Reformation and the political theory of the Scottish Enlightenment'.[99]

However, we must remember that this is not a rigorously homogenous tradition. For one thing, it incorporated thinkers from English and Irish Real Whig backgrounds as well as native Scots. It is also crucial to appreciate that the discourses discussed in this chapter were rooted in different historical periods and betray different concerns and emphases. The contractarian discourse of the Reformation

---

95 *Letters of Crito*, p. 50.
96 *Letters of Crito*, p. 49.
97 Lehmann, p. 374.
98 Lehmann, p. 374.
99 Robbins, pp. 177–220; Allan, p. 109; Christopher Harvie, 'The Covenanting Tradition', in *Sermons and Battle Hymns: Protestant Popular Culture in Modern Scotland*, ed. by Graham Walker and Tom Gallagher (Edinburgh, 1990), pp. 8–23 (p. 12).

and Covenanting periods foregrounds popular sovereignty and the right to resist tyranny. With Real Whiggism, the focus is on maintaining the balance of the constitution, and the need to oppose ministerial corruption. The political discourse of the Scottish Enlightenment emphasises participation and the need for active citizenship, the notion of colonial rights, and the superior virtue of small polities as against large, unwieldy empires. At the root of these discourses, nevertheless, is a common core of principles: that governments are not directly ordained by God but rather set up by people for their own welfare and convenience; that government is a covenant or contract between ruler and ruled; that the people are sovereign and their allegiance is conditional; that authority ascends from below; that the welfare of a state depends on the participatory citizenship of its people. These are the principles which unite the political discourses discussed in this chapter, and which may be counted among Burns's own 'first principles in Religion and Politics' (*Letters*, I, 77). It remains to be seen how Robert Burns was introduced to the languages of radicalism, and this subject will form the basis of the next chapter.

CHAPTER TWO

'Learn'd and Clark': A Radical Schooling

Writing to Byron in 1813, Walter Scott declared that Burns 'had an education not much worse than the sons of many gentlemen in Scotland'.[1] An element of hyperbole is discernible here. Burns attended no high school or university, and what formal schooling he did receive was snatched in short bursts when the demands of farm labour permitted. Two and a half years at a local village school, under a schoolmaster hired by his father, was effectively the substance of Burns's formal schooling. This short stint, during which he learned reading, writing and grammar, was over by late 1768, when Burns was nine. Later, in 1773, Burns boarded with his old schoolmaster for three weeks, to revise his English grammar and to learn some French. He completed two further brief spells of schooling, improving his handwriting at Dalrymple parish school for a few weeks in 1772, and learning mathematics and mensuration at Kirkoswald in the summer of 1775.

As a scholastic career, this is meagre enough. On the other hand, it is crucial to appreciate that Burns's education was far more extensive than his formal schooling. It could hardly be otherwise, given the fiercely intellectual presence of William Burnes, a man who bought and borrowed books for his sons and remorselessly engaged them in 'improving' conversations. We must recall, too, that Burns's schoolmaster, John Murdoch, boarded with each of his employers in turn, and was an influence well beyond the hours of school. Moreover, when he took up a post as English teacher in Ayr, Murdoch continued to visit the family, often bringing colleagues along for impromptu seminars at Mount Oliphant farmhouse. A culture of learning was evident, not merely in Burns's home environment but in the wider community, and any discussion of the poet's education must consider his participation in those key institutions of the 'popular Enlightenment' – the book club, the debating society and the Masonic lodge.

Perhaps, then, Scott's assessment isn't so far from the truth. Burns was indeed, as he boasted in a mock elegy written in 1787, 'learn'd and clark'.[2] Through a variety of formal and informal channels, he acquired an education that belies his popular image as the 'heaven-taught ploughman'. In this chapter I discuss the political dimension to that education, exploring the political writers and texts to which Burns's schooling exposed him. How, and by what means, was Burns exposed to the

---

1 *The Critical Heritage*, p. 258.
2 'Elegy on the Death of Robert Ruisseaux' (K, 141), l. 17.

political ideas and idioms discussed in the previous chapter? Where did he absorb the language of liberty? In seeking answers to such questions, we should be conscious that book-learning formed only one aspect of Burns's political education. It cannot be stressed too strongly that the formative element in Burns's 'radical schooling' was his early experience of unremitting labour, grinding poverty, judicial violence and the threat of dispossession. It is also true that Burns's most immediate exposure to radical discourse was through a strong oral culture celebrating the Covenanting matryrs. Debating societies and Masonic lodges, and the New Light circles in which he moved, helped further Burns's political education.

However, these were not the only channels through which Real Whig politics reached Burns. In what follows, while I acknowledge the significance of these less formal factors, my discussion will concentrate on Burns's formal schooling under John Murdoch and on one key textbook in particular: Arthur Masson's *A Collection of English Prose and Verse, For the Use of Schools*. This is not a subject that has attracted much attention. Overwhelmingly, discussions of Burns's early reading have adopted a narrow stylistic perspective, with critics habitually deploring the influence of 'alien' English literary models on Burns's poetry.[3] The question of the ideological or political import of Burns's reading matter has been overlooked. This is unfortunate, for, viewed in this light, the supposedly 'anglicising' material absorbed by Burns is far from alien to his own regional culture in the Presbyterian south-west: the Whiggish sentiments of poets like Addison, Thomson and Akenside were hardly foreign to Covenanting Ayrshire. From a political point of view, Masson's *Collection* is a particularly illuminating document. Surprisingly neglected by Burns scholars, the poet's school reading-book had a profound influence, not just on the development of Burns's political ideas, but on the evolution of his satirical techniques. Murdoch and Masson will be discussed in detail later in the chapter. For now, we begin with the informal elements of Burns's schooling and his involvement in a lively culture of popular education.

Burns and Popular Education

In a letter of 1791 to Sir John Sinclair, editor of that lasting monument of the late Scottish Enlightenment, the *Statistical Account of Scotland*, Burns delivers himself of a paean to popular education:

> To store the minds of the lower classes with useful knowledge, is certainly of very great consequence, both to them as individuals, and to society at large. Giving them a turn for reading and reflection, is giving them a source of innocent and laudable amusement; and besides, raises them to a more dignified degree in the scale of rationality.   (*Letters*, II, 107)

---

3 See, for instance, David Daiches, *Robert Burns*, 2nd edn (London, 1966), pp. 41–3; McIntyre, p. 16.

What Burns articulates here is a civic theory of popular learning. For Burns, the knowledge acquired by the lower classes should above all be 'useful', though this criterion need not be interpreted narrowly: later in the letter Burns counts novels, works of history, sermons and magazines in a list of worthwhile books. As well as utility, Burns emphasises the social impact of education, its value not simply to individuals, but to the community as a whole, 'to society at large'. Finally, education is about esteem and self-respect: it enables the lower classes to improve their position in a hierarchy defined, not by wealth or titles, but by intelligence and – that key Enlightenment virtue – 'rationality'.

The occasion for this hymn to civic education is itself significant. Burns is writing to provide Sinclair with the history of a local circulating library or book club – the Monkland Friendly Society – formed by a group of tenant farmers in Nithsdale, under the patronage of Burns's friend and neighbour, the radical Whig Robert Riddell of Glenriddell. Burns was the effective treasurer and librarian of the society, whose members paid an entry fee and a monthly levy for the purpose of purchasing books. The Monkland group was one of several book clubs and reading societies with which Burns was involved throughout his life. As a young man in Ayrshire he helped to found the Tarbolton Bachelors' Club, a debating society for the young men of his village. Later he belonged to the Mauchline Conversation Club, a book club proper, which amassed a respectable library, its early orders – perhaps predictably – including the *Mirror* and the *Lounger*.

Book clubs were a burgeoning phenomenon in the period, and seem to have been associated particularly with Presbyterian and Dissenting communities. English and Irish Dissenters shared the Scots Presbyterians' enthusiasm for popular education.[4] It was from the Presbyterian reading societies of Ulster that the school of vernacular 'weaver poets' emerged in the 1790s.[5] The popularity of these organisations was partly a matter of economics: the book clubs permitted the lower classes to share the cost of book-buying at a time of rising prices. They were also venues in which ideas might be exchanged, and opinions aired and tested, in a context of democratic debate. Presbyterian and Dissenting culture placed a high value, not just on the acquisition of knowledge, but on its diffusion, its circulation, its communication. The monthly meeting, at which members would discuss their reading and conduct formal debates, was a staple feature of such clubs. Often there was a convivial element to the meetings, although alcohol consumption was usually regulated: the Tarbolton Bachelors' Club's stipulation that members were to drink no more than three pence-worth of beer per meeting seems to have been fairly common (it was shared, for instance, by the Ballynahinch Reading Club in Down).[6]

One striking feature of the book clubs' constitutions was their democratic procedures. The choice of books to be purchased by the Monkland Friendly Society

4 Paulin, *Day-Star*, pp. 36–7.
5 On Ulster book clubs, see J. R. R. Adams, 'Reading Societies in Ulster', *Ulster Folklife*, 26 (1980), 55–64.
6 Adams, 'Reading Societies', p. 57.

was 'always ... decided by the majority', and 'members had their choice of the volumes in rotation' (*Letters*, II, 107). In the Tarbolton Bachelors' Club, each decision – from the election of a president (a new one was chosen each month) to the choice of subjects for debate – was carried by majority vote.[7] Moreover, some of the topics we know were debated at the Bachelors' Club – for instance, *Whether is the savage man, or the peasant of* a *civilized country, in the most happy situation?* – invited highly politicised discussions.[8] Whether or not the authorities were justified in regarding the book clubs as nurseries of sedition, 'hotbeds of radicalism',[9] they undoubtedly exercised the political consciousness of the lower classes. One conservative commentator, describing northeast Ulster in terms that apply equally well to Burns's Ayrshire, observed that 'the mass of the people are Presbyterians, can read and write and are fond of speculating on religion and politics'.[10]

It is important to dissociate this movement of popular education from any connotations of 'self-help' in the Victorian sense. The book clubs were not geared towards personal financial advancement; the aim was not to help individuals to raise themselves out of their class. The tenth regulation of the Tarbolton Bachelors' Club expressly excluded anyone 'whose only will is to heap up money'.[11] This is a point which perplexes James Currie in his discussion of the Tarbolton Bachelors' Club and the Mauchline Conversation Club. Why, Currie wonders, did the members of these societies devote such energy to acquiring knowledge and refining their taste, when they had no real prospect of improving their station? He gets a response from Robert's brother Gilbert, whose long letter on the subject of book clubs is included in Currie's fourth edition of the *Works*.[12]

For Gilbert, education has nothing to do with the attempt to 'rise above one's station'; indeed, he believes that the acquisition of riches must invariably involve 'degradation of character'. Rather, the education of the lower classes should be 'directed to their improvement as men, as the means of increasing their virtue'. Above all, education is important in making plain to a man 'what duties are incumbent on him as a rational creature, and a member of society'. The 'taste' and 'delicacy of sentiment' promoted by works like the *Mirror* and *Lounger* are 'the strongest guard and the surest foundation of morality and virtue'. The function of learning is not to raise a man to a higher station but to teach him the dignity of the station he holds:

> [T]he man of enlarged mind feels the respect due to him as a man; he has learned that no employment is dishonourable in itself; that while he performs

7 The 'Rules and Regulations' of the Bachelors' Club are given in *The Works of Robert Burns*, ed. by James Currie, 4th edn, 4 vols (London, 1803), I, 363–67.
8 Currie, I, 118.
9 Adams, 'Reading Societies', p. 56.
10 Richard Musgrave, *Memoirs of the Different Rebellions in Ireland* (Dublin, 1801), p. 155.
11 Currie, I, 367.
12 Currie, I, 377–95.

aright the duties of that station in which God has placed him, he is as great as a king in the eyes of Him whom he is principally desirous to please.

Learning dispels the mystique which surrounds birth and wealth, and reveals a more pertinent standard of worth – what Robert Burns calls the 'scale of rationality'. Like his brother, Gilbert applauds the civic benefits of education: whether in parish schools or book clubs, education produces 'a virtuous and enlightened populace'. With this phrase, Gilbert recalls the penultimate stanza of 'The Cotter's Saturday Night' (K, 72), in which the speaker prays that

> A *virtuous Populace* may rise the while,
> And stand a wall of fire, around their much-lov'd ISLE.   (ll. 179–80)

What this allusion implies is that education is the guarantor of civic virtue among the lower classes. It is education which inoculates the common people from '*Luxury*'s contagion, weak and vile!' (l. 177), and which instils the manly independence and patriotism which Robert's poem celebrates. In a poem whose moral centre is an act of Presbyterian book-learning – the 'priest-like Father' reading the 'sacred page' (l. 118) of scripture to the family – the connection between education and virtue is constantly being asserted. This is the civic idiom familiarised by contemporary social theorists like Adam Ferguson, for whom a nation's vigour is measured by the patriotism of its common people. For Burns – and indeed for Gilbert – it is education which promotes this patriotism.

  The civic theory of popular education held by Robert and Gilbert may be part of their Presbyterian environment, but it can also be traced more directly to the influence of one man. In the letter to Currie, Gilbert explicitly links his views on education with those of his 'worthy teacher, Mr Murdoch'. That Robert's views were shaped by the same influence is suggested by the letter he wrote to Murdoch in 1783, reporting on his progress to his former dominie (*Letters*, I, 16–18). Reassuring his old teacher that he has not become a 'sordid' man of affairs, Burns presents himself as a voracious reader, who endeavours to 'form [his] conduct' after the 'glorious models' of Shenstone, Thomson, Macpherson and others. The literary training he received from Murdoch has ensured that Burns enters adulthood as a man of public spirit. Clearly, this ultimately political understanding of education as a training in civic virtue can be traced to the influence of the young scholar who ran the Alloway school between 1765 and 1768. [13]

'*A Masterly Teacher*': Burns and John Murdoch

The Presbyterian culture in which Burns was raised, which required every layman to read the scriptures for himself, placed a high social value on learning and education. A succession of parliamentary Acts, the most important of which was the

---

13 On Murdoch, see William Will, *John Murdoch: Tutor of Robert Burns* (Glasgow, 1929), reprinted from *Burns Chronicle*, 4 (1929), 60–89.

Act of 1696, had made provision for a school in every parish, to be established and financed at the expense of the parish heritors (local landowners), and conducted under the supervision of the kirk session, who would appoint and oversee the schoolmaster. In urban areas, it was the responsibility of town councils to provide schools, and so a system of burgh schools existed alongside the parish school network.

The education system thus established by law was not always sufficient to meet the demand for literacy in eighteenth-century Scotland. This was particularly apparent in rural areas. The school-in-every-parish programme had made 'considerable progress' by the end of the seventeenth century and was 'virtually complete' by the 1790s.[14] Nevertheless, there were areas of eighteenth-century Scotland – and Ayrshire was one – in which the system was incomplete. It was also the case that, due to the rise in population, some parishes found that a single school was not enough. However, where the parish schools system was insufficient, local inhabitants themselves organised private or 'adventure' schools to educate their children. In the second half of the century there was a 'veritable explosion in the number of private schools' in the Scottish countryside.[15]

At one time an independent parish, Alloway had been incorporated into the parish of Ayr in 1690, and so had no parish school of its own.[16] There was an adventure school at Alloway Mill, and it was here that Burns began his schooling in early 1765 and was 'grounded a little in English'.[17] However, the school closed shortly after Burns's enrolment when the schoolmaster, William Campbell, left to become master of the workhouse in Ayr. It was then that William Burnes, in conjunction with four of his neighbours, engaged an eighteen-year-old scholar from Ayr, John Murdoch, to teach their children.

There has been a tradition of rather glib disparagement of Murdoch by Burns scholars, for whom an occasionally pompous prose style has seemed sufficient reason to damn the dominie as a worthless pedant. In fact, a promising young scholar educated at Ayr and Edinburgh, Murdoch was something of a catch for his Alloway employers. When he left the Alloway school it was 'to teach and reside in the family of an opulent farmer'.[18] Returning to Ayr in 1772, Murdoch was 'appointed (being one of five candidates examined) to teach the English school'.[19] After four years at Ayr, Murdoch moved to London, working as a teacher of English and French (in 1792 he gave English lessons to Talleyrand), and composing a number of textbooks, including *The pronunciation and orthography of the French language* (1788) and the *Dictionary of Distinctions* (1811).[20] Though he fell on hard

14 T. M. Devine, *The Scottish Nation 1700–2000* (Harmondsworth, 1999), p. 92.
15 Devine, *Scottish Nation*, p. 94.
16 John Strawhorn, *Ayrshire at the Time of Burns* (Kilmarnock, 1959), p. 259.
17 Murdoch to Joseph Cooper Walker, in Will, p. 25.
18 Gilbert Burns, letter to James Currie, 24 October 1800, in Currie, I, 382.
19 Currie, I, 90.
20 James Mackay, *Burns: A Biography of Robert Burns* (Edinburgh, 1992), p. 502.

times in later life, Murdoch was evidently a scholar of higher calibre than the ruck of village dominies.

If Murdoch remains a neglected figure in analyses of the poet's early development, this may reflect a general feeling that, in De Lancey Ferguson's words, 'Murdoch's service was too brief to have much permanent effect on Burns's mind'.[21] However, this view overlooks a number of key factors. What must be borne in mind is not simply the fact of Murdoch's regular residence with the Burneses in the period 1765–68, but also the extraordinary bond which grew up between Murdoch and William Burnes. It is impossible to read Murdoch's letters without being struck by his reverence and affection for the 'rational Christian friend' he described as 'by far the best of the human race that ever I had the pleasure of being acquainted with' and 'the man who, of all mankind that I ever knew, stood highest in my esteem'.[22] It seems likely that Murdoch assisted William Burnes in producing the religious Manual by which Robert was instructed, and we should certainly view the two men as collaborators in Robert's education.

Moreover, when Murdoch returned to Ayrshire in 1772 he renewed his acquaintance with the Burnes family, sending them 'Pope's works, and some other poetry'.[23] Robert's three-week sojourn with his old schoolmaster took place in 1773, when his pupil was, according to Murdoch, 'with me day and night, in school, at all meals, and in all my walks'.[24] And when Robert returned home to help with the harvest, Murdoch kept up a close relationship with the poet and his family:

> I did not, however, lose sight of him; but was a frequent visitant at his father's house, when I had my half holiday, and very often went accompanied with one or two persons more intelligent than myself, that good William Burnes might enjoy a mental feast. Then the labouring oar was shifted to some other hand. The father and the son sat down with us, when we enjoyed a conversation, wherein solid reasoning, sensible remark, and a moderate seasoning of jocularity, were so nicely blended as to render it palatable to all the parties. Robert had a hundred questions to ask me about the French, &c., and the father, who had always rational information in view, had still some question to propose to my more learned friends, upon moral or natural philosophy or some such interesting subject.[25]

Who these 'more learned friends' might be is a question worth posing. In the narrative of his brother's life which he wrote for Mrs Dunlop, Gilbert recalls that, during Robert's stay in Ayr, Murdoch introduced his star pupil to a number of colleagues and friends, including the Francophile Dr Malcolm and Mr Robertson, the school's writing master. Mr Paterson, an Aberdeenshire man who had been 'one

---

21 *Pride and Passion*, p. 41.
22 Will, pp. 23, 28, 33.
23 Currie, I, 66.
24 Murdoch to Joseph Cooper Walker, in Will, p. 27.
25 Murdoch to Joseph Cooper Walker, in Will, p. 28.

of the established teachers in Ayr' when William Burnes settled at Alloway, is another possible participant in the Mount Oliphant seminars. After his death, his widow gave Gilbert and Robert access to Paterson's library, from which they borrowed the *Spectator* and Pope's *Homer*.[26]

For the isolated residents of Mount Oliphant, Murdoch was a point of contact with the learned and largely New Light intellectual circles of Ayr. He was also their channel to a much wider intellectual world in his role as librarian of the Ayr Library, to which William Burnes was a subscriber.[27] In the ideal scheme of education which Gilbert Burns outlines to Currie, he writes: 'I would have the schoolmaster act as librarian, and in recommending books to his young friends, formerly his pupils, and letting in the light of them upon their young minds, he should have the assistance of the minister'.[28] Murdoch did indeed act as the boys' librarian, and it is possible that the Burnes's minister, the Rev. William Dalrymple, assisted the dominie in recommending books. An erudite New Light minister, author of devotional works and a former Moderator of the General Assembly, Dalrymple was another intermediary between the Burnes household and Ayr's academic and clerical establishment.

It is worth noting at this point that many of the New Light ministers and laymen with whom Burns associated were graduates of Glasgow University, the intellectual centre of Burns's south-west, and one of the major disseminators of Real Whig principles in the British Isles.[29] Many of its influential professors – Francis Hutcheson, William Leechman, John Millar – promoted the Real Whig canon of Harrington, Sidney, Fletcher and Molesworth.[30] Nor was enthusiasm for Real Whiggery confined to the classroom. One student debating club at Glasgow was named the 'Oceana' after Harrington's great work.[31] Another student society, the Trinamphorian Club, corresponded with Molesworth in the 1720s, and received his enthusiastic backing in its struggle to vindicate the traditional right of the student body to participate in the election of the University Rector.[32] The university thus developed a tradition of political activism to match its academic promotion of Real Whiggism. John Millar, Professor of Civil Law between 1761 and 1801 and an active member of the Friends of the People, was particularly significant in this regard. Not only did he teach Thomas Muir, Lauderdale, the Earl of Buchan and other prominent reformers, but his writings were part of the 'principal diet of a rising generation of liberals . . . who led the Scottish agitation for reform'.[33] Given

---

26 Currie, I, 67–9.
27 Mackay, *Burns*, p. 42.
28 Currie, I, 393.
29 Robbins, pp. 17, 185, 214, 303, 356.
30 Ian McBride, 'The school of virtue: Francis Hutcheson, Irish Presbyterians and the Scottish Enlightenment', in *Political Thought in Ireland Since the Seventeenth Century*, ed. by D. George Boyce and others (London, 1993), pp. 73–99 (p. 86).
31 McFarland, p. 21.
32 Stewart, *A Deeper Silence*, pp. 82–90; McBride, 'The school of virtue', pp. 84–86.
33 Lehmann, p. 3.

this radical climate, it is no surprise that, of the thirty Presbyterian clerics implicated in the Irish Rebellion of 1798, fully two-thirds were Glasgow graduates.[34] Burns's associates among the Ayrshire New Light – Dalrymple, McMath, McQhuae and McGill – were products of this 'school of virtue' at Glasgow.

John Murdoch's own involvement with this New Light circle ended, somewhat abruptly, in 1776, when he was obliged to leave Ayr after a squabble with William Dalrymple. It seems certain, nevertheless, that Murdoch was a seminal influence on the poet's development. Though he only benefited from Murdoch's 'expert tuition'[35] for two and a half years, Burns's intercourse with Murdoch was fairly constant and intense in the periods 1765–8 and 1772–6. It was partly through Murdoch that Burns was introduced to the New Light circles of Ayr, and it was Murdoch, a 'Whig of the left', who instilled in Burns his civic view of popular education.[36] In the remainder of this chapter I look in greater detail at Burns's early schooling under Murdoch, and consider the significance of Burns's English lessons and of the reading-book he used.

A Real Whig Reading-Book? Masson's Collection *and the Politics of Burns*

In the autobiographical letter to Dr Moore, Burns recalls his first awareness of literary appreciation:

> The earliest thing of Composition that I recollect taking pleasure in was, The vision of Mirza and a hymn of Addison's beginning – "How are Thy servants blest, O Lord!" I particularly remember one half-stanza which was music to my boyish ear –
>
>> "For though in dreadful whirls we hung,
>> "High on the broken wave" –
>
> I met with these pieces in Mas[s]on's English Collection, one of my school-books.   (*Letters*, I, 135)

Masson's *Collection* was one of a handful of books used regularly in the classroom at Alloway: according to Murdoch, 'The books most commonly used in the school were, the *Spelling Book*, the *New Testament*, the *Bible*, Mason's [sic] *Collection of Prose and Verse*, and Fisher's *English Grammar*'.[37]

In eighteenth-century Scotland, the teaching of English to young children involved three principal stages. First, pupils were taught the basic elements of reading, via the A. B. C., the Shorter Catechism and the Bible. Next they studied Spelling Books in order to test and improve their vocabulary. Finally the pupils

---

34 McFarland, p. 247.
35 Mackay, *Burns*, p. 49.
36 Catherine Carswell, *The Life of Robert Burns* (London, 1930; repr. Edinburgh, 1990), p. 55.
37 Murdoch to Walker, in Will, pp. 25–6.

pored over collections of extracts from approved authors.[38] Masson's *Collection* was the book chosen by Murdoch for the third stage of this process. An anthology of short prose pieces and poems, the *Collection* is a varied volume, whose 320 pages encompass moral fables, episodes from ancient and modern history, Bible stories, hymns and psalms, soliloquies from Shakespeare and Home's *Douglas*, political orations from classical Greece and Rome, elegant letters, extracts from periodicals (the *Spectator*, the *Adventurer*, the *Rambler*) and selections from the poetry of Milton, Dryden, Addison, Pope, Thomson and Akenside.[39]

An Aberdonian, educated at Aberdeen Grammar School and Marischal College, Arthur Masson was a teacher of languages, first in Aberdeen and Glasgow, and latterly in Edinburgh. He was an associate of Hugh Blair and a pupil of Thomas Sheridan, and, like them, his concern was to instill 'proper' linguistic standards into young Scots. In one of the regular newspaper advertisements for his Edinburgh school, Masson promised to teach pupils 'how to read with propriety our English poets'. Another advertisement revealed that Masson was currently visiting London in order to further 'his improvement in the English Language, which above all others ought to be the study of every Briton'. He also gave classes in elocution and pronunciation on the model of Sheridan's famous lectures.[40] His *Collection* was a pedagogical tool in the process of training Scots provincials in the proprieties of polite metropolitan English. Its extracts from English poetry and prose would provide young Scots with a kind of junior version of the Belles Lettres courses taught by Hugh Blair and others in the Scottish universities.

As much recent scholarship has shown, the teaching of English, at school and university level, in eighteenth-century Britain was pioneered by Scots and provincial English Dissenters.[41] On one level, the aim was to educate provincial Britons in 'correct' English usage. But the teaching of English was also designed to inculcate the *political* values espoused by Scots Presbyterians and English Dissenters, to instruct young men in the principles of British liberty as understood by these denominations. Certainly, the material in Masson's *Collection* seems to have been selected with this aim in view, as the shibboleths of Protestant libertarianism are canvassed throughout. A section 'Of the Persecutions in the Reign of Queen MARY' (pp. 22–25) relates the sufferings of Protestant martyrs with indignantly

---

38 Alexander Law, 'Scottish Schoolbooks of the Eighteenth and Nineteenth Centuries', *Studies in Scottish Literature*, 18 (1983), 1–32 (p. 2).

39 Arthur Masson, *A Collection of English Prose and Verse, For the Use of Schools*, 4th edn (Edinburgh, 1764). Since Murdoch began to teach in Alloway in 1765, I make the assumption that this is the edition Burns studied.

40 Alexander Law, *Education in Edinburgh in the Eighteenth Century* (London, 1965), pp. 150–153.

41 Franklin E. Court, *Institutionalizing English Literature: The Culture and Politics of Literary Study, 1750–1900* (Stanford, 1992); Thomas P. Miller, *The Formation of College English: Rhetoric and Belles Lettres in the British Cultural Provinces* (Pittsburgh, 1997); *The Scottish Invention of English Literature*, ed. by Robert Crawford (Cambridge, 1998).

Gothic relish. The 'Story of the gun-powder treason' (pp. 26–28) condemns papist perfidy in predictable fashion, while the selection from 'Mrs Rowe's Letters, Moral and Entertaining' (pp. 188–208) contains a letter in which a virtuous young Protestant woman runs away from home rather than submit to her father's desire that she marry 'a bigotted papist' (pp. 193–97).

Beyond this overtly sectarian element, much of the material in Masson promotes a political agenda that might be termed Real Whig. The true end of government, the nature of kingship, the propriety of resisting tyranny, and the nature of Liberty: these are the issues repeatedly raised in the *Collection*. This applies not merely to the extracts from classical political oratory, but also to many of the poems, fables and accounts of historical events. It would not be a gross exaggeration to describe Masson's *Collection* as a kind of Real Whig reading-book. When Snyder argues that Burns 'shaped his standards of value in conformity with those which he found exemplified in Masson's anthology',[42] his words have a political as well as an aesthetic application.

However, before discussing Masson's *Collection* as a formative factor in Burns's political education in more detail, there is a pressing point to address. It may be doubted how much solid learning, let alone political philosophy, Burns could have absorbed at this early age. Notwithstanding John Murdoch's own reflections on this score – 'Let not parents and teachers imagine that it is needless to talk seriously to children. They are sooner fit to be reasoned with than is generally thought'[43] – it seems questionable to attribute any great significance to a book Burns read before the age of ten. Was not De Lancey Ferguson correct to argue that the material in Masson was 'too declamatory to be really within the grasp of a six- or seven-year-old intelligence'?[44]

Ferguson's proposition is persuasive. There are, however, several factors which weigh against it. It is important to bear in mind that, since Burns's school books were few, he studied those books very intensely: 'Burns had few books in his boyhood; consequently he almost memorized the few he had. A surprisingly large number of his favourite quotations can be traced to the poetic selections in Masson'.[45] Given the uncommonly 'retentive memory' of which Burns boasts, and to which Dugald Stewart attests, it is not surprising that Burns had many of Masson's extracts by heart.[46] Moreover, though some of its items might strike modern readers as difficult and demanding, the *Collection* was expressly designed for young children. Before he became a teacher of languages, Arthur Masson himself had taught English to young children, and his *Collection* was intended to answer the needs of such teachers.[47]

42 Franklyn Bliss Snyder, *The Life of Robert Burns* (New York, 1932), p. 44.
43 Murdoch to Cromek, in Will, pp. 33–34.
44 *Pride and Passion*, p. 40.
45 J. De Lancey Ferguson, 'Introduction', *The Letters of Robert Burns*, I, xlv.
46 See the autobiographical letter to Dr Moore, *Letters*, I, 133–46, and Stewart's letter in Currie, I, 143.
47 Law, *Education*, p. 149.

It is also true that Burns, more than most children his age, was accustomed to handling complex ideas and arguments. Gilbert Burns recalled that, at Mount Oliphant, the boys' father 'conversed familiarly on all subjects with us, as if we had been men', with the result, according to Murdoch, that Robert and Gilbert 'began to talk and reason like men much sooner than their neighbours'.[48] Moreover, it is quite possible that Burns actually possessed a copy of Masson and that his familiarity with the anthology extended well beyond his early period of schooling with Murdoch. Indeed, the very density of references to Masson in Burns's poetry suggests that Burns read and re-read the *Collection* throughout his youth and adolescence. At the very least, Masson's *Collection* indicates the kind of topics and writers that would have featured in the discussions of Burns and Murdoch, perhaps during those informal seminars at Mount Oliphant which lasted until Murdoch's departure for London in 1776.

What, then, of the political material in Masson's *Collection*? For purposes of clarity, I will divide this material into three sections. First, there is a group of fables, stories and historical vignettes in the early part of the book, which touch on the proper exercise and limits of political authority. Second, there are poetic selections from the work of seminal Real Whig writers, including Addison, Thomson and Akenside, which often have a political bearing. And finally, there is a group of classical political orations, such as the 'Speech of Fabritius to King Pyrrhus' or 'The second Olynthian of Demosthenes', in which issues of public corruption and the integrity of politicians are discussed.

One of the short group of 'Fables' with which the *Collection* begins is the 'Fable of the young prince and the bees' (pp. 2–3). A young prince, walking in a garden, stops to observe a hive of bees and to admire their industrious 'polity' or 'little commonwealth'. The queen bee addresses the young prince, drawing the moral of the scene before him:

> The view you have before you, young prince, must be entertaining, but may be made instructive. We suffer nothing like disorder, nor licentiousness among us: they are most esteemed, who by their capacity and diligence, can do most for the public weal. Our first places are always bestowed where there is most merit; and last of all, we are taking pains day and night for the benefit of man. Go, and imitate us, introduce that order and discipline among men, you so much admire in other creatures.

The bees' 'polity', as described by the queen, is a meritocracy. The most important offices in the state are filled without reference to birth or title or wealth, but simply according to the worth of the candidate, with worth defined, in civic humanist terms, as public spirit, the readiness to 'do most for the public weal'.

While the mechanical regularity of the bees' commonwealth might be rebarbative to Burns, the values of social cooperation and disciplined public service articulated in the fable are ones Burns upholds in his early political poems. Like Burns's early

48 Currie, I, 63; Murdoch to Walker, in Will, p. 30.

satires, the fable promotes a civic humanist ideal of public service, in which virtue consists in an individual's willingness to work for the public good, and government has the welfare of the public as its proper end. Of course, one extension of this principle is that, where rulers work to frustrate the proper end of government, then they may legitimately be resisted, and removed by force. The propriety of such resistance is made clear in 'The twelve Caesars', the section of Masson's *Collection* which offers a potted history of the Roman Empire.

In 'The twelve Caesars' (pp. 13–16), the public's duty to cashier tyrants is taken for granted. Caligula, we learn, was so 'far from entertaining any desire to benefit the public' that his 'behaviour compelled [the Romans] to cut him off for the security of their own persons, in the year of our Lord forty one'. Nero meets the same fate: 'His subjects having groaned under his tyranny fourteen years, and not able to endure it longer, put an end both to that and his life at once'. Aulus Vitellius, having claimed the emperorship through his military defeat of Otho, soon reveals tyrannical tendencies which necessitate his removal:

> *Aulus Vitellius*, returning victor to *Rome*, was saluted emperor by the senate. His luxury and cruelty soon rendered him so odious, that the people rose upon him, and after treating him with the vilest indignities, threw his dead body into the Tiber.

Domitian, who degenerated from the wise and virtuous example of his two immediate predecessors, Vespasian and Titus, receives his just reward when he is 'murdered by some of his nearest relations'. As these passages indicate, Masson's *Collection* leaves its reader in no doubt that the wages of tyranny is death. Given this unequivocal endorsement of tyrannicide in Burns's school reading-book, it is not surprising that Burns should have felt as he did about the 'deserved fate' of Louis XVI and Marie Antionette:

> What is there in the delivering over a perjured Blockhead & an unprincipled Prostitute into the hands of the hangman, that it should arrest for a moment, attention, in an eventful hour, when, as my friend Roscoe in Liverpool gloriously expresses it –
>
> > "When the welfare of Millions is hung in the scale
> > "And the balance yet trembles with fate!"   (*Letters*, II, 334)

This matter-of-fact acceptance of tyrannicide is, of course, a familiar part of Burns's religious inheritance in Covenanting Ayrshire, and the political significance of covenanting is made apparent in Masson's *Collection*, in the section entitled 'Abridgement of the history of the bible' (pp. 53–63). Chapter VI of this abridgement discusses the sufferings of the Jews under the tyrannical kings of Syria:

> They were exposed to divers persecutions, whereof the last and most cruel, was that of king *Antiochus*, who plundered and profaned the temple of *Jerusalem*, and made use of torments, in order to force the *Jews* to renounce their religion; as may be seen in the history of the *Maccabees*. This was he that forced *Mattathias*

and many *Jews* to enter into a covenant together for the preservation of their religion and liberty.

This last reference, to a covenant for the defence of civil and religious freedom, could hardly fail to resonate in an Ayrshire schoolroom.

If some extracts in Masson provide cautionary tales of tyrants and their merited ends, several others celebrate the virtues of exemplary rulers. In particular, there are three accounts of virtuous, public-spirited kings: King Alfred, King Canute and an unnamed King of Persia. These passages draw on the ideal of the Patriot King associated with the opposition Whigs of the 1740s and 1750s. This was an ideal of uncourtly kingship, which celebrated the virtuous monarch as a selfless servant of his people. Its classic statement was Bolingbroke's *The Idea of a Patriot King* (1749), a work which denied the divine right of kings, and argued that the true end of government was the good of the people, by whose consent the monarch governed. Portrayals of Patriot Kings pervade the dramatic literature of the period, in works such as Henry Brooke's *Gustavus Vasa* (1738), Mallet's *Mustapha* (1739), and Mallet and Thomson's *Alfred* (1740). It is this dissident Whig ideal of the Patriot King that shapes the kingly parables in Masson's *Collection*.[49]

The 'Story of Alfred' (pp. 18–20) is a panegyric on the perfect ruler. Eschewing all kingly luxury, Alfred devotes his time to exertions on behalf of his people. He is just, wise, and above all virtuous: 'No man was more frugal than he of two valuable things, his time, and his revenue; and no man wiser in the disposal of both'. This celebration of Alfred in Burns's schoolbook is telling, for Alfred holds an important place in Burns's personal pantheon of libertarian heroes, alongside nationalist icons like Wallace and Bruce. In the 'Ode [For General Washington's Birthday]' (K, 451), which eulogises the United States as the vanguard libertarian polity and bemoans the political apostasy of England and Scotland, Alfred is the recipient of an anguished apostrophe:

> Alfred, on thy starry throne,
>   Surrounded by the tuneful choir,
> The Bards that erst have struck the patriot lyre,
> And roused the freeborn Briton's soul of fire,
>   No more thy England own. –
> Dare injured nations form the great design,
>   To make detested tyrants bleed?
> Thy England execrates the glorious deed!
>   Beneath her hostile banners waving,
>   Every pang of honor braving,
> England in thunders calls – 'The Tyrant's cause is mine!'
>   That hour accurst, how did the fiends rejoice,
> And hell thro' all her confines raise th' exulting voice,

49 On the idea of the Patriot King, see Clark, *English Society 1660–1832*, pp. 114–21.

That hour which saw the generous English name
Linkt with such damned deeds of everlasting shame!   (ll. 29–43)

Here, Alfred stands as the exalted symbol of an English tradition of liberty which has been trampled underfoot by the country's present rulers. Ignoring England's own exemplary history of resistance to tyrannical rulers, Pitt's government is waging war on an 'injured nation' – France – which has achieved its own glorious revolution. Again we see Burns's unflinching approval of tyrannicide – 'the great design', 'the glorious deed'. The poem is written in 1794, when Britain is at war with Revolutionary France, and Pitt's ministry is suppressing the domestic reform movement in the treason trials of Thomas Hardy, John Horne Tooke and other English radicals. (The Scots reformers Muir and Palmer had been transported the previous year.) Invoking Alfred at this time of crisis, Burns is tapping into a longstanding radical or republican discourse which celebrates Alfred as the framer of the English constitution and the instigator of such judicial benefits as trial by juries. As in John Ryland's *Life and Character of Alfred the Great* (1784), British radicals of the period routinely invoked Alfred at the head of a 'liberal pantheon' that included Chaucer, Milton, Sydney, Harrison, Hampden, Vane and Marvell.[50]

As a reform-minded Scottish writer invoking the name of Alfred and the traditions of English liberty, Burns of course had significant predecessors in James Thomson and David Mallet, whose *Alfred: A Masque* (1740) was a favourite work of the anti-Walpole Whigs. Set during the ascendancy of the Danes, the play depicts the fugitive king as the prototype of a series of great English monarchs – Edward II, Elizabeth I, William III – who successfully avoided the temptations of courts and the flattery of courtiers ('the vermin of a court'), and governed sagely in the interests of the commonwealth by 'build[ing] on an eternal base, / On liberty and laws, the public weal'.[51] Burns knew the play well and quotes from it regularly in his letters; indeed, lines 'from Thomson's Alfred' are among Burns's 'very favorite' quotations (*Letters*, II, 165).

Following the discussion of Alfred in Masson's *Collection* is a vignette of another Patriot King, the 'Story of Canute' (pp. 20–21). Canute's attempt to turn back the waves is conventionally read as a parable of kingly hubris and vainglory; however, in this telling the incident is designed by the king as a lesson to his sycophantic courtiers on the limits of monarchical power. Vexed and disgusted by the flattery of his underlings, Canute forces them to look on while he commands the tide to retreat. His aim is to dispel the mystique surrounding royalty:

> Then rising from his seat, and looking around him, he desired all present to behold and consider the weakness of human power, and that none truly deserved the name of a king, but he whose eternal laws both heaven, earth, and seas obey. From that time he never wore a crown, esteeming earthly royalty nothing else than poor contemptible vanity.

50 Roe, pp. 108–9, 139, 209.
51 *The Works of James Thomson*, 4 vols (London, 1757), III, 225, 242.

Like a rugged Covenanter, Canute disdains the baubles of earthly royalty. Indeed, the Convenanters' slogan – 'No King but Christ' – might stand as the story's epigraph.

The 'Story of Alibaeus the Persian' (pp. 28–31) introduces another example of the Patriot King. A Persian king sets out in disguise to travel his country and meet his people 'in their natural simplicity and liberty'. He announces his journey as follows:

> I am ignorant of the real manners of men, everything that approaches me is disguised: 'tis art, and not nature, that we see in courts: I am therefore resolved to know what a rural life is, to study that kind of men who are so much despised, but who yet seem to be the prop of human society; I am weary of seeing nothing but courtiers, who observe me only to over-reach me with their flatteries; I must go see the labourers and shepherds who do not know me.

The king sets out on his travels, and passes 'thro' several country villages, where he saw the inhabitants dancing and playing, and enjoying their innocent diversions, and was extremely well pleased to observe such cheap and tranquil pleasures at such a distance from court'. He meets an intelligent young shepherd, Alibaeus, who enlightens the king as to the true state of his country:

> As he was crossing a flowery meadow, watered with a small rivulet, he perceived a young shepherd beneath the shade of an elm, playing on a pipe near his feeding flock. Upon inquiry he found his name was *Alibaeus*, whose parents lived in a village hard by. He was beautiful, but not effeminate; lively, but not wild; unconscious of his own charms; never dreaming, that in any respect, he differed from the shepherds around him, tho' without education, his reason had enlarged itself in a surprising manner. The king, having entered into conversation with him, was charmed with his discourse, for by him he was freely informed of some things concerning the state of the people, which a king cannot learn from the crowd of flatterers that surround him. Sometimes he would smile at the ingenuous simplicity of the youth, who spoke out his mind, without sparing anyone in his answers.

Alibaeus becomes an adviser to the king, and in due course chief minister to the king's successor, but he never ceases to miss the rural simplicity of his early life.

Evidently, there is much in the 'Story of Alibaeus' that suggests Burns's early poetry. There is the perception of the common country people as the prop of human society, as in 'The Cotter's Saturday Night'. There is the praise of wholesome rural festivity, as in 'The Twa Dogs'. But most of all, the story foreshadows 'A Dream', a poem in which Burns takes the role of a plain-spoken rural bard, cutting through the flatteries of courtiers to tell his monarch the truth about his country. This is the strategy Burns uses in several of his early satires – he adopts the persona of the 'humble bardie', the simple man who, with apparent naivety and innocence, speaks out his mind 'without sparing anyone'.

The fables and stories in the early part of Masson's *Collection*, dealing with the scope and limits of governmental authority, have an explicitly political import. But the *Collection* is politically significant in less obvious ways. For one thing, it introduces Burns to a number of important Real Whig writers whose work he will go on to study at greater length. Addison, Thomson and Akenside were seen by contemporaries primarily as poets of Liberty, champions of opposition Whiggism and fierce critics of Old Corruption. It was from these authors (as well as from more overtly political writers like Junius) that Burns absorbed that Real Whig idiom – of 'liberty' and 'independence' pitted against 'luxury' and 'corruption' – which pervades his political writings, and to which his regional religious background had already exposed him.

Joseph Addison is represented in Masson by 'A Letter from Italy To the Right Honourable Charles Lord Halifax, In the Year MDCCI' (pp. 89–93), a poem which, as well as providing the river imagery of Burns's epistle 'To W. Simpson, Ochiltree', celebrates Britain as the votary of Liberty and the protector of Europe from wars instigated by 'presumptuous kings':

> 'Tis liberty that crowns *Britannia*'s isle,
> And makes her barren rocks and her bleak mountains smile.
>   Others with towering piles may please the sight,
> And in their proud aspiring domes delight;
> A nicer touch to the stretch'd canvas give,
> Or teach their animated rocks to live:
> 'Tis *Britain*'s care to watch o'er *Europe*'s fate,
> And hold in balance each contending state,
> To threaten bold presumptuous kings with war,
> And answer her afflicted neighbours' pray'r.

In what amounts to a kind of British anticipation of Revolutionary France's Declaration of Fraternity, Addison enlists Great Britain as the guardian of Europe's liberties. The 'Letter from Italy', with its blasts of libertarian rhetoric, was a favourite of Burns's. In a letter of 1794 to Captain Miller, enclosing a copy of 'Robert Bruce's March to Bannockburn', Burns quotes from Addison's poem –

> O, Liberty –
> Thou mak'st the gloomy face of Nature gay,
> Giv'st beauty to the sun, & pleasure to the day!

– before presenting 'Bannockburn' as his own composition on the same libertarian theme (*Letters*, II, 277).

The *Collection* also includes 'The Campaign' (pp. 94–105), Addison's 'triumphalist Whig poem',[52] which contains the phrase 'haughty Gaul' – 'The haughty *Gaul* beheld with tow'ring pride, / His ancient bounds enlarg'd on ev'ry side' – which Burns deploys in 'The Dumfries Volunteers'. The poem expresses that suspicion of courtly luxury which animates so much of Burns's poetry. Addressing 'happy Britain', Addison notes approvingly that, like the bees' commonwealth in Masson's fable, Great Britain bestows its highest offices on grounds of merit alone:

52 Paulin, *Day-Star*, p. 132.

> Thy fav'rites grow not up by fortune's sport,
> Or from the crimes, or follies of a court;
> On the firm basis of desert they rise,
> From long try'd faith, and friendship's holy ties.

As these passages indicate, the modern view of Addison as the advocate of polite, spectatorial sociability is dangerously incomplete, overlooking as it does Addison's status as an uncompromising Real Whig, a fiery chastiser of Old Corruption. *Cato: A Tragedy* (1713), which Burns had read by 1786, was the party manifesto of opposition Whiggism:

> A Day, an Hour of virtuous Liberty,
> Is worth a whole Eternity in Bondage.[53]

Addison's Whiggish politics are reinforced by another writer whom Burns discovered in the pages of Masson. It is a decidedly political James Thomson that Burns encountered in his school reading-book. The Whiggish apostrophe to 'Happy *Britannia*' from *Summer* is one of three passages from *The Seasons* (1730) extracted in Masson (pp. 124–133). Here, Britain is a freedom-loving 'ISLAND of bliss!', whose public-spirited inhabitants enjoy the prosperity that liberty brings:

> Happy Britannia! Where the *Queen* of arts,
> Inspiring vigour, *Liberty* abroad
> Walks unconfin'd, even to thy farthest cotts,
> And scatters plenty with unsparing hand.

Like Addison, Thomson celebrates Britain as the home of freedom, 'The dread of tyrants, and the sole resource / Of those that under grim oppression groan'.

   Though he first encountered Thomson in Masson, it was during his stay at Kirkoswald in 1775 that Burns's 'reading was enlarged with the very important addition of Thomson's ... works' (*Letters*, I, 141). Reading *The Seasons* in its entirety, Burns would have encountered much more in the way of 'Opposition Whig propaganda'.[54] Throughout *The Seasons* the politicians who earn Thomson's praises are emphatically Whiggish. When he celebrates the patriots of English history, it is the great Whig heroes – Hampden, Russell, Sidney, Shaftesbury – who crowd the stage (*Summer*, ll. 1514–55). In later panegyric passages the patriots of Scotland (*Autumn*, ll. 894–949) and of classical antiquity (*Winter*, ll. 431–529) are celebrated for their public spirit and their heroic resistance to tyranny. Not merely a meditation on country themes, then, Thomson's *Seasons* is a product of 'country' ideology, exalting the 'patriot virtues' of the Country Whigs against the 'corrupted

---

53 Joseph Addison, *Cato: A Tragedy, As it is Acted at the Theatre-Royal in Drury-Lane, By Her Majesty's Servants* (London, 1713), p. 20.
54 Mary Jane Scott, 'James Thomson and the Anglo-Scots', in *The History of Scottish Literature*, ed. by Cairns Craig and others, 4 vols (Aberdeen, 1987), II, 81–99 (p. 94).

power' of Walpole and George II (*Winter*, ll. 656–70).[55] It is on the basis of this political dimension to Thomson's work that Caroline Robbins labels him 'the laureate of the Commonwealthmen'.[56]

As we have seen, Burns was familiar with Thomson and Mallet's Whiggish drama, *Alfred: A Masque*. There is one other play of Thomson's which Burns is known to have read: the tragedy, *Edward and Eleonora* (1739). Again, this was an explicitly political play; so much so, that its performance was banned by the Lord Chamberlain. The character of Edward, a virtuous young prince dismayed at his father's tyrannical behaviour, was widely believed to represent the current Prince of Wales in his opposition to George II. Regardless of this topical application, the play remains radically whiggish, containing unchallenged endorsements of the duty of subjects to admonish and restrain their erring monarch, to 'save him from his ministers'.[57] The principles of Buchanan and the Whig resistance theorists are alive and well in the work of Thomson (who had, after all, been a student for the Presbyterian ministry).

It was as a poet of Liberty, as much as a poet of Nature, that Thomson was celebrated by contemporaries of Burns. In 1792 there appeared a volume entitled *Essays on the Lives and Writings of Fletcher of Saltoun and the Poet Thomson*, in which Thomson is associated with the great Scottish theorist of Real Whiggism. The author of this work was David Erskine, eleventh earl of Buchan. Half-brother to Burns's friend Henry Erskine, Buchan was a peer of decidedly liberal sympathies, a supporter of the American and French Revolutions, a Friend of the People, and a correspondent of Washington. He had a family history of rebelliousness, one of his Covenanting forbears having emigrated to South Carolina as a result of his involvement in conventicling. In 1791, he invited Burns to a memorial festival in honour of Thomson, and though Burns was unable to attend, he composed some verses for the occasion (see his 'Address, To the Shade of Thomson' (K, 331)), verses which indeed appeared in Buchan's *Essays*. Burns had no high opinion of Buchan, regarding him as a bit of a blowhard (see his 'Extempore – on some Commemorations of Thomson' (K, 332)). Nevertheless, Buchan's activities usefully remind us of the extent to which Thomson was being recovered by Burns's contemporaries as a laureate of liberty. For Buchan, 'the highest encomium of Thomson is to be given him on account of his attachment to the cause of civil and religious liberty'.[58]

If Thomson had a rival among the Augustans as the laureate of the Real Whigs, then it was Mark Akenside, another of the poets Burns first encountered in Masson.

---

55 James Thomson, *The Seasons and the Castle of Indolence*, ed. by James Sambrook (Oxford, 1972), pp. 78–80, 113–15, 140–43, 146.
56 Robbins, p. 259.
57 *Works*, IV, 11.
58 David Steuart Erskine, 11th Earl of Buchan, *Essays on the Lives and Writings of Fletcher of Saltoun and the Poet Thomson: Biographical, Critical, and Political* (London, 1792), pp. 214–5.

Though he turned Tory in later life, Akenside made his name as a poet of liberty, a scourge of Old Corruption. A Newcastle Presbyterian, he was educated (like Goldsmith) at the universities of Edinburgh and Leyden. Like Thomson, Akenside had originally intended to train as a Presbyterian minister, and it was this that drew Samuel Johnson's attention when he condemned Akenside's politics in *Lives of the Poets*:

> Whether, when he resolved not to be a dissenting minister, he ceased to be a dissenter, I know not. He certainly retained an unnecessary and outrageous zeal for what he called and thought liberty; a zeal which sometimes disguises from the world, and not rarely from the mind which it possesses, an envious desire of plundering wealth or degrading greatness; and of which the immediate tendency is innovation and anarchy, an impetuous eagerness to subvert and confound, with very little care what shall be established.[59]

Naturally, the Tory Johnson was unsympathetic to this dissenting radical; nevertheless, his remarks again remind us of the political dimension to the work of Akenside. Now remembered chiefly as an adapter and populariser of Newtonian science, Akenside was renowned in his own time above all as a radical Whig. He is invoked by William Drennan, the Belfast United Irishman, in a memorial for a dead friend, whom Drennan describes as

> a Genuine Whig . . . nurtured under the philosophy of Hutcheson, and early inspired by the poetry of Akenside; the study of the former gave him that chastity of the moral sense which binds political and personal duty in the same strict tie of honesty and honour; and the divine muse of the latter threw that sacred flame of liberty into his breast, which burned while he continued to exist.[60]

Drennan is here alluding to Akenside's 'Ode on Lyric Poetry', in which the poet promises 'to throw incense on the vestal flame / Of Liberty'.[61] In Masson's *Collection* (pp. 133–36), Akenside is represented by an extract from his chef-d'oeuvre, *The Pleasures of Imagination* (1744). The passage excerpted is the discussion of taste from Book III, in which the beauties of nature are lauded as being open to all who can savour them:

> Oh! blest of heav'n, whom not the languid songs
> Of luxury, the *Syren!* not the bribes
> Of sordid wealth, nor all the gaudy spoils
> Of pageant honour can seduce to leave

59 Samuel Johnson, *The Lives of the Most Eminent English Poets; with Critical Observations on their Works*, 4 vols (London, 1781), IV, 449–50.
60 William Drennan, 'Character of Alexander Henry Haliday, M. D.', *Fugitive Pieces in Verse and Prose* (London, 1815), p. 155.
61 Mark Akenside, *Poems*, 2 vols (London, 1776), II, 55.

> Those ever blooming sweets, which from the store
> Of nature fair imagination culls
> To charm th'enliven'd soul! What tho' not all
> Of mortal offspring can attain the heights
> Of envied life; tho' only few possess
> *Patrician* treasures or imperial state;
> Yet nature's care, to all her children just,
> With richer treasures and an ampler state
> Endows at large whatever happy man
> Will deign to use them . . .

The glories of Nature are not merely the poor man's compensation for material want; they can only be fully relished by those who are free from the enervating trammels of wealth. As Burns puts it in the 'Epistle to Davie' (K, 51):

> What tho', like Commoners of air,
> We wander out, we know not where,
>   But either house or hal'?
> Yet *Nature*'s charms, the hills and woods,
> The sweeping vales, and foaming floods,
>   Are free alike to all.   (ll. 43–48)

It is not difficult to see why Johnson took exception to Akenside's politics. Of the pleasures which Akenside celebrates in his most famous poem, there is none he rates higher than the pleasure of imagining the great acts of civic virtue, such as Brutus's slaying of the tyrant Caesar. For Akenside, there is a fitness in such acts which the mind finds congenial: nothing our fancy can trace, whether in the natural or supernatural world, is more sublime, wonderful or beautiful than virtue. In this way, suggests Akenside, imagination is reinforced by truth and beauty, and leads us to pursue the paths of public virtue and to emulate the 'ancient honour' of the classical patriots (Book I, ll. 490–500, 559–604; Book II, ll. 712–771).[62]

The Whiggish qualities of Akenside's best-known poem are readily discernible, but it is on the lengthy *Ode to the Country Gentlemen of England* (1758)[63] that Akenside's reputation as the poet of the Real Whigs and champion of liberty primarily rests. Palpably influenced by Fletcher's *Discourse of Government with Relation to Militias*, the poem opens with a depiction of the warlike landholder of old, equally at home wielding the sword, speaking in council, or steering the plough. Compared with their virtuous predecessors, Europe's contemporary barons are anonymous, private figures:

> But who are ye? from Ebro's loitering sons
> To Tiber's pageants, to the sports of Seine;
> From Rhine's frail palaces to Danube's thrones,

62 *Poems*, I, 47–8, 50–52, 86–88.
63 *Poems*, II, 115–23.

> And cities looking on the Cimbric main,
> Ye lost, ye self-deserted? whose proud lords
> Have baffled your tame hands, and given your swords
> To slavish ruffians, hir'd for their command.

The English gentlemen must heed the dire example of mainland Europe. Though secure from foreign invasion by virtue of its island condition, Albion must beware of 'mighty armies station'd round the throne'. To safeguard the balance of the constitution, Akenside exhorts the English country gentlemen to 'arm [their] rural state', to take the initiative in organising local militias, instead of dissipating their resources in pursuing court patronage, burning 'slavish incense' at 'some courtly shrine'. As we shall see in the next chapter, there are clear affinities between Akenside's view of the obligations of English country gentlemen and Burns's critique of the Scots aristocracy in poems such as 'The Twa Dogs' and 'The Author's Earnest Cry and Prayer'.

In the previous chapter, I pointed to the coalescence of Calvinist or Real Whig ideology with the discourse of classical and Renaissance civic humanism. In the remainder of this chapter, I turn to the classical material in Masson's *Collection*. The section on the history of the Caesars has already been discussed, but there is a group of classical political orations in the *Collection* which is worthy of further attention. The 'Speech of Romulus after founding Rome', the 'Speech of Quinctius Capitolinus' and the 'Speech of Atherbal to the Roman Senate' are all accomplished instances of classical oratory. However, the two orations most relevant to our discussion are the 'Speech of Fabritius to King Pyrrhus', and 'The second Olynthian of Demosthenes, Translated by Lord Lansdowne'.

The 'Speech of Fabritius to King Pyrrhus' (pp. 167–8) takes place in the wake of a Roman military defeat. The Tarentines, with the assistance of King Pyrrhus of Epirus, have beaten the Roman army. Fabritius is one of a group of Roman senators sent to negotiate a treaty with Pyrrhus. A man of great abilities and civic virtue, Fabritius chooses to live in poverty, owning only a small house and a patch of land which he works himself. Assuming that Fabritius is unhappy in these conditions, King Pyrrhus sees an opportunity to corrupt the senator with bribes. Fabritius nobly rejects the King's offers:

> As to my poverty, you have indeed, Sir, been rightly informed. My whole estate consists in a house of but mean appearance, and a little spot of ground; from which, by my own labour, I draw my support. But if by any means you have been persuaded to think that this poverty makes me less considered in *my country*, or in any degree unhappy, you are entirely deceived . . . With regard to *honours, my country* places me, poor as I am, upon a level with the richest: for *Rome* knows no qualifications for great employments, but virtue and ability. She appoints me to officiate in the most august ceremonies of religion; she intrusts me with the command of her armies; she confides to my care the most important negotiations. My poverty does not lessen the weight and influence of my counsels in the senate; the *Roman* people honour me for that very poverty,

which you consider as a disgrace: they know the many opportunities I had in war to enrich myself, without censure; they are convinced of my disinterested zeal for their prosperity; and if I have anything to complain of in the return they make me, 'tis only the *excess* of their applause. What value then can I put upon your gold and silver? What king can add any thing to my fortune? always attentive to discharge the duties incumbent on me: I have a mind free from SELF-REPROACH, and I have an HONEST FAME.

What is important about this passage is not just the exemplary conduct of Fabritius, who emerges as a paragon of civic rectitude, but the depiction of a society organised in such a manner that the poor but virtuous man can wield political influence; it is his virtue and not his poverty that is regarded. In this respect, the Fabritius speech points forward to Burns's famous letter of April 1793 (*Letters*, II, 207–10), written under the pressure of an Excise Board enquiry into his political conduct, in which Burns defends the political competence of the poor, independent commoner:

Does any man tell me ... that it does not belong to my humble station to meddle with the concerns of a People? – I tell him, that it is on such individuals as I, that [a (*deleted*)] for the hand of support & the eye of intelligence, a Nation has to rest. – The uninformed mob may swell a Nation's bulk; & the titled, tinsel Courtly throng may be its feathered ornament, but the number of those who are elevated enough in life, to reason & reflect; & yet low enough to keep clear of the venal contagion of a Court; these are a Nation's strength.

If the sentiments here recall Fabritius, it is also true that Fabritius' speech seems proleptically Burnsian. That concluding declaration – 'I have a mind free from SELF-REPROACH, and I have an HONEST FAME' – might have come from one of Burns's letters. Indeed, it reads like a prose version of the lines from the 'Epistle to Davie':

> The honest heart that's free frae a'
>   Intended fraud or guile,
> However Fortune kick the ba',
>   Has ay some cause to smile.   (ll. 35–38)

If the idiom of Burns's political works owes something to the Fabritius speech, even more telling is 'The Second Olynthian of Demosthenes, translated by Lord Lansdowne' (pp. 168–180). Here Demothenes is inciting the Athenian people to support the Olynthians in their struggle against the depredations of Philip of Macedonia. If the Olynthians are not given swift and substantial military assistance, Demosthenes argues, then Athens will be the next item on Philip's expansionist agenda. Throughout the discourse, Demosthenes defends his duty to speak freely and even harshly, because the citizenry has so often been led astray by flatterers and sycophants:

If I assume at this time a more than ordinary liberty of speech, I conjure you to suffer patiently those truths, which have no other end but your own good: you have too many reasons to be sensible how much you have suffered by hearkening to *Sycophants*. I shall therefore be plain in laying before you the grounds of past miscarriages, in order to correct you in your future conduct.

It is the baneful influence of ministers over their subordinates that has prevented the voice of the truly public-spirited from gaining a hearing:

> But since we have been pestered up by a vile race of hypocrites and *Sycophants*, who dare not open their mouths till they have learnt their lessons, till they have servilely inquired what they shall say, what they shall propose, what they shall vote, and in what way they may make themselves agreeable: in a word, since advices publickly given, must first be whispered by some great man or minister, and you bespeak as it were, and prepare your own poison, how can it otherwise happen, but your debates must be corrupted, your councils ineffectual, your reputation blasted, and disgrace accumulated upon disgrace, while those illustrious parasites flourish and prosper by their country's ruin.

Demosthenes then contrasts the corruption of Athens's current leaders with the true civic virtue of an older generation of statesmen:

> Visit the houses of *Aristides*, *Miltiades*, or any other of those patriots of antiquity, you will find nothing, not the least mark or ornament, to distinguish them from the meanest of their next neighbours. They meddled not in government to enrich themselves, but the public; they had no schemes of ambition but for the public, nor knew any interest, but the public ... The magistrate was then subservient to the people; punishments and rewards were properties of the people; all honours, dignities, and preferments were disposed by the voice and favour of the people; but the magistrate now has usurped the right of the people, and exercises an arbitrary authority over his ancient and natural lord.

In its chastisement of corrupt public representatives who 'dare not open their mouths till they have learnt their lessons' and who 'flourish and prosper by their country's ruin', this speech reads like a paraphrase of Burns's early satirical address, 'The Author's Earnest Cry and Prayer, to the Right Honorable and Honorable, the Scotch Representatives in the House of Commons' (K, 81). This is a poem in which Burns accuses the Scottish MPs of selling Scottish interests down the river in return for ministerial patronage. To keep their '*posts* an' *pensions*' (l. 27), the Scottish MPs avoid speaking up for the beleaguered Scotch whisky industry, crippled by a punitive tax regime; they dare not speak out lest 'a *Minister* grow dorty, / An' kick [their] place' (ll. 135–6). In its tone, its method, its structure and its content, Burns's satire draws heavily on Demosthenes' speech, and it is no accident that Demosthenes is invoked in the poem. Listing some of the Scots MPs whose virtue he has newly impugned, the speaker ingenuously compares them to Demosthenes and Cicero, slyly pointing up their own civic failings by comparison with these classical patriots:

> *Erskine*, a spunkie norland billie;
> True Campbels, *Frederic* an' *Ilay*;
> An' Livistone, the bauld *Sir Willie*;
>   An' mony ithers,
> Whom auld Demosthenes or Tully
>   Might own for brithers.   (ll. 79–84)

With those droll final two lines, which neatly change the stanza's direction in classic Habbie fashion, the ostensible compliment flares into a withering put-down. If anything, these 'billies' would be the *objects* of Demosthenes' indignant eloquence.

The other element that needs comment here is Demosthenes' assumption of 'more than ordinary liberty of speech'. Again, this is the line Burns takes in the early satires. Flattery and sycophancy have obscured the truth for too long. Their mists must be blasted away by the force of plainspoken integrity. It is for the benefit of the MPs and monarchs in 'A Dream' and 'The Author's Earnest Cry and Prayer' that the poet will unleash his 'raucle tongue'. We can see, then, that the two personae between which Burns wavers in his satires – that of the naïve 'simple bardie' whose corrosive critique of his leaders is apparently inadvertent, and that of the plainspoken, independent commoner, who knowingly censures his corrupt rulers – are each represented in Masson's *Collection*.

In a sense, then, Masson's *Collection* provided the foundation of Burns's political education. It introduced him to political theory, to debates over the scope and extent of political authority and the relationship between executive and legislature. It equipped him with a political vocabulary, derived from the Real Whig authors of the earlier eighteenth century, whose idiom, with its glorification of 'independence' and 'liberty' and its polemic against 'luxury' and 'corruption', was by no means unrelated to the old Scots Whiggism of the Ayrshire countryside. And it provided him with satirical techniques – both the cutting naïveté of Alibaeus and the plainspoken censure of Demosthenes.

Of course, Masson's *Collection* was not the only source of Real Whig influence on Burns. The New Light and Freemasonic circles in which Burns moved as a young man were pervaded by the Real Whig ethos of Glasgow University. The debates at the Tarbolton Bachelors' Club and in the taverns of Mauchline and Tarbolton exposed Burns to a more popular, Covenanting version of the Presbyterian political legacy. And of course Burns continued to extend his political reading with writers like Henry Fielding, the 'most radical of the Whigs of George II's reign',[64] polemicists like Junius and Timothy Thunderproof, and the thinkers of the Scottish Enlightenment. Perhaps Burns gained a second-hand knowledge of Buchananite political theory from Robertson's *History of Scotland*, which is listed among the valuable books belonging to the Monkland Friendly Society (*Letters*, II, 108). Or perhaps he read the series of articles on Buchanan in *The Bee* (a periodical to which

64 Robbins, p. 287.

Burns subscribed), in which Buchanan was hailed as a 'herald of civil and religious liberty' and an advocate of the 'rights of man'.[65] In any case, it was through Masson that Burns was introduced to Buchananite, Real Whig discourse. That the end of government was the good of the public; that the people had an ultimate right to resist tyranny; that the participation of the citizens in defence and government was vital to a nation's strength; that public spirit and not hereditary rank was the proper qualification for citizenship: these were the principles instilled in Burns by his schooling. It was on these values that Burns forged his responses to the pressing political issues of the time: the war with the American colonies, the parliamentary reform movement, the ministerial crises of the early 1780s, the campaign to abolish slavery. And it was these same values and that Real Whig idiom that shaped the political poems and satires of Burns's early period.

65 *The Bee*, 5 (1791), 232.

PART TWO

EARLY POLITICAL POEMS

CHAPTER THREE

'A Raucle Tongue': Early Political Poems and Satires

Towards the end of his short life, Burns wrote a pointed little squib reflecting his own experience of politics (K, 536):

> IN politics if thou woulds't mix,
>   And mean thy fortunes be;
> Bear this in mind, be deaf and blind,
>   Let great folks hear and see.[1]

The concentrated bitterness of these lines - the poem is a tiny phial of disillusion – has its roots in the conservative backlash which overtook the Scottish reform movement in the 1790s. What Marilyn Butler has termed 'the Scottish "Terror", 1793–95'[2] casts a dark shadow over the last years of the poet's life. Burns's own exposure to government intimidation in the 1790s will be discussed in Chapter 8, but it is worth pointing out that, even in the pre-Revolutionary 1780s, political verse was what Burns himself might have termed a 'kittle business' for a lower-class writer. Mean though his fortunes were, however, Burns opted to run the risks. He did mix in politics, and more often than not it was the 'great folks' who suffered the invective of a man with a keen eye for political abuses, a man who, as Henry Mackenzie regretted, 'indulged his sarcastic humour in talking of men, particularly if he thought them proud, or disdainful of Persons of inferior rank'.[3] Sarcastic humour may have been a feature of Burns's temperament, as several contemporaries attest,[4] but a readiness to chastise his social superiors was also one of the fruits of the poet's education. That the citizen must scrutinise the conduct of his governors, and judge them by the 'Calvinist and humanist vision of the active and industrious social leader',[5] was a cardinal lesson of Burns's schooling. It was

---

1 Kinsley dates the poem to 1795 or 1796, though Patrick Scott Hogg quotes a Robert Ainslie letter suggesting that a version of the poem was composed in 1793; see *The Lost Poems*, p. 49.

2 Marilyn Butler, 'Burns and Politics', in *Robert Burns and Cultural Authority*, pp. 86–112 (p. 102).

3 Henry Mackenzie, quoted in *Burns As Others Saw Him*, ed. by W. L. Renwick (Edinburgh, 1959), p. 4.

4 See in particular Maria Riddell's memoir, in *The Critical Heritage*, pp. 101–7, and David Sillar in *Burns As Others Saw Him*, pp. 1–2.

5 Allan, p. 194.

also a lesson that Burns was willing to act upon, not least in the poems to be discussed in this chapter.

In his important study of Burns's poems and songs, Thomas Crawford presents 'the political poems completed before the end of 1786' as a coherent body of work. For Crawford, what unites these poems is their refraction of high politics through the idiom and imagery of a vernacular consciousness, 'the close juxtaposition of Parliament and parish pump, of Court and ale-cup commentators'.[6] That is true, but what also requires emphasis is the political sophistication of these early poems, the extent to which they are ballasted by political ideas of the kind discussed in the previous section – ideas about representation, the origin and limits of political authority, the true end of government, and the proper relationship between executive and legislature. Of course, Burns was not a political theorist but a poet, and in what follows I shall pay close attention to questions of poetic genre, diction, register, metre and other formal aspects of Burns's verse. But I also aim to read Burns's early political poems with an eye to their intellectual and discursive framework, and to demonstrate that there is a schooled political intelligence at work in these poems, informing their procedures and shaping their perspective on contemporary events. For the most part, my discussion will concentrate on a group of four political poems first published in the Kilmarnock edition of *Poems, Chiefly in the Scottish Dialect* (1786): 'The Vision', 'The Twa Dogs', 'The Author's Earnest Cry and Prayer', and 'A Dream'. These poems will be at the heart of my discussion, though I will also refer to other works of the same period, including poems written in or before 1786 but first published in the 1787 Edinburgh edition ('A Fragment', 'The Brigs of Ayr') and a poem written in 1786 but never published in the poet's lifetime ('Address of Beelzebub'), as well as pointing out some pertinent parallels with Burns's later political writings.

Early Political Poems

If the popular image of 'Burns the Jacobin' is misleading, this is for one simple reason: it draws attention to the wrong revolution. For it was not the French Revolution but its American forerunner that most powerfully shaped Burns's politics. The revolt of the American colonies was the defining political event of Burns's early manhood. Sixteen years old at the outbreak of the War of Independence, Burns came to regard the new United States as a model of the virtuous civic polity. But if the American Revolution was to provide an enduring focus for Burns's political aspirations, on a more immediate level it offered ample scope for satirical attacks on the British elite. In a satirical ballad on the American war, 'A Fragment' (K, 38), Burns pokes knowing fun at the hapless British leaders whose conduct of the war was so lamentably inept:

> B—*rg*—*ne* gaed up, like spur an' whip,
>   Till *Fraser* brave did fa', man;

6 *Burns*, p. 147.

> Then lost his way, ae misty day,
>   In *Saratoga* shaw, man.
> C—*rnw*—*l*—*s* fought as lang's he dought,
>   An' did the Buckskins claw, man;
> But *Cl*—*nt*—*n*'s glaive frae rust to save
>   He hung it to the wa', man.
>
> Then *M*—*nt*—*gue*, an' *Guilford* too,
>   Began to fear a fa', man;
> And *S*—*ckv*—*lle* doure, wha stood the stoure,
>   The German Chief to thraw, man:
> For Paddy *B*—*rke*, like ony Turk,
>   Nae mercy had at a', man;
> An' *Charlie F*—*x* threw by the box,
>   An' lows'd his tinkler jaw, man.   (ll. 25–40)

Though an early work – it was probably written in 1784 – the piece is notable for its poise, its witty irreverence and its surefooted canter through the maze of contemporary politics. Marshalling a numerous cast of characters, Burns parades his knowledge, not merely of the war's key military engagements, but of the shifting political alliances and myriad personalities involved in the ministerial crises of the early 1780s. Stylistically deft in its handling of a modified Christis Kirk stanza, whose connotations of bumbling buffoonery Burns neatly exploits, the ballad is even more remarkable for its political nous. Here is a poor provincial farmer writing with the assurance and authority – if not the linguistic 'propriety' – of a Westminster insider.

'A Fragment' serves notice of Burns's prowess as a satirist and political commentator. However, as Burns acknowledged in a letter to Mrs Dunlop (*Letters*, I, 392), and as later events were to prove, politics was 'dangerous ground' for a writer of Burns's class. A poet of 'humble' birth, using raucously popular language, might conceivably prove acceptable to a polite readership if presented as an untaught, spontaneous genius of the kind celebrated in Scottish Enlightenment aesthetics. However, a poet from this background conducting mordant expositions of the power relations in his society, in a language calculated to degrade his social superiors, was a rather different proposition. Burns was keenly aware that trenchant political satire might neither be expected nor applauded from the pen of a tenant farmer. He was equally aware that, for his Kilmarnock poems to achieve commercial success, he had to win the approval of that genteel audience acknowledged in his Preface as 'his readers, particularly the Learned and the Polite, who may honor him with a perusal'.[7] From the outset, then, there are tensions between the kind of poetry that Burns wishes to write and the kind of poetry that a polite readership is willing to tolerate from a working-class writer. We can see Burns negotiating these tensions in the important long poem, 'The Vision' (K, 62).

---

7 Robert Burns, *Poems, Chiefly in the Scottish Dialect* (Kilmarnock, 1786), v–vi.

'The Vision' is a poem of spiritual crisis, in which an obscure rural poet – evidently a version of Burns himself – begins to doubt the viability, the advisability of poetic creation for a man of his class. Like Burns, the speaker is an impoverished tenant farmer struggling to scratch a living. The opening stanzas – perhaps the finest example in Scottish literature of that conventional contrast between a wintry landscape and a cosy firelit interior – introduce us to a weary, disheartened figure:

> THE sun had clos'd the *winter-day*,
> The Curlers quat their roaring play,
> And hunger'd Maukin taen her way
> To kail-yards green,
> While faithless snaws ilk step betray
> Whare she has been.
>
> The Thresher's weary *flingin-tree*,
> The lee-lang day had tir'd me;
> And when the Day had clos'd his e'e,
> Far i' the West,
> Ben i' the *Spence*, right pensivelie,
> I gaed to rest.
>
> There, lanely, by the ingle-cheek,
> I sat and ey'd the spewing reek,
> That fill'd, wi' hoast-provoking smeek,
> The auld, clay biggin;
> And heard the restless rattons squeak
> About the riggin. (ll. 1–18)

The tone of world-weariness is abetted by those regular iambs, long vowels and the monotonous full rhymes which clog the first three lines of each stanza. The vision of a cosmic repose, encompassing everything from the retiring hare to the Day itself, points up the enervation of the speaker, who wants to share in this peace ('I gaed to rest'), yet finds himself troubled, 'restless' as the vermin in the rafters. What vexes the speaker is the thought of the wasted hours he has devoted to poetry, when he might have been pursuing a more profitable course:

> Had I to guid advice but harket,
> I might, by this, hae led a market,
> Or strutted in a Bank and clarket
> My *Cash-Account*;
> While here, half-mad, half-fed, half-sarket,
> Is a' th' amount. (ll. 25–30)

Disillusioned, the speaker is vowing to leave off poetry forever, when a beautiful, tartan-robed lass – whom he takes to be 'some SCOTTISH MUSE' (l. 51) – enters the farmhouse. This is Coila, named after Burns's native district of Kyle, come to allay the poet's misgivings. In a lengthy address which takes up most of the second section or Ossianic 'duan' of the poem, Coila assures the speaker that there *is* a legitimate role for the poet of humble origins, that he should be proud to follow the vocation of a 'rustic Bard' (l. 177). Before Coila speaks, however, there is a long digressive passage which describes her billowing mantle, on which appear scenes depicting the region of Kyle, its topography and inhabitants.

In the Kilmarnock version of 'The Vision', Coila's mantle is described in four stanzas which make fleeting reference to Kyle's rivers and hills and the county town of Ayr. In the Edinburgh version, a further seven stanzas are added, and in the version in the Stair MS (which represents the poem as originally composed) there are twenty-three stanzas devoted to the mantle. In these more expansive versions, the description of Coila's robe encompasses not merely the physical characteristics of Kyle, but its illustrious inhabitants, past and present. 'Many a Patriot-name . . . / And Hero' (ll. 130–1) is cited here: soldiers, statesmen, judges, imperial governors, writers, academics; all who have been diligent in the service of the community, and who are untouched by the modern tendency towards luxury and self-interest. Each is praised for his civic virtue, be it the martial valour of Colonel Fullarton, the public rectitude of Lord Justice Clerk, or the literary prowess of James Boswell. In this section of the poem, Burns is celebrating those members of the Ayrshire elite who *do* approach the ideal of the active and virtuous social leader. Essentially, these are the 'some exceptions' to the rule of aristocratic corruption to whom Burns refers in 'The Twa Dogs'.

The fact that Burns decided to abridge the description of Coila's mantle when publishing 'The Vision' might suggest a desire for concision. But it might also indicate Burns's awareness of the extent to which the whistle-stop tour of Kyle in duan 1 undermines the advice which Coila gives to the poet in duan 2. If Coila's speech has a single aim it is to reconcile the poet to his second-class status as a humble regional poet whose work has no connection with the public sphere of politics and high culture. Coila explains to the poet that there are numbers of aerial spirits under the direction of Scotia – 'the great *Genius* of this Land' (l. 145) – who direct the activities of Scotland's inhabitants:

> 'They SCOTIA's Race among them share;
> 'Some fire the *Sodger* on to dare;
> 'Some rouse the *Patriot* up to bare
>   'Corruption's heart:
> 'Some teach the *Bard*, a darling care,
>   'The tuneful Art.   (ll. 151–6)

While some of Scotia's aerial helpers have responsibility for statesmen, bards and soldiers of the kind eulogised in duan 1, there is an inferior order of spirits who guide the steps of less illustrious charges:

> 'To lower Orders are assign'd,
> 'The humbler ranks of Human-kind,
> 'The rustic Bard, the lab'ring Hind,

'The Artisan;
'All chuse, as, various they're inclin'd,
'The various man.   (ll. 175–80)

As one of these inferior spirits, Coila has responsibility for the speaker, whom she
identifies as one of the 'humbler ranks', a 'rustic Bard' to be classed alongside farm-
servants and artisans. Coila's division of Scottish society into higher and lower
orders reproduces the traditional civic humanist hierarchy, whereby public
responsibility is the preserve of a moneyed class who are untainted by the stultifying
and degrading process of earning a living, while a 'mechanical' labouring class lack
the leisure to devote their attention to the public good. 'We look for elevation of
sentiment, and liberality of mind', writes Adam Ferguson, 'among those orders of
citizens, who, by their condition, and their fortunes, are relieved from sordid cares
and attentions'.[8]

If we take the speaker of 'The Vision' as a version of the author, then Burns would
appear to be acknowledging the constraints of his social position, accepting that he
has no right to participate in or even to comment on the public life of his nation. If
Coila is right, then Burns is part of that mechanical class which is unfitted for
citizenship. He cannot aspire to join the civic order of men described in duan 1,
cannot make the transition from 'rustic Bard' (l. 177) to '*Bard*' (l. 155). Coila's
account of the rustic bard's poetic development in stanzas 13 to 19 of duan 2 grants
the speaker competence in only three types of poetry: nature poetry, love poetry
and 'manners-painting strains' (l. 241) – that is, depictions of quaint rural folkways
and customs. His domain is a restricted '*humble sphere*' (l. 260) cut off from the civic
arena. And here we light on the fundamental paradox of the poem. 'The Vision' is
a manifesto poem, in which the poet encounters his Muse and listens to her
instructions. What makes the poem intriguing is that the manifesto does not
belong to Burns. It is a manifesto for the kind of poet Burns knows his genteel
public would wish him to be. Stay happy in your humble sphere, the speaker is told.
Leave the conduct and criticism of public affairs to your social superiors. Trust in
providence to order society fairly, and remain deaf and blind to the doings of
great folks.

Clearly, Burns's poetic oeuvre demonstrates his rejection of the restrictive role
recommended by Coila. But even within 'The Vision' itself, the possibility of
following Coila's advice has been undermined in advance by duan 1. Coila advises
the poet to ignore public affairs and write an apolitical landscape poetry; however,
the very possibility of such a poetry has been exploded by the earlier description of
Coila's mantle. What that description demonstrates is that landscape is never
neutral or apolitical. As in James Thomson's *The Seasons*, on which this section of
'The Vision' is modelled, landscape bears the impress of social power relations. The
landscape of Kyle is a text with military, judicial, political dimensions. The 'wild,
romantic grove' (l. 115) described by the speaker is the haunt of 'An *aged Judge* ... /

8 *Essay*, p. 186.

Dispensing good' (l. 120); the picturesque 'ruins pendent in the air' (l. 92) are the former abodes of families who fought for Scottish independence. Even when Coila announces her status as a regional muse in duan 2 –

> 'Of these am I – COILA my name;
> 'And this district as mine I claim,
> 'Where once the *Campbells*, chiefs of fame,
> > Held ruling pow'r   (ll. 199–202)

– she uses a formulation which defines Kyle in terms of political authority ('ruling pow'r'). In this way, Coila subverts her own assumption that landscape can be divorced from politics.

Indeed, a subtle vein of self-subversion runs throughout Coila's address, as elements of her language and imagery work to counteract her argument. When Coila describes the natural scenery which inspired the youthful poet, she mentions the 'dashing roar' (l. 212) of the sea. The rhyme-word here ('roar') recalls the earlier appearance of the same rhyme-word in the reference to the 'venal Senate's roar' (l. 159) in duan 1. In this way, politics intrude into the reader's consciousness at the very moment when Coila is seeking to float the illusion of an apolitical land-scape poetry. The effect is similar when Coila uses an arboreal analogy in her attempt to reconcile the poet to his humble sphere:

> 'Tho' large the forest's Monarch throws
> > 'His army shade,
> 'Yet green the juicy Hawthorn grows,
> > 'Adown the glade.   (ll. 255–8)

The position of the lowly hawthorn – beyond the monarch's shade or, by implication, beyond the patronage and influence of the crown – is the very position of independence from which one may speak out most freely against monarchical shortcomings (a point Burns will later make in 'A Dream'). In other words, Coila's imagery can be used to support an argument *for* a politically interventionist provincial poetry, as well as an argument against that kind of verse. Moreover, the hawthorn's green, sappy boughs themselves carry what, from Coila's point of view, are unfortunate political connotations: there is no great distance between this 'juicy Hawthorn' and the radicals' Tree of Liberty. It is as if Burns is determined to sabotage Coila's speech: he gives Coila a script that will appeal to his polite readers, but he can't resist undermining her pompous oration, insinuating the flaws in her argument.

Burns attempts to have it both ways in 'The Vision', to be his own kind of poet and to write for a genteel audience. This is why, as David Daiches points out, the poem is radically divided, its two duans failing to coalesce.[9] There seem, for instance, to be two different Coilas, one for each duan of the poem. In duan 1, the treatment of the muse is typically Burnsian. In Burns's invocations of the muse – in the second

9 Daiches, p. 134.

'Epistle to J. Lapraik', for instance – there is often a strong sense that the poet must achieve a mastery over the muse. The muse is a 'hizzie' – a word which can mean whore as well as wench or girl – whom the poet must take in hand. And this seems, initially, to be the case in 'The Vision'. We open in an atmosphere of recent physical exertion, with the semi-naked – 'half-sarket' (l. 29) – poet sprawled at his fireside. The Muse – again a *'Hizzie'* (l. 41) – slips into the farmhouse, in a scenario which recalls the nocturnal lovers' visits which feature so regularly in Burns's songs. Blushing and submissive, she keeps her gaze averted from the poet, 'Her *eye* . . . turn'd on empty space' (l. 59), and receives the poet's sexual stare – that lustful 'glowr[e]' (l. 45) which Tam o' Shanter will later bestow on Nannie. And, again like Nannie, the Muse is showing plenty of leg: emerging from her tartan mantle is a well-formed limb – 'Sae straught, sae taper, tight and clean' (l. 65) – which mesmerises the poet. She is a characteristic Burnsian muse – a mixture of the bashful and the sexually available.

By duan 2, however, all this has changed. The Muse – now identified as 'COILA' (l. 199) – has lost her sexual aura and acquired instead the demeanor of a sibling, 'an elder Sister's air' (l. 137). In a reversal of Burns's usual practice, it is now the Muse who masters the poet: she claims him as her property and delivers a lengthy lecture in the imperative mood ('regard . . . know . . . strive . . . trust . . . preserve . . . wear') to which he listens mutely. She is no longer the familiar 'hizzie' of duan 1, but a strait-laced, imperious figure who condescendingly lectures the poet. And what is particularly eloquent here is the poet's uncharacteristic silence. The role in which Coila casts him, the role of the humble bard, contented with his lot, is one that stifles the poet's voice, reduces him to silence. There is good reason why we don't hear the poet's response to Coila's oration: a poet of Burns's stamp, who heeds the advice given by Coila, has nothing left to say. Ultimately, therefore, Burns has to reject Coila's 'counsels' (l. 265), as he evidently does in the more political poems in the Kilmarnock volume. Her advice does indeed become a 'passing thought' (l. 275) which the poet ignores as he turns to chastise a 'venal senate' in poems like 'The Author's Earnest Cry and Prayer', 'A Dream' and 'The Twa Dogs'.

The decision to open the Kilmarnock volume with 'The Twa Dogs' was a bold one. It was also a decision which would never have been taken by the submissive 'rustic bard' of Coila. The poem is not merely polemical in a manner that Coila would abhor, but it consciously invites comparision with 'A Vision' (it shares a number of features, including the dialogic format and the Ossianic references), and seems in some ways to 'answer' that earlier poem. The opening couplet –

> 'TWAS in that place o' *Scotland*'s isle,
> That bears the name o' auld king COIL,

– does not only introduce a fairytale note quite appropriate to a poem which features talking dogs; it also transports us back to the territory of Coila. However, unlike the region depicted on Coila's mantle, from which the lower classes have been edited out, the 'COIL' of 'The Twa Dogs' includes what Carlyle called the 'rough scenes of Scottish life, . . . the smoke and soil of a too harsh reality'.[10] The pain and fatigue of farm labour; the constant threat of hunger and cold; the oppression of 'racked rents' (l. 51); the tyranny of landlords and factors; the prospect of destitution: all this is vividly present in 'The Twa Dogs'. Coming immediately after a preface which craves the indulgence of 'the Learned and the Polite', there is a bracing frankness in a poem which exposes the shameful condition of Scotland's rural poor, and points an admonitory finger at the Scottish ruling class.

The poem takes the form of a dialogue between two Ayrshire dogs – Caesar, a smart Newfoundland who belongs to a local laird, and Luath, a ploughman's collie – who meet one afternoon and exchange their opinions of the '*lords o' the creation*' (l. 46). The first part of the colloquy is dominated by Luath, who enlightens Caesar as to the true condition of the tenant farmers and cotters, before Caesar delivers a trenchant exposé of gentry manners. Before the dialogue, proper, however, there is a short opening section which introduces us to the participants. Here Burns constructs an idyll of carefree, joyous activity. We watch the dogs chasing around, play fighting, digging up moles and snuffling one another with 'social *nose*' (l. 39). The immediately striking characteristic of the dogs is their refreshing freedom from class prejudice. Caesar might be the pet of the local laird, but he has none of the hauteur of his master's class:

> But tho' he was o' high degree,
> The fient a pride na pride had he,
> But wad hae spent an hour caressan,
> Ev'n wi' a Tinkler-gipsey's *messan*:
> At *Kirk* or *Market*, *Mill* or *Smiddie*,
> Nae tawtied *tyke*, tho' e'er sae duddie,
> But he wad stan't, as glad to see him,
> An' stroan't on stanes and hillocks wi' him.   (ll. 15–22)

The humour of this passage lies in the conceit by which pissing in public becomes an index of a civilised mind, free from narrow prejudice. If Caesar is no snob, then Luath, for his part, is commendably free from national chauvinism, caring nothing for the fact that Caesar is an incomer, 'nane o' Scotland's dogs' (l. 10). For all the class and national differences between them, the dogs are fast friends, 'unco pack an' thick the gither' (l. 38). Above all, it is the sociability of the dogs that is emphasised, their joy in each other's company and in the company of their kind. They show an instinctive camaraderie, untrammeled by the distorting considerations of wealth and rank which afflict human beings. Indeed, the dogs display a benevolence and generosity which their masters cannot rival. Caesar and Luath may look down their noses at creatures of an entirely different species, but human beings treat their *own* kind in this way. As an incredulous Caesar observes:

10 Thomas Carlyle, unsigned review in *Edinburgh Review*, 48 (1828), in *The Critical Heritage*, p. 354.

> L—d man, our gentry care as little
> For *delvers*, *ditchers*, an' sic cattle;
> They gang as saucy by poor folk,
> As I wad by a stinkan brock.   (ll. 89–92)

The gentry treat their tenants and cotters like 'cattle' or indeed like dogs: inferior creatures to be used for their masters' benefit, 'keepet for his Honor's pleasure' (l. 8). This, then, is the central inversion in a poem whose dominant principle is inversion: the community of the dogs is more humane than that of their masters.

The extent of mankind's inhumanity is made apparent in the early exchanges of the dogs, and it is Caesar who broaches the subject. He describes the opulence of the Laird's table, the wanton luxury of his lifestyle, and wonders how poor folk manage to survive on their meagre fare. In reply, Luath acknowledges the justice of Caesar's assessment:

> Trowth, *Caesar*, whyles they're fashed eneugh;
> A *Cotter* howckan in a sheugh,
> Wi' dirty stanes biggan a dyke,
> Bairan a quarry, an' sic like,
> Himsel, a wife, he thus sustains,
> A smytrie of wee, duddie weans,
> An' nought but his han'-daurk, to keep
> Them right an' tight in *thack an' raep*.
>
> An' when they meet wi sair disasters,
> Like loss o' health, or want o' masters,
> Ye maist wad think, a wee touch langer,
> An' they maun starve o' cauld an' hunger.   (ll. 71–82)

There is an understated pathos here, and Luath's matter-of-fact tone is the key to the success of this passage. He is merely confirming the accuracy of Caesar's impression, not complaining stridently about the hardships of the poor, and his spare, expository language has the force of unvarnished truth. His second line – 'A *Cotter* howckan in a sheugh' – has a kind of haiku starkness and clarity typical of the passage as a whole. But Luath also points to the compensations of the poor folks' lot. They have the pleasures of family life and good fellowship, and they relish those moments of freedom when they may enjoy a sociable glass of beer and indulge their passion for political discussion:

> An' whyles, twalpennie-worth o' *nappy*
> Can mak the bodies unco happy;
> They lay aside their private cares,
> To mind the Kirk an' State affairs;
> They'll talk o' *patronage* an' *priests*,
> Wi' kindling fury i' their breasts,
> Or tell what new taxation 's comin,
> An' ferlie at the folk in LON'ON.   (ll. 115–22)

If anything is a 'ferlie' or wonder here, it is the fact that, despite living on the brink of destitution, the poor folk can put their own problems to one side and devote their attention to the public good. The same thing, unfortunately, can't be said of their superiors. 'The Twa Dogs' reverses the traditional civic hierarchy, showing poor tenant farmers and cotters who look to the public good, while aristocrats and Members of Parliament are engrossed in their private ambitions. Indeed, we have already been given a hint of the divergent values of the social classes in the very names given to the dogs. Luath's ploughman master signals his elevation of mind by choosing, from an epic poem, the name of a noble warrior's dog. The Laird, by contrast, names his pet for a succession of tyrannous rulers who pursued private ambitions at the expense of the public good, and who – as Burns learned in Masson – often met bloody ends at the hands of their outraged subjects.

The satirical climax of the poem is a coruscating, hell-for-leather denunciation of the British ruling class. Again, Burns introduces this controversial material with admirable discretion. It is Luath who innocently triggers the tirade, by launching a fulsome tribute to the public-spirited gentry who serve their country as parliamentarians. His encomium, however, is cut short by an exasperated Caesar, who butts in to set the record straight. From Caesar we learn the inside story, from the dog's – if not the horse's – mouth:

> Haith lad, ye little ken about it;
> *For Britain's guid!* guid faith! I doubt it.
> Say rather, gaun as PREMIERS lead him,
> An' saying *aye* or *no* 's they bid him:
> At Operas an' Plays parading,
> Mortgaging, gambling, masquerading:
> Or maybe, in a frolic daft,
> To HAGUE or CALAIS takes a waft,
> To make a *tour* an' take a whirl,
> To learn *bon ton* an' see the worl'.
>
> There, at VIENNA or VERSAILLES,
> He rives his father's auld entails;
> Or by MADRID he takes the rout,
> To thrum *guittarres* an fecht wi' *nowt*;
> Or down *Italian Vista* startles,
> Wh—re-hunting amang groves o' myrtles:
> Then bowses drumlie *German-water*,
> To make himsel look fair an' fatter,
> An' clear the consequential sorrows,
> Love-gifts of Carnival Signioras.
> *For Britain's guid!* for her destruction!
> Wi' dissipation, feud an' faction!   (ll. 149–70)

Here, the civic humanist distaste for 'luxury' combines with a Calvinist animus against excessive sensual indulgence to produce a blistering indictment of upper-class corruption. The satirical, flyting vigour of this passage ought not to obscure its close affinities with Presbyterian moralising and the hellfire sermon. The dangerous social consequences which accompanied man's failure to discipline his appetites and passions was a constant preoccupation of the Scottish Calvinist mind. It was also one with which Burns was familiar at an early stage: the religious *Manual* which his father composed for Burns's instruction warns the reader to cultivate 'a mind regular and having the animal part under subjection to the rational'.[11] Caesar's depiction of a prodigal, hedonistic Member of Parliament is only one of Burns's many Calvinist salvoes against upper-class dissipation. In a letter of 1783, he criticises the Ayrshire nobility for 'imitating English, and French, [and] other foreign luxuries & fopperies' (*Letters*, I, 19). In a late political squib from 1794, he attacks the well-to-do members of a Dumfries loyalist club who 'In uproar and riot rejoice the night long' ('Extempore [on The *Loyal Natives*' Verses)]' (K, 450)). In one of the election ballads he mocks the Duke of Queensberry's devotion to 'the all-important cares / Of fiddles, wh—res and hunters' ('Epistle to Robt. Graham Esq: of Fintry on the Election for the Dumfries string of Boroughs, Anno 1790' (K, 318)). And of course there is the reference to those oppressors of the poor who 'riot in excess' in the 'Epistle to Davie' (K, 51).

This forceful Presbyterian censoriousness which is discernible in Burns's political poetry seems at odds with the carnivalesque impulses in some of his other works. It is noticeable, however, that, while Burns may celebrate the temperate, recreational festivity of the lower orders, he tends to condemn the festivity of the upper classes as wasteful, luxurious and socially harmful. The necessarily frugal indulgences of the poor in 'The Twa Dogs' ('twalpennie-worth o' *nappy*' on a holiday) are celebrated as a healthful break from labour, part of 'common recreation' (l. 126). But the sports of the rich are not so innocent. There is a desperation about the gentry's festivity; it is designed not to replenish spent energy but rather to obliterate the ennui of an idle life, of 'days, insipid, dull an' tasteless' (l. 209). Moreover, its effects are not just personally but socially pernicious: card-playing ladies 'Stake on a chance a farmer's stackyard' (l. 227); dissipated gentlemen squander the hard-earned resources of the community in senseless 'debauches' (l. 216). This is not a fruitful cycle of labour and recreation, but a barren oscillation between idleness and debauchery.

Festivity in Burns's poetry has the same ambivalence which François Laroque has identified in Shakespearean festivity. On the one hand is a popular, communal festivity, celebratory and carnivalesque – a 'banquet for all the world'; on the other, a more sinister, exclusive or class-based debauchery, which is not regenerative but destructive. Laroque's observation on Shakespearean festivity holds good for the work of Burns:

---

11 William Burnes, *A Manual of Religious Belief, Composed by William Burnes (The Poet's Father), For the Instruction of His Children* (Kilmarnock, 1875), p. xlix.

Once it has been cut off from its roots and has forfeited popular approval, festivity is doomed to become an instrument of torment, an occasion of sacrifice, even an abettor of the forces of evil.[12]

In the satires of Burns, the festivity of the upper classes is of this sinister variety. And the social reverberations of upper-class indulgence are not just economic but political. In 'The Twa Dogs', the MP's lavish lifestyle neutralises his ability to represent the people; it is financed not only by rents from his property but by angling for ministerial patronage, 'gaun as PREMIERS lead him, / An' saying *aye* or *no*'s they bid him'. The MP is led a dog's life by his ministerial masters, and here we are reminded of the opening description of Caesar and his imposing, ostentatious collar:

> His locked, letter'd, braw brass-collar,
> Show'd him the *gentleman* an' *scholar*.   (ll. 13–14)

This image of the shiny metal collar – a mark of distinction which is also a badge of servitude – has a resonance which encompasses the parliamentarian derided by Caesar: held on a 'lead' (l. 151) as tightly as any dog, the MP is the pampered pet of the executive. What this debauched figure symbolises, then, is the ability of the executive to corrupt the legislature through the dispensation of patronage – what Burns later refers to as the 'alarming System of Corruption [which] has pervaded the connection between the Executive Power and the House of Commons' (*Letters*, II, 173). The MP described by Caesar is a servant, not of the people but of the executive; he is working not 'for Britain's guid', but to please the 'PREMIER'. We see here the first indication of Burns's concern at a system of political patronage which is threatening to destroy that great eighteenth-century desideratum, 'the balance of the constitution'.

In 'The Author's Earnest Cry and Prayer, to the Right Honorable and Honorable, the Scotch Representatives in the House of Commons' (K, 81), the constitutional concerns which are adumbrated in 'The Twa Dogs' become the central focus of the poet's attention, as Burns continues his disparaging scrutiny of his society's leaders. Though the poem centres on an apparently light-hearted topic, whisky was in fact an emotive political issue in Burns's Scotland, an issue which focused important concerns about taxation and representation. Throughout the eighteenth century, successive British governments had attempted to increase the tax on whisky. In Scotland, this policy was seen as a calculated assault on a key Scottish industry, motivated by national animosity and designed to promote the interests of wealthy English distillers.[13] The topic of whisky duties was therefore an

---

12 François Laroque, *Shakespeare's Festive World: Elizabethan Seasonal Entertainment and the Professional Stage*, trans. by Janet Lloyd (Cambridge, 1991), p. 270.

13 For a discussion of the excise laws relating to the whisky industry in the period, see Henry Hamilton, *An Economic History of Scotland in the Eighteenth Century* (Oxford, 1963), pp. 104–10.

issue designed to cause maximum embarrassment to Scotland's MPs. It showed the London parliament favouring the interests of England and attacking the 'spirit' of Scotland. It illustrated the impunity with which Parliament could contravene the Treaty of Union. And above all, it demonstrated the impotence of Scotland's representatives; they were backing an anti-Scottish executive, instead of defending the people of Scotland.

As we have seen, Burns believed in the right of the common people to call their rulers to account, to chastise those rulers when they failed in their duties. At the same time, he was alive to the dangers, for a poet of his class, in voicing reckless and unguarded criticism of his superiors. One solution to this dilemma was a technique described by Burns as '*Ironic* satire, sidelins sklented' ('To W. Simpson, Ochiltree'); that is, he lets loose the most trenchant criticism under a screen of ingenuousness and deference. The technique is wielded with great skill in 'The Author's Earnest Cry and Prayer', one of Burns's most slyly 'double-voiced' works, in which almost every word that the metre stresses is pregnant with irony, is overlaid with the accents of mockery. As in 'The Twa Dogs', the contraints of Burns's social position work to his artistic advantage, producing a work which is more effective – more humorous, more supple and more pointed – than any piece of earnest denunciation.

'Ironic satire' is used to good effect from the start. The poem's title recalls the 'cry and prayer' in 2 Chronicles, 6.19, in which Solomon implores God to deal justly with 'thy people Israel'. The implication here is that the MPs should deal justly with the people of Scotland. But the title also reflects ironically on the vanity and conceit of the politicians; the speaker offers up a 'prayer' to the MPs, suggesting that they regard themselves as deities in relation to ordinary, lower-class Scots. Given that the poem goes on to strip every scrap of political integrity from Scotland's parliament-arians, there is also a retrospective irony in the title's longwinded appellation – 'the Right Honorable and Honorable, the Scotch Representatives in the House of Commons'. The epithet 'honorable' acquires an ironic ring just as surely as it does in Anthony's oration in *Julius Caesar* ('and Brutus is an honorable man').

The technique of ironic satire continues in the opening stanza:

> YE IRISH LORDS, ye *knights* an' *squires*,
> Wha represent our BRUGHS an' SHIRES,
> An' dousely manage our affairs
> > In *Parliament*,
> To you a simple Bardie's pray'rs
> > Are humbly sent.   (ll. 1–6)

Ostensibly, this is a deferential flourish, a doffing of the cap. Effectively, however, the stanza denies any legitimacy to Scotland's politicians. The Scots MPs have no genuine democratic mandate; they are in a position to hold office only because of their social standing, because they are 'LORDS', '*knights*', '*squires*'. Indeed, some of them – as 'IRISH LORDS' – don't even hail from Scotland. That repeated 'our' aligns the poet with the people of Scotland against this privileged few; he is addressing the politicians on Scotland's behalf. The fact that the poet is obliged to argue Scotland's case with the MPs indicates that they themselves have failed to do so. There is, then, a heavy freight of sarcasm on that verb – 'represent' – on which the second line's metre encourages us to linger. In fact, the poem suggests, parliamentary politics in Scotland is not *about* representation so much as political management; the MPs 'dousely manage our affairs'. Here, Burns's technique of aggressive deference is brilliantly illustrated in the adverb 'dousely', which means soberly and prudently, but also – and this is why Burns uses it – meekly and obligingly, or even, as Crawford notes, 'tamely'.[14] By the time we reach the end of the opening stanza, the notion that a 'simple' bardie is 'humbly' addressing his superiors has become just another layer of irony.

In this opening stanza, Burns has deftly alluded to the shortcomings of the electoral system under which the Scots are governed, and it is worth pausing for a moment to consider how that system operated. After the Union, Scotland returned forty-five MPs to Westminster. The thirty county members were returned by an electorate of fewer than 3,000 people. The fifteen burgh members were chosen by the self-selecting oligarchies who controlled local government. Tom Devine has calculated that, in the later eighteenth century, around 0.2 per cent of Scotland's population had the vote. This was a much lower proportion than in England or Ireland, where the franchise was much more widely distributed. Indeed, there were almost as many voters in the city of Dublin as there were in the whole of Scotland.[15] Almost no-one in Scotland had any say in choosing his elected representatives (a point Burns makes when he addresses the MPs, with masterful ambivalence, as 'ye chosen FIVE AND FORTY' (l. 133)). And because the Scottish electorate was so tiny, and since the Scottish MPs were such a negligible force in relation to the 600-odd members of the Commons, the government found it relatively easy to manage the Scottish representatives. As W. Hamish Fraser observes, 'Scottish politicians were perceived, with some justification, as the most venal and the most ready to sell their votes in return for government patronage'.[16]

Burns's poem is an exhortation to these notoriously venal creatures, inciting them to resist the lures of government patronage and to demand redress for Scotland's grievances, to 'echo thro' Saint Stephen's wa's / Auld Scotland's wrangs' (ll. 71–2). Adopting the persona of a 'simple Bardie' (l. 5), Burns implores the members to work for the repeal of the Wash Act of 1784, which had placed severe excise duties on Scotch whisky. The tone of the poem is mainly jocular, but that does not diminish the stinging rebuke implicit in the circumstance of a 'nameless wight' (l. 55) having to exhort his upper-class representatives to perform their public duty and fight Scotland's corner in the British parliament. That the Scottish members have so far proved reluctant to trouble the House with Scotland's grievances is put down to their involvement with the system of parliamentary patronage:

14 *Burns*, p. 150.
15 Devine, *Scottish Nation*, p. 196.
16 W. Hamish Fraser, *Scottish Popular Politics: From Radicalism to Labour* (Edinburgh, 2000), p. 4.

> Does ony *great man* glunch an' gloom?
> Speak out an' never fash your thumb!
> Let *posts* an' *pensions* sink or swoom
>   Wi' them wha grant them:
> If honestly they canna come,
>   Far better want them.
>
> In gath'rin votes ye were na slack,
> Now stand as tightly by your tack:
> Ne'er claw your lug, an' fidge your back,
>   An' hum an' haw,
> But raise your arm, an' tell your crack
>   Before them a'.   (ll. 25–36)

The 'simple Bardie' then advises the apparently tongue-tied parliamentarians on how best to present their case:

> Paint Scotland greetan owre her thrissle;
> Her *mutchkin stowp* as toom 's a whissle;
> An' damn'd Excise-men in a bussle,
>   Seizan a *Stell*,
> Triumphant crushan 't like a muscle
>   Or laimpet shell.
>
> Then on the tither hand present her,
> A blackguard *Smuggler*, right behint her,
> An', cheek-for-chow, a chuffie *Vintner*,
>   Colleaguing join, –
> Picking her pouch as bare as Winter,
>   Of a' kind coin.   (ll. 37–48)

Like a painter of allegories, Burns composes a vivid tableau of Scotland's predicament. He represents the nation as an aged crone, reduced to poverty by the destruction of the national industry. And indeed this is a poem whose central preoccupation is 'representation', in both the political and artistic senses of the word. Burns has to take on the task of (artistic) representation, since the 'Scotch representatives' in the House of Commons – in Burns's words, 'the Representative part of the Legislature' (*Letters*, II, 208) – are not doing their job of (political) representation. 'The Author's Earnest Cry and Prayer' is thus a poem which demonstrates the very virtues that the MPs lack. It is a work of exhortative eloquence, designed to 'rouse . . . up' (l. 17) the Scottish representatives just as they should have roused up the government ministers. It 'paints' the misery of Scotland just as the Scottish members should already have done. Like 'The Twa Dogs', then, this is a poem which overturns conventional notions about where civic virtue is to be looked for in society. Here we have a lower-class speaker who is able to lift his eyes from his own material struggles and look to the public good ('mind the kirk and state affairs'), while his upper-class representatives, who are free from the pressures of immediate want, are wholly engrossed in lining their pockets.

If there is one dominant feature of Burns's technique in this poem, it is the tact with which he makes the venality of the MPs transparently clear, while avoiding the risk of seditious libel. One of the key methods by which Burns achieves this feat is the ironic use of the rhetorical question. Having painted a graphic portrait of Scotland's distress, the speaker poses an indignant query:

> Is there, that bears the name o' SCOT,
> But feels his heart's bluid rising hot,
> To see his poor, auld Mither's *pot*,
>   Thus dung in staves;
> An' plunder'd o' her hindmost groat,
>   By gallow's knaves?   (ll. 49–54)

The force of this stanza lies in the fact that, unlike most rhetorical questions, this one does suggest an answer different from that which the questioner apparently assumes. *Yes*, there *is* a group of Scots whose heart's blood does *not* boil in patriotic rage at Westminster's contemptuous treatment of Scotland – they are the Scots MPs. This device of the ironic rhetorical question is so successful that Burns uses it again a few stanzas later, asking the MPs if they can bear to watch auld Scotland in tears without jumping to her protection. Again, shockingly, the question must be answered in the affirmative.

Sensing that the appeal to public duty will not be sufficient to move Scotland's representatives to action, Burns then plays on their fears, threatening an eruption of popular violence, with discontented Scots vindicating their own liberties in arms, if the MPs fail to secure redress for Scotland:

> Arouse my boys! exert your mettle,
> To get auld Scotland back her *kettle*!
> Or faith! I'll wad my new pleugh-pettle,
>   Ye'll see 't or lang,
> She'll teach you, wi' a reekan whittle,
>   Anither sang.

> An' L—d! if ance they pit her till 't,
> Her tartan petticoat she'll kilt
> An' durk an' pistol at her belt,
>   She'll tak the streets,
> An' rin her whittle to the hilt,
>   I' th' first she meets!   (ll. 85–90, 97–102)

Though the imagery has a comic exuberance, the threat which it makes is serious enough. Clearly, Burns's political horizon allowed him to envisage a resort to arms when the covenant between government and people has broken down. The speaker's injunction to 'get auld Scotland back her *kettle!*' requires careful consideration in this connection. Given that Burns later uses 'kettle' as a synonym for the constitution – 'The *kettle* o' the Kirk and State' ('The Dumfries Volunteers') – we are faced with an intriguing possibility: could Burns here be calling for the restoration of the Scottish Parliament as well as the repeal of the punitive English excise laws? At any rate, it is notable that the personification of Scotland has changed from an old, feeble woman – 'poor, auld Mither' (l. 51), 'The kind, auld, cantie Carlin' (l. 62) – to a revolutionary amazon whose raunchily warlike appearance foreshadows the Liberté of Delacroix.

Among Burns's lesser-known prose works, and one which throws light on the issues raised in 'The Author's Earnest Cry and Prayer', is a letter sent to the *Edinburgh Evening Courant* in 1789, written under the pseudonym of John Barleycorn (*Letters*, I, 371–75). This is an open letter to Prime Minister Pitt, composed on behalf of the Scottish distillers, in protest at a new round of prohibitive whisky duties. These duties threatened to ruin, not the distillers alone, but farmers, cotters and all who worked the land, 'from the landlord of a Province down to his lowest hind'. Now, Burns was in no doubt as to why this 'most partial tax' had been imposed on the Scots. It was designed, he says, 'to favour a few opulent English Distillers, who ... were of vast Electioneering consequence'. The interests of Scotland had been 'sacrificed, without remorse, to the infernal deity of Political Expediency!' Again, the corrupting influence of Westminster politics was threatening the welfare of Scotland.

This corruption of Scottish public life under the Union is the central preoccupation of 'The Author's Earnest Cry and Prayer'. Not only is Scotland's economic welfare jeopardised by the Union; much more importantly, the civic virtue of the nation is degraded and debased by the unequal connection with England. It is not enough, from a civic humanist perspective, for a country to be governed wisely. It must be governed by its own inhabitants. Government by a foreign power – even if that government is enlightened and humane – cannot be salutary. The liberty that does not depend on the active exertions of the inhabitants of a country is no liberty at all. 'Liberty is a right which every individual must be ready to vindicate for himself', wrote Adam Ferguson, 'and which he who pretends to bestow as a favour, has by that very act in reality denied.'[17] This is the situation against which 'The Author's Earnest Cry and Prayer' registers its protest. That the office of the statesman has been degraded is the import of the main body of the poem. But that other crucial civic office – that of the soldier – has likewise been debased, and this is Burns's subject in the 'Postscript'.

The Postscript is an ironic salute to the martial virtue of the Scots. Where once the Scots fought, in true civic humanist fashion, for the independence of their nation, now the Highland soldiers are the mercenary shock troops of British imperialism. The speaker of the Postscript is no longer the 'simple Bardie' of the first part of the poem, but an unnamed ignoramus who glories in Scotland's current

17 *Essay*, p. 266.

military exploits. He begins by lauding Scotland's whisky-sodden hard-men against the wine-swilling cowards of the Mediterranean:

> Let half-starv'd slaves in warmer skies,
> See future wines, rich-clust'ring, rise;
> Their lot auld Scotland ne'er envies,
> > But blyth an' frisky,
> She eyes her freeborn, martial boys,
> > Tak aff their Whisky.   (ll. 145–50)

We know from the earlier part of the poem that 'auld Scotland', far from being 'blyth an' frisky', is a downtrodden, haggard crone. Given the legacy of poverty and political impotence which Scotland has been shown to endure, we are surely meant to see the Scottish soldiers in the British army as being closer to 'half-starv'd slaves' than 'freeborn, martial boys'. There is nothing free or virtuous in their military service. Instead, as the speaker boasts, the Scottish soldiers are unthinking automatons, who slaughter at royal command:

> But bring a SCOTCHMAN frae his hill,
> Clap in his cheek a *highlan gill*,
> Say, such is royal GEORGE's will,
> > An' there's the foe,
> He has nae thought but how to kill
> > Twa at a blow.   (ll. 163–8)

This is the utter degradation of military virtue. The virtuous citizen, vindicating his own and his nation's liberties in arms, has become the hireling thug of the state. In this stanza, Burns reflects the concerns which many radicals shared at the corrupting influence of standing armies. In *The Origin of the Distinction of Ranks* (1779), John Millar writes:

> The tendency of a standing mercenary army to increase the power and prerogative of the crown, which has been the subject of much declamation, is sufficiently obvious. As the army is immediately under the conduct of the monarch; as the individuals of which it is composed depend entirely upon him for preferment; as, by forming a separate order of men they are apt to become indifferent about the rights of their fellow-citizens; it may be expected that, in most cases, they will be disposed to pay an implicit obedience to his commands, and that the same force which is maintained to suppress insurrections, and to repel invasions, may often be employed to subvert and destroy the liberties of the people.[18]

Burns might have written his 'Postcript' to illustrate Millar's remarks. His mercenary Highlander, 'disposed to pay an implicit obedience' to King George's commands, is the tool of an increasingly overbearing monarchy. Clearly, this

18 Lehmann, p. 286.

drunken redcoat would have no compunction about following 'royal GEORGE's will', whether the 'foe' was a foreign soldier or a domestic reformer. What Burns suggests in this Postscript is that, until Scotland's national liberty – symbolised in the poem by whisky – is redeemed, then the country's martial spirit will continue to be prostituted in this squalid fashion. This, perhaps, is the meaning of the poem's rather opaque concluding toast: 'FREEDOM and WHISKY gang thegither, / Tak aff your whitter' (ll. 185–6).

One trait of her old national liberty which Scotland *has* maintained is the freedom of her speech: 'Auld Scotland has a raucle tongue' (l. 127). And as an indictment of the Scottish ruling elite, 'The Author's Earnest Cry and Prayer' is significant as much in its style as its substance. Burns's familiar, colloquial mode of address – 'Arouse my boys!' (l. 85), 'For G—d-sake, Sirs!' (l. 103) – obliterates the epic distance which supposedly separates the MPs from the lower-class speaker. This familiar tone, together with some savage mock-humility – 'Alas! I'm but a nameless wight, / Trode i' the mire out o' sight!' (ll. 55–6) – dramatises Burns's contempt for his supposed superiors, who have so little merited their exalted position. His tongue-in-cheek comparison of the Scots MPs with Demosthenes and Cicero merely underscores their betrayal of the civic ideal.

There is a further dimension to the politics of style in Burns's political satires. The cultivation of a low, plain-spoken style which can be presented as 'artless' reinforces the 'country' ideology of these poems, their praise of rural independence and condemnation of courtly corruption, 'the venal contagion of a Court' (*Letters*, II, 210). It is crucial to the success of a poem like 'The Author's Earnest Cry and Prayer' that the speaker should address his exalted audience in a low, unvarnished style. Such a style testifies to the speaker's independence, his freedom from courtly pretence and hypocrisy. He is not obliged to wheedle, to 'round the period an' pause' (l. 68) like compliant MPs. He demonstrates his integrity through the irreverence of his style, his use of 'a raucle tongue'. His earthy, pungent Scots – a demotic and democratic 'crack' (l. 35) – is the tongue in which to tell the 'honest, open, naked truth' (l. 20).

Burns's style in the satires is an expression of political dissent. It is comparable in significance to the 'opposition poetics' cultivated by various English republican poets after the Restoration of Charles II. Steven Zwicker has shown how poets like Marvell cultivated a plain-spoken, often irreverent style as part of their dissident 'country' politics, and eschewed a high courtly style as indicative of moral depravity and corruption. This was a poetics which took its stand on such concepts as 'the authenticity of satiric bluntness' and 'the equation of immorality and stylistic excess'.[19] We can perceive just such principles at work in the political satires of Burns's early period. In 'A Dream' (K, 113), for instance, the 'satiric bluntness' with which Burns reminds the King of the loss of the American colonies –

19 Steven N. Zwicker, 'Lines of Authority: Politics and Literary Culture in the Restor- ation', in *Politics of Discourse: The Literature and History of Seventeenth-Century England*, ed. by Kevin Sharpe and Steven N. Zwicker (Berkeley, 1987), pp. 230–70 (p. 246).

> Your *royal nest*, beneath *Your* wing,
>   Is e'en right reft an' clouted   (ll. 32–33)

– is associated with 'authenticity', with the notion that '*Facts* are cheels that winna ding, / An' downa be disputed' (ll. 30–31). This remains a general principle throughout Burns's political satire: Burns demonstrates his independence from court influence through his independence from the courtly standard of speech; the use of 'plain, braid Scots' promises a 'plain, braid story' ('The Brigs of Ayr'). Burns's mixed Scots-English style is a counterpart of the 'distinctive country poetic' adopted by Marvell and the English republicans.[20] It is as part of this commitment to 'opposition poetics' that Burns cultivates the persona of the uncouth, country poet, the 'Bard of rustic song' ('A Bard's Epitaph'). This persona is reminiscent of David Lindsay's John the Common Weill, or the John Upaland of the Reformation satirists: a representative, plain-spoken rustic, where rusticity connotes honesty and integrity.[21] By contrast, the submissiveness, the tameness of the Scottish MPs in 'The Author's Earnest Cry and Prayer' is evinced by their fastidious, courtly language, their ability 'with rhetoric clause on clause / To mak harangues' (ll. 69–70). Tellingly, the familiar, irreverent style which Burns employs in the political satires was identified by contemporaries as characteristic of Presbyterianism and its 'levelling' doctrines. In *The Scotch Presbyterian Eloquence*, an episcopalian satire first published in 1692 but reprinted throughout the eighteenth century, Presbyterian writers and preachers are chastised not only for incendiary political doctrines but for the offensive 'rusticity' of their language and their familiar and irreverent treatment of persons of quality.[22]

Perhaps the most licentious, and certainly the most controversial, blast of irreverent 'Presbyterian eloquence' among Burns's early satires is 'A Dream', the mock laureate ode to George III which Burns daringly included in the Kilmarnock volume.[23] Despite an equivocal reference to the Pretender, this is a poem which reminds us that anti-Hanoverianism was as much a radical Whig as a Jacobite principle by the 1780s. Burns challenges George III's absolutist pretensions in the name, not of the exiled dynasty, but of a sovereign people. As in 'The Author's Earnest Cry and Prayer', Burns adopts the deliberately lower-class persona of the 'humble poet', and again he uses a provocatively uncouth idiom, his independence

---

20 Zwicker, p. 246.
21 For John Upaland, see 'Ane Exhortatioun derect to my Lord Regent and to the rest of the Lordis accomplisis', in *Satirical Poems of the Time of the Reformation*, ed. by J. Cranstoun, 2 vols (Edinburgh, 1891–93), I, 52–56.
22 Gilbert Crockatt and John Monro, *The Scotch Presbyterian Eloquence*, 4th edn (London, 1719), pp. 3–4, 29, 90.
23 The mock laureate ode was a new genre, pioneered by George Ellis in *Probationary Odes for the Laureateship* (1785); see *Parodies of the Romantic Age: The Poetry of the Anti-Jacobin and Other Parodic Writings*, ed. by Graeme Stones and John Strachan, 5 vols (London, 1999), II, 4–10.

from the courtly standard of speech signalling his independence from court corruption.

'A Dream' was written in response to Thomas Warton's laureate ode 'For His Majesty's Birthday, 1786',[24] which Burns had read in a newspaper. The 1780s was a period of widespread public anxiety at the apparently high-handed practices of George III, who was regarded by many as having extended the scope of monarchical power in a way that threatened the balance of the constitution and undermined 'Revolution Principles'. The view that, in the words of John Dunning's famous parliamentary motion of 1780, 'the influence of the crown has increased, is increasing, and ought to be diminished', was widely shared.[25] In this context, it seemed the height of absurdity and mendacity for Warton to hail George III as a ruler of classical integrity, 'Who bids his Britain vie with Greece' (l. 64), and who, like a modern-day Hiero or Ptolemy, 'Diffusing opulence and public good' (l. 42), combines virtuous kingship with patronage of the arts. In Burns's view, such sentiments were, in the laureate's own words, 'the tinsel gifts of flattery' (l. 4), and it was Burns's task to emulate Warton's Grecian bards and tear these flimsy bays 'from the tyrant's brow' (l. 3).

In 'A Dream', Burns reverses the conventional role of the laureate. Humorously introducing himself as 'My Bardship' (l. 5), Burns warns the king that he 'winna flatter' (l. 20) and proceeds to advise the king to reform parliament ('rax Corruption's neck' (l. 66)), reduce taxation, and improve the quality of his ministers,

> . . . chaps, wha, in a *barn* or *byre*,
>   Wad better fill'd their station
>   Than *courts* yon day.   (ll. 43–45)

Implicit here is the principle of the covenant: the notion that the king has duties and that his subjects, however humble, may call him to account. To demonstrate that this particular monarch is in pressing need for such counsel and admonition, Burns alludes caustically to the loss of the American colonies:

> 'Tis very true, my sovereign King,
>   My skill may weel be doubted;
> But *Facts* are cheels that winna ding,
>   An' downa be disputed:
> Your *royal nest*, beneath *Your* wing,
>   Is e'en right reft an' clouted,
> And now the third part o' the string,
>   An' less, will gang about it
>   Than did ae day.   (ll. 28–36)

This stanza – with its indecorously homely proverb, and its reference to the king's dominions as a 'royal nest' – is a classic example of Burns's reductive, carnivalesque

24 *The Poems of T. Warton, and J. Warton* (Chiswick, 1822), pp. 131–3.
25 Dickinson, 'Radicals and Reformers', p. 125; Clark, *Language of Liberty*, pp. 282–3.

style. Burns's language here is characterised by a strong 'carnivalistic frankness',[26] and indeed Burns might be said to have infused the boisterous atmosphere of the popular King's Birthday celebration into his mock laureate ode.[27] Burns refers to the loss of the colonies in order to suggest that the king's 'skill may weel be doubted', and to stymie those flatterers who would persuade the king that he is infallible and can 'ne'er do wrang' (l. 16). A throw against the perceived rehabilitation of divine right kingship under George III, the poem ties in with Burns's sarcastic references to 'this very reign of heavenly Hanoverianism' and 'the illustrious & sapientipotent Family of H—' in a later letter to Mrs Dunlop (*Letters*, I, 337).

A crucial feature of 'A Dream', as of Burns's other political satires, is the concern with taxation, the notion that 'auld *Britain*' has been taxed 'Till she has scarce a tester' (l. 49). The reason why taxation is such a prominent issue in Burns's political satires is that, in civic theory, it is the revenue gained from taxation which enables the executive to corrupt the legislature with sinecures and pensions. The 'new taxation' in 'The Twa Dogs', and the 'sair taxation' (l. 48) in 'A Dream', represent the corrupting power of the executive, the source of the '*posts* an' *pensions*' in 'The Author's Earnest Cry and Prayer'. Whenever Burns discusses the suborning of the legislature he almost invariably raises the issue of taxation. In the epistle 'To a Gentleman who had sent him a News-paper, and offered to continue it free of expense' (K, 282), Burns speaks of 'royal George ... managing St. Stephen's quorum' (l. 21–2), and sarcastically suggests that the sources of government revenue have proliferated to such an extent that a tax on sexual intercourse may be expected at any moment. Burns reads the paper, he says, to find out

> How cesses, stents, and fees were rax'd,
> Or if bare a—s yet were tax'd.   (ll. 27–8)

Behind the coarse humour a serious political point is being made: the growth in taxation is abetting the spread of corruption.

From the above discussion of three early poems – 'The Twa Dogs', 'The Author's Earnest Cry and Prayer', and 'A Dream' – it should be apparent that Burns's political poetry is founded on a coherent political philosophy and a reasoned response to contemporary politics. The critique of corruption, the call for independent politicians, the anxiety concerning taxation, the protest at the suborning of the legislature: all this shows Burns utilising the Calvinist and civic humanist discourses discussed in the previous chapter. And while these civic premises can be inferred from the early satires, they are in fact explicitly set out in a series of political letters which Burns composed a couple of years later, in response to an Excise Board enquiry into his supposed 'disaffection'. In this series of political

---

26 Mikhail Bakhtin, *Problems of Dostoevsky's Poetics*, ed. and trans. by Caryl Emerson (Minneapolis, MN, 1984), p. 174.

27 Christopher A. Whatley, 'Burns: Work, Kirk and Community in Later Eighteenth-Century Scotland', in *Burns Now*, ed. by Kenneth Simpson (Edinburgh, 1994), pp. 92–116 (pp. 107–11).

letters written in 1792/93, Burns articulates the political theory behind the earlier satires. Essentially, Burns subjects the contemporary British political system to a classic civic humanist analysis, as in the following passage from a letter to Robert Graham of Fintry:

> As to REFORM PRINCIPLES, I look upon the British Constitution, as settled at the Revolution, to be the most glorious Constitution on earth, or that perhaps the wit of man can frame; at the same time, I think, & you know what High and distinguished Characters have for some time thought so, that we have a good deal deviated from the original principles of that Constitution; particularly, that an alarming System of Corruption has pervaded the connection between the Executive Power and the House of Commons. – This is the Truth, the Whole truth, of my Reform opinions . . .
>
> (*Letters*, II, 173)

The British constitution, having lost the struggle against corruption, requires to be renovated, returned to its original principles. In a letter to John Francis Erskine of Mar (a political ally before whom Burns has no cause to dissimulate), Burns reasserts his conviction that, while 'in its original principles' the British constitution may be sound, there has recently arisen 'a system of corruption between the Executive Power & the Representative part of the Legislature' (*Letters*, II, 208). In other letters from the same period Burns reiterates this charge of corruption. He encourages the editor of a reformist newspaper to 'Lay bare, with undaunted heart & steady hand, that horrid mass of corruption called Politics & State-Craft!' (*Letters*, II, 158). And in the 'Political Catechism' set down in a letter to Alexander Cunningham, Burns defines politics as 'a science . . . wherewith, by means of nefarious cunning, & hypocritical pretence, we govern civil Polities for the emolument of ourselves & our adherents' (*Letters*, II, 182).

Although these prose comments date from 1792/93, they undoubtedly express the principles behind the early political satires. A civic critique of public corruption is at the centre of poems such as 'The Author's Earnest Cry and Prayer', and 'The Twa Dogs' which bemoan the burgeoning influence of the king's ministers, the corruption of the legislature by the executive, and the unscrupulous uses of public revenue. The MPs in 'The Author's Earnest Cry and Prayer' cannot speak out for the public good as they see it, for fear they might lose their places at court. The early satires, then, rest on a coherent civic theory of politics. Burns interprets contemporary politics in terms of a 'Machiavellian moment', a crisis of corruption. The balance of the constitution has broken down, and the mechanism is not now working for the public good but for the private profit of the administration and its placemen. Like his admired Junius, Burns regards the Lords and Commons as 'seven hundred persons notoriously corrupted by the Crown', and aims to expose 'that state of abandoned servility and prostitution, to which the undue influence of the Crown has reduced the other branches of the legislature'.[28]

---

28 *The Letters of Junius*, 2 vols (London, 1806), I, ix, xvi.

The theme of a political system beset by corruption is one to which Burns reverts throughout his career. He explores it in that (largely uninspired) series of election ballads in which he exposes 'the sirens of Flattery, the harpies of Corruption, & the furies of Ambition, these infernal deities that on all sides and in all parties preside over the villainous business of Politics' (*Letters*, II, 44). Long before John Galt's *The Member* (1832), Burns's election ballads – most effectively 'Buy Braw Troggin' (K, 494) – expose the jobbery and venality surrounding British parliamentary elections:

> WHA will buy my Troggin,
>   Fine ELECTION WARE;
> Broken trade o' *BR*[OUGHTON]
>   A' in high repair.   (ll. 1–4)

It is this preoccupation with corruption which explains what Burns himself describes as 'the fanfaronade of independance to be found in his works' (*Letters*, II, 209). In civic thought, independence is the antidote to corruption. It is the crucial political virtue, the qualification for citizenship. Consequently, independence is one of the key terms in Burns's political vocabulary. In the 'Epistle to a Young Friend' (K, 105), Burns advises his correspondent to

> . . . gather gear by ev'ry wile,
>   That 's justified by Honour:
> Not for to *hide* it in a *hedge*,
>   Nor for a *train-attendant*;
> But for the glorious priviledge
>   Of being *independant*.   (ll. 51–56)

This is independence, not in the national but the civic sense, denoting the economic self-sufficiency necessary to disinterested participation in the affairs of the public; the freedom from bribery and undue influence.

In classic civic theory, independence involves economic self-sufficiency, the possession of 'gear'. But Burns adapts the civic principle to fit his own circumstances, and the situation of Scotland as he sees it. For Burns, the defining feature of independence is the freedom to act as one's conscience dictates, and not be directed by another's private interest. It is not a question of independent means but of independent minds. The 'man of independant mind' ('Song – For a' that and a' that') may be a man of little or no wealth, but one who nevertheless thinks for himself, like the Bard of 'The Brigs of Ayr' (K, 120), 'nurst in the Peasant's lowly shed, / To hardy Independence bravely bred' (ll. 7–8). This is the independence Burns boasts of in 'A Dream' –

> For me! before a Monarch's face,
>   Ev'n *there* I winna flatter;
> For neither Pension, Post, nor Place,
>   Am I your humble debtor.   (ll. 19–22)

It is the same independence alluded to in 'A Dedication to Gavin Hamilton Esq' (K, 103):

> This may do – maun do, Sir, wi' them wha
> Maun please the Great-folk for a wamefou;
> For me! sae laigh I need na bow,
> For, LORD be thanket, *I can plough*.   (ll. 11–14)

As we shall see in Chapter 8, the independence available to the poor tenant farmer was a quality which Burns came to prize all the more when, upon accepting a commission with the excise, his own independence became severely curtailed.

In some of his early satires, as we have seen, Burns indicts the ruling classes for a failure of political leadership. Other satires focus on the deplorable *social* effects of upper-class corruption. It is in the 'Address of Beelzebub' (K, 108), a poem written in 1786 but never published during his lifetime, that Burns launches his most trenchant and unrestrained satirical attack on irresponsible social leadership. The poem was occasioned by activities of several highland landlords – Campbell of Breadalbane, Mackenzie of Applecross, and Macdonald of Glengarry – who allegedly combined to prevent the intended emigration of five hundred impoverished Highlanders from Glengarry's estates. According to the *Edinburgh Advertiser* of 30 May, 1786, the Highlanders' intention of emigrating to Canada was reported to a meeting of the Highland Society by Campbell of Breadalbane, who revealed

> that five hundred persons had agreed to emigrate from the estates of M'Donald of Glengarry; that they had subscribed money, purchased ships, &c., to carry their design into effect. The noblemen and gentlemen agreed to co-operate with government to frustrate their design; and to recommend to the principal noblemen and gentlemen in the Highlands to endeavour to prevent emigration, by improving the fisheries, agriculture, and manufactures, and particularly to enter into a subscription for that purpose.

Burns provides a less sympathetic account of the Society's activities in the poem's ironic dedication:

> To the Right Honorable JOHN, EARL OF BREADALBANE, President of the Right Honorable the HIGHLAND SOCIETY, which met, on the 23d of May last, at the Shakespeare, Covent Garden, to concert ways and means to frustrate the designs of FIVE HUNDRED HIGHLANDERS who, as the Society were informed by Mr McKenzie of Applecross, were so audacious as to attempt an escape from theire lawful lords and masters whose property they are by emigrating from the lands of Mr McDonald of Glengarry to the wilds of CANADA, in search of that fantastic thing – LIBERTY –

The poem opens with Beelzebub commending the landlords for preventing the Highlanders' emigration. Had they reached the New World, he reflects, the 'Poor, dunghill sons of dirt an' mire' (l. 19) might have followed the example of the

American colonists, and aspired to 'PATRICIAN RIGHTS' (l. 20). Feigning indignation at the very thought, Beelzebub slyly articulates what we are undoubtedly meant to regard as the true attitude of the landlords to those under their jurisdiction:

> THEY! an' be d—mn'd! what right hae they
> To Meat, or Sleep, or light o' day,
> Far less to riches, pow'r, or freedom,
> But what your lordships PLEASE TO GIE THEM?   (ll. 27–30)

By playing on the secret convictions of the lords – that their tenants are a species of property, to dispose of as they see fit – Beelzebub aims to egg them on to greater acts of evil. Glengarry is warned that his rack renting of the tenants, and his impounding of their goods, merely serves to ruffle 'their stubborn Highlan spirit' (l. 38), and so a more rigorous course of action is recommended:

> But smash them! crush them a' to spails!
> An' rot the DYVORS i' the JAILS!
> The young dogs, swinge them to the labour,
> Let WARK an' HUNGER mak them sober!
> The HIZZIES, if they're oughtlins fausont,
> Let them in DRURY LANE be lesson'd!
> An' if the wives, an' dirty brats,
> Come thiggan at your doors an' yets,
> Flaffan wi' duds, an' grey wi' beese,
> Frightan awa your deucks an' geese;
> Get out a HORSE-WHIP or a JOWLER,
> The langest thong, the fiercest growler,
> An' gar the tatter'd gipseys pack
> Wi' a' their bastarts on their back!   (ll. 39–52)

This vision of unrestrained commercial exploitation and violence has a vivid infernal energy, a shocking brio. Beelzebub's inverted panacea, where the ills of a single landowner are remedied by the exploitation of an entire community, contains some of the most powerful lines in Burns. Whether Burns accurately represents the motives of the Highland Society over the Glengarry affair may indeed be open to question.[29] Nevertheless, the poem presents the potential depravity of a person encouraged to believe that another class of humans exists solely for his own profit and gratification; a person relying on what Adam Smith calls 'the vile maxim of the masters of mankind', namely, 'All for ourselves, and nothing for other people'.[30]

All the same, the poem is no easy, self-righteous denunciation of Glengarry and his like. By the form of the poem – a dramatic monologue – the reader is effectively aligned with the monologue's auditors, Breadalbane and Glengarry, and undergoes

---

29 Thomas Crawford, *Boswell, Burns and the French Revolution* (Edinburgh, 1990), p. 23.
30 *Wealth of Nations*, I, 418.

their infernal temptation. This is what makes the poem so effective: the reader is permitted to savour the intoxicating prospect of wielding an absolute authority. Beelzebub's insinuations and instructions, so horrifying when considered abstractly, exert a guilty fascination. As with any vigorous and relished contempt, his contempt for the Highlanders is in some degree contagious. If Beelzebub aims to activate Glengarry's baser instincts, he does the same for the reader. What would be straightforwardly repugnant as an intellectual proposition is less glibly dismissable when experienced as an embodied viewpoint. Burns's dramatic approach in this poem is thus far more powerful than the conventional Augustan moralising on the abuses of power: having experienced something of its temptations, the reader is the better apprised of the need for checks and restraints on power.

The 'Address of Beelzebub' takes Burns's civic humanist critique of his society's leadership to a new level of sophistication; the poem is a triumphant aesthetic success, 'Burns's most underrated dramatic monologue'.[31] However, the poem's sophistication and black humour should not blind us to its deeply religious and moralistic implications – namely, that the conduct of Glengarry and Breadalbane is satanic, that it betokens a blasphemous disregard for the word of God and the religion of Christ. We are reminded again of the 'Epistle to Davie' (K, 51):

> Alas! how aft, in haughty mood,
> GOD's creatures they oppress!   (ll. 77–78)

Again, Burns is not invoking the standards of secular democracy so much as those of Presbyterian moralism. This is the 'religio-political language' which Burns habitually employs in his radical poems.[32]

'The Brigs of Ayr' (K, 120), written in the autumn of 1786 and first published in the 1787 Edinburgh edition, is a more uneven poem than the 'Address of Beelzebub', but one which has important political resonances. It centres on the *topos* of ancients against moderns, taking the form of a dialogue between the Auld Brig of Ayr and a newer counterpart. The Auld Brig is Gothic, ugly, but solid and durable – 'teughly doure' (l. 80); the New Brig elegant, but flimsy. As the dialogue advances, the opposition develops wider connotations. Firstly, there is a religious aspect: the Auld Brig as a kind of rugged, architectural Covenanter, opposing the New Brig's elegant Moderatism. The Auld Brig praises the 'douce' and 'godly' townspeople of earlier days (ll. 151–60), while the New Brig disparages the Auld Brig's puritanical 'notion, / That sullen gloom was sterling, true devotion' (ll. 146–7). The opposition between the two structures also acquires a politico-philosophical dimension: the Auld Brig presents a sturdy, civic humanist defence of Gothic liberty against degenerate modernity, while the New Brig advocates a polite, commercial ethic.

These are the central oppositions of the poem. At no point can Burns be said to take definite sides in the debate. Neither Brig seems to have the better of the exchanges, which are rather unsatisfactorily cut short by the arbitrary introduction

---

31 Robert Burns, *Selected Poems*, ed. by Carol McGuirk, p. 238.
32 Patrick Scott Hogg, 'Robert Burns under the microscope', *Herald*, 25 January 1996.

of a train of allegorical figures led by 'The Genius of the Stream'. However, though the debate is unresolved, the tendency of commentators has been to align Burns with the Auld Brig's position, and this seems warrantable.[33] Certainly, there is a familiar Burnsian tenor to the Auld Brig's tirade against modern degeneracy:

> Nae langer Rev'rend Men, their country's glory,
> In plain braid Scots hold forth a plain, braid story:
> Nae langer thrifty Citizens, an' douce,
> Meet owre a pint, or in the Council-house;
> But staumrel, corky-headed, graceless Gentry,
> The herryment and ruin of the country;
> Men, three-parts made by Taylors and by Barbers,
> Wha waste your weel-hain'd gear on d—d *new Brigs* / and *Harbours*!
>
> (ll. 166–73)

No doubt this speech is something of a verbal caricature, a depiction of a stereotypical 'ancient' attitude. Nevertheless, the Auld Brig's Fergusonian lament over the comparative degeneracy of contemporary social leaders is one which Burns regularly echoes in his poems and letters. Moreover, the civic outlook of the Auld Brig chimes with the persona cultivated by Burns in the opening section of the poem, in which he appears as a 'hardy' peasant-poet, 'train'd to arms in stern Misfortune's field' (l. 10), and not to be counted among 'The servile, mercenary Swiss of rhymes' (l. 12). It is tempting, then, to read 'The Brigs of Ayr' as reflecting Burns's disillusion with standards of behaviour in contemporary public life, and his hankering for a more severe Calvinist and civic humanist ethos among his society's leaders.

But the presentation of the Auld Brig, if largely favourable, remains ambivalent. We approach the crux of this ambivalence in considering the epithet 'Gothic'. In one instance, the narrator's description of the Auld Brig as 'Gothic' carries favourable connotations of sturdiness and independence:

> *Auld Brig* appear'd of ancient Pictish race,
> The vera wrinkles Gothic in his face:
> He seem'd as he wi' Time had warstl'd lang,
> Yet, teughly doure, he bade an unco bang.   (ll. 77–80)

In another instance, however, the New Brig uses 'Gothic' as an aesthetic term and in a pejorative sense to impugn the Auld Brig's inelegant appearance:

> There 's men of taste wou'd tak the *Ducat-stream*,
> Tho' they should cast the vera sark and swim,
> Ere they would grate their feelings wi' the view
> Of sic an ugly, Gothic hulk as you.   (ll. 103–106)

---

33 See, for example, Crawford, *Burns*, p. 197.

These two competing usages admirably illustrate the ambivalent status of the 'Gothic' as a concept in eighteenth-century thought. As Pocock observes, the term 'Gothic' was 'one of high praise in the language of politics, while remaining a synonym for barbarism in the language of cultural history and aesthetics'. As this dichotomy suggests, 'there was implicit in the creed of civic humanism a real doubt whether citizenship and culture were not at least partly incompatible – the "Spartan" image at work once more'.[34] This doubt is very much present in 'The Brigs of Ayr', in which Burns associates culture and elegance with a stage of society which, from the civic point of view, is degenerate, and civic liberty with a stage of society which, from a cultured perspective, is primitive. In effect, the dialogue between the two bridges is a dialogue between culture and liberty. It is Burns's inclination toward the latter option that explains his eagerness to present himself as a rugged, unrefined poet, a 'simple Bard, rough at the rustic plough' (l. 1). In adopting this persona, Burns avoids the embarrassment which – on civic and Calvinist counts – attaches to his position as a creative artist. He adopts the only poetic role which is compatible with civic principles: that of the Bard, the uncultured poet.

It is, of course, one of the ironies of Burns's political poetry that this strategic positioning of himself as a simple, uncultured rustic should have proved so successful, obscuring the intellectual context in which his poems were produced. Undoubtedly, this uncultured persona has abetted the critical tradition which reads Burns's political satires as the splenetic, incoherent outbursts of an embittered peasant. What I hope to have shown in this chapter is that Burns's satires are the work, not of a boorish backwoodsman, but of a man whose perception of contemporary politics was shaped by a critical engagement with a variety of political discourses, including civic humanism, Real Whiggism and Presbyterian contractarianism. As I have also sought to demonstrate, Burns does not simply absorb these discourses uncritically, but rather adapts them to his own circumstances. In particular, Burns revises the conventional association of civic virtue with landed property, arguing that independence of mind and not of means is the proper basis of political integrity. By adopting the persona of a lower-class 'humble Bardie' in his political satires, Burns suggests that even the humblest member of society is competent to censure and admonish his governors, that, as Buchanan says, 'even poor and almost unknown men from among the lowest ranks of the people' may fittingly speak out against misgovernment.[35] In his imaginative engagement with a range of radical discourses, Burns demonstrates the error of those commentators who ascribe his political satire exclusively to personal animosity or class jealousy. If Burns's politics were, in Hugh Blair's snooty jibe, the politics of the smithy, they were forged on the anvil of a powerful radical tradition.

34 J. G. A. Pocock, *Politics, Language and Time: Essays on Political Thought and History* (London, 1972), p. 95.
35 Buchanan, p. 81.

CHAPTER FOUR

'My Friends, My Brothers!': Bardic Fraternity in the Kilmarnock Verse Epistles

When Burns made his first appearance as a published poet, he did so in a volume which displayed his talent for epistolary verse. Leaving aside the clutch of songs, epitaphs and epigrams with which *Poems, Chiefly in the Scottish Dialect* (1786) closes, there are thirty poems in Burns's debut collection. Eight of these – over a quarter of the book – are verse epistles, bantering salutations to Ayrshire friends and cronies.[1] The sheer volume of epistolary verse is perhaps the most striking feature of the Kilmarnock book. It is as if, reluctant to venture into print as a solitary bard, Burns required the sponsoring presence of his friends and fellow-poets. Davie Sillar, John Lapraik, William Simpson, James Smith and John Rankine are powerful – if silent – presences in the Kilmarnock *Poems*. They share the stage with Burns, as addressees of the book's most vigorous and fluent verses. Though the Edinburgh critics would celebrate Burns as a one-off, spontaneous genius, they were reading against the grain of a volume in which he appears above all as a literary team-player, member of an Ayrshire poetic school, one of a fraternity of local bards.

Reading the epistles, we are transported to the intimate underworld of Kyle's unpublished rhymers. Although we are reading these verses in a printed book, they take us back to the period before such a book existed, to the *manuscript* epistles which Burns actually sent to his Ayrshire comrades in the months before his book appeared. In the epistle 'To J. Smith' (K, 79), for instance, we find Burns, in the winter of 1785/86, worrying about the prospect of committing his poems to print:

> This while my notion 's taen a sklent,
> To try my fate in guid, black *prent*;
> But still the mair I'm that way bent,
>   Something cries, 'Hoolie!
> 'I red you, honest man, tak tent!
>   Ye'll shaw your folly.

---

1 They are: 'To J. Smith'; 'Epistle to Davie, a Brother Poet'; 'Epistle to a Young Friend'; 'A Dedication to Gavin Hamilton Esq'; 'Epistle to J. Lapraik, An Old Scotch Bard'; 'To the Same' (also known as 'Second Epistle to J. Lapraik'); 'To W. Simpson, Ochiltree'; and 'To J. Rankine, Enclosing some Poems'.

'There's ither Poets, much your betters,
'Far seen in *Greek*, deep men o' *letters*,
'Hae thought they had ensur'd their debtors,
           'A' future ages,
'Now moths deform in shapeless tatters,
           'Their unknown pages.'

Then farewell hopes of Laurel-boughs,
To garland my poetic brows!
Henceforth, I'll rove where busy ploughs
           Are whistling thrang,
An' teach the lanely heights an' howes
           My rustic sang.

I'll wander on with tentless heed,
How never-halting moments speed,
Till fate shall snap the brittle thread;
           Then, all unknown,
I'll lay me with th' *inglorious dead*,
           Forgot and gone!   (ll. 37–60)

There is some ambiguity here, in this valediction to the hopes of fame. We are not
sure whether these are the words of one who has decided not to publish his work at
all (in which case he must have changed his mind), or one who has simply
abandoned in advance any hope of poetic celebrity. What is not ambiguous,
however, is Burns's bright anticipation at the prospect of continued obscurity. The
gusto of that 'farewell' is palpable: the word marks a threshold, as Burns gives over
the anxious desire for fame and embraces a carefree anonymity. The 'whistling' of
those ploughs suggests both a relaxed freedom from care and also the 'rustic sang' (l.
54) of the (largely anonymous) Scottish folk tradition. Burns, by implication,
anticipates a life of pastoral freedom as a nameless ploughman poet.

Once Burns has committed it to print in the 1786 *Poems*, the epistle to Smith
inhabits a paradox. Here we have a printed poem which requires to be read as an
unpublished manuscript; a poet, whose name is emblazoned on the title page of his
book, presenting himself as 'all unknown'. At the very moment when 'he appears in
the public character of an Author' (as he puts it in his Kilmarnock preface), Burns
looks forward to a life of rural obscurity. As Jeffrey Skoblow has observed, this air of
paradox pervades the Kilmarnock book, notably in the preface, in which Burns
acknowledges his desire 'to be distinguished', while asserting his status as 'an
obscure, nameless Bard'. The poet who must count among his readers 'the Learned
and the Polite' wants nevertheless to remain an unselfconscious part of his rustic
environment.[2] Burns seems reluctant to cross the threshold which separates the oral
and manuscript world of the local rhymer from the printed world of the accredited

2 Skoblow, pp. 115–19.

poet. He wants to keep a foot in the bardic camp, and this – more than anything else – explains why so much of the book is epistolary. It is through the epistles that Burns can most successfully hold at a distance his status as an 'official', published poet and assert his involvement in a local bardic culture. In the epistles he is Rab Mossgiel, village rhymer, not Robert Burns, Poet.

For all that, 'To J. Smith' is evidently not the work of a poet cut off from contemporary literary culture. The reference to the *'inglorious dead'* (l. 59) is, of course, an allusion to Thomas Gray's 'Elegy Written in a Country Churchyard', and it provides a key to Burns's self-presentation in the epistles. If the speaker of Gray's 'Elegy' is a poet who mediates the experience of the voiceless lower classes for a polite audience, then the Burns of the Smith epistle pointedly rejects this role. Instead of purporting to speak for the 'rude forefathers of the hamlet', Burns casts himself as one of them: he is the 'mute, inglorious Milton' whose grave Gray's speaker surveys.[3] The fact that Burns is now a published poet is, he assures us in his preface, something of an accident: 'it was not till very lately, that the applause, perhaps the partiality of Friendship, wakened his vanity so far as to make him think any thing of his was worth showing; and none of the following works were ever composed with a view to the press'. It is the applause of local bards like John Lapraik and Willie Simpson – the 'coaxin billie' whose 'flatterin strain' is acknowledged in the epistle 'To W. Simpson, Ochiltree' (K, 59) – that has prompted Burns to publish. In other words, the very dynamic of publication reinforces Burns's connections with a local bardic community.

Gray's village Milton, however, is not the only poet suggested by those repeated 'unknowns' in the epistle to Smith. There is another poet, lying 'unknown' in a churchyard, whose fate interests Burns. The poet is Robert Fergusson, and the churchyard is in Edinburgh's Canongate. When he was living in the capital in 1787, Burns wrote to the Bailies of the Canongate requesting permission to erect a headstone on Fergusson's grave:

> Gentlemen,
>
> I am sorry to be told that the remains of Robert Ferguson [sic] the so justly celebrated Poet, a man whose talents for ages to come will do honor . . . to our Caledonian name, lie in your church yard among the ignoble Dead unnoticed and unknown.   (*Letters*, I, 90)

This reference to 'the ignoble Dead' is a telling one. In the context of the letter, the fact that Fergusson lies in the kirkyard undistinguished from his lowly peers is intended as a reproach on the authorities. And yet, the possibility remains that Burns is not 'sorry' at all, that in fact he envies Fergusson's position: the phrase 'ignoble Dead' reminds us that Fergusson has achieved the consummation sought

---

3 Thomas Gray, 'Elegy Written in a Country Churchyard', *The Complete Poems of Thomas Gray, William Collins, Oliver Goldsmith*, ed. by Roger Lonsdale (London, 1969), pp. 103–42.

by Burns in the epistle to Smith: 'Then, all unknown, / I'll lay me with th' *inglorious dead*, / Forgot and gone!' (ll. 58–60).

Once 'justly celebrated', Fergusson's vogue is now over, returning him to the condition of Gray's 'unnoticed' peasants. Burns here connects his own vernacular forerunner with Gray's 'rude forefathers of the hamlet', and so with the local bards of the Kilmarnock epistles. Fergusson has experienced fame and has come through the other side, as it were, and it may be that Fergusson is among those poets of fleeting celebrity (and classical learning) whose now 'unknown pages' give pause to the as yet unpublished Burns in the Smith epistle. Still, it is not Fergusson's current obscurity but his traumatic experience of fame that intimidates Burns. In his 'Epitaph. Here lies Robert Fergusson, Poet' (K, 142), an elegy written in a city churchyard, Burns views Fergusson's literary celebrity as a kind of nightmare, in which the Edinburgh poet was constrained to please the great and good, while their niggardly patronage kept him in misery: 'Luxury and Wealth lay by in state, / And thankless starv'd what they so much admir'd' (ll. 7–8).

Burns perceives in Fergusson's 'thankless' celebrity a demoralising precedent for himself as he prepares to leave the shelter of the bardic community to take his place as a published poet. From the beginning, Burns had a very clear-sighted awareness of what publication would mean to him, of the humiliating relationships of patronage and condescension in which it would involve him. Nor did it take long for critics to pull social rank on Burns and so plunge him into what he describes as 'the anxieties of Authorship' (*Letters*, I, 87). In Henry Mackenzie's influential *Lounger* review of December 1786, the ploughman poet is praised for his 'genius', but the review ends by recommending Burns to the charity of the rich:

> To repair the wrongs of suffering or neglected merit; to call forth genius from the obscurity in which it has pined indignant, and place it where it may profit or delight the world; these are exertions which give to wealth an enviable superiority, to greatness and to patronage a laudable pride.[4]

Here, in only the second review of his *Poems*, Burns is being held up as a suitable object of polite condescension, and reminded of the 'superiority' of his moneyed readers. This is the situation which Burns dreaded in advance, and which makes Mackenzie's image of the poet thirsting for celebrity so implausible. If Burns 'pined indignant' at anything during this period, it was at critics like Mackenzie with their monumental snobbery. Indeed, even before the *Lounger* review appeared, Burns already seems nostalgic for the days before 'my Authorship' (*Letters*, I, 101). In 'The Brigs of Ayr' (K, 120), written in autumn 1786 when the bandwagon that will take him to Edinburgh is already rolling, Burns pictures himself as 'a simple Bard, / Unknown and poor, simplicity's reward' (ll. 47–8). In one of the first letters he wrote from Edinburgh, two days after his arrival in the city, addressed to Sir John Whitefoord (the Master of his Masonic Lodge), Burns muses on the distasteful

4 *The Critical Heritage*, p. 71.

elements of literary fame, referring ruefully to 'that prostitution of heart and talents [poets] have at times been guilty of' (*Letters*, I, 68). In the midst of his Edinburgh celebrity – and therefore in the midst of his humiliation, his reluctant 'prostitution' – Burns hankers for obscurity. To the Rev. Greenfield he complains of having been '*dragged* forth . . . to the full glare of learned and polite observation' (*Letters*, I, 74, my emphasis), a phrase repeated in a letter to Mrs Dunlop (see *Letters*, I, 85). To the Rev. George Lowrie he declares himself ready to go 'back to my shades, the coverts of my unnoticed, early years' (*Letters*, I, 89). After his Edinburgh experience, it is indeed with something like relief that Burns shirks the 'encumbering robe of public notice' (*Letters*, I, 73–4) and embraces the obscurity, the anonymity of song-work with Johnson and Thomson and residence in the remote south-west.

Burns's Edinburgh period must be seen as an interlude of often painful national eminence in a poetic career mainly conducted in provincial obscurity. And while Burns may have resented the financial hardship of the Ayrshire and Dumfries years, he did not regret his circumscribed celebrity. In his Edinburgh letters, Burns more than once insists that his own opinion of his abilities was settled long before his current éclat, and that his ambition is rather to please his 'Compeers, the rustic Inmates of the Hamlet' (*Letters*, I, 88) than to achieve lasting fame as an author. One might dismiss this as the rationalisation of a writer who knows his fifteen minutes will shortly be up, but there can be little doubt that Burns viewed celebrity with a jaundiced eye. As Jeffrey Skoblow observes, Burns did almost everything he could to keep his work *out* of polite public notice: 'Each of Burns's characteristic gestures in the field of textuality . . . is a gesture of disappearance . . . Scots, vulgarity, obscenity, privacy, anonymity: the textual Burns is designed to resist its condition'. As Skoblow points out, 'only eighty-four of the 632 items collected in Kinsley's edition appear in the various editions of *Poems* Burns published'.[5] The Kilmarnock volume itself was published partly at the behest of friends. It was also published under a virtual pseudonym; two months before his poems went to press, Burns was spelling his surname 'Burness'. Given Burns's addiction to such gestures of disappearance, it is difficult not to discern a note of (perhaps unconscious) entreaty in the final words of the Kilmarnock preface: 'let him be condemned, without mercy, to contempt and oblivion'. A preface which ends on the word 'oblivion' seems the perfect expression of Burns in this mood.

So where does this leave the epistles? It might be argued that the epistles, those missives of an *unpublished* local bard, those vital relics of Burns's obscurity, are in some respects his most characteristic poems. The poet who distrusts fame is most at home in verses written, not for those 'readers . . . who may honor him with a perusal', but for his own circle of friends. Paradoxically, of course, it is the act of publication that releases the subversive potential of these 'homely' epistles, implying as it does that the correspondence of local bards is worthy of public notice. When we recall the cultural position of this epistolary poet – that he is not the Pope of 'Epistle

5 Skoblow, p. 124.

to Dr Arbuthnot', writing as the enervated arbiter of the nation's literary life, but an obscure Ayrshire bard shooting the vernacular breeze with the local rhymers – then the extent of Burns's daring becomes apparent. In a poem like 'To W. Simpson, Ochiltree', Burns opens a window onto a republic of letters which, though local and 'unkend-of' (l. 39), cockily aspires to international reach and significance:

> Th' *Illissus*, *Tiber*, *Thames* an' *Seine*,
> Glide sweet in monie a tunefu' line;
> But *Willie* set your fit to mine,
>   An' cock your crest,
> We'll gar our streams an' burnies shine
>   Up wi' the best.   (ll. 49–54)

The very inclusion of the verse epistles in Burns's debut volume is an act fraught with political significance. Burns confronts the world of 'the Learned and the Polite' with the world of the Mauchline 'ram-stam boys', giving voice to the mute ingloriousness of his community. Through the epistles, Burns is opening the floor of literature to those whom his schoolbook had called 'that kind of men who are so much despised, but who yet seem to be the prop of human society', or whom George Buchanan had labelled 'poor and almost unknown men from among the lowest ranks of the people'.

The subversive potential of this gesture was not lost on Burns's early critics. Regretting that 'delicacy should be so often offended in perusing' the Kilmarnock volume, Henry Mackenzie blames Burns's friends, 'the society in which he must have mixed'.[6] It is a safe bet that Mackenzie has in mind here Burns's epistles, the poems which bring that indecorous society onto the page. The epistles are not – like 'The Cotter's Saturday Night' or 'The Brigs of Ayr' – dedicated to bankers or lawyers, but are written mainly to men of Burns's own class, in whose convivial company the constraints of decorum are loosed. The epistles are composed in a frankly non-standard idiom - a kind of pub-talk or 'blether' – and in a mode of bantering informality lucidly explicated in Mikhail Bakhtin's comment on 'intimate genres':

> Intimate genres and styles are based on a maximum internal proximity of the speaker and addressee (in extreme instances, as if they had merged). Intimate speech is imbued with a deep confidence in the addressee, in his sympathy, in the sensitivity and goodwill of his responsive understanding. In this atmosphere of profound trust, the speaker reveals his internal depths.[7]

Or, as Burns puts it in the 'Epistle to a Young Friend' (K, 105): 'Ay free, aff han', your story tell, / When wi' a bosom crony' (ll. 33–4). The epistles *are* 'free'; they are off-hand and unguarded, especially in their treatment of Burns's social superiors,

---

6 *The Critical Heritage*, p. 70.
7 M. M. Bakhtin, *Speech Genres and Other Late Essays*, ed. by Caryl Emerson and Michael Holquist, trans. by Vern W. McGee (Austin, 1986), p. 97.

such as the 'sordid sons o' Mammon's line' (l. 95) anathematised in the 'Second Epistle to J. Lapraik' (K, 58), or the heartless 'Enbrugh Gentry' (l. 22) cursed in 'To W. Simpson, Ochiltree'.

In some respects, this makes the epistles more radical even than those poems – 'A Dream', 'The Author's Earnest Cry and Prayer' – in which Burns actively confronts the powers-that-be. In the epistles we *overhear* what the lower orders think of their masters, much in the manner of 'The Twa Dogs' – a strategy which allows for uninhibited frankness and asperity while also relegating the upper classes to an off-stage role. Moreover – and this, too, is part of their politics – the epistles place the reader in a subordinate position, looking over Burns's shoulder at verses meant principally for the eyes of another. The reader is 'an accidental party to the discourse' of the poems. We are outsiders, interlopers, 'eavesdroppers and Peeping Toms'.[8] The epistles shut us out. They establish a closed community, a kind of poetic equivalent of the Tarbolton Bachelors' Club, whose constitution stipulated that 'No member, on any pretence whatever, shall mention any of the club's affairs to any other person but a brother member, under the pain of being excluded'.[9] Despite being published in *Poems*, the epistles retain the status of private letters. As such, they are resistant to the processes of literary criticism: they are inadmissible as evidence, they do not offer themselves for our appraisal. For Burns and his correspondents, the business of criticism is an inside job, one which they perform *within* the epistles, in their 'roosing' of one another's work and their comparative references to Ramsay and Fergusson. The result is a kind of self-regulating community that requires no corroboration, no endorsement from the outside world. To a degree perhaps never again achieved in his oeuvre, Burns creates a space in which the terms of debate, the rules of engagement, are of his own making. In the epistles, Burns is on home ground.

Brothers in Misfortune, Brothers in the Muse

The epistles are the poetic currency of Burns's bardic brotherhood. On what, however, does this brotherhood rest: what common bond unites Burns, Sillar, Lapraik and the others? What does Burns share with these local 'unknown' bards? The title of the 'Epistle to Davie, a Brother Poet' points forward to another, shorter poem which provides a clue. In his lines 'On Fergusson' (K, 143), Burns hails the Edinburgh poet as:

> O thou, my elder brother in Misfortune,
> By far my elder Brother in the muse.   (ll. 3–4)

Like Robert Fergusson, the recipients of Burns's epistles tended to be his brothers in misfortune. James Smith had lost his father at the age of ten. John Lapraik had

8 Skoblow, pp. 173, 177.
9 Currie, I, 366.

been ruined in the Ayr Bank failure of 1773, had recently served time in a debtor's prison and at the time of Burns's epistle was struggling to make a living as a farmer. Davie Sillar had failed as a schoolmaster, and was now setting up as a grocer. John Rankine, like Burns, was a tenant farmer, trying to ride out the economic crisis brought on by the American War. These were men who had experienced personal sorrow and financial hardship and who knew the weary business of struggling to make a living in the Ayrshire of the 1780s, a county in which the decline of farming and manufacturing had, as Burns informed his Montrose cousin in 1783, seen 'hundreds driven to a starving condition' (*Letters*, I, 19).

His correspondents are poor men. For Burns, though, the mutual poverty of the epistolary comrades does have its advantages. For one thing, it confirms the disinterested nature of their friendship. No-one hopes to gain, in any material sense, from these relationships. They are founded on natural social impulse, not calculation of interest. It is noticeable that Burns seems almost to require a situation of shared poverty before he can express sentiments of friendship with proper conviction. When greeting a social superior in 'A Dedication to Gavin Hamilton Esq' (K, 103), Burns has to envisage his prosperous landlord a 'victim sad of Fortune's strife' (l. 130), anticipating a time when Hamilton has become 'as poor a dog' (l. 124) as Burns is. Only then can Burns strike the true fraternal note:

> If friendless, low, we meet together,
> Then, Sir, your hand – my FRIEND and BROTHER.
>
> (ll. 133–4)[10]

In one sense, then, the brotherhood of Burns's epistles is a brotherhood of misfortune, a camaraderie of hardship: 'Affliction's sons are brothers in distress' (l. 87), as he puts it in 'A Winter Night' (K, 130). But this hardship is not simply the basis of true friendship, it is the road to self-knowledge. The 'Misfortunes' detailed in the 'Epistle to Davie' 'gie the wit of *Age* to *Youth*; / They let us ken oursel' (ll. 91–2). And what they let us ken, above all, is the fundamental equality of men. When caressed by Fortune, it may be possible to suppose oneself innately superior to the mass of mankind. In 'A Winter Night' (K, 130), it is 'pamper'd Luxury' (l. 50) who views the peasant as

> 'A creature of another kind,
> 'Some coarser substance, unrefin'd,
> 'Plac'd for her lordly use thus far, thus vile, below!   (ll. 56–58)

But at the ground level occupied by Burns and his comrades, such lofty pretensions are risible. Like the Adam Ferguson who writes of 'the resolute ardour with which a man adheres to his friend, or to his tribe, after they have for some time run the

---

10 Burns's compulsive need to reinscribe in a lower-class context his socially superior addressees is seen also in the opening stanza of 'The Cotter's Saturday Night. Inscribed to R. Aiken, Esq', in which Burns imagines 'What Aiken in a *Cottage* would have been' (l. 8). Robert Aiken was an Ayr solicitor.

career of fortune together', [11] Burns views shared misfortune as the wellspring of genuine friendship.

Sillar, Simpson and Lapraik, however, are not merely Burns's brothers in misfortune: they are also his brothers in the muse. 'Poetry and poverty', as Karl Miller remarks: 'his epistles are charged with that conjunction.'[12] And the point to note here is that, for Burns, this is a *necessary* conjunction: pounds sterling and 'sterling Wit' ('To J. Smith') are radically incompatible. In his letter of December 1786 to Sir John Whitefoorde, Burns presents the poet as a being fated to a life of penury:

> I do not think prodigality is, by any means, a necessary concomitant of a poetic turn; but I believe a careless, indolent in attention to oeconomy, is almost inseparable from it; then there must be, in the heart of every bard of Nature's making, a certain modest sensibility, mixed with a kind of pride, that will ever keep him out of the way of those windfalls of fortune, which frequently light on hardy impudence and foot-licking servility.
>
> (*Letters*, I, 68)

Poverty might be the poet's curse, but Burns also wants to argue that poetry compensates for material want. For the community as a whole, poetry and song provide welcome recreation in the breaks between labour, as in the *'sang about'* session described in the 'Epistle to J. Lapraik'. But for the poet himself, the afflatus of creation is sweet recompense for hardship and poverty. Wit for want is a fair bargain, argues Burns in 'To J. Smith':

> The star that rules my luckless lot,
> Has fated me the russet coat,
> An' damn'd my fortune to the groat;
> But, in requit,
> Has blest me with a *random-shot*
> O' countra wit.   (ll. 31–36)

The farmer who is 'damn'd' economically is 'blest' with the gift of creativity: poetry is his saving grace.

The epistles themselves enact this redemption of poverty by poetry. The 'Epistle to Davie' opens with Burns describing the bitter winter weather in which he sits down to write his poem in his poorly insulated farmhouse, 'While frosty winds blaw in the drift, / Ben to the chimla lug' (ll. 7–8). The 'Second Epistle to J. Lapraik' opens with a description of the exhausting farm labour which Burns has newly completed – 'Rattlin the corn out-owre the rigs, / Or dealing thro' amang the naigs / Their ten-hours bite' (ll. 8–10). In each case, the hardship is transformed by the practice of poetry: Burns forgets the cold, or he forgets his tiredness, in the joyous

11 *Essay*, p. 17.
12 Karl Miller, 'Introduction', *Landscape Poets: Robert Burns*, ed. by Miller (London, 1981), p. 9.

activity of composing. The 'Epistle to Davie' ends with an image of the poet dismounting from his hot, sweat-drenched Pegasus, the poetic gallop of the previous ten stanzas having dispelled the frozen atmosphere of the poem's opening lines. In their very existence, then, the epistles demonstrate why Davie should not be 'sour, / To see how things are shar'd' (ll. 16–17), and why Lapraik has no need to 'envy the *city-gent*' or the 'paughty, feudal *Thane*' (ll. 61, 66). Secure in the possession of intrinsic merit, Lapraik and Davie should maintain a stoical indifference to fortune. Burns's advice in the second Lapraik epistle is simple: 'Ne'er mind how Fortune *waft* an' *warp*; / She's but a b—tch.' (ll. 47–8).

Almost all of the epistles open with some lines in praise of the recipient, and in each case Burns is careful to select for eulogy qualities intrinsic to the man, distinctions owed to nature and not to the artificial marks of rank or wealth or piety. Lapraik is praised for native poetic genius or 'ingine', Rankine is 'ready-witted', Simpson is 'winsome', and Smith is hailed as the all-round natural man:

> That auld, capricious carlin, *Nature*,
> To mak amends for scrimpet stature,
> She's turn'd you off, a human-creature
>   On her *first* plan,
> And in her freaks, on ev'ry feature,
>   She's wrote, *the Man*.   (ll. 13–18)

The aim of these eulogies is clear: they are devices in a rhetorical strategy designed to persuade his fellow bards to remain content with their true intrinsic merit as recognised by Burns, and not to jeopardise this intrinsic worth in the pursuit of its empty forms, whether these be the forms of worldly success or of ostentatious piety.

In the epistles, Burns presents himself as the exemplar of this high-minded indifference to the gifts of fortune. Addressing the 'Pow'rs' in 'To J. Smith', Burns inventories the goods he would gladly forego if he could only be assured of native poetic ability:

> 'Gie dreeping roasts to *countra Lairds*,
> 'Till icicles hing frae their beards;
> 'Gie fine braw claes to fine *Life-guards*,
>   'And *Maids of Honor*;
> 'And yill an' whisky gie to *Cairds*,
>   Until they sconner.
>
> 'A *Title*, DEMPSTER merits it;
> 'A *Garter* gie to WILLIE PIT;
> 'Gie Wealth to some be-ledger'd Cit,
>   'In cent per cent;
> 'But gie me real, sterling Wit,
>   'And I'm content.'   (ll. 127–38)

So long as Burns can turn a line of verse, he is indifferent to the goods of fortune.

Even formal education is one of the extrinsic benefits Burns will do without. His reiterated prayer is for intrinsic poetic ability alone: 'Gie me ae spark o' Nature's fire' ('Epistle to J. Lapraik'); 'Gie me o' *wit* an' *sense* a lift' ('Second Epistle to J. Lapraik'); 'Grant me but this, I ask no more, / Ay rowth o' rhymes' ('To J. Smith').

The epistles are presented as testimony that this intrinsic 'poetic' worth is sufficient to carry one through the hazards of fortune. These poems are a kind of aesthetic and spiritual stocktaking; they come to stand as a defiant and exemplary assertion of personal identity: '*I, Rob, am here*' ('Second Epistle to J. Lapraik'). Burns's endurance is not merely celebrated as a personal triumph, but is offered as an inspirational, morale-boosting example. In this respect, especially if read in conjunction with 'The Vision', the epistles form something similar to the old Puritan spiritual autobiography or conversion narrative, but with 'poetry' taking the place of religion. Or perhaps the true comparison is with another group of exhortatory epistles – those of St Paul. In his missives to Ayrshire's bardic faithful, Burns acts as the apostle of poetry, where 'poetry' is to be understood not simply as an art form but as a way of life, a body of values, a commitment to selfless sociability and mutual assistance. In the epistles to Sillar, Lapraik and Simpson, Burns seeks to reassure Ayrshire's bards that poetry is worth pursuing despite the poverty it entails. In effect, Burns plays the role of Coila in 'The Vision', visiting these potentially despondent poets and urging them to stick to their craft.

What prevents the epistles from degenerating into a species of secular sermon, however, is the extent to which this pep talking, boosterist Burns is himself beset by misgivings and doubts. At the heart of the epistles is a tension between the devil-may-care persona Burns cultivates and the often desperate reality of Ayrshire rural life, a reality which the poems are – to a greater or lesser degree – constrained to acknowledge. The persona Burns adopts is that of the roistering ram-stam boy, determined to seize each chance of pleasure while defying the mores of the prudent majority and, in the words of one early critic, 'cheerfully supporting the fatigues of a laborious employment'.[13] It is the tendency for this cheerfulness to pall that gives to the epistles a sense of urgency and struggle. Though they tack and veer with airy deftness, what ballasts these poems, what lies beneath the waterline, so to speak, is the consciousness of poverty and the dread of destitution. The agricultural crisis of the 1780s impinges heavily on poems which reflect, sometimes obliquely, on financial inequality and the dire condition of the rural poor. The poem in which these tensions are most dynamically apparent is the 'Epistle to Davie, a Brother Poet'.

---

13 James Anderson, unsigned review in *Monthly Review*, 85 (December 1786), 439–48, in *The Critical Heritage*, pp. 71–74 (p. 72).

But either house or hal'

At points in the epistles, Burns can come across like the author of a modern self-help manual, offering feel-good soundbites of the 'look to the future', 'don't dwell on your regrets' variety. What the 'Epistle to Davie' shows is how hard it is to take that advice – how hard it is not to grudge the rich their comforts, and not to fear the very real prospect of destitution. A genial outlook may be tricky to sustain – 'It's hardly in a body's pow'r, / To keep, at times, frae being sour' (ll. 15–16): nevertheless, insists Burns, this is what must be attempted. In some ways Burns's first substantial poem, the 'Epistle to Davie' is a complex work, whose declamatory and didactic elements fail to subdue the tensions and doubts at the heart of the poem. More sombre and serious than the other Kilmarnock epistles, lacking their swagger and easy conviction, it is an attractively uncertain poem. The Cherrie and the Slae stanza, with its halting, equivocal rhythm, is nicely suited to the poem's shifting moods, its brooding, anxious tone. This is a poem of poignantly imperfect bravado in which Burns takes a long look at poverty and destitution and attempts, not altogether successfully, to allay his own fears at the prospect.

The poem opens, like 'The Vision' or 'Man was Made to Mourn', with a bleak winter landscape, and the poet huddled against the cold, hunched over his fire. He is brooding on the hardship of his lot, the injustice of

> . . . how things are shar'd;
> How *best o' chiels* are whyles in want,
> While *Coofs* on countless thousands rant,
> And ken na how to wair't.   (ll. 17–20)

As in the other epistles, however, this despondency is swiftly checked. It's no use making a bad job worse, says Burns, by 'pining at out state' (l. 87). Davie should 'ne'er fash [his] head' (l. 21) about poverty and 'ne'er mind a feg' (l. 26) about growing old. Burns is attempting to reassure Davie – and indeed himself – that their present situation is tolerable and even that the dreaded eventuality of destitution might not be so terrible either. The arguments marshalled by Burns are not in themselves unpersuasive. Though poor, he tells Davie, we still have our health. We enjoy the pleasures of love, friendship and poetry. Even were we reduced to beggary, we would still have the satisfaction of conscious integrity – an 'honest heart that's free frae a' / Intended fraud or guile' (ll. 35–6) – and would no longer have to struggle to preserve our position in society. We would enjoy the beauties of nature, we would amass a great deal of self-knowledge and – that venerable sop to the poor through the ages – we might gain our reward in heaven more readily than the rich, those debauched wealthy libertines who 'riot in excess! / Baith careless, and fearless, / Of either Heaven or Hell' (ll. 80–82).

And yet, beneath the deft rhetorical manoeuvres and the succession of well-turned arguments, the black shape of Burns's dread remains visible. It surfaces in stanza III, as Burns takes a fleeting glance into the abyss:

> To lye in kilns and barns at e'en,
> When banes are craz'd, and bluid is thin,
>   Is, doubtless, great distress!   (ll. 29–31)

The exclamation mark here acknowledges the extent of the understatement, while the crazed bones and thin blood suggest that the 'e'en' to which Burns refers is the evening of life as well as that time of day when the destitute seek shelter. That death might be the outcome of a winter's night spent out of doors perhaps explains the poem's rather desperate concern with the world to come. The word 'blest' appears five times in a poem whose anxiety over personal salvation recalls the gloomy religious pieces of Burns's Irvine period. In this prayer, written in the prospect of destitution, Burns is trying to convince himself that God is on his side. But what stamps every line of the poem is the fear that he is already damned.

It is not surprising, then, that Burns's arguments to Davie lack conviction and fail to withstand close scrutiny. In the opening verse, Burns betrays confusion over the cause of his discontent. He begins by resenting the material comforts enjoyed by the prosperous: 'I grudge a wee the *Great-folk*'s gift, / That live sae bien an' snug' (ll. 9–10). Then he changes tack and asserts that material comforts are irrelevant; what really riles him is the arrogance of the rich:

> I tent less, and want less
>   Their roomy fire-side;
> But hanker, and canker,
>   To see their cursed pride.   (ll. 11–14)

This tension between spiritual and material wealth pervades the poem. Burns wants to move the discussion onto a spiritual plane, where the social eminence of the rich can be condemned for producing a damnable arrogance or 'cursed pride', while the poor can be offered the hope of salvation, of being 'blest'. Burns wants to believe that it is on the spiritual level, and not the material, that we encounter 'The real guid and ill' (l. 94). The problem, however, is that Burns's high-minded argument is continually being undermined by his very vivid presentiment of physical hardship. And what is significant here, what brings home the horror of Burns's situation, is that the hardship described in stanzas one and six is that of his *current position* as a tenant farmer, *not* that of his envisaged destitution. The position to which Burns precariously clings is itself one of relative misery, the position of those who 'drudge and drive thro' wet and dry, / Wi' never-ceasing toil' (ll. 72–3). It is this knowledge that makes Burns's arguments poignantly unconvincing. Destitution, he argues, will 'let us ken oursel' (l. 92). But does Burns *want* to know himself? Does he really desire to find out how he would respond to destitution? If there is one emotion communicated by the 'Epistle to Davie', it is the poet's desperate fear of such self-knowledge and of the testing which would take place in those 'kilns' where vessels are tried in the heat or in those 'barns' (l. 29) where the wheat is separated from the chaff.

Perhaps the most valiantly idealistic stanza in the poem is the fourth, in which

Burns shares with Davie his vision of jolly beggary in a pastoral Ayrshire landscape:

> What tho', like Commoners of air,
> We wander out, we know not where,
>   But either house or hal'?
> Yet *Nature*'s charms, the hills and woods,
> The sweeping vales, and foaming floods,
>   Are free alike to all.
> In days when Daisies deck the ground,
>   And Blackbirds whistle clear,
> With honest joy, our hearts will bound,
>   To see the *coming* year:
>   On braes when we please then,
>   We'll sit and *sowth* a tune;
>   Syne rhyme till't, we'll time till't,
>   And sing't when we hae done.   (ll. 43–56)

In this portrait of wandering vagabonds, 'Commoners of air', Burns is drawing on the imagery of carefree beggars deployed in popular songs like 'The Merry Beggars' or 'The Happy Beggars', both of which appear in Vol IV of Ramsay's *Tea-Table Miscellany* (1740).[14] It is noticeable, however, that Burns's vision of idyllic beggary takes place in the spring. In a poem which is dated 'January' and which opens with a blizzard, the unspoken question must be: what happens to this idyll when winter takes hold? Burns hints at the answer in another depiction of apparently jovial mendicancy written around this time – 'Love and Liberty. A Cantata' (K, 84). This scene of roistering beggars *does* take place in winter, when 'hailstanes drive wi' bitter skyte' (l. 4), and so we are constantly aware that the 'merry core' (l. 7), who have pawned their clothes to purchase drink, leaving garments scarcely sufficient to 'coor their fuds' (l. 240), will be pitched out into the cold and frost when the party's over. Their bravado, like that of Burns himself in the 'Epistle to Davie', is frantic, unsustainable. The real condition of being 'But either house or hal' ' is one of misery, not liberty, as Burns acknowledges in the tenderly empathetic address 'To a Mouse, On turning her up in her Nest, with the Plough, November, 1785' (K, 69). In this portrait of sudden homelessness amid 'Winter's *sleety dribble*' (l. 35), the epistles' easy swagger is in short supply. The terrified field-mouse, 'turn'd out, for a' thy trouble, / But house or hald' (ll. 33–4), too evidently figures Burns's own fate, should he find himself evicted from his farm. To the question implicitly posed in his epistles – 'Are you a man or a mouse?' – Burns here discovers an uncomfortable answer. For all his big talk to Simpson and Lapraik, Burns recognises something of himself in the trembling frame of the 'tim'rous *beastie*' (l. 1). The poem ends on the emotion that underwrites all Burns's braggadocio in the verse epistles: 'An' *forward*, tho' I canna *see*, I *guess* an' *fear*!' (ll. 47–8).

---

14 Thomas Crawford surveys the British tradition of 'popular beggar pastoral' in
    Society and the Lyric (Edinburgh, 1979), pp. 185–212.

'The heart *ay's the part ay*'

In a letter to one of his Dumfries drinking companions in early 1794, Burns wrote: 'Some of our folks about the Excise Office, Edinburgh, had & perhaps still have conceived a prejudice against me as being a drunken dissipated character. – I might be all this, you know, & yet be an honest fellow . . . ' (*Letters*, II, 281–2). The figure of the honest man, the man of true and not titular worth, stands at the centre of Burns's moral universe. The phrase resounds through his work like a keynote; it is the highest accolade, the fittest epitaph, the measure of all things. In the 'Second Epistle to J. Lapraik', as we shall see, it is 'The social, friendly, honest man' who alone 'fulfils *great Nature's plan*' (ll. 87, 89).

What the honest man stands for in Burns is a conception of morality which has clear affinities with Protestant notions of the 'inner voice' of Conscience. The honest man is the man of consistent inner integrity. He is not the pious man, the man whose worth is accredited by an organised church and expressed through rituals and observances; rather, he disciplines himself. This is a view of morality not as a set code but as the spontaneous promptings of conscience or the Hutchesonian moral sense.[15] In the 'Epistle to a Young Friend', Burns advises his correspondent to listen to this inner voice of conscience, not to the sanctions of church authorities:

> The *fear o' Hell*'s a hangman's whip,
>   To haud the wretch in order;
> But where ye feel your *Honor* grip,
>   Let that ay be your border:
> It's slightest touches, instant pause –
>   Debar a' side-pretences;
> And resolutely keep it's laws,
>   Uncaring consequences.   (ll. 57–64)

The coercion of the external law may be necessary for the 'wretch' who can only be kept in order by a 'hangman's whip'. However, for the chosen few – including Burns and his young friend – the external law has no force. It is the law which comes from inside that one must obey; one must respond to its most delicate promptings, its 'slightest touches', even when these are in conflict with positive law or social convention. For Burns, it is always better to follow the promptings of conscience than to be 'very punctilious in the Christian Law' (*Letters*, I, 343).

This type of sentiment raises once again the issue of Burns's affinity with William Blake. The comparison of Burns with Blake has been made often, and to illuminating effect.[16] Recent work on Blake by Jon Mee and Edward Thompson, exploring the role of 'antinomianism' in Blake's thought, suggests that another

---

15 For Burns's absorption of Hutchesonian ideas, see Joseph Walter McGinty, 'Literary, Philosophical and Theological Influences on Robert Burns', 2 vols (unpublished doctoral dissertation, University of Strathclyde, 1995), I, 138–44.

16 See, for instance, Leopold Damrosch, 'Burns, Blake and the Recovery of Lyric',

point of comparison might be made.[17] For the ethos of Burns's epistles might legitimately be called 'antinomian', in the sense employed by Thomson and Mee. By antinomianism, here, is not meant the doctrine that those who are possessed of grace are beyond the moral law and may sin with impunity (a doctrine which Burns satirises in 'Holy Willie's Prayer', 'A Dedication To Gavin Hamilton Esq' and the bawdy song 'I'll tell you a tale of a Wife'). Rather, Burns's epistles inculcate the equally 'antinomian' principle that conduct is to be regulated from within – by the 'inner voice' of conscience – and not by rules of behaviour imposed from without. Antinomianism does not imply that believers are subject to no restraining power; instead, believers are subject to the surer, more reliable curb of their own moral sense.[18] Burns's 'reliance upon the inner light of the heart and mind' is, in this sense, characteristically antinomian.[19]

The antinomian ethos of the epistles is evidenced by the recurrence of imagery connected with the heart; 'The *heart* ay 's the part ay / That makes us right or wrang' ('Epistle to Davie'). This is a fundamental antinomian image, going back to St Paul's letter to the Corinthians, which argues for the law written 'not in tables of stone, but in fleshy tables of the heart' (II Corinthians 3. 3). With this passage, Paul identifies Christ as the initiator of the new covenant spoken of in Jeremiah 31. 33: 'I will put my law in their inward parts, and write it in their hearts'. Paul's words announce that man's bondage to the Mosaic Law – both ceremonial and moral – is over; it has been superseded by the era of Grace. Those who have grace, who have embraced Christ, have no need to follow the moral law or bow down before priestcraft; they have a surer guide inside them. As Blake observes: 'henceforth every man may converse with God & be a King & Priest in his own house'.[20]

Carol McGuirk has observed that Burns divides humanity into two classes: an 'elect' of good-hearted, impulsive people set against the reprobate mass of prudent, thrifty rule-observers.[21] McGuirk here echoes Hoxie Fairchild's contention that Burns saw himself as 'one of the heart's elect'.[22] This concept of 'sentimental election' is central to Burns's epistles. In 'To J. Smith', it is a select group, depicted almost as a specially licensed, crack military unit – 'The hairum-scairum, ram-stam boys, / The rattling squad' (ll. 165–66) – who are saved from the massed ranks of 'douse folk, that live by rule' (l. 151). The argument of the epistles is authentically

Studies in Romanticism, 21 (1982), 637–60; Andrew Noble, 'Burns, Blake and Romantic Revolt', in *The Art of Robert Burns*, pp. 191–214.

17 Jon Mee, 'Is there an Antinomian in the House? William Blake and the After-Life of a Heresy', in *Historicizing Blake*, ed. by Steve Clark and David Worrall (London, 1994), pp. 43–58; Thompson, *Witness Against the Beast*.

18 Thompson, *Witness Against the Beast*, p. 12.

19 McGinty, II, 400.

20 Annotations to R. Watson's *Apology for the Bible*, in *The Complete Poetry and Prose of William Blake*, ed. by D.V. Erdman (New York, 1982), p. 615; quoted in Mee, p. 53.

21 Carol McGuirk, *Robert Burns and the Sentimental Era* (Athens, GA, 1985), pp. 26–30.

22 Hoxie Neale Fairchild, *Religious Trends in English Poetry*, 6 vols (New York, 1939–68), III, 56.

antinomian: these poems posit an elite group of 'honest men' who are above the petty laws followed by everyone else, and who regulate their own conduct according to their inner benevolent impulses. The epistles confirm Fairchild's contention that 'Burns had spurned the antinomianism of the Evangelicals for antinomianism of a more attractive sort – the glorious freedom of the children of sensibility'.[23]

There is in the epistles a Pauline sense of the rule-observing life as spiritual deadness. The 'douce folk, that live by rule' in the Smith epistle have no dynamism, no native impulse, as if their very blood lay static in their veins: they are 'tideless-blooded' (l. 152), their hearts are a 'standing pool' (l. 155). This imagery looks back to St Paul's description of the law as 'the ministration of death', and his assertion that 'the letter killeth, but the spirit giveth life' (II Corinthians 3. 6–7). In a letter of June 1789 to Mrs Dunlop, Burns makes a similar distinction between torpidly mechanical virtue and the true 'enthusiasm' of instinctive moral impulse:

> What a poor, blighted, rickety breed are the Virtues & charities when they take their birth from geometrical hypothesis & mathematical demonstration? And what a vigorous Offspring are they when they owe their origin to, and are nursed with the vital blood of a heart glowing with the noble enthusiasm of Generosity, Benevolence and Greatness of Soul?
>
> *(Letters*, I, 420)

This passage recalls Hutcheson's statement that our sense of moral good and evil operates without rational calculations of personal advantage, just as our aesthetic sense of beauty and harmony does not depend upon 'any Knowledge of *Mathematicks*'.[24] Like Hutcheson's philosophy, Burns's epistles are organised around a Pauline opposition between fluid impulse and mechanical rationality, between the internal conscience and the external code, between 'the *morality of the heart*' and 'the letter of the law' (*Letters*, I, 418).

Spontaneity thus becomes a kind of cardinal virtue for Burns, and one which extends to the composition of poetry. The rejection of rule-bound classicism and the claim to spontaneous, unfettered composition feature in almost all of Burns's epistles. Indeed, the very form of the epistle conventionally lent itself to such claims. The supposedly unmethodical nature of the epistolary form was exploited in the epistolary novels of the period – in Smollett's *The Expedition of Humphry Clinker* (1771), for instance, with its dashes and broken sentences designed to indicate spontaneous composition. Here is Mr. Dennison writing to Lydia Melford:

> – I speak the language of my own heart; and have no prompter but nature. – Yet there is something in this heart, which I have not yet disclosed – I flattered myself – But, I will not – I must not proceed – Dear Miss Liddy![25]

23 Fairchild, *Religious Trends*, III, 43.

24 Francis Hutcheson, *An Inquiry into the Original of our Ideas of Beauty and Virtue* (London, 1725), p. 124.

25 Tobias Smollett, *The Expedition of Humphry Clinker*, ed. by Peter Miles (London, 1993), p. 17.

Samuel Richardson, who in the Preface to *Clarissa* (1747–9) celebrates '*instantaneous* descriptions', made frequent use of the present tense in his epistolary novels, as a way of bringing the action right up to the moment of inscription.[26] In the Preface to *Sir Charles Grandison* (1754), Richardson characterises the epistolary style as writing 'to the *Moment*, while the Heart is agitated by Hopes and Fears'.[27] So familiar a device did this become that Fielding satirises it in *Shamela* (1741): 'Mrs Jervis and I are in bed, and the door unlocked; if my master should come – Odsbobs! I hear him just coming in at the door . . . '.[28] In 'To J. Smith', Burns makes a similar use of the present tense both to suggest spontaneous, unmethodical composition and to give the reader the impression of instantaneous communication:

> Just now I've taen the fit o' rhyme,
> My barmie noddle's working prime,
> My fancy yerket up sublime
>   Wi' hasty summon:
> Hae ye a leisure-moment's time
>   To hear what's comin?   (ll. 19–24)

This suggestion that the poet, no more than his reader, knows what is coming next, is a feature of the epistles, as in the 'Epistle to a Young Friend':

> But how the subject theme may gang,
>   Let time and chance determine;
> Perhaps it may turn out a Sang;
>   Perhaps, turn out a sermon.   (ll. 5–8)

To reinforce the impression of immediacy in the epistles Burns frequently describes his present circumstances at the very moment of composition. Often the moment of writing which Burns evokes is a random hour snatched from the demanding routine of farm labour, as in the 'Second Epistle to J. Lapraik':

> WHILE new-ca'd kye rowte at the stake,
> An' pownies reek in pleugh or braik,
> This hour on e'enin's edge I take,
>   To own I'm debtor,
> To honest-hearted, auld Lapraik,
>   For his kind *letter*.   (ll. 1–6)

This evocation of a buckshee hour opportunistically dedicated to the muse anticipates the epistle 'To the Rev. John M'Math' (K, 68), where an onset of rain

---

26 Samuel Richardson, *Clarissa: Or, The History of a Young Lady*, ed. by Angus Ross (Harmondsworth, 1985), p. 35.

27 Samuel Richardson, *The History of Sir Charles Grandison*, ed. by Jocelyn Harris, 3 vols (London, 1972), I, 4.

28 Henry Fielding, *Joseph Andrews and Shamela*, ed. by Martin C. Battestin (London, 1965), p. 313.

during harvesting allows the poet to 'dedicate the hour / In idle rhyme' (ll. 5–6). These passages invite us to regard the epistles as poems composed in a hurry by a poet working within a tight timescale. We are to view the epistles as a kind of smash-and-grab poetry, opportunistically snatched when circumstances permit, not methodically worked at. That evocative phrase – 'this hour on e'enin's edge' – with its sense of a moment just about to pass, a particular shade of sky just about to deepen, is highly characteristic of Burns's epistles. It conveys that impression of a writing perpetually poised on the cusp of the moment, 'maintained at a continuous present'.[29]

The illusion of spontaneity is continued in the epistles by Burns's repeated reference to the physical act of writing, again evident in the 'Second Epistle to J. Lapraik':

> Sae I gat paper in a blink,
> An' down gaed *stumpie* in the ink:
> Quoth I, 'Before I sleep a wink,
>   'I vow I'll close it;
> 'An if ye winna mak it clink,
>   'By Jove I'll prose it!'
>
> Sae I've begun to scrawl, but whether
> In rhyme, or prose, or baith thegither,
> Or some hotch-potch that's rightly neither'
>   Let time mak proof;
> But I shall scribble down some blether
>   Just clean aff-loof.   (ll. 31–42)

'Scrawl', 'scribble': the terms used to describe the process of inscription suggest speed and flurry, give an impression of the poet as harassed amanuensis, struggling to keep up with the dictation of his Muse. Note, too, how the modulation from past tense ('I gat') into present ('I've begun') brings the poem right up to the present moment, so that we seem to see the poem being jotted down before our eyes. Throughout the epistles, Burns's references to his pen – 'my auld pen's worn to the grissle' ('Epistle to J. Lapraik'), 'My pen I here fling to the door' ('To J. Smith') – remind us of the fluid individuality of script behind the fixed impersonality of print, and present us with the image of the poet in the process of composition. Like Richardson, Sterne, Boswell and other writers of 'sensibility', Burns aims to 'give the impression of literature as process, as created on the spot out of the events it describes'.[30]

Any suggestion of pre-planning or deliberate strategy in the formation of this utterance is rigorously excluded. The terms used to describe poetry and the poetic

---

29 Northrop Frye, 'Towards Defining an Age of Sensibility', in *Poets of Sensibility and the Sublime*, ed. by Harold Bloom (New York, 1986), pp. 11–18 (p. 14).

30 Frye, pp. 12–13.

act are such as might almost suggest glossolalia: 'the fit o' rhyme', 'blether / Just clean aff-loof'. Burns's claim is that his is a poetry composed with no purpose – 'an *aim* I never fash' ('To J. Smith') – in a language not shaped by conscious strategy – 'plain, braid lallans' ('To W. Simpson, Ochiltree') – and inspired by alcohol – 'set him to a pint of ale' ('Epistle to J. Lapraik'). What emerges from the self-projections in the epistles is the image of Burns as a poet by happenstance, one who is prompted into spontaneous utterance at the instigation of his feelings, through the inspiration of a Muse or by the intoxication of alcohol, but never one who might deploy premeditated strategy, conscious learning and craftsmanship in the purposeful production of a methodised poem.

The solemn league and covenant of friendship

The claim to aesthetic spontaneity must be understood as part of a wider concern with moral spontaneity in the epistles. The celebration of benevolent impulse and spontaneous fellow-feeling is crucial to a genre whose 'central purpose . . . is to display friendship'.[31] One of the key correspondences, therefore, between Burns and the thinkers discussed in Chapter 1 of this book is his view of man as a naturally and instinctively social animal. Burns shares the Calvinist and civic humanist understanding of society as a good in itself. Society is not an expedient combination for the better provision of material goods, but the embodiment of the divine purpose, as the 'Second Epistle to J. Lapraik' makes clear:

> Were this the *charter* of our state,
> 'On pain o' *hell* be rich an' great,'
> *Damnation* then would be our fate,
>   Beyond remead;
> But, thanks to *Heav'n*, that 's no the gate
>   We learn our *creed*
>
> For thus the royal *Mandate* ran,
> When first the human race began,
> 'The social, friendly, honest man,
>   'Whate'er he be,
> ''Tis *he* fulfils *great Nature's plan*,
>   'And none but *he*.'   (ll. 79–90)

Here, once more, is the idiom of election: the children of sensibility are saved, while the grubbers after guineas will be damned. At times, indeed, Burns seems to take upon himself the task of sorting out the sheep from the goats, as if his elbow-chair were the seat of judgement. In the 'Epistle to J. Lapraik' he despatches the mammonites to outer darkness while welcoming his comrades to the throne of grace:

---

31 John C. Weston, 'Robert Burns' Use of the Scots Verse-Epistle Form', *Philological Quarterly*, 49 (1970), 188–210 (p. 190).

Awa ye selfish, warly race,
Wha think that havins, sense an' grace,
Ev'n love an' friendship should give place
   To *catch-the-plack*!
I dinna like to see your face,
    Nor hear your crack.

But ye whom social pleasure charms,
Whose heart the *tide of kindness* warms,
Who hold your *being* on the terms,
   'Each aid the others,'
Come to my bowl, come to my arms,
    My friends, my brothers!   (ll. 115–26)

The religious tenor of the epistles – three of them involve prayers and one includes a 'sermon' – is no accident. Friendship, in these poems, has a sacred quality. In one of his prose letters, Burns refers to 'the solemn league and covenant of friendship' (*Letters*, II, 59), and throughout the epistles friendship is seen in almost sacramental terms, as a holy communion at which Burns is both celebrant and communicant: 'Come to my bowl, come to my arms, / My friends, my brothers!'

Burns's view of humanity's god-given sociability has political ramifications. It provides the basis for a strongly civic political ideology, an ideology rooted in the principle of duty to one's fellows. Burns's epistles, indeed, undertake an audacious reconstruction of the conventional civic hierarchy. In the epistles, Burns and his correspondents (local poets and farmers, freethinkers and freemasons) are presented as an archetypal civic community: a society of equals, whose selfless cultivation of virtue, integrity and public spirit distinguishes them from the 'selfish, warly race' whose sole concern is with '*catch-the plack*'. In the classical republic, of course, it was the landed elite who formed the virtuous citizen class, while the disenfranchised poor took care of domestic 'economy'. In Burns's epistolary republic, however, it is the poet's humble correspondents who devote their scanty leisure hours to public pursuits (learning, poetry, political discussion), while their supposed superiors – the 'cits' and 'lairds' – are wholly engrossed with money-grubbing. The epistles enact a radical inversion of the traditional civic hierarchy: republican virtue now exists among common people, while the traditional civic leaders stand condemned by their own standards.

Burns's contempt for his degenerate social superiors finds expression through the gendered imagery deployed in the 'Second Epistle to J. Lapraik', where Burns pokes fun at his correspondent for being jealous of merchants and lairds:

Do ye envy the *city-gent*,
Behint a kist to lie an' sklent,
Or purse-proud, big wi' cent per cent,
   An' muckle wame,
In some bit *Brugh* to represent
    A *Baillie*'s name?

> Or is't the paughty, feudal *Thane*,
> Wi' ruffl'd sark an' glancin cane,
> Wha thinks himsel nae *sheep-shank bane*,
>   But lordly stalks,
> While caps an' bonnets aff are taen,
>   As by he walks?   (ll. 61–72)

Burns hold up for ridicule the 'womanly' characteristics of these powerful men. The city-gent has the 'muckle wame' of a pregnant woman – he has been emasculated by the pleasures of the belly – while the feudal Thane wears a fussily effeminate 'ruffled sark'. With these images, Burns is drawing on a long-standing civic humanist discourse which associates luxury with effeminacy, and which regards 'economics' as a womanly pursuit. If classical 'virtu' is 'that which becomes a man', then these milk-and-water cissies have lost any right to its name. By contrast, the true civic heroes are those – like Burns and his comrades – whose 'gen'rous manly bosoms' ('Epistle to J. Lapraik') are moved by a zeal for the public good.

Despite the familiar image of 'Burns the Democrat', then, Burns is concerned as much with the *duties* of the citizen as with his democratic rights – the duty to love one's neighbour, to live by the principle 'Each aid the others!', to 'tak a neebor's part' ('Epistle to a Young Friend'). In 'A Winter Night' Burns condemns the oppressor of the poor for impiously pursuing 'the selfish aim, / To bless himself alone!' (ll. 63–4). In the 'Epistle to Davie', Burns views oppression, not as the curtailment of abstract human rights but as the impious disregard for one's fellow creatures:

> Think ye, that sic as *you* and *I*,
> Wha drudge and drive thro' wet and dry,
>   Wi' never-ceasing toil;
> Think ye, are we less blest than they,
> Wha scarcely tent us in their way,
>   As hardly worth their while?
> Alas! how aft, in haughty mood,
>   GOD's creatures they oppress!
> Or else, neglecting a' that 's guid,
>   They riot in excess!
>   Baith careless, and fearless,
>   Of either Heaven or Hell;
>   Esteeming, and deeming,
>   It a' an idle tale!   (ll. 71–84)

This is the poet as hellfire preacher, denouncing the immorality of the rich, fighting oppression with Christian values. In Burns, as in the thinkers discussed in chapter 1, the civic duty to the community combines with the biblical injunction to love one's neighbour. The religious and moralistic tenor of the 'Epistle to Davie' is of a piece with Burns's attacks on the corruption and incompetence of the governing elite, such as the card-playing landowners in 'The Twa Dogs', the careerist MPs in 'The Author's Earnest Cry and Prayer', the profit-hungry aristocrats in the 'Address of Beelzebub', and the bungling monarch in 'A Dream'. The verse epistles form a crucial complement to this moralistic political poetry. The healthy civic community of the epistles, characterised by mutual benevolence and *esprit de corps*, operates as a microcosmic model against which the breakdown of civic values in the larger community is measured.

Burns's verse epistles are political, if in a less overt or rigorous manner than the poems discussed in the previous chapter. They do not raise questions of government corruption or the suborning of the legislature by an overweening executive, but they remain political on a different level. They show the civic virtue of a community far removed from the metropolitan world of status and power and wealth. They assert the efficacy of non-material values – good-fellowship, fraternity, sympathy – against the corrupt self-seeking of the governing class. And in their celebration of friendship there is a radicalism, a politicised sociability, of the kind made familiar by the activists of the period – the *Friends* of the People, the *Friends* of Liberty, the *Friends* of the Constitution. As Robert Crawford observes, Burns did not have to wait for the French Revolution to reveal to him the political significance of brotherhood: 'the fraternity which [Burns] knew was not simply that of *liberté*, *égalité*, *fraternité*; it was also the fraternity of the various brotherhoods to which he belonged – whether that of the freemasons or of the Crochallan Fencibles'.[32] The verse epistles have their origin in one of Burns's brotherhoods – the brotherhood of local bards and political dissenters that he gathered around him in Ayrshire. However, Sillar, Lapraik and the others were not the only local fraternity to whom Burns owed allegiance. There was another important group of 'brothers' whom Burns regarded as comrades in the struggle against tyranny and oppression. This was the 'candid, lib'ral band' of the Ayrshire New Lights, and their relationship with Burns is explored in the following section.

---

32 Crawford, 'Robert Fergusson's Robert Burns', in *Robert Burns and Cultural Authority*, pp. 1–22 (p. 13).

PART THREE

THE NEW LIGHT

CHAPTER FIVE

'A Candid, Lib'ral Band': Burns and the New Light

An' when ye gravely try your skill
On *ordination* an' *free-will*,
E'en whiggish drones chap in a gill,
You're sic a bright man;
For a' you're owre like *Rabin Hill*,
A black New-light-man.

(James Orr, 'Epistle to N— P—, Oldmill',
Posthumous Works (1817))

The struggle between the Old Light and New Light parties in the eighteenth-century Scottish kirk contained, even for contemporaries, an element of farce. The bickering of churchmen, and particularly of co-religionists, is an inherently risible subject, and Burns lampoons the whole controversy as a 'moonshine matter' in his 'Epistle to W. Simpson, Ochiltree'. But if it provoked his detached amusement, the division in the Scottish kirk also prompted some of Burns's most engaged and vehement verses. The reason for this paradox is simple. If the clerical manoeuvring of the competing parties could seem comical, the issues raised by the debate – liberty of conscience, the right of private judgement, the proper limits of ecclesiastical, and indeed secular authority – go to the heart of Burns's religious and political concerns.

Burns's attachment to the New Light cause was not just an intervention in a parochial dispute. Rather, New Light Presbyterianism may be accounted one of the seminal intellectual influences on Burns, one through which he was exposed to the modern ideas of the European Enlightenment as well as to certain values of traditional Presbyterianism. The principles of New Lightism – private judgement, practical benevolence, universal tolerance, defiance of tyranny – were intellectually attractive to Burns, and informed many of the books he most admired. Equally, Burns enjoyed the sense of being part of a progressive, avant-garde group of independent thinkers, taking a defiant stand against entrenched authority. New Lightism satisfied Burns's clubbable instincts, his relish for cameraderie, at the same time as it fulfilled his strong sense of independent-mindedness; like Freemasonry, it accommodated both Burns's sociability and his individualism. As a central element of Burns's intellectual and social context, the New Light merits more detailed attention than it has generally been given in studies of the poet. In this chapter, I aim to give a short account of the genesis and development of New Light

Presbyterianism and to assess Burns's own relationship with the New Light party and with New Light ideas. The question of how these relationships helped to shape Burns's religious satires will be treated in Chapter 6.

'A black New-Light-man'

'You know my sentiments respecting the present two great Parties that divide our Scots Ecclesiastics', wrote Burns to Mrs Dunlop in July 1789 (*Letters*, I, 422). That Burns should have such decided sentiments regarding the division in the Scottish kirk was hardly surprising. Burns's father, a committed New Light layman who took his domestic religious duties seriously, regularly engaged his sons in religious discussions. Burns, moreover, was brought up under the tutelage of prominent New Light ministers in Ayr and Tarbolton, before being confronted, at age twenty-five after the move to Mossgiel, with the rebarbative Old Light principles of the Rev. William Auld, parish minister of Mauchline. Not that New Light ideas had been passively or uncritically absorbed by the poet. On the contrary, with its emphasis on private judgement, the New Light encouraged Burns to develop and to articulate his own religious opinions. As a young man in Tarbolton Burns had already begun to make a name for himself as a noisy advocate of liberal views. He would hold forth with heterodox ideas during the debates between sermons on a Sunday:

> Polemical divinity about this time was putting the country half-mad; and I, ambitious of shining in conversation parties on sundays between sermons, funerals, &c. used in a few years more to puzzle Calvinism with so much heat and indiscretion that I raised a hue and cry of heresy against me which has not ceased to this hour. (*Letters*, I, 136)

It was at Mauchline, however, that Burns's polemical religious opinions achieved poetic voice. At Mauchline Burns was galvanised by antagonism; here he encountered strident theological orthodoxy and authoritarian church discipline, as both himself and several of his friends fell foul of the Mauchline kirk session. Importantly, too, Burns was now the head of a household in his own right, and bullishly conscious of the religious competence of the lay Presbyterian householder (the 'priest-like Father' of 'The Cotter's Saturday Night'). While opposing clerical aggrandisement, Burns evidently relished the religious duties of the Presbyterian layman, who was expected to be priest in his own home. A self-ironising, but probably accurate picture of Burns catechising the Mossgiel servants appears in 'The Inventory' (K, 86):

> An' ay on Sundays duly nightly,
> I on the questions *targe* them tightly;
> Till faith, wee Davock's turn'd sae gleg,
> Tho' scarcely langer than your leg,
> He'll screed you aff Effectual Calling,
> As fast as ony in the dwelling.   (ll. 40–45)

It is likely that such duties sat well with Burns's strong sense of his own religious competence, and that his new status as a householder emboldened the poet in his attacks on the Old Light.

It was with the Mauchline satires, including 'The Holy Tulzie', the epistle 'To the Rev. John M'Math', and 'Holy Willie's Prayer', that Burns established himself as a New Light polemicist. Of 'The Holy Tulzie' he later recalled: 'With a certain side of both clergy and laity it met with a roar of applause' (*Letters*, I, 144). These poems brought Burns the attention and admiration of New Lights throughout the county. He now associated on familiar terms with New Light ministers (McGill, Wodrow, McMath, McQuhae) and with prominent New Light laymen like Gavin Hamilton and Robert Aiken. In Ayrshire, as in Ulster at this time, New Light Presbyterians were often ardent Freemasons, drawn to the craft by its non-dogmatic, fraternal ethos, and Burns's friendships with the Ayrshire New Lights were cemented in the county's Lodges. Burns became for a time the New Lights' champion – Carlyle's 'fighting man of the New-Light Priesthood', Henley's 'laureate of the New Light party' – springing to the defence of beleaguered liberals in a series of caustically belligerent satires.[1]

However, while the poet's overall support for the New Light cause is not open to doubt, it is necessary at this point to enter a caveat. If, in the epistles to McMath and Goldie, Burns takes the position of an uncompromising New Light partisan, in some of the less polemical kirk satires – 'The Holy Fair' and even 'The Ordination' – his sympathies are not so clear-cut. Neither the condemnation of the Old Lights nor the praise of the New is as decided as it might be. It is well to bear in mind John C. Weston's observation that

> in several kirk satires the warmth, fun, and colourful humanity of the popular religion shows through the ridicule of Calvinism, and in at least one ('Holy Fair') the Moderates get their lumps for being boring, English, and sycophantic.[2]

For much of his youth Burns had been ardently and uncritically orthodox – in his own words, possessed of 'an enthusiastic, idiot piety' (*Letters*, I, 135) – and it can be argued that an appreciation of 'enthusiasm' survived his conversion to New Light principles. As Raymond Bentman argues, the 'enthusiasm' of the Evangelicals was something to which Burns remained sympathetic even as he deplored other aspects of their creed:

> The Evangelicals upheld a religion that was warmer, more passionate, more immediately gratifying. They believed in a kind of passion that Burns, in other contexts, also believed in.[3]

---

1 *The Critical Heritage*, p. 377; Henley and Henderson, II, 356.
2 Weston, 'Robert Burns's Satire', p. 43.
3 Raymond Bentman, *Robert Burns* (Boston, 1987), p. 7.

However, this caveat in turn requires to be qualified, for the New Lights themselves endorsed a version of 'enthusiasm' in the notion of a Hutchesonian 'moral sense' which prompts to virtue from within. The situation is a complex one, and it is perhaps a reflection of this complexity that, in the kirk satires no less than the election ballads, Burns makes an uncertain showing as a party hack.

From these brief remarks, it should already be apparent that the popular understanding of Burns's kirk satires is radically flawed. The image of Burns as the scourge of Presbyterianism, attacking 'the kirk itself and all that it stood for',[4] is a poor caricature of his position. The most cursory grasp of the biography, never mind the poems, would reveal that Burns's engagement with Presbyterianism is far more nuanced than this. His regular church attendance, his lifelong interest in church politics, his sermon-tasting, his numerous epistolary references to family worship and catechising: all this suggests that, whatever Burns's quarrels with the kirk, he quarrelled very much as a competent Presbyterian layman, aware of his rights and determined to assert them. As Fairchild argues in his masterful treatment of the poet's religious opinions, Burns 'always remained, according to his own peculiar lights, a son of the Kirk'.[5]

In this chapter I am not concerned primarily with the poet's personal religious faith, the tenor of his spirituality, or the nature of his belief in God. This topic has been well covered by Walter McGinty, who devotes a large part of his thesis to a study of 'Burns's Personal Religion', and who argues convincingly that 'three recurrent themes' dominate the poet's religious reflections: 'a belief in a benevolent God, a speculation on an existence beyond the grave, and an acknowledgement of his own accountability' before God.[6] Nor do I intend to focus minutely on the poet's doctrinal beliefs. Broadly, Burns may be said to have departed from the strict Calvinist doctrines of original sin and predestination, although his position is not wholly consistent.[7] While he describes himself as being 'in perpetual warfare with' the doctrine of original sin (*Letters*, I, 303), his letters sometimes betray an almost Swiftian perception of human depravity, and in one he alludes to the 'native incorrigibility' of his own heart (*Letters*, II, 283). Burns's position on predestination and the doctrine of justification through faith is similarly ambivalent. On the evidence of the letter of 8 January 1788 to Agnes McLehose (the fullest statement of his personal religious beliefs), Burns appears to accept the Arminian position: that is, he believes that those who sincerely endeavour to live righteously will be rewarded in heaven, and that 'it must be in every one's power to embrace [God's] offer of "everlasting life" ' (*Letters*, I, 201). And yet in the same letter Burns concedes that 'A mind pervaded, actuated and governed by purity, truth and charity . . . does not *merit* heaven', implying an acceptance that god-given grace is requisite for salvation.

4 Richard Hindle Fowler, *Robert Burns* (London, 1988), p. 67.
5 *Religious Trends*, III, 20.
6 McGinty, II, 360–473 (p. 435).
7 McGinty, II, 405–6. However, McGinty also finds that 'there were elements of Burns's belief that were entirely compatible with a Calvinistic view' (II, 406).

Ultimately, the uncertainty over Burns's doctrinal labels – whether he may legitimately be categorised as 'Arminian' or 'Socinian' – is of little moment. Burns was no dogmatist or sytematic theologian, and his putative attachment to specific heterodox doctrines matters less than his principled opposition to the enforcement of orthodoxy, and his commitment to a practical, benevolent form of Christianity.

The minutiae of the poet's doctrinal beliefs, then, will not be my primary concern in what follows; my aim is rather to determine what the New Light movement meant for Burns, how it informed and influenced his work. In the eyes of Burns, the New Light was much more than simply a church party: it represented an orientation, a complex of beliefs, a *Weltanschauung*. Understood in these terms, the New Light is central to Burns's outlook and achievement. This chapter will consist of two sections. In the first section I give a short account of the New Light or Moderate party in the Church of Scotland, its ideology, organisation and development. In the second section, I discuss some of the theological and other writings which influenced Burns's religious opinions. These include the religious *Manual* composed by Burns's father, and the writings of William Dalrymple, William McGill, John Taylor and John Goldie, as well as Sterne's *Tristram Shandy* and John Moore's *Zeluco*.

The Rise of Moderatism

The Moderate or New Light party in the Church of Scotland was first formally organised during a dispute over lay patronage in 1752. The Patronage Act of 1712, imposed on the Scottish kirk in direct contravention of the Union settlement, had restored the right of lay patrons (usually a local landowner, but in about a third of parishes the crown) to nominate ministers to vacant charges. This replaced the settlement of 1689–90, by which the elders and Protestant heritors of a parish might nominate the minister, subject to the consent of the congregation. The Patronage Act created a groundswell of unrest, as congregations sought to resist the presentation of unpopular nominees. When the General Assembly, in line with the law of the land, sought to enforce these presentations, many presbyteries were recalcitrant and sometimes openly rebellious.[8]

The Moderate party came into being when a group of the younger clergy (who were not necessarily supporters of patronage) banded together to uphold the authority of the General Assembly. From this period onwards, the Moderate-led Assembly made it a policy to force reluctant presbyteries to induct the nominees of the patron. The proper hierarchical subordination of church courts (regarded as an essential counterweight to the parity of ministers in Presbyterianism) was thus a central concern of the Moderate party as it emerged in 1752, and which, as a well-disciplined and tightly organised body, was able to dominate proceedings in the

8 Richard Sher and Alexander Murdoch, 'Patronage and Party in the Church of Scotland, 1750–1800', in *Church, Politics and Society: Scotland 1408–1929*, ed. by Norman MacDougall (Edinburgh, 1983), pp. 197–220 (pp. 207–211).

General Assembly, the Church of Scotland's highest court, until the turn of the nineteenth century. The Moderates' dominance was particularly marked during the 1760s and '70s when the party was led by the extremely able figure of William Robertson.

As Richard Sher has emphasised in his seminal study of the Moderate literati, the power of the Moderates rested on a secure institutional foundation. Holding influential positions in the universities and in church administration, the Moderates were able to direct and dominate proceedings in the General Assembly. Under the influence of Moderate professors the universities habitually returned Moderate candidates to the Assembly, where the party 'maintained a tight grip on permanent assembly offices such as the principal clerk and church procurator'. Robertson's personal prominence was made possible by the fact that, as Principal of Edinburgh University, he was able to attend the Assembly every year, unlike many of his evangelical opponents, who attended in rotation with other members of their presbyteries.[9]

For all this astute politicking, however, the New Light was much more than an effective ecclesiastical party, 'Dr Robertson's administration'. At its broadest, Moderatism signified an ethos or orientation dating back to the early part of the century, if not before, and current far beyond the confines of clerical circles. For some commentators, admittedly, the early or proto-Moderates like Simson or Hutcheson are to be viewed as a separate phenomenon from the Robertson Moderates, on account of their opposition to patronage.[10] Clearly, however, there is a broader continuity in outlook and orientation beneath the less momentous differences in policy and strategy. One obscures more than one reveals by excluding Francis Hutcheson or William Leechman from the rubric of Moderatism, or by confining its application to the clergy.[11] There is a case, too, for retaining a less institution-centred definition of Moderatism. In the context of Edinburgh and the General Assembly, Moderatism may indeed have operated primarily as an institutional 'regime', but this was not necessarily so in the provinces. For Robert Burns in Ayrshire and Dumfriesshire, as we shall see, the New Light constituted an intellectual tendency or loose affiliation of embattled freethinkers rather than the supposed governing party in the General Assembly. Certainly, for the purposes of this chapter, what matters is not 'the specific policies and programs'[12] of the Moderate party in the church, so much as the philosophy of Moderatism and its cultural significance. Mathieson's definition of Moderatism as a general Zeitgeist ('Moderatism, in the full acceptation of that term, was only another name for the

---

9 Sher, *Church and University*, pp. 93–147.
10 Sher, *Church and University*, pp. 16–17, 153.
11 The forerunners of the Robertson Moderates in the early part of the eighteenth century are studied in Henry Sefton, '"Neu-lights and Preachers Legall": some observations on the beginnings of Moderatism in the Church of Scotland', in *Church, Politics and Society*, pp. 186–96.
12 Sher, *Church and University*, p. 17.

spirit of the age'[13]) may be excessively idealistic, but Moderatism cannot be reduced to an interest group, an ecclesiastic cabal.

The roots of Moderatism or the New Light, considered as a social and cultural formation rather than a cabal of Edinburgh ministers, lie in the newfound security of the Presbyterian church following the revolution settlement of 1689–90. Presbyterian government had been restored by the revolution settlement and guaranteed by the Act of Security of 1706 (although many Presbyterians remained suspicious of the ensuing Union).[14] This meant that, despite the British parliament's imposition of the Toleration and Patronage Acts (1712), the position of Scottish Presbyterianism had been copper-fastened. Many now saw no need for Presbyterians to unite in a phalanx behind codified statements of orthodoxy, and argued that a greater degree of latitude might be reclaimed by the individual. The new requirement that clergy and lay communicants subscribe to the Westminster Confession of Faith seemed outmoded and authoritarian to those influenced by New Light notions of free enquiry.

Several key developments in the early decades of the century demonstrated just how pervasive the New Light ethos had become. The most important of these was undoubtedly the Simson case. When John Simson, Professor of Divinity at Glasgow, was charged with heresy (first Arminianism in 1715 and then Arianism in 1726), his treatment by the church courts was tellingly lenient: although he was eventually suspended from his teaching duties, he was not deposed and continued to enjoy his salary.[15] The leniency shown to Simson was not, however, extended to the antinomian zealots within the kirk. In 1720 the General Assembly was forthright in its condemnation of Edward Fisher's *Marrow of Modern Divinity* (1646), an old English antinomian treatise republished by Scottish evangelicals in 1718.[16] The defeat of the 'Marrowmen' signalled the kirk's utter repudiation of extreme antinomian views, and its determination to contain the zealots. The spread of liberal, New Light opinions was evidenced also by the appointment of Hutcheson and Leechman to chairs at Glasgow, the successful (if controversial) production of a play written by a Scottish clergyman, John Home's *Douglas*, and the steady decline in rigorous kirk discipline.[17]

Not all of the significant developments within eighteenth-century Presbyterianism, however, originated in Scotland. In tracing the rise of Moderatism in early eighteenth-century Scotland we must not overlook the influence of English Presbyterianism (especially the writings of John Taylor), and, more importantly, of

13 William Law Mathieson, *The Awakening of Scotland: A History from 1747 to 1797* (Glasgow, 1910), p. 234.

14 Michael Lynch, *Scotland: A New History*, 2nd edn (London, 1992), p. 321.

15 J. H. S. Burleigh, *A Church History of Scotland* (London, 1960), pp. 287–91.

16 A. L. Drummond and J. Bulloch, *The Scottish Church, 1688–1843: The Age of the Moderates* (Edinburgh, 1973), pp. 32–37.

17 T. C. Smout, *A History of the Scottish People 1560–1830* (1969; repr. London, 1972), pp. 213–22.

Irish Presbyterianism. Particularly in the West of Scotland, with its close cultural links to Ulster, the influence of the Irish New Lights was seminal. A long history of mutual intercourse connected western Scotland with the North of Ireland, and denominational ties played a central role in this relationship. Students for the Presbyterian ministry in Ireland, debarred by their religion from entering Trinity College Dublin, came to study at Glasgow University and, to a lesser extent, at Edinburgh. At Glasgow University, 'Scoto-Hiberni' comprised just under a fifth of the student body throughout the eighteenth century.[18] Neither Scottish nor Irish Presbyterianism in this period can be adequately understood in isolation from the other: in this field as in others, we need to be aware of what one historian has termed the 'ideological community' connecting Scotland and Ulster.[19]

Indeed, the very term 'New Light' was first applied, in an eighteenth-century Presbyterian context, during the subscription controversy in the Synod of Ulster. This dispute, which led to the secession of the Presbytery of Antrim in 1726, was over the issue of compulsory subscription to the Westminster Confession of 1643. In 1705 clerical subscription had been made obligatory by the Synod of Ulster. However, with the days of rigorous Anglican persecution now a memory, and with the relative security implied by the 'regium donum' (a yearly grant from the king to the Presbyterian clergy), such an imperious requirement of orthodoxy could not be warranted by the demands of unity, and a growing number of Ulster ministers began to claim the freedom of conscience to which peacetime Calvinism entitled them. In 1705, a reading and debating club known as the Belfast Society was formed by a group of liberal-minded ministers and divinity students.[20] Among its members was the young Antrim minister John Abernethy, who asserted his right of private judgement in a sermon entitled 'Religious obedience founded on personal persuasion', delivered in 1719 and published the year after. This sermon, dubbed 'New Light' by an orthodox opponent, initiated a controversy which was resolved in 1726 by the placing of all the nonsubscribing ministers into the Presbytery of Antrim, and the exclusion of that Presbytery from the Synod of Ulster. Abernethy's sermon has some claim to be regarded as the first statement of New Light principles.[21]

'New Light' thus initially betokened an opposition to man-made confessions of orthodoxy, and this opposition remained central to the movement in Scotland as in Ulster. In Scotland, certainly, the New Lights did continue to subscribe the Westminster Confession, but many – particularly in the 1770s and 1780s – declared their principled opposition to man-made creeds, and did not hesitate to underplay

18 McFarland, pp. 4–6.
19 McFarland, pp. 1, 23. On the general political and cultural connections between the two areas, see Graham Walker, *Intimate Strangers: Political and Cultural Interaction Between Scotland and Ulster in Modern Times* (Edinburgh, 1995), esp. pp. 3–8.
20 On the Belfast Society, see Stewart, *A Deeper Silence*, pp. 74–80.
21 A. T. Q. Stewart, *The Narrow Ground: Aspects of Ulster 1609–1969* (London, 1977), p. 98.

or disregard whatever they found obnoxious in the Confession.[22] In the western counties, if we may judge from the works of Burns, it was the opposition to man-made confessions, rather than any predilection for church patronage, which was the definitive feature of the New Light Presbyterians. If so, this no doubt reflects their close intercourse with the New Lights of Ulster.

The influence of liberal Irish Presbyterianism in the West of Scotland was ensured, not just by the general level of intercourse between the two areas, but by the particular activities of one important individual: Francis Hutcheson, Professor of Moral Philosophy in the University of Glasgow between 1730 and 1746. As noted in Chapter 1, the Ulsterman Hutcheson was an inspirational figure, a compelling extemporaneous speaker whose lectures attracted large audiences.[23] His pupil Adam Smith described him as 'the never to be forgotten Dr Hutcheson'.[24] Like many northern Irish Presbyterians, Hutcheson maintained close contacts with English and southern Irish dissenters, and the influence of Rational Dissent is evident in his thought. Hutcheson taught that religion was amenable to reason, that the law of God was discoverable in the order of the universe as well as in revealed religion. Morality was not to be derived from doctrine but established empirically by its effects: '*that Action is best*, which accomplishes the *greatest Happiness* for the *greatest Numbers*; and *that, worst*, which, in *like manner*, occasions *Misery*'.[25] Hutcheson was in fact the first to articulate this classic utilitarian formula, one which Burns himself echoes in a letter to Mrs Dunlop: 'Whatever mitigates the woes, or increases the happiness of others, this is my criterion of goodness; and whatever injures society at large, or an individual in it, this is my measure of iniquity' (*Letters*, I, 419). In his religious – as opposed to moral philosophical – writings, Hutcheson was strongly influenced by the Antrim New Lights and their defence of the principle of private judgement. 'There is', wrote Hutcheson in his *Short Introduction to Moral Philosophy*, 'a sense deeply infixed by nature, of each one's *right of private judgement*, or of judging for himself in all matters of duty, especially as to religion'.[26]

Hutcheson's influence on the Presbyterian church can hardly be exaggerated: 'a whole generation of students for the ministry from Ireland and Scotland sat at his feet and absorbed his dispassionate ethics'.[27] Nor was it only the Moderates who were indebted to the Irishman. Although a New Light, Hutcheson was an opponent of lay patronage, and in his *Considerations on Patronages* (1735) he advanced the

---

22 Ian D. L. Clark, 'From Protest to Reaction: The Moderate Regime in the Church of Scotland, 1752–1805', in *Scotland in the Age of Improvement: Essays in Scottish History in the Eighteenth Century*, ed. by N. T. Phillipson and Rosalind Mitchison (Edinburgh, 1970), pp. 200–224 (p. 205); McGinty, II, 346–7.

23 Sefton, p. 188.

24 Letter to Archibald Davidson, 16 November 1787, quoted in *Theory of Moral Sentiments*, p. 301n.

25 *An Inquiry into the Original of our Ideas of Beauty and Virtue*, p. 164.

26 *Philosophical Writings*, p. 167.

27 Drummond and Bulloch, p. 47.

arguments which would become 'the principle doctrine of the Popular party' in the latter half of the century.[28] Through William Leechman, Hutcheson's appointee as Professor of Divinity at Glasgow in 1743, Hutcheson's ideas were made available to later generations of divinity students. The later Moderates, especially those in the western counties who had been educated at Glasgow, must be seen not merely as part of a pro-patronage governing 'machine', but as the inheritors of the liberal, freethinking ethos of Hutcheson and the Irish Presbyterians. [29]

As a party, however, the later Moderates were not equally solicitous of all religious freedoms, and not all criticism of the Moderates can be ascribed to evangelical bigotry. Their support of patronage made the Robertson Moderates inconsistent lovers of liberty; they applied freedom of conscience to doctrinal issues, but not to the settlement of ministers.[30] Their position as beneficiaries of government patronage, and their adherence to an ideal of politeness and gentility, inclined the Robertson Moderates to take a conservative stand on current political questions. Unlike their Old Light opponents, for instance, the Moderates supported the government against the colonists during the American Revolution. The widespread feeling among contemporaries that the Moderates were more concerned with cultivating genteel society than with the cure of souls seems to have had some basis in fact. As Burleigh observes, the *Autobiography* of Alexander Carlyle – voluble on his relations with his heritors, reticent on the subject of parochial duties – rather confirms the justice of this charge.[31] Whether or not they possessed, in Cockburn's words, 'no principle superior to that of obsequious allegiance to patrons', the Moderates did not baulk at alienating the common people, and remained blithely unconcerned at the exponential growth of Presbyterian Dissent.[32] In his anti-Moderate satire, *Ecclesiastical Characteristics* (1753), John Witherspoon sardonically envisages, as the logical extension of Moderate values, a lazy, flockless ministry enjoying inflated stipends in the company of its landed benefactors:

> Who can tell whether, when we shall have brought moderation to perfection, when we shall have driven away the common people to the Seceders, who alone are fit for them, and captivated the hearts of the gentry to a love of our solitary temples, they may not be pleased to allow us more stipends, because we shall have nothing to do but spend them?[33]

28 Sher and Murdoch, 'Patronage and Party', pp. 208–9.
29 On the 'considerable longevity' of Hutcheson's legacy, see McFarland, p. 13.
30 Sher, *Church and University*, p. 68.
31 Burleigh, p. 302.
32 Henry Cockburn, *Memorials of His Time* (Edinburgh, 1856), p. 236.
33 John Witherspoon, *Ecclesiastical Characteristics: Or, The Arcana of Church Policy. Being an Humble Attempt to open the Mystery of Moderation, Wherein is shewn, a plain and easy way of attaining to the character of a Moderate man, as at present in repute in the Church of Scotland*, in *The Works of John Witherspoon*, 9 vols (Edinburgh, 1804–5), VI, 139–222 (pp. 219–220).

Witherspoon's position is a polemical one, but it is not for that reason to be lightly dismissed.

Burns himself was not blind to the shortcomings of the Moderates, and indeed he takes a satiric swipe at New Light politeness and gentility in the portrait of Smith in 'The Holy Fair' (K, 70): 'His English style, an' gesture fine, / Are a' clean out o' season' (ll. 129–30). However, what must be borne in mind is that Burns's New Light is not to be equated with the Robertson Moderates and the Edinburgh clerical elite. For it is not as the party of politeness or the party of patronage that Burns celebrates the New Light. His is the *Ayrshire* New Light, fighting authoritarian Calvinism in its heartland; the New Light shaped by the Real Whig traditions of Glasgow University. Burns reveals the rationale behind his New Light partisanship when he praises William McGill for 'squaring Religion by the rules of Common Sense' (*Letters*, I, 454), or lauds John McMath for his benevolent 'heart . . . / An' winning manner' ('To the Rev. John M'Math'). For Burns the New Light represents two things above all: an emphasis on non-dogmatic tolerant Christianity; and a belief in the Protestant right of private judgement.

Despite the evident utility of labels such as 'Old Light' and 'New Light', however, we must guard against drawing the division too starkly. These were not warring factions, implacably opposed one to the other. It is entirely typical that Witherspoon, in *Ecclesiastical Characteristics*, should quote with evident admiration from Dr Robertson and acknowledge that 'there are many worthy and good men' among the Moderate party.[34] Even the Secession groups tended to maintain strong and amicable links with the main body of the church. In Ulster, the non-subscribing Presbytery of Antrim never became wholly detached from the Synod of Ulster.[35] Moreover, the majority of New Lights were not openly critical of orthodox Calvinist doctrines, but in sermons and lectures simply passed over in silence the doctrines which they did not hold. Doctrinally, the Scottish New Lights were 'ostensibly if tepidly orthodox', and worked amicably alongside Old Light colleagues.[36] Even on the issue of patronage, many New Lights were conciliatory, arguing that the measure was to be accepted only because it was the law of the land; indeed, throughout Robertson's period as Moderate leader, the General Assembly registered an annual protest at the 'grievance' of patronage.[37] While critics argued that the Moderates' strict enforcement of the General Assembly's authority was un-Presbyterian, Moderates pointed out that Presbyterianism required subordination of church courts as well as equality of ministers.[38] In all, the Moderates were 'more devoutly Presbyterian than secular interpretations sometimes allow'.[39]

34 *Works*, VI, 226–7, 255.
35 R. F. G. Holmes, *Our Irish Presbyterian Heritage* (Belfast, 1985), p. 66.
36 Burleigh, pp. 297–8, 303.
37 Sher and Murdoch, 'Patronage and Party', pp. 211–12.
38 Drummond and Bulloch, p. 65.
39 Richard B. Sher, 'Introduction: Scottish-American Cultural Studies, Past and Present', in *Scotland and America in the Age of the Enlightenment*, ed. by Richard B. Sher and Jeffrey Smitten (Edinburgh, 1990), pp. 1–27 (p. 16).

It is important to realise that, while Moderatism may fruitfully be associated with 'the spirit of inquiry and criticism that characterized the Enlightenment',[40] it was at the same time deeply rooted in the Reformed tradition. Crucially, the New Lights saw themselves as renovating the true founding principles of Protestantism, in their concern with private judgement and the primacy of scripture.[41] As McFarland observes, the New Light emphasis on private judgement was not just 'part of a broader liberalising current in European Protestantism'; it also drew on 'the anti-authoritarianism of earlier . . . Presbyterian thought, for its corollary was an attack on the church itself as a corporate institution, divinely ordained to interpret Scripture'.[42] In their opposition to subscription, and their insistence on valuing scripture above any man-made confessions, the New Lights (as they well understood) were renovating traditional Calvinist principles. In the *Institutes*, Calvin had written:

> a most pernicious error widely prevails that Scripture has only so much weight as is conceded to it by the consent of the church. As if the eternal and inviolable truth of God depended upon the decision of men![43]

In essence, this was the position of many New Light Presbyterians, as they asserted their freedom of judgement against the church's Westminster Confession.

The controversy surrounding the *Essay on the Death of Jesus Christ* (1786), written by the Moderate Ayr minister and friend of Burns, William McGill, provides a striking illustration of the New Light's reliance upon traditional Protestant principles. McGill was accused of teaching the doctrines of Socinianism and Arminianism in opposition to the teaching laid down in the Westminster Confession. Defending himself against orthodox attacks, McGill argues that, by placing the authority of a man-made creed (the Westminster Confession) above that of scripture and so denying the right of private judgement, his Old Light accusers are acting like Romanists. In a deft manoeuvre, he charges one of his adversaries, the splenetic William Peebles, with having transgressed the great principles of Protestant liberty, precisely *as laid down in* the Westminster Confession. McGill writes:

> At least from his present publication[44], there is great reason to doubt, whether he [Peebles] has any belief or regard for any of those articles of the Confession of Faith, which asserts the supreme authority of the scriptures, the right of private judgement, and the great principles of protestant liberty, as

40 Burleigh, p. 295.
41 McGinty, II, 331–34.
42 McFarland, p. 11.
43 John Calvin, *Institutes of the Christian Religion*, ed. by John T. McNeill, trans. by Ford Lewis Battles, 2 vols (Philadelphia, 1960), I, 75.
44 *A Sermon by Rev. William Peebles preached to the Magistrates and Council of the Burgh of Newton upon Ayr, 5th November 1788* (Kilmarnock, 1788).

distinguished from the infallibility, implicit faith, and slavery of the church of Rome.[45]

McGill goes on to compare Peebles to 'a father of the holy office of the inquisition'.[46] This imputation of 'Romish' propensities was a standard tactic; New Lights often characterised the enforcement of confessional orthodoxy as 'popish'. John Taylor, the Norwich Presbyterian from whom the New Lights derived many of their ideas, described the enforcement of Trinitarian orthodoxy by Norwich Congregationalists as 'Dissenting Popery'.[47] As we shall see, Burns, too, habitually describes his Old Light adversaries in the stigmatizing terminology of Roman Catholicism.

In placing Burns's kirk satires in context, then, it is above all important to avoid misreading the New Light as a move towards deism or secularism. In Scotland as elsewhere in Europe, the Enlightenment critique of organised religion does not represent a wholesale spurning of a benighted past, nor does it herald a brave new world of modern secularism. With the exception of France, the European Enlightenment was immersed in religion. In Protestant countries, Enlighteners saw themselves as renovating the libertarian founding principles of the Reformation: freedom of enquiry, the right of private judgement, the efficacy of reason. Mark Goldie, whose researches in the field of intellectual history throw much light on this issue, argues that the mainstream of Enlightenment thought represented, 'not predominantly an atheism in revolt against Christianity, but rather a further unfolding of the programme of Christian Reformers'.[48] There was now, however, one important difference: the Enlightenment reformers were attacking, not merely the tyrannous practices of the Roman church, but also those of degenerate Protestants. The battle was no longer against Rome as such, but against Roman practices wherever they appeared. 'Priestcraft', a recent coinage which covered both Catholic and popish Protestant practices, was now the declared enemy.[49]

A New Light Library

Since the days when his father would bring 'improving' books home, Burns was a voracious consumer of religious literature, devouring sermons, devotional tracts and church histories. In the autobiographical letter to Dr Moore, Burns lists among his early reading Thomas Stackhouse's *New History of the Holy Bible* (1737), John Taylor's *Scripture Doctrine of Original Sin* (1740), and the *Physico-Theology* (1713) and

---

45 *The Benefits of the Revolution: A Sermon preached at Ayr on 5th of November 1788 by William McGill, D. D., to which are added Remarks on a Sermon preached on the same day at Newton upon Ayr* (Kilmarnock, 1789), pp. 33–34, quoted in McGinty, II, 331.

46 *Benefits*, p. 40, in McGinty, II, 333.

47 Mathieson, p. 216.

48 Goldie, 'The civil religion of James Harrington', p. 201.

49 Mark Goldie, 'Priestcraft and the birth of Whiggism', in *Political Discourse in Early Modern Britain*, pp. 209–31.

Astro-Theology (1714) of William Derham (*Letters*, I, 138). Writing to Alexander Cunningham in 1790, Burns claims to be 'deeply read' in such popular devotional works as Thomas Boston's *Human Nature in its Fourfold State*, William Guthrie's *Trial of a Saving Interest*, and Walter Marshall's *On Sanctification* (*Letters*, II, 16). Later, as librarian and treasurer of the Monkland Friendly Society, Burns's book orders included Knox's *History of the Reformation* and Hugh Blair's *Sermons*, as well as such 'damned trash' as Edward Fisher's *Marrow of Modern Divinity*, and Howie's *Scots Worthies* (*Letters*, II, 66). Perhaps the best way in to the whole subject of Burns's religious satires is to consider some of the theological writings which helped to form and to focus his own New Light principles.

Foremost among the theological writings which influenced Burns is the religious *Manual* which his father, William Burnes – perhaps assisted by John Murdoch – composed for the family's instruction. This *Manual*, which takes the form of a dialogue between a father and his son, has been described as bearing 'a strong liberal tinge'.[50] Certainly the *Manual* emphasises practical morality over doctrinal ortho-doxy in classic New Light fashion. Faith may indeed be necessary to salvation, says the Father in the dialogue, but he who endeavours to fulfil the moral law to the best of his ability will not fail to be accepted by God:

> The Moral Law as a rule of life, must be of indispensable obligation, but it is the glory of the Christian religion, that if we be upright in our endeavours to follow it and sincere in our repentance, upon our failing or shortcoming, we shall be accepted according to what we have, and shall increase on our strength, by the assistance of the Spirit of God co-operating with our honest endeavours.[51]

In this passage, strict predestinarian Calvinism is modified towards an Arminian position. While accepting that 'the assistance of the Spirit of God is absolutely necessary for salvation', the *Manual* teaches that those who endeavour to fulfil the moral law will naturally receive this assistance.[52] This hopeful, Arminian message is characteristic of the *Manual* as a whole.

Walter McGinty describes the tenor of William Burnes's *Manual* as being a 'milder form of Calvinism ... in keeping with the tone of Dr Dalrymple's writings'.[53] William Dalrymple, Burns's minister at Ayr, was a leading light among the Ayrshire Moderates. In his sermons and writings, Dalrymple preached a mild, lenitive Christianity which emphasised the importance of practical moral conduct: 'That which does not sanctify a man's mind or make him better, doth not subserve religion. Truth is better served by holiness than by argument.'[54] Dalrymple's benevolent Christianity was the staple of the Burnes family's public worship until

---

50 Crawford, *Burns*, p. 40.
51 Burnes, xliv–xlv.
52 Burnes, xlv.
53 McGinty, II, 492.
54 William Dalrymple, *A Sequel to the Life of Christ* (Ayr, 1791), p. 265, quoted in McGinty, II, 498.

the removal to Lochlie in 1777. Dalrymple, however, was not the only New Light controversialist in the Ayr charge. William McGill, Dalrymple's colleague as minister of Ayr, was another of Burns's Moderate friends, whose own theological writings became a central 'battleground' in the struggle between the New Lights and the Old.[55]

On its publication in 1786, McGill's *Practical Essay on the Death of Jesus Christ* was immediately swamped in controversy over its alleged Socinian and Arminian tendencies. A lengthy heresy trial, fought out in the church courts, was finally resolved in 1790, when McGill submitted an equivocal 'apology' to the Synod of Glasgow and Ayr.[56] In 1787, in a letter to Mrs Dunlop, Burns announces his intention of writing a satirical poem in defence of 'my learned and truly worthy friend Dr McGill' (*Letters*, I, 175). Mrs Dunlop advised Burns against meddling in the matter, however, and it is not until 1789 that Burns trounces McGill's Old Light enemies in 'The Kirk's Alarm'.

McGill's *Essay* is a standard piece of New Light theology, biased towards the practical as opposed to the doctrinal aspects of Christianity. In contrast to the strict Calvinists, who held that good works were of no account in securing salvation, McGill asserts the efficacy of practical moral endeavour. 'The virtue and obedience of men', though always imperfect, 'hath been in many cases so acceptable to GOD, that for the sake of it, he hath declared himself willing to shew mercy to some who had no title to it'.[57] In a dig at the strict Calvinist doctrine of justification by faith alone, McGill warns the reader 'to beware of disparaging moral righteousness, and especially to beware of those who make it a point of religion to disparage it'.[58] The New Testament teaches us that all who honestly endeavour to live righteously, and who sincerely repent of their sins, shall gain their reward in heaven. Christ did not die for the elect alone; rather his mission was 'to save even the chief of sinners [I. Timothy 1.15], by turning them away from their iniquities' (a scenario which Burns humorously explores in the final stanza of 'Address to the Deil').[59]

Of the strictly theological writings which influenced Burns, two more deserve particular notice: John Taylor's *Scripture Doctrine of Original Sin*, and the works of John Goldie. Goldie in particular is a fascinating figure, a provincial intellectual of decidedly eclectic interests. A Kilmarnock wine merchant and acquaintance of Burns (he acted as a guarantor for the poet's Kilmarnock edition), Goldie was an inventor as well as an amateur theologian. His *Essays on Various Important Subjects, Moral and Divine*, popularly known as 'Goudie's Bible', was published in 1779. A five-volume work entitled *The Gospel Recovered from its Captive State* appeared in 1784, and in the following year this work was reissued in a six-volume set, the first

55 McGinty, II, 300.
56 For a comprehensive account of the McGill case, see McGinty, II, 299–359.
57 William McGill, *A Practical Essay on the Death of Jesus Christ, in Two Parts: Containing, I. The History, II. The Doctrine, of his Death* (Edinburgh, 1786), p. 276.
58 *Essay*, p. 285.
59 *Essay*, p. 453.

volume of which was a reprint of the *Essays*. The appearance of this new edition was the occasion of Burns's 'Epistle to John Goldie in Kilmarnock, Author of, The Gospel recovered' (K, 63).

The title page of Goldie's *Essays* carries an epigraph from Pope's *Essay on Man* (1733–34) –

> For Modes of Faith, let graceless zealots fight;
> His can't be wrong whose life is in the right.[60]

This adumbrates the central division that Goldie sets up, between an active, practical Christianity and a barren external orthodoxy. In a swipe at the 'graceless zealots', Goldie declares that his book is intended for

> all different denominations of Christians, that love the simplicity of the gospel, and desire to keep clear from the defilement of superstition, that is brought on by the doctrines, traditions, and commandments of fallible men.[61]

Here Goldie draws on the traditional Reformed principle of 'sola scriptura' – that the bible alone should be the basis of religion. One persistent metaphor, recurring obsessively throughout his work, encapsulates Goldie's distinction between true and false religion. This is the image of the stamped gold coin, by which Goldie signifies that true native worth needs no man-made stamp of approval to make it current:

> For I receive nothing barely, because of the image impressed thereupon, but only for the quality upon which the image is impressed; for there is nothing depends so much upon the king's stamp as bad or counterfeit metal, without which image it could not pass current; but that which is of a proper quality will pass as valid for full value, without any impression.
>
> In like manner, we ought to receive no doctrines, because they are said, by men, to have come from God, except they are of a proper quality, not contrary, but agreable to the nature and perfections of the Deity.[62]

This last principle – that true doctrines will be 'agreeable to the nature and perfections of the Deity' – is central to Goldie's exegetical method. When reading scripture, the individual believer ought to use the known character of God (his benevolence, his justness) as a touchstone. Only then will he know whether a given text is to be interpreted in a literal or a figurative sense. When the literal meaning of a text is found to be inconsistent with the attributes of God, then it is certain that the text should be interpreted figuratively.[63]

---

60 *The Poems of Alexander Pope*, ed. by John Butt (London, 1963), p. 535.
61 John Goldie, *Essays on Various Important Subjects, Moral and Divine: Being an Attempt to Distinguish True from False Religion* (Glasgow, 1779), p. 2.
62 *Essays*, p. 8. See also pp. 68–9, 84, 98.
63 *Essays*, pp. 16–17.

This is an exegetical principle which Goldie has apparently borrowed from John Taylor, the English Presbyterian clergyman whose works were exceptionally influential among the Scottish New Lights. In his *Scripture Doctrine of Original Sin* (1740), Taylor writes:

> For the scriptures can be no rule to us if the understanding God hath given us is not a Rule in judging their sense and meaning. Nothing ought to pass for divine Revelation which is inconsistent with any of the known Perfections of the divine nature.[64]

Both Taylor and Goldie maintain that the strict Calvinist doctrines of predestination and original sin are inconsistent with the goodness and benevolence of God. Therefore, the scriptural passages from which these doctrines are derived ought to be interpreted in a figural and not a literal sense. When a text's literal meaning is inconsistent with the character of God, then that text must be interpreted figuratively. (In fairness to Calvin, it should be noted that Calvin himself had been among the most influential critics of biblical literalism, arguing that scripture had been 'accommodated' to our imperfect human understandings and was not always to be taken literally.[65])

Burns follows Taylor and Goldie in regarding the doctrines of original sin and predestination as inconsistent with the character of 'an all-powerful and equally beneficent God' (*Letters*, II, 283). Moreover, like Taylor and Goldie, Burns's opposition to the strict Calvinist dogmas is related to his insistence on interpreting the bible according to his own lights: 'Still I am a very sincere believer in the Bible; but I am drawn by the conviction of a Man, not the halter of an Ass' (*Letters*, I, 349). For Burns and the New Lights, the Westminster Confession was just such a halter, and the attempts to compel assent to its tenets were a denial of Christian liberty. In the work of Goldie and Taylor, Burns encountered not just a benevolent, tolerant brand of Christianity, but a resolute commitment to the right of private judgement.

In a letter of 6 October 1790 to Mrs Dunlop, written in a flush of joyous optimism following a recent recovery from illness, Burns celebrates the life-giving properties of religious faith. Having praised the writings of the Rev. Samuel Bourn (whom Mrs Dunlop has been reading), Burns bursts out:

> – We can no more live without Religion, than we can live without air; but give me the Religion of Sentiment & Reason. – You know John Hildebroad's famous epitaph –

> > 'Here lies poor old John Hildebroad;
> > 'Have mercy on his soul, Lord God,
> > 'As he would do, were he Lord God,
> > 'And thou wert poor John Hildebroad.' –

64 John Taylor, *The Scripture Doctrine of Original Sin*, 2nd edn (London, 1741), p. 3, quoted in McGinty, II, 402–3.
65 *Institutes*, I, 121.

This speaks more to my heart, & has more of the genuine spirit of Religion in it, than is to be found in whole waggon-loads of Divinity. (*Letters*, II, 57)

This last section of the passage echoes Parson Yorick in *Tristram Shandy*:

I wish there was not a polemic divine, said Yorick, in the kingdom; – one ounce of practical divinity – is worth a painted ship-load of all their reverences have imported these fifty years.[66]

Burns had discovered Sterne's novel by 1781 – he later referred to the book as one of his 'bosom favorites' (*Letters*, I, 141) – and it is evident that imaginative literature, no less than the explicitly theological works we have so far been considering, helped to shape the poet's religious sensibility. In many ways, *Tristram Shandy* is as crucial a 'New Light' text for Burns as the essays of John Goldie, and we can imagine Burns's gratification on reading such passages as the incident of Corporal Trim's catechism in volume five. Suspecting that Trim is merely reeling off words he doesn't comprehend, Walter Shandy demands to know what Trim understands by 'honouring his father and mother'. Trim replies that he means allowing them 'three half-pence a day out of my pay, when they grow old':

– And didst thou do that, Trim? said Yorick. – He did indeed, replied my uncle Toby. – Then, Trim, said Yorick, springing out of his chair, and taking the corporal by the hand, thou art the best commentator upon that part of the Decalogue; and I honour thee more for it, Corporal Trim, than if thou hadst had a hand in the *Talmud* itself.[67]

Trim's practical application of the commandment provides a more authoritative and eloquent interpretation that any that could be offered by the scholars and divines.

Sterne's parable of 'practical divinity' illustrates the democratising tendency of New Light principles. Moral authority, no longer vested in trained commentators and biblical adepts, is the property of anyone who lives a virtuous life. Prizing practical benevolence and kindness above doctrinal orthodoxy, the New Lights argued that true 'Christian' virtues might be found, not just among all social classes, but among all varieties of people across the globe. Burns's lines from 'A Dedication to Gavin Hamilton Esq' (K, 103),

> Ye'll get the best o' moral works,
> 'Mang black *Gentoos*, and Pagan *Turks*,
> Or Hunters wild on *Ponotaxi*,
> Wha never heard of Orth—d—xy,   (ll. 41–44)

make a gesture which becomes familiar in the writings of those influenced by the

66 Laurence Sterne, *The Life and Opinions of Tristram Shandy, Gentleman*, ed. by
    Graham Petrie (Harmondsworth, 1967), p. 379.
67 *Tristram Shandy*, p. 385.

New Light; the portrayal of benevolent savages, pointedly depicted as more truly virtuous than some impeccably orthodox Christians. Of relevance in this connection is Dr John Moore's *Zeluco* (1786), and its depiction of a classic benevolent savage, Hanno the slave. An Edinburgh doctor and correspondent of Burns, John Moore was the recipient of the famous autobiographical letter. His *Zeluco* was highly regarded by the poet, who made a series of pencil annotations in his own copy of the novel. Moore writes to Burns on 29 March 1791:

> I remember you once hinted before, what you repeat in your last, that you had made some remarks on *Zeluco*, on the margin. I should be very glad to see them, and regret you did not send them before the last edition, which is just published. Pray transcribe them for me; I sincerely value your opinion very highly, and pray do not suppress one of those in which you *censure* the sentiment or expression. Trust me, it will break no squares between us - I am not akin to the Bishop of Grenada.[68]

Burns's annotated copy of the novel, now in the Thomas Cooper Library of the University of South Carolina, reveals that the account of Hanno the slave particularly interested the poet.

The story of Hanno, a West Indian slave working on Zeluco's plantation, appears in Chapter XV of Moore's novel. Having refused to undertake the whipping of a fellow slave who was falsely accused of wrongdoing, Hanno is himself beaten to death on the orders of Zeluco. When a good-natured soldier brings a priest to Hanno's death bed to administer the last rites, Hanno surprises them both with his magnanimous attitude towards his cruel master:

> 'Now,' said the soldier, when the ceremony was over, 'now, my honest fellow, you may bid the devil kiss your b—de, for you are as sure of heaven as your master is of hell; where, as this reverend father will assure you, he must suffer to all eternity.'
>
> 'I hope he will not suffer so long,' said Hanno, in a faint voice; and speaking for the first time since the arrival of the priest.
>
> 'Have a care of what you say, friend,' said the priest in a severe tone of voice; you must not doubt of the eternity of hell's torments. – If your master goes once there, he must remain for ever.'
>
> 'Then I'll be bound for him,' said the soldier, 'he is sure enough of going there.'
>
> 'But I hope in God he will not remain for ever,' said Hanno – and expired.[69]

This account of a heterodox benevolence which scandalises the priest and renders the rite an absurdity clearly appealed to Burns. In his own annotated copy of the

---

68 Currie, II, 350–51.
69 John Moore, *Zeluco: Various Views of Human Nature Taken From Life and Manners, Foreign and Domestic*, 2 vols (London, 1789), I, 130–131.

novel, Burns endorses the final page of the Hanno chapter with the words, 'A glorious story!'.[70]

It is hardly surprising that such works as *Zeluco* and *Tristram Shandy*, with their 'New Light' emphasis on practical morality over doctrinal orthodoxy, should have impressed Burns. Throughout his letters Burns registers his abhorrence of that religion which focuses barrenly on abstract points of doctrine. In a letter of January 1788 to Agnes McLehose, Burns writes: 'I hate the very idea of controversial divinity; as I firmly believe, that every honest, upright man, of whatever sect, will be accepted of the Deity' (*Letters*, I, 204). Writing to Alexander Cunningham in September 1792, Burns mocks 'the sightless soarings of SCHOOL DIVINITY' (*Letters*, II, 146). Finally, in a letter to Mrs Dunlop on New Year's Day 1795, Burns deistically celebrates the consoling power of faith, regardless of creed or denomination:

> I have nothing to say to any body, as, to which Sect they belong, or what Creed they believe; but I look on the Man who is firmly persuaded of Infinite Wisdom & Goodness superintending & directing every circumstance that can happen in his lot – I felicitate such a man as having a solid foundation for his mental enjoyment; a firm prop & sure stay, in the hour of difficulty, trouble & distress; & a never-failing anchor of hope, when he looks beyond the grave.
>
> (*Letters*, II, 333)

Burns's ideal believer uses his faith, not to mark himself off from the adherents of other creeds, but to fortify himself on the journey through life. Beyond commending this practical religiosity, there is, for Burns, 'nothing to say'.

However, while the New Lights downplayed dogma and condemned sectarian squabbling, it would be a mistake to conclude that they set no store by denominational differences. The very right of private judgement which the New Lights cherished was, in their eyes, associated with certain denominations more than with others. High Anglicanism and, above all, Roman Catholicism, were regarded by New Lights as authoritarian and hierarchical, while Presbyterian and Dissenting denominations – at least in principle – advocated a right of private judgement which was properly conducive to enlarged and tolerant views. Unthinking acquiescence in the views of the clergy, leading to an intolerant attitude towards those of other denominations, was associated particularly with Roman Catholicism. In Moore's *Zeluco*, for instance, it is a Roman Catholic Portuguese merchant who embodies blind acceptance of dogma and complete intolerance of other creeds:

> It had never occurred to his mind that there could be any doubt of the truth of those tenets in which his father and mother had instructed him, and which he heard venerable-looking men in sacred habits proclaim from all the pulpits of Lisbon. He was decidedly of opinion, that none but monsters of wickedness, who ought to be burnt in this world by way of preparing them for the next,

70 Moore, I, 132.

could harbour any doubt on such important points; he had indeed occasionally heard it hinted, that some of these doctrines were incomprehensible, and others contradictory; but this did not convey to his judgement any reason for doubting of their truth.[71]

Again, this is a passage that Burns has marked by asterisks in his copy. Moore's Portuguese merchant may stand alongside Sterne's Dr Slop, the Catholic bigot in *Tristram Shandy*, as an embodiment of Catholic shortcomings. Carol McGuirk has even suggested that Sterne's Dr Slop 'probably inspired Burns's frequent equation of Auld Licht Calvinism with Catholicism'.[72]

Insofar as Protestants were guilty of the same slavish obedience to clerical authorities and man-made confessions as were Catholics, then they were held to have betrayed the true principles of Reformed religion: namely, the primacy of scripture, and the right of private judgement. As we have seen, William McGill attacked his Old Light enemies by linking them with Catholicism. It is important to grasp the significance of this point. Although New Light Presbyterians advocated Catholic Relief, they remained unequivocally critical of Catholicism itself, regarding it as inherently authoritarian and superstitious. Even John Goldie, who parades his lack of denominational rancour, refers disparagingly to 'the Popish world' and deplores 'the degree of superstition [Catholics] possess, their saints and holidays being almost without number'.[73] Similarly, while Burns proudly declares his affection for individual Catholics – alluding to Bishop John Geddes, he informs Mrs Dunlop that 'the first [that is, finest] Cleric character I ever saw was a Roman Catholick' (*Letters*, I, 175) – he regularly expresses his distaste for Catholicism. Far from being incompatible with 'progressive' ideas, a suspicion of Catholicism (though not of individual Catholics) was in fact the *concomitant* of New Light liberalism.[74]

It is one of the central claims of this chapter that Burns's opposition to the Ayrshire Old Lights does not represent the poet's divorce from his Presbyterian environment. The principles which informed his attack on the Old Light were securely part of his Reformed inheritance: an emphasis on practical morality as opposed to what John Goldie calls 'the circumstantials of religion';[75] an understanding of God as benevolent and merciful; an emphasis on the competence of the layperson and on the right of private judgement in reaching an interpretation of God's word and creation; and an opposition to all church authorities insofar as they approach the 'tyranny' of Roman Catholicism. Burns's kirk satires represent a very Presbyterian phenomenon: the competent layman's attack on priestcraft. In the epistles to McMath and Goldie, Burns is participating in a tradition of

---

71 Moore, I, 212–213.

72 Robert Burns, *Selected Poems*, ed. by Carol McGuirk, pp. 201–2.

73 *Essays*, p. 51.

74 Marianne Elliott, *Watchmen in Sion: The Protestant Idea of Liberty* (Derry, 1985), p. 9; McBride, *Scripture Politics*, p. 2.

75 *Essays*, p. 51.

anticlericalism (or 'priest-skelping' as he calls it) which has deep roots in Presbyterian culture, particularly in Burns's own part of Scotland. The twin dynamics of the religious satires – the opposition to priestcraft and the critique of empty formalism – locate Burns very firmly within a Reformed Protestant context.

Burns, of course, was keenly aware of the historical resonance of his attack on the rigidly righteous. As a young man holding court between sermons in Tarbolton, impugning Old Light shibboleths in a kirkyard corner or a grubby tavern, he felt himself to be participating in the great historical struggle against priestcraft. This was a struggle, after all, in which his county – that 'country where civil, and particularly religious liberty have ever found their first support, and their last asylum' – had played no petty part.[76] But Burns's own most telling contribution would come with the great kirk satires.

76 *Reliques of Robert Burns*, ed. by R. H. Cromek (London, 1808), p. 344.

CHAPTER SIX

'Priest-Skelping Turns': The Kirk Satires

Writing to Alexander Cunningham on 27 July 1788, in the facetious vein which he often adopts with that correspondent, Burns describes as follows his plans for his eldest son:

> By the bye, I intend breeding him up for the Church; and from an innate dexterity in secret Mischief which he posses [*sic*], & a certain hypocritical gravity as he looks on the consequences, I have no small hopes of him in the sacerdotal line.
>   (*Letters*, I, 299)

In this humorous aside, Burns is making one of his most characteristic rhetorical gestures – the mocking and demystifying of the clerical office. The remark to Cunningham recalls a series of similar moments in Burns's work: the image of Death driving a cargo of clergymen to hell in 'Lines Addressed to Mr. John Ranken' (K, 48), for instance, or the mock astonishment with which the speaker of 'Death and Dr Hornbook' (K, 55) reveals that 'Ev'n Ministers' have been known to tell a 'rousing whid'. Behind the humour of such moments lies an entrenched and well-defined intellectual position. This is the perennial Protestant jealousy of clerical aggrandisement, the principled revulsion from the bondage of 'priest-craft'. The notion that the clergyman – or indeed the kirk elder – is a man like any other, and must be kept in his place, is a constant preoccupation of Burns's religious satires.

The satirical bravado of Burns's 'priest-skelping' poems, however, is in short supply in his earliest religious works. During the winter of 1781–2, while temporarily resident at Irvine, Burns composed a series of pious and somewhat po-faced religious poems, which sit rather uneasily with the angry turbulence of his later religious satires. They include 'Winter, A Dirge', 'A Prayer, in the Prospect of Death', 'Stanzas on the same Occasion', 'A Prayer, under the Pressure of violent Anguish', 'The First Psalm' and 'The *First Six Verses* of the Ninetieth Psalm'. These poems were written during a period of personal crisis for Burns. He had gone to Irvine to set up as a flax-dresser, but the venture had collapsed ignominiously, leaving the poet 'not worth sixpence' (*Letters*, I, 142). Coming at a time when his father's health was deteriorating ominously and the family was plagued with debt, the failure of Burns's business venture filled the poet with a keen sense of his own worthlessness. In his First Commonplace Book, Burns recalls the mood of the period:

There was a certain period in my life that my spirit was broke by repeated losses and disasters, which threatened, and indeed effected the utter ruin of my fortune. My body too was attacked by that most dreadful distemper, a Hypochondria, or confirmed Melancholy . . . [1]

Burns's response to these 'losses and disasters' seems to have been a gloomy conviction that he was being justly punished for a corrupt, vicious nature. The speaker in the poems from the Irvine period regards his sufferings as divinely ordained. 'But he whose blossom buds in guilt / Shall to the ground be cast' (ll. 13–14): the uncompromising message of 'The First Psalm' (K, 19) is endorsed by the speaker of 'Winter, A Dirge' (K, 10), who humbly addresses the 'POW'R SUPREME, whose mighty Scheme, / These *woes* of mine fulfil' (ll. 17–18). Such suffering at the hands of 'an angry GOD' ('Stanzas on the same Occasion' (K, 14)) is the natural condition of sinning humanity, destined to endure 'Life's *joyless* day' ('To Ruin' (K, 12)). The Weltschmertz which pervades these poems is partly a response to personal disappointments, but it also has deep roots in Protestant culture. Like the Covenanting writers who expressed their eagerness to be 'off the stage', Burns uses theatrical metaphors – 'this scene of care', 'this earthly scene' – to suggest the hollow insubstantiality of existence, the transient drama of human sorrow. It is only the terror of hell that stops the speaker embracing the deliverance of death. 'A Prayer, in the Prospect of Death' (K, 13) tentatively raises the prospect of divine forgiveness, but in 'Stanzas on the same Occasion', the speaker is once more smarting beneath God's 'sin-avenging rod' (l. 9). Even here, however, the speaker acknowledges the justice of his fate, and proclaims the inveteracy of his sinfulness. Were he spared now, he would merely commit more sins:

> Fain would I say, 'Forgive my foul offence!'
>   Fain promise never more to disobey;
> But, should my Author health again dispense,
>   Again I might desert fair Virtue's way;
> Again in Folly's path might go astray;
>   Again exalt the brute and sink the man;
> Then how should I for Heavenly Mercy pray,
>   Who act so counter Heavenly Mercy's plan?
> Who sin so oft have mourn'd, yet to temptation ran?
>
> (ll. 10–18)

For such an early work – the poem probably dates from 1781–2 – these are remarkably accomplished lines. The measured cadences of the Spenserian stanza (used by Burns for the first time here), along with the alternating, masculine rhymes of the first four lines, help to create that tone of balanced, even clinical self-assessment that Burns is seeking to convey. The emphatic triple tolling of 'Again' at the start of lines 4, 5 and 6 signals the recurrence of the speaker's moral lapses while

1 Kinsley, III, 1014.

marking his own exasperation at his sinfulness. The disjunction between 'Heavenly Mercy pray' and 'Heavenly Mercy's plan' points up the distance which separates the speaker's spiritual condition from that required by God, while suggesting his desire to make the two converge.

However, while guilt and resignation are the keynotes of the Irvine poems, even in these early self-mortifying pieces a bristling, defensive belligerence, a desire to challenge the complacency of the pious, begins to assert itself. Keenly alive to his own sinfulness, Burns comes to resent those who would veil their own shortcomings. Increasingly, his critical gaze turns outwards, and dismay at his own frailty is replaced by disgust at the duplicity of others. As early as 1777, in 'A Penitential thought, in the hour of Remorse' (K, 5), the teenage Burns had attacked the hard-heartedness of the 'Seeming good', those who 'think [it] sin to pity' the 'poor, despis'd, abandon'd vagabonds' (ll. 10–11). Now, from around 1784 onwards, he conducts a series of satirical attacks on religious hypocrisy and 'seeming' goodness.

This transition, from pious lamentation to caustic satire, requires some comment, and it may be useful to turn briefly to a group of songs which Burns composed at around the same time as the Irvine poems. 'Though fickle Fortune has deceiv'd me' (K, 16), 'My father was a farmer' (K, 21), and 'Fragment (Altho my bed were in yon muir)' (K, 22) are spirited lyrics from the perspective of an impoverished countryman. Far from being the manifestation of divine displeasure, the speaker's poverty in these works is ascribed to the whims of 'fickle Fortune'. And instead of resignation, his attitude is one of Stoic indifference to Fortune's favours: 'I do not much regard her. O' ('My father was a farmer'). As in the early 'Song (Behind yon hills where Lugar flows)' (K, 4) and 'Song (Tibby I hae seen the day)' (K, 6), the speaker hymns the pleasures to be had with an honest country lass, and thumbs his nose at those girls who deem a ploughboy beneath their notice.

These songs written in defiance of 'fickle Fortune' and in contempt of haughty young women help to account for the transition from piety to satire in Burns's religious poetry. Burns comes to regard the hauteur and arrogance of the ultra-orthodox churchgoers, those who are unshakeably assured of their own salvation, in the same light as he views the snobbery of the rich farmers' daughters. In both cases, Burns perceived an outward propriety masking those natural carnal desires, those 'headlong, furious passions' which he was ready to acknowledge in himself. It is no coincidence that Burns's first kirk satire involves an attack on both religious sanctimony and sexual hypocrisy.

'Address to the Unco Guid, or the Rigidly Righteous' (K, 39) was probably written in 1784. The 'Unco Guid' whom Burns addresses are the Presbyterian Pharisees of late eighteenth-century Ayrshire, those who make virtue consist in conspicuous devotion and external regularity of conduct. Burns's contempt for them is evident from the opening verse, with its mock deferential awe, its sarcastic lingering on 'pious' and 'holy':

> O YE wha are sae guid yoursel,
>   Sae pious and sae holy,
> Ye've nought to do but mark and tell
>   Your Neebours' fauts and folly!
> Whase life is like a weel-gaun mill,
>   Supply'd wi' store o' water,
> The heaped happer 's ebbing still,
>   And still the clap plays clatter.   (ll. 1–8)

The relished broadness of speech, the long drawled vowels – 'sae guid yoursel' – and scornful sibilants, flout the fastidious regularity of the Unco Guid. The image of the 'weel-gaun mill' encapsulates Burns's quarrel with the Unco Guid: what they take to be genuine righteousness is merely a mechanical regularity, the living stream of impulse artificially dammed and channelled. All this is a far cry from 'Stanzas on the same Occasion', in which the speaker, discussing his 'headlong, furious passions', regretted his inability 'To rule their torrent in th' allowed line'. Now, it seems, such regulation is to be despised as the cowardly thwarting of natural passions.

Set against this coterie of douce rule-observers, the speaker of 'Address to the Unco Guid' represents sinning humanity. He does so, not just in the sense of typifying, but also in a narrower, legal sense, in that he undertakes to 'propone defences' (l. 14) for mankind, to act as 'counsel for poor mortals' (l. 10), before the self-appointed tribunal of the Unco Guid. The case for 'poor mortals' rests on the significance of those external observances by which the pious set so much store: their conspicuous religiosity, their professed orthodoxy, their ostentatious abstention from irregular pleasures or 'Debauchery and Drinking' (l. 36). Against this legalistic emphasis on outward forms of behaviour, the poem insists on the primacy of internal motive. Like Francis Hutcheson, Burns insists that an act of true virtue involves a benevolent motive or intention.[2] Paradoxically, given his stated objections to Calvinist soteriology, Burns values the inner spiritual condition over mechanical 'good works'. The Unco Guid may be outwardly regular and disciplined, but how can one tell what is in their hearts? Their continence may be founded on any number of spurious motives. It may be prompted by spiritual vanity, 'That purity ye pride in' (l. 22). It may have its source in worldly prudence; the desire to avoid, not damnation proper, but 'D—mnation of expences!' (l. 40). Or, in the case of sexual abstemiousness, it may be the enforced consequence of a want of allure:

> Ye high, exalted, virtuous Dames,
>   Ty'd up in godly laces,
> Before ye gie poor *Frailty* names,
>   Suppose a change o' cases;
> A dear-lov'd lad, convenience snug,
>   A treacherous inclination –

---

2 See *An Inquiry into the Original of our Ideas of Beauty and Virtue*, pp. 107–9, 150.

> But, let me whisper i' your lug,
> Ye're aiblins nae temptation. (ll. 41–48)

The chasteness of these women – 'Ty'd up in godly laces' – may indeed go no deeper than their gaudily modest attire. And this imagery of restriction – 'Ty'd up' – looks back not just to the image of the mill in stanza one or the 'castigated pulse' (l. 25) of stanza four; it also points forward to the imagery of impeded blood-flow in the epistles, associating the Unco Guid with those described in the epistle 'To J. Smith' as being 'tideless-blooded', whose 'hearts are just a standing pool'.

Taken in itself, the poem suggests, bodily mortification deserves neither praise nor censure; what determines its value is the motive, the inner condition of the heart. In arguing thus, Burns is echoing Hutcheson and the moral sense philosophers; but he is also renovating a typically Calvinist principle. In the *Institutes*, Calvin inveighs against superstitious abstemiousness, as in the practice of fasting:

> God does not greatly esteem fasting of itself, unless an inner emotion of the heart is present, and true displeasure at one's sin, true humility, and true sorrowing arising from the fear of God. Indeed, fasting is not otherwise useful than when it is joined as a lesser help to these. For God abominates nothing more than when men try to disguise themselves by displaying signs and outward appearances in place of innocence of heart. Therefore, Isaiah very severely inveighs against the Jews' hypocrisy in thinking they were satisfying God when they had only fasted, whatever impiety and impure thoughts they harboured in their hearts. 'Is this the fast that the Lord has chosen?' [Isa. 58. 5–6, conflated], and what follows. Hypocritical fasting, then, is not only a useless and superfluous weariness but the greatest abomination.[3]

It is out of the same opposition to formalism that Calvin goes on to deplore 'the too superstitious admiration of celibacy' and 'immoderate affection for virginity'.[4] He appears, indeed, to share Burns's attitude to 'high, exalted, virtuous dames'. Far from 'throwing aside the conventional teaching of Calvinism'[5] in this poem, Burns is echoing Calvin's view of self-mortification as an unhealthy constriction of natural impulse. That is, Burns's anti-formalism, his 'New Light' emphasis on 'the Religion of the Bosom', is a renovation of Reformed Protestant principles in opposition to the authoritarianism and formalism of the Old Light. To this extent, there is substance to A. B. Jamieson's remark that 'Burns often came nearer to true Calvinism ... than ever the Auld Lights did'.[6] For Burns, as for St Paul, the mechanical observance of rules is the 'ministration of death'.

At the beginning of the 'Address to the Unco Guid', the speaker appears to accept the legalistic outlook of his adversaries. He treats the Unco Guid as competent judge

3 *Institutes*, II, 1245.
4 *Institutes*, II, 1252–1253.
5 Keith, p. 106.
6 Jamieson, pp. 47–48.

and jury: he directs them to certain pieces of evidence, invites them to make comparisons and meets anticipated objections, all in the manner of a skilful advocate. Indeed, the poem is an adept piece of judicial rhetoric. The legalistic paradigm, however, is gradually undermined. Throughout the poem, terms of conditionality – 'would', 'suppose', 'aiblins' – suggest the vulnerability of the premise on which the Unco Guid rely – namely, that it is possible to reach decisive judgement of others. In this way, Burns undermines the competence of the jury. The comprehensive knowledge which permits decisive judgement is available only to God; he alone can judge conclusively, can judge the motive and not merely the action:

> Who made the heart, 'tis *He* alone
>   Decidedly can try us,
> He knows each chord its various tone,
>   Each spring its various bias:
> Then at the balance let 's be mute,
>   We never can adjust it;
> What 's *done* we partly may compute,
>   But know not what 's *resisted*.   (ll. 57–64)

What Burns insists on in this last verse is the irreducible otherness of the individual. We cannot view another's experience from the inside. We must acknowledge the primacy of conscience in others, and not seek to judge them by their obedience to the law. Accordingly, the poem concludes on an appeal for tolerance, but this appeal is launched, not from the perspective of 'enlightened' rationalism, but from the perspective of a deep-rooted antinomian opposition to legalism, a Pauline exaltation of spirit over letter.

    Though 'Address to the Unco Guid' maintains the earnest tone of Burns's early religious poems, its use of vernacular Scots for purposes of satirical reduction points forward to the more openly burlesque strategies of later ecclesiastical poems. The 'Epistle to J. Rankine, Enclosing some Poems' (K, 47) was written in late 1784, but it marks a departure. The tone is different. The poetry has shifted gear, from the measured, almost ponderous public accents of 'Address to the Unco Guid', to a pacier, defter, more intimate and slippery form of address. And the strategy is different too. There is no attempt to vindicate a point of view in front of a hostile jury. Burns no longer bothers to engage the Unco Guid intellectually. The contemptible, risible nature of the 'saunts' is simply assumed in a discourse directed knowingly to a friend and fellow roaring boy, John Rankine. As we might expect in an epistle despatched from one indicted fornicator to another, the tone is cocksure, in all senses of the word:

> O ROUGH, rude, ready-witted Rankine,
> The wale o' cocks for fun an' drinkin!
> There 's monie godly folks are thinkin,
>   Your *dreams* an' tricks
> Will send you, Korah-like, a sinkin,
>   Straught to auld Nick's.   (ll. 1–6)

The prospect of damnation is no longer cause for anguished reflection (as it was in the early religious poems), but merely the cue for a wisecrack.

After its joshing first stanza, the poem modulates into the burlesque mode which would become such a trademark feature of Burns's religious poems. This is the first appearance of the burlesque in Burns, but already the poet's handling is wonderfully assured, as he pretends to berate Rankine for poking fun at clergymen and elders:

> Hypocrisy, in mercy spare it!
> That *holy robe*, O dinna tear it!
> Spare 't for their sakes wha aften wear it,
>   The lads in *black*;
> But your curst wit, when it comes near it,
>   Rives 't aff their back.
>
> Think, wicked Sinner, wha ye're skaithing:
> It's just the *Blue-gown* badge an' claithing,
> O' Saunts; tak that, ye lea'e them naething,
>   To ken them by,
> Frae ony unregenerate Heathen,
>   Like you or I.   (ll. 13–24)

The emphatic last four syllables resonate beyond the burlesque sentence of which they are part. Beneath the holy robes of dissimulation, the pious have the same desires and passions as everyone else: 'Like you or I', they are men of flesh and blood. In the very next stanza, Burns abruptly drops the burlesque mode and resumes his direct address to Rankine, discussing the poems which he has enclosed with the epistle:

> I've sent you here, some rhymin ware,
> A' that I bargained for, an' mair . . .   (ll. 25–6)

The effect is devastating. Having roasted the 'saunts' in two virtuoso stanzas, Burns then drops them without a word, turning to more important matters. The remaining nine stanzas of the poem are given over to an extended allegory of Burns's own fornication summons, with some cursory lampooning of the kirk session as a '*Poacher-Court*' (l. 47). The allegory is humorous enough and conducted with some spirit, and it is continually surprising to recall that this highly risqué work made it into the final pages of Burns's Kilmarnock volume. (The fact that Hugh Blair stupidly failed to interpret the allegory doesn't diminish the audacity of this inclusion.) However, the real power of the poem lies, not in the bawdy allegory, but in the distillate of rancour found in the twelve brilliant lines of burlesque.

The burlesque mode is one which Burns exploited in several of his kirk satires – most prominently in 'The Holy Tulzie', 'Holy Willie's Prayer' and 'The Ordination' – but I want now to turn to one of the less familiar 'kirk epistles', 'To W. Simpson, Ochiltree' (K, 59). Where the epistle to Rankine delivers a snub to the Old Lights in its very structure, despatching them in a brusque two stanzas, the epistle to

Simpson goes one stage further. Here the discussion of ecclesiastical matters is relegated to a Postscript. It is only after the main business of the poem is over – after the fraternal greetings have been made, and an extensive discourse on Scottish poetry completed – that the distasteful subject of kirk politics is reluctantly broached. Simpson has asked Burns to give a definition of the term 'New Light':

> My memory 's no worth a preen;
> I had amaist forgotten clean,
> Ye bad me write you what they mean
>   By this *new-light*,
> 'Bout which our *herds* sae aft hae been
>   Maist like to fight.   (ll. 109–114)

In a footnote to this stanza, Burns defines New Light as 'A cant-term for those religious opinions, which Dr TAYLOR of Norwich has defended so strenuously'. As this would indicate, Burns tends to understand the New Light as a body of opinion, or even as an intellectual orientation, and not primarily as an organised church party.

Burns's Postscript allegorises the development of the religious conflict in the Scottish kirk as a dispute between rival astronomical theories. Originally, the Postscript argues, everyone accepted the traditional view that the moon is regularly replaced by a new one as it gradually wears out:

> In thae auld times, they thought the *Moon*,
> Just like a sark, or pair o' shoon,
> Woor by degrees, till her last roon
>   Gaed past their viewin,
> An' shortly after she was done
>   They gat a new ane.   (ll. 121–26)

Later, however, a group of New Lights appeared, who maintained that the moon is in fact orbiting the earth. The outraged Old Lights sought to vindicate the orthodox viewpoint by force and persecution, until the lairds obliged them to desist:

> This game was play'd in monie lands,
> An' *auld-light* caddies bure sic hands,
> That faith, the *youngsters* took the sands
>   Wi' nimble shanks,
> Till *Lairds* forbad, by strict commands,
>   Sic bluidy pranks.   (ll. 151–56)

Now there are triumphant New Lights 'amaist on ev'ry *knowe*' (l. 159), while the disgruntled Old Lights are left to plot their next move. The allegory ends with a pitiful vision of the Old Lights planning a balloon flight to the moon, in an attempt to vindicate their exploded theories.

Burns's allegory presents the dispute between Old Lights and New as centring on the right of private judgement. The Old Lights are associated with unthinking acceptance of received truths – 'It ne'er cam i' their heads to doubt it' (l. 128) – while the New Lights, 'weel learn'd upo' the beuk' (l. 133), are associated with the virtues of scholarship and scientific learning; freedom of rational enquiry confronts the authoritarian defence of received opinion. This is a confrontation which Burns sets up throughout his writings on religion. Burns regularly asserts the need 'to join FAITH and SENSE' ('The Kirk's Alarm' (K, 264)), to subject the tenets of faith to the reason of the individual believer; and he habitually casts the New Lights as the champions of truth and free enquiry.

The dispute between Old Lights and New is viewed by Burns as part of an international struggle ('This game was played in monie lands') between traditional, immemorial beliefs and the insights of a new rationalism; a struggle which was decisively won by the progressive forces. This Postscript, then, casts doubt on Burns's habitual depiction of the New Light as a persecuted minority of fearless *philosophes*. As his allegory indicates, the days when the Old Lights could enforce orthodoxy with hangings (as in the execution of Thomas Aikenhead, the Edinburgh student hanged for blasphemy in 1697), are long gone; the New Lights, safely in the ascendant, can now afford to be 'quite barefac'd' (l. 162) in espousing their beliefs.

But the astronomy allegory serves more than one purpose. As well as allowing Burns to imply that New Light and Old Light beliefs carry different degrees of rational persuasiveness, the astronomy conceit also suggests there is an arcane, esoteric quality to the whole dispute. In the final stanza of the Postscript, Burns decides that both Old and New Lights are engaged in a futile struggle over indifferent matters, and holds himself aloof from the whole sorry spectacle:

> Sae, ye observe that a' this clatter
> Is naething but a 'moonshine matter;'
> But tho' dull *prose-folk* Latin splatter
> > In logic tulzie,
> I hope we, *Bardies*, ken some better
> > Than mind sic brulzie.   (ll. 181–86)

In the first half of the epistle, Burns had celebrated the pleasures of artistic composition and poetic camaraderie, against the sterile money-grubbing of the 'warly race' who 'drudge an' drive' for riches. Here he once again presents poetry as a disinterested, spiritual activity far removed from the sterile wrangling of theological disputants. As Chambers and Wallace remark, Burns fought for the New Lights 'as opponents of orthodoxy, rather than as the advocates of a rival and equally dogmatic theology'.[7] In so far as the dispute between New Lights and Old centred on abstruse points of dogma, Burns was scornful of both sides. Indeed, one of the keynotes of Burns's kirk satires is the attack on dogmatic, formalistic religion, from whatever theological source. In the kirk satires, a New Testament religion

---

7 *The Life and Works of Robert Burns*, ed. by Robert Chambers, rev. by William Wallace, 4 vols (Edinburgh, 1896), I, 168.

founded on impulse and conscience – what Burns calls 'the Religion of the bosom' (*Letters*, I, 204) – confronts an authoritarian, almost Talmudic emphasis on formal observances – what we might label 'the Religion of the law'.

In a letter to John Ballantine dated January 1787, Burns gently satirises his pious Edinburgh landlady for her formalistic approach to the practical duties of the Christian; according to Burns, his landlady 'vigorously and perseveringly practices some of the most distinguishing Christian virtues, such as, attending Church, railing against vice, &c' (*Letters*, I, 83). It is this external, ossified Christianity that, in a more censorious fashion, Burns attacks in his kirk satires. Nowhere is Burns's impatience with the dead letter of form and ceremony more explosively vented than in the poem whose official title is 'A Poet's Welcome to his love-begotten Daughter; the first instance that entitled him to the venerable appellation of Father' (K, 60), but which also appears, in the Rosenbach MS, as 'The Poet's Welcome to his Bastart Wean'.

This poem is Burns's pledge to his illegitimate daughter that the irregular circumstances of her birth shall not affect his love for her. His daughter shall be as well clothed, fed and educated 'As any brat o' Wedlock's bed' (l. 35) in her own social class. The poet shall never cavil or demur at acknowledging his fatherhood but shall 'brag the name o't' (l. 48). The poem is offered in lieu of a birth certificate; it is a personal guarantee that the girl will be looked after and acknowledged as the poet's responsibility. The tone is one of mingled tenderness and defiance:

> Wee image o' my bonie Betty,
> As fatherly I kiss and daut thee,
> As dear and near my heart I set thee,
>   Wi' as gude will,
> As a' the Priests had seen me get thee
>   That 's out o' h—.   (ll. 19–24)

Here Burns skilfully exploits the incremental momentum of the Habbie stanza to suggest mounting emotion, the modulation from tenderness into resentful aggression. These last two lines, turning the searchlight of moral scrutiny onto those who would wield it, form a masterstroke of oblique contempt.

But for all that Burns's noble defiance in this poem is directed against 'Kirk and Queir' (l. 16), his insouciant approach to ceremony has a very Presbyterian ring. Burns's reluctance to place great significance on form and ceremony was in fact shared to a large extent by the Presbyterian Church – for instance, in the case of the marriage ceremony. Currie notes the laxity of the Church of Scotland's law respecting marriage,

> the validity of which requires neither the ceremonies of the church, nor any other ceremonies, but simply the deliberate acknowledgement of each other as husband and wife, made by the parties before witnesses, or in any other way that gives legal evidence of such an acknowledgement having taken place . . .

Marriages conducted in Scotland without the ceremonies of the church, are considered as *irregular*, and the parties usually submit to a *rebuke* for their conduct in the face of their respective congregations, which is not however necessary to render the marriage valid.[8]

The church itself attached little mystique to the form or ceremony of marriage. There is in fact no great ideological distance – though there is a vast difference in tone – between the kirk's position and Burns's own assessment of the ceremony of matrimony, whimsically expressed in his Shandyean letter to John Arnot in April 1786:

> Still, Sir, I had long had a wishing eye to that inestimable blessing, a wife. – My mouth watered deliciously, to see a young fellow, after a few idle, common-place stories from a gentleman in black, strip & go to bed with a young girl, & no one durst say black was his eye; while I, for just doing the same thing, only wanting that [insignificant (*deleted*)] ceremony, am made a Sunday's laughing stock, & abused like a pick-pocket.   (*Letters*, I, 35)

Like Burns, the kirk viewed the actual ceremony as a matter of no great moment, so long as the two parties acknowleged their mutual commitment. If the kirk was famously severe in its sanctions against sexual 'incontinence', this was counter-balanced, as Currie observes, by the laxity of its marriage law.

However, if Burns was often vehement in his opposition to religious ceremony and show, he was not always consistent. There is an entry in the *Journal of the Highland Tour* in which the poet inveighs against the spartan atmosphere of Presbyterian worship:

> What a poor, pimping business is a Presbyterian place of worship, dirty, narrow and squalid, stuck in a corner of old Popish grandeur such as Linlithgow and, much more, Melrose! Ceremony and show, if judiciously thrown in, absolutely necessary for the bulk of mankind, both in religious and civil matters.[9]

This statement sits ill with the outright rejection of religious ceremony in 'Address to the Unco Guid', 'The Cotter's Saturday Night', or 'The Poet's Welcome' (and indeed with the scorn of 'civil' pomp in such songs as 'Is there for honest Poverty'). However, it is important to bear in mind the generic context of this remark. Burns is writing a tour journal, and endeavouring to play the part of the sophisticated, genteel traveller. Ceremony is necessary, we note, not for Burns himself, but simply to keep the groundlings amused. We can be sure that Burns did not deem himself, in this context, one of 'the bulk of mankind'.

Nor was the man to whom Burns addressed his next kirk satire to be classed among the unthinking mass of mankind. The 'Epistle to John Goldie in Kilmarnock, Author of, The Gospel recovered' (K, 63) is one of the strongest of

---

8 Currie, I, 21.
9 *Robert Burns's Tours of the Highlands and Stirlingshire 1787*, ed. by Raymond Lamont Brown (Ipswich, 1973), p. 17.

Burns's ecclesiastical epistles. Written to show solidarity with a fellow freethinker as a new edition of his writings is published, the poem hails Goldie as the scourge of the hypocrites. A series of vivid personifications in the first four stanzas depicts Goldie vanquishing Bigotry, Superstition, Orthodoxy and – that Enlightenment bugbear – Enthusiasm:

> Enthusiasm 's past redemption,
> Gane in a gallopin consumption:
> Not a' her quacks wi' a' their gumption
>   Can ever mend her;
> Her feeble pulse gies strong presumption,
>   She'll soon surrender.   (ll. 13–18)

The 'blame' for the rout of the Old Light forces is laid squarely with Goldie and John Taylor, on account of their writings:

> It's you and Taylor are the chief
> To blame for a' this black mischief;
> But could the L—d's ain folk get leave,
>   A toom tar-barrel
> And twa red peats wad bring relief
>   And end the quarrel.   (ll. 25–30)

As is usual in the epistles, Burns operates as a motivator, boosting his correspondent's morale, urging him to keep the faith, egging him on to greater exertions:

> E'en swinge the dogs; and thresh them sicker!
> The mair they squeel ay chap the thicker;
> And still 'mang hands a hearty bicker
>   O' something stout;
> It gars an Owther's pulse beat quicker,
>   And helps his wit.   (ll. 37–42)

Burns recommends that Goldie take a good swig of alcohol to help with his compositions. This injunction ties in with the familiar celebration of unpremeditated, spontaneous composition in the epistles, but in this case it has an added propriety in that Goldie is not only an author but a wine merchant. As with most of Burns's epistles, the poem comes to a rather cursory close, in this case with two stanzas reiterating the inspirational properties of alcohol.

The epistle to Goldie dates from August 1785. The very next month Burns sent an epistle to another local champion of religious freedom, the Rev. John McMath of Tarbolton. A Moderate minister at Tarbolton, McMath was assistant (and later successor) to Dr Wodrow, and figures as an object of dread to the Old Light speaker in 'The Holy Tulzie' (K, 52):

> Auld Wodrow lang had wrought mischief,
> We trusted death wad bring relief;
> But he has gotten, to our grief,
>   Ane to succeed him;
> A chap will soundly buff our beef
>   I meikle dread him.   (ll. 73–78)

McMath was another member of that fraternity of liberal thinkers whom Burns sought to bind together in his network of familiar epistles.

'To the Rev. John M'Math, Inclosing a copy of Holy Willie's Prayer, which he had requested' (K, 68) divides, both linguistically and thematically, into two main sections. In the first section (the opening six stanzas), Burns conducts a vigorous, satirical attack on the Old Light party, using a heavily Scotticised register. In the second section (the remaining ten stanzas), the poem turns from satire to earnest declaration, as Burns expounds his religious beliefs in a series of apostrophes – to Pope, to Religion, to Ayr, to McMath himself. This section is in a lightly Scotticised English, Burns's favoured register for public declamation.

Like many of Burns's epistles, the poem opens with a brilliantly vivid scene-setting stanza:

> WHILE at the stook the shearers cow'r
> To shun the bitter blaudin' show'r,
> Or in gulravage rinnin scow'r
>   To pass the time,
> To you I dedicate the hour
>   In idle rhyme.   (ll. 1–6)

Here, as in the second epistle to Lapraik, the poem is placed against a background of agricultural labour. The poet is writing during an unforeseen break in harvesting occasioned by the onset of rain. Accordingly, as is usual in Burns's epistles, there is the suggestion of unpremeditated, spontaneous composition. This first stanza also points up Burns's apartness from the rest of the labouring community. While the others shelter behind stooks or indulge in horseplay, Burns uses the time to produce a poem. This implies that Burns is something above the common run of farm workers, and a fit correspondent for a minister. On a more impressionistic level, the first stanza sets up a tension between violent intensity – the 'bitter blaudin' show'r' before which the shearers 'cow'r' – and airy, light-hearted recreation or 'gulravage'. This tension is illuminating. Our horizon of expectation, as readers of a Scots epistle, includes the geniality and inconsequential knockabout fun suggested by 'gulravage'; we are not prepared for what Burns in fact gives us, namely, a 'bitter blaudin' show'r' of invective against the Old Lights.

Having alluded to his earlier kirk satires, Burns feigns anxiety lest the Old Lights should loose their 'holy thunder' (l. 11) on him. Then, as if to illustrate just how seriously he takes the threats of the kirk, Burns gives gleeful expression to a seemingly uncontainable torrent of contempt:

> But I gae mad at their grimaces,
> Their sighan, cantan, grace-prood faces,
> Their three-mile prayers, an' hauf-mile graces,
>   Their raxan conscience,
> Whase greed, revenge, an' pride disgraces
>   Waur nor their nonsense.   (ll. 19–24)

Once again, Burns's ire is directed against formalism, against those who use ostentatious devotion in place of righteousness of heart, who only 'take religion in their mouth' (l. 55). The Old Light use 'gospel colors' (l. 47) and 'zeal for gospel laws' (l. 53) as a 'screen' (l. 48) for their 'malice' (l. 57), as is seen in their vindictive and unChristian treatment of Gavin Hamilton, '*Gaun*, miska't waur than a beast' (l. 25). In true libertarian Protestant vein, Burns chides the Old Lights for their almost popish reliance on external ceremony ('three-mile prayers'), recalling John Goldie's attack on those who 'will conform to any outward ceremonies . . . but not to the rules of virtue, as required of us by God'.[10]

Although the poem is addressed to a minister, Burns attacks the trickery of the clerical class. He makes no attempt to dampen the fire of his anticlericalism, wishing for the satirical skill of Pope, the better to expose the chicanery of the Old Light clergy:

> O Pope, had I thy satire's darts
> To gie the rascals their deserts,
> I'd rip their rotten, hollow hearts,
>   An' tell aloud
> Their jugglin' hocus pocus arts
>   To cheat the crowd.   (ll. 37–42)

Again, this echoes John Goldie, who had compared the Devil to a priest on account of his 'masterly abilities . . . to deceive the world'.[11] Burns's reference to crowd-pleasing tricks also anticipates the image of the preacher as mountebank in 'Love and Liberty' (K, 84):

> Observ'd ye yon reverend lad
>   Mak faces to tickle the Mob;
> He rails at our mountebank squad.
>   Its rivalship just i' the job.

This is a classic Protestant image, a venerable staple of anticlerical propaganda. Burns here takes up the classic position of the Protestant layman: he is the unmasker, the gaff-blower, keen to bear active witness ('tell aloud') against the ploys of the clergy. At moments like these, Burns comes close to endorsing the view of organised religion as 'the trick of the crafty FEW, to lead the undiscerning MANY' (*Letters*, II, 283).

---

10 *Essays*, p. 56.
11 *Essays*, p. 82.

Having berated the Old Lights largely in vernacular Scots, Burns turns to a formal, lightly Scotticised English when he apostrophises true religion – 'All hail, Religion! maid divine!' (l. 61), and dedicates himself to her service:

> With trembling voice I tune my strain
> To join with those,
> Who boldly dare thy cause maintain
> In spite of foes. (ll. 69–72)

Earlier, Burns had belittled the threat of the Old Lights and their impotent 'holy thunder'. Now, by contrast, a horde of genuinely menacing, unscrupulous enemies ('crowds . . . mobs') confront the brave New Lights, who fearlessly maintain the cause of true religion against all comers. Burns now presents the New Lights as an embattled minority of Ayrshire dissidents:

> O Ayr, my dear, my native ground,
> Within thy presbytereal bound
> A candid lib'ral band is found
> Of public teachers,
> As Men, as Christians too renown'd
> An' manly preachers. (ll. 79–84)

It is as part of this fearless gang of intrepid freethinkers that Burns evidently sees himself and his epistolary correspondents.

Towards the beginning of the epistle to McMath, Burns uses the elements of clerical apparel as synecdoche for ministers and elders: he has written 'mony a sonnet / On gown, an' ban', an' douse black bonnet' (ll. 7–8). Throughout his anticlerical writings Burns habitually draws attention to the outward appearance of the clergy – 'the lads in black', 'black-gowns', 'a gentleman in black'. In so doing he suggests that there is nothing inherently different between the clergy and the laity, but only a badge of office, a uniform. Without it they are the same as everyone else – 'Like you or I'. It is the suggestion that the clergy, or even the lay zealots, are intrinsically better than everyone else, that riles Burns most. 'They ken nae mair wha's reprobate / Than you or I', complains the speaker in 'The Bonniest Lass'.[12] According to orthodox Calvinism, of course, no-one *could* know who was saved and who damned.[13] Nevertheless, in practice, the temptation would have been to regard the rigidly orthodox as those favoured with God's grace. What Burns objects to in this confident division of men into saved and damned on the grounds of outward orthodoxy, is precisely what he hates about the division of men into nobles and commoners on the grounds of birth: namely, that it provides an artificial standard of value, by which the empty title of merit is made to stand for the living quality. In a letter to Alexander Cunningham in 1792, Burns revealingly links the Unco Guid with aristocrats in their arrogant self-satisfaction:

12 *The Merry Muses of Caledonia*, ed. by James Barke and Sydney Goodsir Smith (London, 1965), pp. 90–91.
13 See Calvin, *Institutes*, II, 968–70.

They are orderly; they may be just; nay, I have known them merciful: but still your children of Sanctity move among their fellow-creatures with a nostril snuffing putrescence, & a foot spurning filth, in short, with that conceited dignity which your titled Douglases, Hamiltons, Gordons, or any other of your Scots Lordlings of seven centuries standing, display [am (*deleted*)] when they accidentally mix among the many-aproned Sons of Mechanical life.

(*Letters*, II, 147)

Through mere adherence to the tenets of orthodoxy and the cultivation of ostentatious piety, the zealot is credited with the righteousness which, for Burns, belongs only to the person who actively vindicates his worth in the world through his benevolent actions. The empty symbol of worth receives the homage due to the living presence; it is a species of moral idolatry.

One particular outbreak of moral idolatry which ignited Burns's indignation, and which prompted some of his most effective anti-orthodox poems, concerned a dispute between his friend and landlord Gavin Hamilton, and the kirk session of Mauchline. Hamilton had been arraigned by the session on charges which included irregular attendance at kirk and neglect of family worship, and though the higher church courts – the district Presbytery and regional Synod – subsequently found in Hamilton's favour, his treatment by the session was an outrage to Burns, the more so since one of Hamilton's most active enemies in the Mauchline session was an elder of impeccable orthodoxy but questionable morals called William Fisher. The dispute between Fisher and Hamilton came to seem for Burns a confrontation between imputed and genuine worth, between the letter and the spirit of merit.

The most important poetic upshot of this affair is of course 'Holy Willie's Prayer' (K, 53), but of neglected merit is the Kilmarnock volume's 'A Dedication to Gavin Hamilton Esq' (K, 103). This is a work which may legitimately be classed as a verse epistle, having many hallmarks of the form: the beguiling, intimate tone; the rambling, diffuse structure; the celebration of the correspondent as an ally in the struggle against religious and social hypocrisy. For part of the poem Burns, in familiar satiric vein, adopts the persona of an orthodox Old Light who is ready to acknowledge that, yes, Hamilton does show instances of practical benevolence – he gives to the needy, keeps his word, suffers ill-usage with patience, bears no grudges; but yet, this moral gold lacks the stamp of orthodoxy which alone makes it current in the eyes of the elect:

> That he's the poor man's friend in need,
> The GENTLEMAN in word and deed,
> It's no through terror of D—mn—t—n;
> It's just a carnal inclination.   (ll. 45–48)

A disposition towards 'carnal' morality is no sure evidence of election; far more reliable, in the eyes of the Old Light, is the ostentatious display of piety:

> Learn three-mile pray'rs, an' half-mile graces,
> Wi' weel spread looves, an' lang, wry faces;

> Grunt up a solemn, lengthen'd groan,
> And damn a' Parties but your own;
> I'll warrant then, ye're nae Deceiver,
> A steady, sturdy, staunch *Believer*.   (ll. 61–66)

In these passages Burns obliquely praises Hamilton while wittily indicting Old Light formalism. Again, however, it is necessary to point out that Burns is here attacking a perversion of Calvinism rather than Calvinism itself. To oppose a conception of worth as consisting in the formal observance of a set code with the idea that worth must be repeatedly vindicated by the consistent goodness of one's actions in the world, is to range oneself on the side of Calvin. As Weber remarks, 'the God of Calvinism demanded of his believers not single good works, but a life of good works combined into a unified system'.[14]

As should be evident by now, the motivating principles of Burns's kirk satires are anticlericalism and anti-formalism. Burns attacks priestcraft, or the tendency of Old Light Presbyterianism to reproduce the 'errors' of Roman Catholicism. However, Enlightenment anticlericalism ought not to be confused with atheism or even secularism. Mark Goldie's comment on English anticlerical discourse during the age of Enlightenment holds good for Scotland:

> We can accept that there was a militant anticlericalism in English political discourse, but we must also recognise that it was grounded in an unfolding tradition of Christian reformism. Atheism, if it existed at all, was marginal. The broad stream of critical reflection on religion was hostile not to piety but to the vanity of dogmatizing, not to scripture but to theocracy.[15]

Enlightened opposition to priestcraft is a continuation of the reforming desire for a 'pure' religion purged of priestly superstitions and inventions; a simple, scriptural religion such as that depicted at the end of 'The Cotter's Saturday Night' (K, 72), set against a gaudy, ceremonious religion whose *'Italian trills'* (l. 115), 'pompous strain' and 'sacredotal stole' (l. 150), are evidently intended to signify Catholicism. Calvin's remark that 'wherever there is great ostentation in ceremonies, sincerity of heart is rare indeed' might almost stand as a paraphrase of these lines from 'The Cotter's Saturday Night':

> Compar'd with this, how poor Religion's pride,
> In all the pomp of *method*, and of *art*,
> When men display to congregations wide,
> Devotion's ev'ry grace, except the *heart*!   (ll. 145–48)

As Henley saw, then, the thrust of Burns's ecclesiastical poetry is anticlerical in the tradition of Knox, rather than straightforwardly anti-Calvinist.[16] Burns's revolt

14 Max Weber, *The Protestant Ethic and the Spirit of Capitalism*, trans. by Talcott Parsons (1930; repr. London, 1992), p. 117.
15 Goldie, 'Priestcraft and the birth of Whiggism', p. 211.
16 Henley and Henderson, IV, 236n., 257.

against orthodoxy is sanctioned by Presbyterian tradition, resting as it does on a belief in the right of private judgement and in the competence of the laity, a refusal to defer unconditionally to any ecclesiastical authority, and a Calvinistic opposition to formalism. His ecclesiastical satires do not represent Burns's dislocation from his community's religious heritage; on the contrary, Burns is working within a tradition of anticlericalism which has always been a strong element within Presbyterian thought, particularly in his own south-west.

This is a point which it is important to stress, since Henry Buckle's depiction of the eighteenth-century Scots as a priest-ridden people is still rehearsed by certain commentators on Burns. In fact, as Henry Grey Graham argued, the contrary was closer to the truth, and what obtained in Scotland was rather a 'people-ridden clergy'.[17] Scrutinised at every turn in his conduct and doctrine, liable to be disciplined by his session if found wanting, the Presbyterian minister was continually made aware of the conditional and delegated nature of his authority. This was particularly evident in the Covenanting counties, with their long traditions of lay assertiveness. The south-west, indeed, was the area of eighteenth-century Scotland in which resistance to the authority of kirk sessions was strongest. In this area alone, the level of illegitimate births increased during the century, as did the proportion of offenders willing to defy the session. The fact that this area was also the historical stronghold of Presbyterianism is only an apparent paradox. As historians have argued, the Presbyterian traditions of religious rebelliousness in fact help explain the laity's stubborn resistance to clerical domination.[18]

As a gloss on Robert Burns's kirk satires, Goldie's contention that Enlightenment anticlericalism was 'hostile not to piety but to the vanity of dogmatizing, not to scripture but to theocracy' is highly apposite. Burns's ecclesiastical satire is not merely compatible with a sincere religiosity ('All hail, Religion! maid divine!'), but has its roots in specific elements of the Reformed tradition. Like other New Lights, Burns opposed the Old Light Presbyterianism on impeccable Reformed principles: the competence of the layman; the primacy of scripture; the right of private judgement. The fact of Burns having been a Scots Presbyterian accounts in large measure for the principles of independence which animate his satires on the kirk. As Christina Keith argues, 'it was just the principles Burns had imbibed from the Kirk, that made him so furious with the hypocrisy he now saw in it. It was just the Calvinist in him that cared.'[19] In a sense, Burns's revolt against orthodoxy is, in Angus Calder's terms, a fresh modulation within Knox's tradition.[20] This is what we might term the Calvinist paradox: you most fully possess the tradition by going outside it; you accede to its power in the act of renouncing it.

17 Graham, *Social Life*, II, 100.
18 R. Mitchison and L. Leneman, *Sexuality and Social Control: Scotland, 1660–1780* (Oxford, 1989), pp. 145–6; Whatley, pp. 103–4.
19 Keith, p. 80.
20 Angus Calder, 'Missionary Scotland?', *Cencrastus*, 21 (1985), 35–39 (p. 39).

PART FOUR

EROTICA

CHAPTER SEVEN

'The Democracy of Sex': Burns's Bawdry

In a study of the dissident elements in Burns's work, the poet's bawdy writings merit particular attention. In these scurrilous, defiantly vulgar works, Burns takes his most daring liberties with the concepts of decorum, order and hierarchy. The celebration of anarchic, untrammeled impulse which fuelled the verse epistles finds its fullest scope in Burns's 'underground' poems. Songs like 'The Trogger' and 'Wha'll m— w me now' are bawdy hymns to sexual desire, to the imperative, clamorous urge, which will find its way around all the dams of law and etiquette and social convention. Alasdair Gray has written that, for Burns, 'sexual love was . . . the most essential human activity' as well as 'the greatest of human pleasures',[1] and there is a deal of truth in this. Throughout Burns's erotic verse, sexual love forms a standard of measurement: placed in the balance with 'TITLE . . . TREASURE . . . REPUTATION's care' ('Love and Liberty'), it demonstrates how flimsy, how lightweight are these seemingly weighty matters. The kirk, the crown, the Houses of Parliament: the sex drive outweighs them all:

> The kirk and state may join and tell;
> To do sic things I manna:
> The kirk and state may gae to h—ll,
> An' I shall gae to Anna.[2]   (ll. 25–28)

As this verse indicates, the apparently private expression of sexual love has a political resonance: it demonstrates the impotence of church and state, and points up the hubris of their totalitarian pretensions. The sex urge cannot be suppressed by edict; it is universal, it runs, as one of Burns's bawdy songs has it, 'frae the queen to the tinkler' ('Bonie Mary'). What Dietrich Strauss calls 'der egalisierenden Natur des Koitus'[3] is the guiding thread of Burns's bawdry. As David Daiches puts it in his discussion of Burns's erotic poetry: 'Other writers may talk of the democracy of the grave; Burns found it more amusing to contemplate the democracy of sex'.[4]

---

1 Alasdair Gray, 'On Neglect of Burns by Schools and His Disparagement by Moralists and Whitewashers With Some Critical Remarks', *Studies in Scottish Literature*, 30 (1998), 175–80 (p. 176).
2 *The Merry Muses of Caledonia* ([n.p.], 1799; repr. Columbia, SC, 1999), p. 10.
3 Dietrich Strauss, *Die erotische Dichtung von Robert Burns* (Frankfurt am Main, 1981), p. 214.
4 Daiches, p. 280.

While it would be easy to overstate the political significance of Burns's bawdry, there is an undoubted area of overlap between Burns's political and his erotic writings. Political satire was, especially in the fraught 1790s, an underground activity occupying the same illicit sphere as bawdry, so it is not surprising that, in the repressive climate of the 'Scottish Terror', Burns found his bawdy and his political interests coalescing. There is a poem written in 1793, 'To Captn G—, on being asked why I was not to be of the party with him and his brother K—nm—re at Syme's' (K, 437), in which Burns speculates jocularly on the reason why he has not been invited to a social evening hosted by his friend John Syme:

> Is 't lest with bawdy jests I bore,
>   As oft the matter of fact is?
> No! *Syme* the theory can't abhor –
>   Who loves so well the practice. –
>
> Is it a fear I should avow
>   Some heresy seditious?
> No! *Syme* (but this is entre nous)
>   Is quite an old Tiresias. –   (ll. 9–16)

That Burns should discuss bawdy humour and sedition in such close proximity is no coincidence. At a time when the state was striking fear into the hearts of reformers, Burns found in 'bawdy jests' the means of subjecting the British (and indeed European) establishment to mockery and ridicule. As we can see from songs like 'Why should na poor folk mowe' and 'Act Sederunt of the Session', bawdry was for Burns, among other things, a way of conducting a sardonic commentary on the values and institutions of official culture.

As this political dimension would suggest, bawdry was not a frivolous poetic sideline or hobby in which Burns indulged merely for the amusement of his friends. The many scholars and editors who have attempted to quarantine this section of Burns's work, denying that it has any fundamental relation to his 'official' writings, do the poet a disservice. In contrast to Franklyn Bliss Snyder, who declares that Burns 'never intended' his bawdy productions 'to be thought of as forming any part of his literary work',[5] I believe that Burns's erotic verse is an integral aspect of his oeuvre. For Burns, *all* poetry was in some sense transgressive. In the autobiographical letter to Dr Moore, Burns writes of the occasion when he 'first committed the sin of RHYME' (*Letters*, I, 137). The terminology is significant: the writing of poetry *was* a sin in Burns's early environment. It transgressed the sober values of his father. It transgressed the morality of the kirk. In the epistles, Burns presents poetry as an oppositional activity, ranged against the dominant commercial-Calvinist ethos of Scottish society. Given all this, it is not surprising that bawdry appears to Burns as a necessary and indeed central poetic mode. For Burns, bawdry was the ultimate extension of poetry's inherently dissident bias. Bawdry was proof poetry, the undiluted distillate of verse.

5 Snyder, *The Life of Robert Burns*, p. 426.

The Bawdy Burns

'There is, there must be some truth in original sin', Burns wrote to Robert Cleghorn: 'My violent propensity to B—dy convinces me of it. – Lack a day if that species of composition be the Sin against "the Haly Ghaist," "I am the most offending soul alive"'(*Letters*, II, 255). Burns's bawdy propensity surfaced early – a song, 'My Girl She's Airy', and a poem, the 'Epistle to J. Rankine, Enclosing some Poems', both occasioned by his affair with Elizabeth Paton, date from 1784.' And the bawdy urge remained constant: Burns not only composed original bawdry throughout his life, he also recast many of the 'indecent' folk songs he encountered in his work for James Johnson's *Scots Musical Museum* and George Thomson's *Select Collection of Original Scotish Airs*. As late as June 1796, in the month before his death, Burns was informing Maria Riddell that he found relief from his rheumatic pains in the writing of bawdry:

> No! if I must write, let it be Sedition, or Blasphemy, or something else that begins with B, so that I may grin with the grin of iniquity, & rejoice with the rejoicing of an apostate Angel. (*Letters*, II, 382)

That Burns not only rejoiced in bawdry, but studied it with rigorous application, is evident from his letters to George Thomson, which reveal a profound knowledge and appreciation of Scotland's traditions of erotic song. It is also important to bear in mind that, as Carol McGuirk argues, Burns probably composed much more in this vein – and particulary much more 'political bawdry' – than has survived the depredations of his moralising editors.[6] In all, Burns undoubtedly became, what he called William Smellie, a 'Veteran in . . . B—dry' (*Letters*, II, 10).

In February 1792, Burns wrote to John McMurdo, Chamberlain to the Duke of Queensberry:

> I think I once mentioned something to you of a Collection of Scots Songs I have for some years been making: I send you a perusal of what I have gathered. – I could not conveniently spare them above five or six days, & five or six glances of them will probably more than suffice you. – When you are tired of them, please leave them with Mr Clint of the King's Arms. – There is not another copy of the Collection in the World, & I should be sorry that any unfortunate negligence should deprive me of what has cost me a good deal of pains. (*Letters*, II, 138)

The manuscript for whose safety Burns was so solicitous was his collection of erotic verses, including both his own compositions and 'walkers', as he called the bawdy songs picked up on his folk-collecting field work. And though the material which his notebook contained might be unpublishable, it was not for that reason confined to Burns's private use. In addition to John McMurdo, Robert Cleghorn seems to have borrowed the collection: in a hasty note dashed off to Cleghorn in August 1790, Burns asks: 'Why don't you return me my Collection of [*word missing*] Songs?'

6 Robert Burns, *Selected Poems*, ed. by Carol McGuirk, p. 277.

(*Letters*, II, 48). Another connoisseur of bawdry, Andrew Erskine, requested a loan
of the erotic notebook in 1793. If the precious collection was not often loaned out,
Burns did invite others to view it. In a letter of December 1789 to Provost Robert
Maxwell of Lochmaben, enclosing a copy of the bawdy song 'I'll tell you a tale of a
Wife', Burns invites Maxwell to 'come & see the rest of my Collection' (*Letters*, I,
462). Individual songs from the collection were regularly incorporated into Burns's
letters to friends (especially Cleghorn, William Dunbar, Alexander Cunningham
and William Stewart), and the productions of his 'high-kilted Muse' were no doubt
also aired at the meetings of the Crochallan Fencibles, an Edinburgh drinking club
of which Burns was a member. Nevertheless, the printed publication of Burns's
bawdry had to wait until four years after his death, when songs which Burns had
written or reworked were among those included in an anthology of Scottish bawdry
published in 1799 as *The Merry Muses of Caledonia*.[7]

The provenance of this volume, and its likely source(s), continues to cause
controversy. The work may have been based on Burns's manuscript collection,
variously reported to have been sold by Burns on his deathbed, inveigled from Jean
after Burns's death, or sent to Liverpool to Burns's biographer, James Currie, along
with the rest of the poet's papers. It may have been based on a more or less accurate
copy of Burns's MS collection, perhaps transcribed when the MS was in Robert
Cleghorn's possession, or when it was lying around the King's Arms pub (see the
letter to McMurdo, above). It may even be that the *Muses* was based on 'versions set
down from memory', conceivably by a member of the Crochallan Fencibles.[8] The
two most thorough researchers of Burns's bawdry – G. Legman and James
Kinsley – are inclined to believe that the 1799 book was compiled by Burns's friend
Peter Hill, an Edinburgh bookseller and Crochallan Fencible to whom Burns's MS
collection was probably sent for copying in 1793, and that Hill based his volume on
the MS collection, 'supplemented from other holograph versions – and from other
poems or collections of poems current among the Crochallan Fencibles'.[9] G. Ross

---

7 This work was republished throughout the nineteenth century, acquiring accretions
  of bawdry which had no connection with Burns. The reliable modern editions are:
  The Merry Muses of Caledonia, ed. by James Barke and Sydney Goodsir Smith
  (London, 1959, 2nd edn 1965); *The Merry Muses of Caledonia Collected and in Part
  Written by Robert Burns*, ed. by G. Legman (New York, 1965), which is a facsimile of
  the (incomplete) Rosebery copy of the first edition; and *The Merry Muses of
  Caledonia; A Collection of Favourite Scots Songs, Ancient and Modern; Selected for the Use
  of the Crochallan Fencibles* ([n.p.], 1799; repr. Columbia, SC, 1999), which is a
  facsimile of the only known complete copy of the 1799 edition, and is accompanied
  by an introductory pamphlet, *Robert Burns and The Merry Muses*, by G. Ross Roy.
8 J. De Lancey Ferguson, 'Sources and Texts of the Suppressed Poems', Preface to
  The Merry Muses of Caledonia, ed. by James Barke and Sydney Goodsir Smith, 2nd
  edn (London, 1965), pp. 15–22 (p. 21).
9 James Kinsley, 'Burns and the *Merry Muses*', *Renaissance and Modern Studies*, 9
  (1965), 5–21 (pp. 20–21); G. Legman, *The Horn Book: Studies in Erotic Folklore and
  Bibliography* (London, 1970), pp. 164–9.

Roy raises the further possibility that William Smellie, founder of the Crochallan Fencibles, printer of Burns's Edinburgh edition and editor of the first edition of the *Encyclopaedia Britannica*, 'had a hand in the production of the first edition of *The Merry Muses*'.[10]

The provenance of the 1799 book remains a matter of conjecture. What *can* be said with confidence is that the proportion of *The Merry Muses* attributable to Burns is much greater than some of Burns's editors have been willing to admit. The brazen fraudulence of Currie – who, in his 1800 edition of the *Works*, interpolated the sentence 'A very few are my own' into the letter to McMurdo quoted above – was replicated a century later by Duncan McNaught, who, in his 1911 edition of *The Merry Muses*, 'indulged in re-writing and falsification in yet another futile attempt to show Burns the author of fewer pieces than he was'.[11] Today, however, following the researches of Kinsley and Legman, it is accepted that we have holograph authority for over twenty of the pieces in the 1799 *Merry Muses* (and indeed for nine bawdy songs not included in the *Muses*), and that there are further songs whose authorship by Burns may be asserted or denied on the basis of internal evidence. As R.D.S. Jack observes, the research on Burns's bawdry undertaken in the 1960s now 'allows a literary critic objectively to assess Burns's contribution to the extensive and often inspired bawdy literature of Scotland'.[12]

Folk Humour, Carnival and Grotesque Realism

The bawdy literature of Burns, like the bawdy literature of Scotland, is first and foremost a humorous literature. It is therefore doubly antipathetic to certain traditional forms of criticism, being not only erotic but comic. It lacks the seriousness by which the erotica of Donne or Marvell qualify for canonical status. Of course, as Peter Wagner points out, 'the notion that erotic poetry must be grave, solemn and spiritual to deserve attention is a fairly modern one, and developed in the eighteenth century'.[13] It goes without saying that an adequate study of Burns's erotic verse must abandon the fetish of 'seriousness', and get to grips with the poet's bawdy humour. This humour, moreover, is of a particular kind. It has a quality of ambivalence which makes it more than simply satirical, and indeed it may be that 'satire' is an inadequate rubric under which to discuss Burns's politico-erotic verse.

In much of Burns's political bawdry, there is discernible neither the fixed moral standpoint nor the unambivalent censorious tone which characterise the satirist. Let us consider, for instance, the irreverent treatment of politicians in such poems – in 'A Dream', where Prince William appears as 'Young, royal TARRY-BREEKS' and Pitt the Younger as 'a true guid fallow's get', or in the lines 'To a Gentleman who

---

10 G. Ross Roy, *Robert Burns and The Merry Muses* (Columbia, SC, 1999), viii.

11 Maurice Lindsay, *The Burns Encyclopedia*, 3rd edn (London, 1980), p. 232.

12 R. D. S. Jack, 'Burns and Bawdy', in *The Art of Robert Burns*, pp. 98–126 (p. 100).

13 Peter Wagner, *Eros Revived: Erotica of the Enlightenment in England and America* (London, 1988), p. 162.

had sent him a News-paper' (K, 282), where the Holy Roman Emperor is characterised as a 'doup-skelper', the heir to the British throne as 'that daft buckie, Geordie W∗∗∗s', and Pitt, Fox and Burke as 'sleekit Chatham Will', 'glaiket Charlie', and 'daddie Burke'. Now, while this irreverent idiom has an undoubted lampooning effect, it lacks the element of condemnatory ethical criticism which pertains to satire. Instead, the striking quality of Burns's writing in this vein is its ambivalence, its half-derisive, half-laudatory tone. The point is not that Burns is even-handed in his treatment of political figures, attending in turn to good qualities and bad, but that *each* of his epithets contains a combined equivocal tone of praise and abuse; the word 'get', for example, or the epithet 'daddie'. This type of discourse occupies a flickering wavelength between affirmation and denunciation; it manifests an ambivalence which sets it apart from satire. Indeed, much of the poetry currently discussed under the rubric of satire might more properly be discussed, I submit, using a concept formulated by Mikhail Bakhtin: the concept of 'folk humour'.

Bakhtin's most sustained and comprehensive discussion of folk humour is to be found in his study of Rabelais, *Rabelais and His World*. In this book, Bakhtin attempts to widen the parameters of Rabelais criticism in order to allow a full consideration of the influence of popular culture on Rabelais' novel. In the past, Bakhtin argues, Rabelais has been approached solely as a representative of the scholarly humanist culture of the Renaissance, while his debt to the popular culture of his era (particularly the culture of popular festivity) has been neglected. This has skewed our perception of Rabelais' novel, many elements of which, though apparently trivial or even incomprehensible from the perspective of high literary culture, reveal their true philosophic depth when viewed as part of a distinct folk culture.

Central to Bakhtin's theory, then, is the conviction that all the various popular forms – the rites, festivals, folktales, ballads, farces and so forth – which flourished in the marketplaces of medieval and Renaissance Europe, participated in one common culture, having its own coherent system of values and symbols, and existing in opposition to the official culture of the elite classes and the Catholic Church. According to Bakhtin, the peoples of Renaissance Europe inherited a coherent popular culture, developed throughout the medieval period, and unified by a particular type of burlesque humour. Throughout the Middle Ages

> a boundless world of humorous forms and manifestations opposed the official and serious tone of medieval ecclesiastical and feudal culture. In spite of their variety, folk festivities of the carnival type, the comic rites and cults, the clowns and fools, giants, dwarfs and jugglers, the vast and manifold literature of parody – all these forms have one style in common: they belong to one culture of folk carnival humour. [14]

---

14 Mikhail Bakhtin, *Rabelais and His World*, trans. by Hélène Iswolsky (Bloomington, Ind., 1984), p. 4. Though written during the 1930s, this book was first published in Russia in 1965, and in English translation in 1968. Subsequent page references are given in the text.

Although the culture of folk humour had persisted in these semi-underground forms for several centuries, a momentous historical dislocation took place in the era of Rabelais, which meant that the expression of folk culture was no longer restricted to the occasional public holiday and to the lower literary genres. With the break-up of the medieval feudal and ecclesiastical order in the sixteenth century, with the rise of Protestantism, of capitalist economic practices, and with the triumph of the vernacular languages over Latin, the rigid medieval separation of high and low culture began to break down. Not only did high literary culture reach the subordinate classes through the development of printing and the diffusion of literacy, but elements of popular culture exerted an unprecedented influence on the forms and genres of high culture:

> The era of the Renaissance . . . was marked in the literary sphere first of all by the fact that the highest potentials of folk humour had attained the level of great literature and had fertilized it. Without being aware of this fact it is impossible to understand either the culture or the literature of the sixteenth century.
>
> (p. 136)

The fact that the 'culture of folk humour . . . could now rise to the high level of literature and ideology and fertilize it' (p. 72) is demonstrated by the novels of Cervantes and Rabelais and by the plays of Shakespeare. The works of these writers reveal a profound engagement with images and motifs of popular culture, with popular vernacular idiom, and with the burlesque, anti-official atmosphere of that most vibrant manifestation of popular festive life: the carnival.

With its ritual reversal of traditional social hierarchy, and its celebration of seasonal renewal, of death and rebirth, carnival becomes for Bakhtin an index and microcosm of the whole folk-humorous culture. Carnival constitutes a separate, unofficial holiday world, with its own time-frame, its own rules and norms, a world turned upside-down. In carnival we encounter 'the suspension of all hierarchic differences, of all ranks and status' (p. 246). The overturning of hierarchy in carnival – the ritual 'uncrowning' of authority figures, the election of mock kings and 'Lords of Misrule' – demonstrates the artificiality of official systems of rank by imagining a completely new allocation of status. Carnival knows that its version of the world is not self-sufficient or ultimately authoritative; but it knows, by the same token, that the same is true of official culture. Below the conventional distinctions of rank, it suggests, everyone is on the same level: 'all were considered equal during carnival' (p. 10).

Carnival equality, however, is not to be interpreted as the expression of popular utopian longing for a less stratified society. Rather, it is the result of a profoundly social view of life, an insistence on the condition of social interdependence which characterises *any* society, despite its official distinctions of rank and status. Implicit in the communal nature of carnival is the recognition that the free-standing individual of early-modern contract theory, the man who *prior* to joining civil society enjoys the use of reason and language, is a bourgeois fiction. Outside society, man could not be man; his consciousness of self, his powers of ratiocination, his moral capacity – all depend upon language, upon a sign system which cannot exist outwith society. In carnival, the human being is never a free-standing individual but always part of a whole, a whole that constantly renews itself.[15]

It is this awareness of social interdependence which explains why folk culture constantly foregrounds the human body and the basic bodily functions common to everyone. A preoccupation with the body in its changing, open-ended state is what Bakhtin calls 'grotesque realism', the aesthetic principle which, above all others, distinguishes the culture of folk humour. In grotesque realism, the body is a levelling principle, it stands for shared humanity, and is never a merely private body:

> In grotesque realism . . . the bodily element is deeply positive. It is presented not in a private, egotistic form, severed from the other spheres of life, but as something universal, representing all the people . . . The material bodily principle is contained not in the biological individual, not in the bourgeois ego, but in the people, a people who are continually growing and renewed.
>
> (p. 19)

The grotesque body differs widely from the self-contained and sealed-up body of classical and neoclassical art, 'its convexities smoothed out, its apertures closed' (p. 29). It is a body involved with its environment, a body of protuberances and orifices, 'the open mouth, the genital organs, the breasts, the phallus, the potbelly, the nose' (p. 26). Folk humour points to the body's ongoing need to fuel up and discharge, and concentrates on those acts which most clearly demonstrate the body's incompleteness – the act of eating, the act of sex. Again, the feasting and fornication do not represent acts of individual gratification; they represent the people as a regenerating whole. Images of sex, images of food and drink, represent 'the triumph of the people as a whole' (p. 302), the people's constant renewal as a collective body.

It is through imagery associated with eating, defecation and copulation that folk humour prosecutes its attack on official seriousness, its 'lowering of all that is high, spiritual, ideal, abstract' (p. 19). So we have the mock drunkards' liturgies and the lecherous priests of Renaissance burlesque. However, the object linked with the imagery of the 'bodily lower stratum' – the anus, genitalia, urine, excrement and so forth – is not merely debunked. A strong positive force attaches to these bodily images, linked as they are with fertility and regeneration. For instance, Bakhtin draws attention to 'the ambivalent character of drenching in urine, the element of fertility and procreating power [as well as debasement] contained in this image' (p. 230). In this way, folk humour is ambivalent, 'degrades and regenerates simul-taneously' (p. 240). In folk humour, the ideas and symbols of official culture are not subjected to a satiric denouncement, but to a laughing, carnivalesque overturning,

---

15 This aspect of Bakhtin's thought is cogently discussed in Tzvetan Todorov, *Mikhail Bakhtin: The Dialogical Principle*, trans. by Wlad Godzich (Minneapolis, MN, 1984), pp. 29–34.

which is not merely negative but involves a regeneration of the object on another (more material) level. The object of folk humour is brought down to a level *shared* by the humorist; it is brought down to earth, to the same level as everyone else.

Although Bakhtin's concept of folk humour is formulated in a study of sixteenth-century culture, there is nothing wilful in applying it to the work of a writer such as Burns. Carnivalesque folk humour continued to exert an influence on the literature of eighteenth- and nineteenth-century Europe. Bakhtin argues that, as carnival proper becomes a less prevalent social phenomenon, it is 'reincarnated in literature'.[16] The literary reincarnation of carnival is a defining feature of the poetry of the eighteenth-century Scottish Vernacular Revival. The work of Allan Ramsay and, especially, Robert Fergusson features poems which not only embody a carnivalesque perspective, but which centre on popular festive events ('The Daft Days', 'The King's Birth-Day in Edinburgh', 'Hallow-Fair', 'Leith Races'). The longevity of the boisterous Christis Kirk genre, whose classic period runs from the fifteenth to the late eighteenth century, again indicates the central role of the carnivalesque in Scottish vernacular poetry.[17]

Folk Humour in Burns's Bawdry

A discussion of the carnival impulse in Burns's bawdry might appropriately begin with a song composed in December 1792, 'Why should na poor folk mowe' (K, 395). On the face of it this song, which Burns describes as a 'tippling Ballad' (*Letters*, II, 174) and which comes to a close with a toast, is a convivial paean to the sexual act, the poor man's one affordable enjoyment:

> WHEN Princes and Prelates and het-headed zealots
> All Europe hae set in a lowe,
> The poor man lies down, nor envies a crown,
> And comforts himsel with a mowe.   (ll. 1–4)

In this opening verse, we seem to be on familiar territory: Burns is celebrating the harmless pleasures of the poor against the destructive power games of the rich, in the manner of 'Nature's Law' or 'I murder hate by field or flood', where sex is essentially the poor man's consolation for the absence of effective political power. This song, however, is not just another discursus on the consolations of phil-andering. Unlike the songs mentioned above, it is not premised on a complete dichotomy between the everyday life of the people and the wielding of effective political power. Instead, this familiar dichotomy is set up in the first verse only to be

---

16 Mikhail Bakhtin, *Problems of Dostoevsky's Poetics*, ed. and trans. by Caryl Emerson (Minneapolis, MN, 1984), pp. 156–60.

17 On the 'Christis Kirk' tradition in Scottish poetry, see Allan H. MacLaine, 'The Christis Kirk Tradition: Its Evolution in Scots Poetry to Burns, *Studies in Scottish Literature*, II (1964–65), 3–18, 111–124, 163–182, 234–250; *The Christis Kirk Tradition: Scots Poems of Folk Festivity*, ed. by Allan H. MacLaine (Glasgow, 1996).

dismantled in the rest of the song. The subsequent three verses list the (unsuccessful) attempts of various European monarchs and nobles to strike the decisive blow against the French, with the suggestion that they would have been better off following the poor man's example and contenting themselves with a 'mowe'. Accordingly, as the song develops we become aware of an effective political power exercised by the masses, and of the circumscribed nature of that seemingly absolute power wielded by the great European monarchs; when translated into practice, the great man's design will be altered, diluted, even frustrated by the supposedly passive, ineffectual masses. Like the Hardy of 'In Time of "The Breaking of Nations" ', who sees in the processes of agriculture and the rituals of courtship emblems of the quiet continuity of common life beneath the trumpeted squabblings of dynasties, Burns regards the power of the masses – as symbolised in sex, and as realised in Revolutionary France – as being greater than the acts of the supposed 'great men'. The 'great men' who propose, as if by personal fiat, to stamp out the Republican experiment, run up against the contingent nature of experience. Even the seemingly successful Catherine the Great in verse five, who imposes her lover on the throne of Poland, has perhaps changed little enough, since the poor, as the chorus reminds us, are still 'mowing':

> And why shouldna poor folk mowe, mowe, mowe,
>   And why shouldna poor folk mowe:
> The great folk hae siller, and houses and lands,
>   Poor bodies hae naething but mowe.   (ll. 5–8)

Here in the chorus, the stratified official world of legal proprietorship and distinctions of rank – the 'great folk' with their 'siller, and houses and lands' – is surrounded by and in danger of being absorbed into the carnival world of lower-class festivity and acknowledged interdependence symbolised by the sexual act. True to the carnival tradition, then, sex in 'Why shouldna poor folk mowe' is important not as a matter of private indulgence but rather as a social phenomenon. 'Mowe, mowe, mowe': the repetition of the verb signifies not just the repeated strokes in the sexual act but the repetition of the act itself, the ongoing, contingent nature of the experience. This is the folk view of life, which emphasises shared physicality – 'poor *bodies*' – and in which the individual is always part of a larger, constantly renewing whole.

Set against this renewing whole are the great monarchs and nobles – the Duke of Brunswick, Frederick William II, the Emperor – who seek to lift themselves above contingent reality, to elect themselves to a fixed and immutable order of worth measured in rank and property, and who believe that they can direct the fate of Europe through unilateral exercises of will. The view that history is a succession of telling interventions by 'great men' is evidently held by the figures in Burns's song, none of whom doubts his ability to impose his will on events: note Brunswick's relaxed and unhurried 'cruising' (l. 9), the cocksure vows of Frederick William and the Emperor. This type of presumption would later be undercut by Brecht when, in 'Questions From a Worker Who Reads', he focuses attention on the unmentioned foot soldiers and dogsbodies on whose labour all the 'acts' of the great men depend.[18] Burns takes a different tactic: he associates these great figures with the act of copulation, the act which most unanswerably demonstrates the participation of each individual in a chain of interdependence. That is, he brings them down to earth by associating them with the bodily lower stratum:

> When Br—nsw—ck's great Prince cam a cruising to Fr—nce
>   Republican billies to cowe,
> Bauld Br—nsw—c's great Prince wad hae shown better sense
>   At hame with his Princess to mowe.   (ll. 9–12)

What this verse presents is two different versions of the same event. First there is the epic-heroic version projected by Brunswick, and then, heralded by the ironic intensification of laudatory epithets ('Bauld Br—nsw—c's great Prince'), there is the actual, contingent outcome of the venture. The second half of the verse conveys the necessary information – that Brunswick's army was defeated – but does so in an image which plunges Brunswick into the world of becoming, the world of contingency. When we imagine Brunswick in the act of copulation, he loses all epic stasis and becomes part of the ongoing, comic world. This is similar to what happens at the end of Swift's 'Cassinus and Peter', when Caelia, the idealised Petrarchan mistress, is brought down to earth by her association with bodily functions; 'Oh! *Caelia, Caelia, Caelia* shits'.[19]

   In Swift's poem, the fact that Caelia shits is presented as a momentous revelation, so as to convey the comically reverential distance at which the speaker holds his mistress. By contrast, what is crucial to the success of Burns's poem is that the image of Brunswick copulating is smuggled quietly into the poem and 'backgrounded', so that it does not advertise its significance. If the image of the great man copulating is too nakedly present, if it has no alibi, then it will defeat its own purpose. It will say to the reader: 'Look: isn't it amazing that these great personages engage in sexual intercourse, just like the rest of us!' (that is, just as if they were ordinary mortals), which would of course reinforce their essentially superhuman status. In order to avoid this, Burns takes the image of the Duke of Brunswick copulating, and passes it off as a neutral description, a way of conveying the information that Brunswick's army was defeated; in so doing, he removes from the image any suggestion of surprise or unlikeliness and in this way the image retains its polemical force.

   The subsequent verses follow the pattern of the verse on Brunswick. First we hear the bluster and the threats from one of the blue-blooded bullies who aims to chastise the errant French. Then, in the second half of the verse, his failure is gleefully recounted. And in each case it is the image of copulation that brings the 'great man' down to earth:

---

18 Bertold Brecht, *Poems: Part Two 1929–1938*, ed. by John Willett and Ralph
     Manheim (London, 1976), pp. 252–3.
19 Jonathan Swift, *Poetical Works*, ed. by Herbert Davis (Oxford, 1967), p. 531.

> Out over the Rhine proud Pr—ss—a wad shine,
>   To *spend* his best blood he did vow;
> But Frederic had better ne'er forded the water,
>   But *spent* as he docht in a mowe.   (ll. 13–16)

Here the breakdown of the epic ascent is implicit from the first, as the terms in which Frederick formulates his vow – 'to *spend* his best blood' – already suggest copulation. We should notice also the change in nomenclature from the first line to the third. One of the characteristic features of the 'great man' theory of history is that convention, according to which the name of the country may stand for that of the monarch ('France', for example, signifying the King of France), as if one man could fight battles, conduct sieges and so forth. Burns plays on this convention to make a point. In the first two lines, when Frederick William II is confidently planning his decisive intervention, his hubris is indicated by calling him 'Prussia'; in the last two lines, when his project has foundered, his ineffectiveness is indicated by calling him 'Frederic', implying that his innate strength is no more formidable than that of a private citizen. Similarly, in the next verse, the cocksure 'Emperor' becomes a forlorn 'laddie':

> By sea and by shore! the Emp—r—r swore,
>   In Paris he'd kick up a row;
> But Paris sae ready just leugh at the laddie
>   And bade him gae tak him a mowe.   (ll. 17—20)

As the War against France continued, Burns expanded the song to include gleeful verses on the Duke of York's unsuccessful Netherlands campaign and the defeat of the Austrians at Jemappes. As one of the choral poor folk ignored by his society's leaders, Burns glories in the continuing success of the poor folk over the water in frustrating the leaders of Europe. The resilience of the French Republic is some kind of poetic justice. It allows Burns to claim that, until Europe's great folk abandon their attempts to lord it over the masses, until they acknowledge their common humanity – as expressed in the shared bodily functions of sex – then they will continue to suffer the humiliation of defeat. In this context, the familiar abusive injunction of which the song is a kind of elaboration, and which comes closest to being articulated in the verse on the Emperor, has some claim to be considered as constructive criticism.

  The treatment of the monarchs and nobles, then, is not merely abusive and one-sided. In true carnival fashion, the humour is ambivalent, it renews as it degrades. Burns does not mount a bitter satirical attack on the song's great personages; he laughingly explodes their pretensions by means of the imagery of the lower stratum. Even the fate wished on Catherine the Great – 'May the deil in her a— ram a huge pr—ck o' brass!' (l. 23) – is comically impossible, has the flamboyancy of a formalised cursing rather than the gravity of a serious attack. On the one hand, the aim is certainly to degrade and debunk the great folk, to bring them down to earth. Nevertheless, though they lose their epic distance and finish, the notables are reborn as full-blooded social folk. Imagined in the process of copulating, they are brought down from their exalted position and reintegrated into the comic life shared by everyone else. Thus the King and Queen become the natural objects of a bar-room toast which focuses on their sexual activities:

> But truce with commotions and new-fangled notions,
> A bumper I trust you'll allow:
> Here 's George our gude king and Charlotte his queen,
> And lang may they tak a gude mowe!   (ll. 25–28)

It is perhaps due to this ambivalent humour, a humour that renews as it degrades, a humour that aims to bring everyone down to the same level, that some commentators have mistakenly regarded the song as apolitical, celebrating an anodyne pluralism of sex. In his 1965 edition of *The Merry Muses*, G. Legman reads the song as a testimony to Burns's withdrawal from political engagement and a recantation of his Republican principles. Legman describes Burns as

> pronouncing a curse on all political houses equally, and vindicating the right of 'the poor man' to nothing more than to 'comfort himself with a m—w'. Even as sexual revolt this is pretty mild, especially in combination with the patriotico-sexual benediction of King George and his Queen with which the song ends . . . [20]

But Burns does not pronounce 'a curse on all political houses equally'. As I hope to have shown, the seemingly apolitical sentiment of the first verse is deceptive; as the song develops, sexual activity itself becomes politicised, representing the interdependent body of the people which, in France, is triumphing over the reactionary monarchs of Europe. Having altogether missed the political significance of sex in the song, it is not surprising that Legman regards the final verse as a sycophantic 'benediction', and remains deaf to the strong political over-tone. 'Lang may they tak a gude mowe': long may they acknowledge their participation in an interdependent whole, and not pursue private interests against the good of the people.

In 'Why shouldna poor folk mowe', Burns uses the carnivalesque drama of death and rebirth as a template for contemporary politics, showing a moribund *ancien régime* bowing to the power of a renascent, revolutionary Europe. The reason why Legman fails to appreciate the radical tenor of the song is because he fails to understand folk humour. In terms of ideological content, the song is no different from other radical works such as 'Is there for honest Poverty'; it expresses the same awareness of human interdependence, the same opposition to aristocratic privilege. In the latter song, however, Burns uses the resources of high culture to mount an abstract rhetorical attack on princes and nobles; in 'Why shouldna poor folk mowe', he subjects them to a carnivalesque uncrowning based on the principles of folk humour.

---

20 *The Merry Muses of Caledonia*, ed. by G. Legman, xiii–xiv.

178 Burns the Radical

An Alternative State

The characteristic movement in 'Why shouldna poor folk mowe' is a downward one: the exalted is brought down to earth. In some of Burns's other bawdy work, this movement is reversed, and the conventionally low is raised to the height of formality and official recognition. In 'The Fornicator' (K, 61), which probably commemorates Burns's impregnation of Elizabeth Paton, Burns imagines an official brotherhood of fornicators, with specified conditions of membership. As the song develops, we witness the elaboration of a Fornicator's Code: the Fornicator must acknowledge his involvement should his partner become pregnant (verse one); he must never forgo an opportunity of sex with a willing partner (verse three); he must provide for any offspring (verse four), and so forth. Fornication itself is restricted to acts of sex for pleasure; sex with a prostitute does not qualify:

> Ye wenching blades whose hireling jades
>   Have tipt you off blue-boram,
> I tell ye plain, I do disdain
>   To rank you in the Quorum;
> But a bony lass upon the grass
>   To teach her esse Mater,
> And no reward but for regard,
>   O that's a Fornicator.   (ll. 33–40)

Burns has transformed the title of Fornicator from a stigma which the culpable can hardly avoid into an accolade to which not everyone may aspire. The song ends with the tongue-in-cheek suggestion that, let your social rank or status be what it will, it is the glorious rank of Fornicator that most surely indicates greatness:

> Your warlike Kings and Heros bold,
>   Great Captains and Commanders;
> Your mighty Cesars fam'd of old,
>   And Conquering Alexanders;
> In fields they fought and laurels bought,
>   And bulwarks strong did batter,
> But still they grac'd our noble list
>   And ranked Fornicator!!!   (ll. 41–48)

In 'The Fornicator', Burns creates an alternative rank, an alternative code of morality, in defiance of his society's official mores. The artificiality of the official system is exposed by a simple device: that of treating non-official phenomena in official terms. In this way, as Bakhtin observes, folk humour creates an alternative state, duplicating the institutions of official culture to create a mock version of the official system. Folk humour 'builds its own world versus the official world, its own church versus the official church, its own state versus the official state'.[21]

---

21 *Rabelais*, p. 88.

Burns begins to erect his alternative state in 'The Fornicator'. He continues the process in a later poem, in which he provides for the newly created brotherhood of fornicators an official judiciary to ensure correct conduct among its members. 'The Court of Equity' (K, 109) concerns the proceedings of a local fornicators' tribunal, presided over by Burns himself, with three of his Mauchline friends serving as Fiscal, Clerk and Messenger at Arms. The court can be seen as a mock version of the Presbyterian parochial court, the 'kirk session': like the session, the court is careful to emphasise the delegated nature of its authority, the fact that it has been 'deputed' (l. 10) and 'by our brethren constituted' (l. 9). Here, however, the object is not to discover and punish fornication, but to penalise the failure to fornicate properly. The type of malefactor whom the court aims to punish includes

> The wretch that can refuse subsistence
> To those whom he has given existence;
> He who when at a lass's by-job,
> Defrauds her wi' a fr—g or dry—b—b;
> The coof that stands on clishmaclavers
> When women haflins offer favors: –
> All who in any way or manner
> Distain the Fornicator's honor.   (ll. 19–26)

The poem is in the form of a 'Libel Summons' (it is sometimes known by that title) served by the court on two suspected transgressors of the Fornicator's code. It is therefore a pseudo-official document, and, as one might then expect, the chief virtue of the poem lies in its representation of language. There is parody of bureaucratic circumlocution: 'The year 'tween eighty five and seven' (l. 4). There is the broad structural humour implicit in the mobilisation of latinate, legal idiom in the context of parochial 'houghmagandie':

> WE, Fornicators by profession,
> As per extractum from each Session,
> In way and manner here narrated,
> Pro bono Amor congregated . . .   (ll. 5–8)

There is also a humorous use of inversions and of the unusual syntax which legal documents tend to adopt as a way of avoiding ambiguity or of exploiting the authoritative, sombre inflection of archaic usages. When egregious syntax and pompous diction are applied to a particularised and unofficial context the result is humorous, most triumphantly so at the point when Sandy Dow is alleged to have been 'clandestinely upward whirlin / The petticoats o' MAGGY BORELAN' (ll. 85–6). Another linguistic high point is the virtuoso passage in which the sexual activities of 'Clockie' [clockmaker] Brown are reported in the professional idiom of his trade:

> FIRST, YOU, JOHN BROWN, there 's witness borne,
> And affidavit made and sworn,
> That ye hae bred a hurly-burly

'Bout JEANY MITCHEL'S tirlie-whirlie,
And blooster'd at her regulator,
Till a' her wheels gang clitter-clatter.   (ll. 61–66)

Towards the end of the summons, the defendants are informed of the penalties they will incur if the court finds them guilty and unrepentant. Sandy Dow, who denies responsibility for Maggy Borelan's pregnancy, escapes with a warning and an order to own up. 'Clockie' Brown, who has compounded his denial with an attempt to 'poosion' (l. 72) the child which Jeany Mitchel is carrying by him, does not escape so lightly. The punishment he is to suffer is typically carnivalesque: he will be tied to the town pump by his penis for a period of between three and seven turnings of a half-hour glass. The summons is subscribed with due formality by President Burns and his Clerk, and witnessed by the Messenger at Arms.

In this same genre of the pseudo-official document, there is a letter of Burns's, written as a cover note to a bawdy song (*Letters*, I, 65–6). The letter is a mock royal decree, in which Burns requests his two correspondents – 'our trusty and well-beloved WILLIAM CHALMERS and JOHN M'ADAM' – to deliver the enclosed song to a sherriff's officer for public burning at the cross of Ayr. Styling himself 'POET-LAUREAT and BARD IN CHIEF in and over the Districts and Countries of KYLE, CUNNINGHAM, and CARRICK, of old extent', and claiming jurisdiction over 'Bards, Poets, Poetasters . . . &tc', Burns is evidently having fun taking off the style of the royal decree, from the imperious capitals and the plural possessive pronouns ('OUR WILL THEREFORE IS . . . '), to the use of augmentation ('nefarious, abominable, and wicked', 'appellation, phrase, and nickname'). He signs off with 'GOD SAVE THE BARD!' The letter is a squib, a *jeu d'esprit*, but it remains important for my purpose in that it shows Burns, in a context involving bawdy song, working with the notion of an alternative state. As well as an order of fornicators and a fornicators' court, we now have a lawgiver for bards.

Alternative versions of official institutions crop up throughout Burns's bawdry. There is the mock legal decree in 'Act Sederunt of the Session' (K, 436):

IN Edinburgh town they've made a law,
    In Edinburgh at the Court o' Session,
That standing pr—cks are fauteors a',
    And guilty of a high transgression. –   (ll. 1–4)

There is the alternative heraldry in one of the bawdy versions of 'Green Grow the Rashes' in *The Merry Muses*:

An' heard ye o' the coat o' arms,
    The Lyon brought our lady, O,
The crest was, couchant, sable c—t,
    The motto, "*ready, ready*," O.[22]   (ll. 13– 16)

---

22 *The Merry Muses of Caledonia* (n.p., 1799; repr. Columbia, SC, 1999), pp. 28–9.

(The burlesque on heraldry, which is, as we shall see, a common theme in Burns's 'conventional' poetry, is itself compelling reason for attributing this version to Burns.)

The convivial club at which Burns aired many of his bawdy productions itself participated in this cult of the alternative state. The Crochallan Fencibles was a mock regiment, named in derision of the volunteer defence forces raised during the war with the Americans. Its office bearers took military titles: William Dunbar, for instance, was the Colonel, and William Smellie, as we have seen, was described by Burns as a 'Veteran' in bawdry. In a letter to Peter Hill, Burns refers to a recent meeting of the Fencibles as 'the last field-day of the Crochallan corps' (*Letters*, II, 79). The mock-institutional character of the Crochallan Fencibles was shared by other convivial clubs of the era. The Crochallans had their counterparts in such clubs as the 'Medmenhamites', a mock religious order of English rakes (including the radical politician John Wilkes), which met in the ruins of a Cistercian abbey in the mid-1750s. Founded by the violently anti-Catholic Sir Francis Dashwood, the Medmenhamites composed a mock liturgy and dispensed mock sacraments.[23]

The Medmenhamites also produced mock literary works, demonstrating that the cultural as well as the political and religious institutions of official culture were fair game for bawdy treatment. *An Essay On Woman* (1763), probably composed by Thomas Potter or John Wilkes, is a bawdy parody of Pope's *Essay on Man*, and includes some competent mimicry, such as the following variation on the Popean zeugma:

> Prick, cunt and bollocks in convulsions hurl'd
> And now a Hymen burst, and now a World.[24]

This poem foreshadows Burns's use of bawdry for purposes of literary parody, most notably in his mock-pastoral 'Ode to Spring' (K, 481), whose savagely satirical opening is given a delightful air of innocence by the polite 'Sir' which ends each second line:

> When maukin bucks, at early f—s,
>   In dewy glens are seen, Sir;
> And birds, on boughs, take off their m—s,
>   Amang the leaves sae green, Sir . . .   (ll. 1–4)

The 'defiance of neoclassical convention' which Damrosch perceives as central to Burns's bawdry is emphatically present in this song.[25] Here Burns blows open the closed system of pastoral by applying it to a bawdy context. Not only the woodland animals, but the mythological figures and the stock Arcadian lovers, are all engaged in sex. Burns, moreover, introduces particular words – 'f—s', 'r—ger', 'a—se' – which the pastoral system cannot naturalise, and which infect the whole song with their incongruity.

---

23 Wagner, p. 57.
24 Quoted in Wagner, p. 55.
25 Damrosch, p. 651.

In the climactic third verse, Burns pushes to humorous extreme the pastoral theme of sympathy between man and landscape (a theme which he elsewhere manipulates to great effect in songs like 'The Banks o' Doon' and 'My Nanie, O'). Here, the rural swain Damon is ludicrously 'in tune' with his environment: as he copulates with Sylvia, he bases his sexual rhythm on the songs of the surrounding birds. As the varieties of birdsong multiply, and as Damon approaches orgasm, the task of conducting a pastoral symphony with his penis becomes too much, and he abandons himself to the natural rhythm of the matter in hand:

> First, wi' the thrush, his thrust and push
>   Had compass large and long, Sir;
> The blackbird next, his tuneful text,
>   Was bolder, clear and strong, Sir:
> The linnet's lay came then in play,
>   And the lark that soar'd aboon, Sir;
> Till Damon, fierce, mistim'd his a—,
>   And f—'d quite out o' tune, Sir.   (ll. 17–24)

That syncopated rhythm in the penultimate line brilliantly signals the breakdown of the pastoral convention. In this song, as in the rest of his bawdy productions, Burns, like Damon, is gloriously 'out of tune' with the conventions of polite literature.

'Official' and 'unofficial' Burns

How, then, does Burns's erotica relate to his poetry as a whole? It should be clear by now that the concerns and methods which shape Burns's bawdy pieces are by no means extraneous to his canonical poetry. The oppositional character of Burns's bawdry – the way it demonstrates the arbitrariness of official forms and practices – aligns it with a familiar strain running through Burns's poetry from the verse epistles to the late political songs, confirming Dietrich Strauss's observation of a complementary relationship between Burns's 'official' and 'unofficial' poetry – that is, between those poems which observed contemporary standards of decorum and those which did not.[26]

This is not to say, however, that Burns's bawdy work lacks distinctiveness in relation to his 'official' canon. On the contrary, its value for the critic lies in the fact that, while it expresses sentiments which are present in the canonical poetry, it does so in a freer, less inhibited fashion. When dealing with certain themes in the poems written for publication, Burns's expression is inevitably confined; but in the bawdry, as Whitman observed, his handling is always 'free and broad'.[27] An acquaintance

---

26 Strauss, p. 295.
27 Walt Whitman, 'Robert Burns as Poet and Person', in *Complete Poetry and Collected Prose*, ed. by Justin Caplan (New York, 1982), pp. 1152–61 (p. 1161).

with the bawdy Burns helps us to gauge the orientation of certain canonical poems, and also deepens our understanding of some familiar Burnsian techniques.

In his bawdy productions, Burns characteristically takes one of the privileged language systems of official culture – the language of the royal decree, the language of literary pastoral – and confronts it with a stubbornly unofficial language: the language of the lower classes, the language of obscenity. In so doing, he reveals the ideological slant in the seemingly 'objective' official register, by showing that there are alternative registers (involving alternative ideological perspectives) which the official discourse cannot homogenise, and which resist official authority. Aware of this, we can perhaps better appreciate those instances in the canonical poems in which Burns plays around with the languages of official culture. In 'Death and Doctor Hornbook. A True Story' (K, 55), for example, the limitations of another official discourse are revealed, when the resources of medical Latin are brought to bear on Hornbook's ludicrous battery of medicines:

> 'Urinus Spiritus of capons;
> 'Or Mite-horn shavings, filings, scrapings,
> > 'Distill'd *per se*;
> 'Sal-alkali o' Midge-tail clippings,
> > 'And mony mae.'   (ll. 128–32)

In 'Address to the Deil' (K, 76), it is the language of literary epic which Burns makes us view from the outside, as a discourse with limits. Milton's portentous address to Satan, which Burns takes as his epigraph,

> O Prince, O chief of many throned pow'rs,
> That led th' embattl'd Seraphim to war,

is followed immediately by Burns's own peremptory, lapel-grabbing address, which incorporates nicknames and vernacular Scots:

> O THOU, whatever title suit thee!
> Auld Hornie, Satan, Nick, or Clootie.   (ll. 1–2)

Again, the effect is to demonstrate that the supposedly monologic official language is, when considered apart from its status, just another element in the complex, heteroglossic mélange of social discourses. As the deil's various sobriquets attest, there is no straightforward fit between word and object.

It is not merely in the treatment of privileged languages but also in the treatment of privileged persons that Burns's bawdry illuminates his canonical work. The folk-humorous treatment of great European leaders in 'Why should na poor folk mowe' is of the same order as the irreverent presentation of British parliamentarians in 'When Guildford good' and of Scots MPs in 'The Author's Earnest Cry and Prayer', and the description of the Prince of Wales 'threshin . . . at hizzies' tails' in 'To a Gentleman who had sent him a News-paper' (K, 282). An awareness of the bawdy work should prevent us from making the same mistake as David Craig in regarding the treatment of the political figures in the canonical poems as puerile and merely 'reductive'. Burns's treatment of MPs, like his treatment of kings and princes in 'Why shouldna poor folk mowe', is ambivalent. To treat MPs as 'local lads saying their piece at a village meeting'[28] might indeed be to bring them down from their position of epic grandeur: but at the same time, it renews them on a more material level, it allows them to be discussed apart from the mystifications of rank and status. Craig evidently feels that Burns has an insufficiently exalted view of his enlightened governors. A genuinely 'reductive' treatment, however, and one which the tractability of the Scots members might well have sanctioned, would be if Burns had anticipated James Gillray's treatment of the English Lords, and depicted the Scots MPs as a herd of cattle, penned ready for the bidders at Smithfield market.[29]

The creation of alternative heraldry, which we noted in connection with 'Green Grow the Rashes', is another device whose use is not confined to the bawdy work. In the fourth Heron election ballad, 'Buy Braw Troggin' (K, 494), the reactionary Rev. James Muirhead is provided with an alternative coat of arms:

> Here's Armorial Bearings,
> Frae the Manse of Urr;
> The crest, an *auld crab-apple*,
> Rotten at the core. (ll. 29–32)

Burns obviously enjoyed this sort of exercise, as a perusal of his letters will testify. Satirising his own laziness in a letter to an unidentified correspondent (*Letters*, II, 92), Burns composes a jocular coat of arms, with two sloths as the supporters and the inverted motto, 'Deil tak the foremost!' And indeed, his famous 'Wood-notes wild' coat of arms (see *Letters*, II, 285), for all that it is solemnly emblazoned on the spines of the Centenary Edition's four volumes, contains more than a little suggestion of parody.

The device of the pseudo-official document, which we noted in connection with Burns's bawdry, occurs throughout the canonical work. There are numerous mock epitaphs, a mock will dictated by a sheep, a jocular elegy, and an alternative laureate's ode, in which the sentiments of Laureate Warton receive much the same revision which Southey's would later undergo in Byron's *Vision of Judgement*. In fact, there are perhaps *two* mock laureate odes: in the 'Ode [For General Washington's Birthday]' Burns creates a King's Birthday Ode for the great republican hero. The bawdy songs, clearly, are integral to the creation of an 'alternative state' in Burns's poetry, an upside-down, carnival world in which sex is required by Act of Session, fornicators have a regulatory body, bards have a king, whores and poets have coats of arms, pet sheep make wills, living men receive elegies, MPs have the status of errand boys or tinkers, and princes and generals are always busy fornicating.

---

28 David Craig, *Scottish Literature and the Scottish People, 1680–1830* (London, 1961), p. 78.

29 See *The Satirical Etchings of James Gillray*, ed. by Draper Hill (New York, 1976), plate 14.

It would be easy to overstate the political significance of this 'alternative state'. Clearly, some of the mock genres are conventional and carry little inherent political freight – the mock elegy and the mock will are stock genres in the vernacular tradition. Nevertheless, as a patriotic Scot and as a voteless farmer, Burns was doubly alienated from the institutional fabric of British society, and he expresses his dissent in a burlesque animus against all things official. The institutional and ideological components of the *ancien régime*, all those forms and practices which require to be invested with mystique, which demand to be seen as natural and inevitable, Burns gleefully exposes. By imagining an alternative, carnival state, Burns demonstrates the artificial and arbitrary character of the existing state. He shows that the components of official culture – the system of rank, the distribution of wealth, the status of 'proper' language – are not given but created.

PART FIVE

POETRY AND POLITICS
IN THE 1790S

CHAPTER EIGHT

'Sacred Freedom': Later Political
Poems and Songs

THE Solemn League and Covenant
Now brings a smile, now brings a tear.
But sacred Freedom, too, was theirs;
If thou 'rt a slave, indulge thy sneer.

('The Solemn League and Covenant' (K, 512))

For the most part, this study has been concerned with Burns's early political writings – that is, with poems and songs written in 1786 or earlier. The reason for this emphasis has been stated: too often, in criticism of Burns, the early political poems have been neglected in favour of the later, by critics eager to view their subject against the backdrop of the French Revolution. In resisting this approach, I have attempted to situate Burns's political verse in the context of indigenous Scottish and British traditions of political discourse, and in so doing to generate fresh readings of some of Burns's most important early works. While its significance for Burns can be overstated, however, the French Revolution remains the defining event of Burns's era. It changed the context in which Burns wrote. It quickened and polarised political life across Europe. It turned abstract principles into matters of immediate political contention. It gave to every public utterance the frisson of controversy. Because of this, the poems and songs written by Burns in the 1790s are perhaps best approached, not in relation to longstanding political discourses and ideological formations, but as interventions in the political moment, as responses to a developing political situation. This chapter charts Burns's poetic excursions across the 'dangerous ground' (*Letters*, I, 392) of post-Revolution politics.

Intially, however, events in France made little impact on Burns. As the Revolution unfolded over the summer of 1789, Burns's eyes were on matters rather closer to home: he was trying to get himself appointed to a Dumfries excise division. He had taken his instruction and received his excise commission the previous summer. Now, with the Ellisland Farm proving – as he had anticipated – a 'ruinous bargain' (*Letters*, II, 22), Burns was ready enter the service. At his own request, he was appointed to the excise division in which he lived, and commenced his duties in September 1789. He pledged allegiance to the King in late October, the same month in which the French king's subjects were forcing their monarch to abandon Versailles and take up residence in Paris. The conjunction is telling: at the very moment when the upheavals in France were galvanising British politics, Burns was signing up as a state functionary, the placeman of a Tory administration, the servant of King George. The tensions in which this involved him – the tension between his official position and his private sentiments, between the reticence of the placeman and the volubility of the poet – were ones with which Burns would wrestle for the remainder of his life. When he wrote or spoke out on public affairs, Burns would do so, not merely as a Scottish bard, but as a government employee. This scenario becomes even more intriguing when we reflect that, just prior to the onset of the French Revolution, Burns had been identified in print as a friend of the Whig opposition.

'A little tinctured with Buff & Blue': Burns and the Whig Opposition

Between the end of 1786 and the spring of 1789, it would have been stretching a point to describe Burns as a political poet. His creative output for this period contains almost nothing of political interest. There is a four-line squib, 'On Johnson's Opinion of Hampden' (K, 191), vindicating the republican hero against Dr Johnson's Tory condescension. There is 'The Fête Champetre' (K, 224), a gentle satire on the bribing of voters during an electoral canvass. And there are some tepid Jacobite effusions, mainly traditional lyrics renovated by Burns. And that about covers it. Admittedly, these had been hectic years for Burns, involving his triumphant first winter in the capital, his tours round Scotland in 1787, his removal to Ellisland, where a new farmhouse had to be built, and the preparations for his entry into the excise. Despite these distractions, however, Burns's artistic output remained respectably high. While in Edinburgh, he had made the acquaintance of James Johnson, a music engraver who was compiling a comprehensive collection of traditional Scottish airs, to be published under the title, *The Scots Musical Museum*. Burns became Johnson's enthusiastic collaborator on the project, collecting and adapting old lyrics and acting as 'editor of the *Museum* in all but name'.[1] But if Burns was now 'absolutely crazed' (*Letters*, I, 168) about songwriting, he was less enthusiastic about political verse. It was not until the spring of 1789 that he began to re-engage with politics.

What re-ignited Burns's interest in 'the villainous business of Politics' (*Letters*, II, 44) was not the commotion in France but rather the regency crisis of 1788–89. When George III was declared insane in November 1788, it seemed, much to the delight of the Whig opposition, that the Prince of Wales would take over as regent. There followed a bitter constitutional wrangle between the Whigs and the Tories over the proposed powers of the regent, until the king resolved the matter by recovering his sanity in February 1789. The crisis produced two poetic responses from Burns: a laborious, mock-heroic 'Ode to the departed Regency-bill – 1789' (K, 258), which flays the frantic manoeuvring of both political parties, and 'A new Psalm for the Chapel of Kilmarnock' (K, 260), an ironic hymn of thanksgiving

---

1 Donald Low, Introduction to *The Scots Musical Museum 1787–1803*, 2 vols (Aldershot, 1991), I, 2.

for the monarch's convalescence. Sending the regency Ode to Mrs Dunlop, Burns bubbles with enthusiasm:

> I have just this moment finished the following political Squib, and I cannot resist the temptation to send you a copy of it – the only copy indeed that I will send to any body except perhaps anonymously to some London newspaper. – Politics is dangerous ground for me to tread on, and yet I cannot for the soul of me resist an impulse of anything like Wit.   (*Letters*, I, 392)

Alive to the need for circumspection, Burns is nevertheless desperate to vent his opinions, whether in the sanctum of his private correspondence or through anonymous publication in the newspapers. He was writing political verse once more and he wanted a public for his poems. To this end, he sought out the address of Peter Stuart, founder of the opposition *Morning Star*, and began to correspond with him. He sent Stuart a number of poems, including the 'Ode', which appeared in the *Star* on 17 April) and 'A new psalm', which appeared on 14 May.[2] The same month, Burns describes his relationship with Stuart in a letter to Mrs Dunlop:

> You must know that the Publisher of one of the most blasphemous party London Newspapers is an acquaintance of mine, and as I am a little tinctured with Buff & Blue myself, I now and then help him to a Stanza.
>
> (*Letters*, I, 403)

Burns was beginning to see himself as something of a Whig propagandist, the hired gun of the opposition forces.

It was in this spirit of partisan Whiggery that he composed his 'Sketch. Inscribed to the Rt. Hon. Ch. J. Fox Esq.' (K, 262), in which he presents his compliments to the opposition leader and claims Fox as his 'Patron' (l. 7). For the most part, admittedly, the poem has precious little to do with Fox, the body of the piece being a series of anodyne reflections on the complexity of human nature, proving – hold the front page – that 'Mankind is a science defies definitions' (l. 28). At the opening of the poem, however, Burns addresses Fox directly:

> Thou, first of our orators, first of our wits,
> Yet whose parts and acquirements seem just lucky hits;
> With knowledge so vast, and with judgement so strong,
> No man, with the half of 'em, e'er could go wrong;
> With passions so potent, and fancies so bright,
> No man with the half of 'em e'er could go right;
> A sorry, poor misbegot son of the Muses,
> For using thy name offers fifty excuses.   (ll. 9–16)

---

2 For Burns's dealings with the London press, see Lucyle Werkmeister, 'Some Account of Robert Burns and the London Newspapers, with special reference to the Spurious *Star* (1789)', *Bulletin of the New York Public Library*, 65 (1961), 483–504; 'Robert Burns and the London Daily Press', *Modern Philology*, 63 (1966), 322–35.

A headstrong, impetuous genius, who wears his learning lightly and who is often led astray by the power of his emotion and the brilliance of his wit: all this seems remarkably familiar. And if Fox sounds suspiciously like Robert Burns's idea of Robert Burns, it comes as no surprise when, at the poem's close, 'Billy' Pitt is cast as the villain of the piece, a pushing, 'wardly' fellow of the sort disparaged in the verse epistles:

> But truce with abstraction, and truce with a muse,
> Whose rhymes you'll perhaps, Sir, ne'er deign to peruse:
> Will you leave your justings, your jars and your quarrels,
> Contending with Billy for proud-nodding laurels?
> (My much-honour'd Patron, believe your poor Poet,
> Your courage much more than your prudence you show it;
> In vain with Squire Billy for laurels you struggle,
> He'll have them by fair trade, if not, he will smuggle;
> Not cabinets even of kings would conceal 'em,
> He'd up the back-stairs and by G— he would steal 'em!
> Then feats like Squire Billy's you ne'er can atchieve 'em,
> It is not, outdo him, the task is, outthieve him.)   (ll. 39–50)

Like Willie Simpson or John Lapraik, Fox is warned not to struggle for honours and fame. A good-natured fellow like himself is ill-equipped in the tussle for treasure: it is the selfish and unprincipled who, like 'Squire' Pitt, will always come out on top.

The 'Sketch' is by no means in Burns's best manner, being marred both by a glibly knowing tone and by the runaway momentum of its anapaestic metre. Still, if it falters as a work of art, the poem remains important as a political testament. It is here that Burns announces his party allegiance, nailing his buff and blue colours to the mast. The significance of this act becomes clear when we reflect that, until this point, Burns's political verse had been pronouncedly Pittite in sympathy. Prior to May 1789, as William Donaldson has pointed out, references to William Pitt in Burns's poems had been mainly favourable, while those to Charles Fox has been largely disparaging.[3] Though commentators have been quick to accuse Burns of political 'confusion', there is nothing incongruous in his early support for Pitt. The political configuration of British politics in the 1790s – where Fox, the reformist icon, confronts Pitt, the reactionary Tory diehard – should not be read back into the previous decade. For most of the 1780s, Pitt's reformist credentials were, if anything, stronger than those of Fox. In 1785, the year before Burns's Kilmarnock edition, Pitt had proposed a reform bill which, if successful, would have abolished thirty-six rotten boroughs, redistributed a number of seats and extended the county franchise. Twice before – in 1782 and 1783 – Pitt had introduced motions on reform. The defeat of these measures may have been a foregone conclusion, but Pitt

---

3 William Donaldson, 'The Glencairn Connection: Robert Burns and Scottish
  Politics, 1786–1796', *Studies in Scottish Literature*, 16 (1981), 61–79 (pp. 62–66).

was not greatly helped by the somewhat lukewarm support afforded by Fox.[4] Accordingly, while Pitt's reputation was that of a serious and committed – if moderate – reformer, Fox's record was less consistent. To many, he seemed shifty and unreliable, an impression hardly helped by his ferocious debauches, his notorious addiction to gambling and wine, and his generally indifferent stewardship of the Whig opposition. It is no surprise, then, that the Burns of the Kilmarnock poems should favour Pitt over Fox. In 'A Dream', Pitt is 'a true guid fallow's get, / A Name not Envy spairges' (ll. 57–8), while in 'The Author's Earnest Cry and Prayer' the leader of the opposition is 'Yon ill-tongu'd tinkler, *Charlie Fox*' (l. 109), who ought to be packed off 'to his dicing box, / An' sportin lady' (ll. 113–14).

Burns's supposed political *bouleversement*, then, is nothing of the sort. It is not that Burns had altered his political sentiments – rather that Pitt and Fox had altered their conduct. In any case, Burns's loyalty, as outlined in a letter of 1787 to Henry Erskine, is less to any particular party or politician than to a core of key ideas and values:

> I have a few first principles in Religion and Politics which, I believe, I would not easily part with; but for all the etiquette of, by whom, in what manner, &c. I would not have a dissocial word about it with any one of God's creatures.
>
> (*Letters*, I, 77)

In fact, it is precisely this question of 'the etiquette of, by whom, in what manner, &c.' that explains Burns's switch of allegiance. For most of the 1780s, William Pitt had seemed to be the politician most likely to put Burns's 'first principles' into practice. By the end of the decade, that person was Charles James Fox. Burns reacted accordingly, and by 1789 was well on his way to becoming the poet laureate of the Whigs. It is true that, in the Dumfries Burghs election of that year, he backed the Tory candidate, but this was because the Whigs' patron was the arrogant and obnoxious Duke of Queensberry, 'a cynical recent convert to the Whigs'.[5] From 1789, as William Donaldson indicates, Burns was ever more openly identified as a Foxite Whig: 'the underlying movement of his sympathies is unmistakeably towards the Opposition'.[6]

A few days after despatching the 'Sketch' to Mrs Dunlop, Burns was once more writing to Peter Stuart of the *Star*, sending new verses and seeking to clarify his arrangement with the paper. Authorising Stuart to make appropriate changes to any poems he may send, Burns undertakes to follow the paper's political line, promising to be a loyal supporter of the Whigs and their political ally the Prince of Wales:

> Any alterations you think necessary in my trifles, make them and welcome. In political principles, I promise you I shall be seldom out of the way; as I could lay down my life for that amiable, gallant, generous fellow, our heir apparent'.
>
> (*Letters*, I, 408)

---

4 Michael J. Turner, *British Politics in an Age of Reform* (Manchester, 1999), pp. 27, 37.
5 Donaldson, 'Glencairn Connection', p. 66.
6 Donaldson, 'Glencairn Connection', p. 66.

Burns is also careful to insist that his submissions are to be printed anonymously, unless he expressly indicates otherwise: 'I must beg of you never to put my name to any thing I send, except where I myself set it down at the head or foot of the piece' (*Letters*, I, 409). Given this explicit stipulation, it is astonishing to discover that Peter Stuart actually printed this letter in its entirety in the *Star* for 7 May. In so doing, he exposed Burns as an active Whig propagandist.

In the spring of 1789, then, partly through his own outspokenness, and partly through the actions of Peter Stuart, Burns stood revealed in his true political colours. In March of the following year, the poet was once more sailing close to the political wind, this time in a theatrical prologue performed in the Dumfries theatre. The 'Scots Prologue, *For Mrs. Sutherland's Benefit Night*, Spoken at the Theatre Dumfries' (K, 315) was written for the wife of Burns's friend George Sutherland, manager of the resident company of actors. Like Burns's earlier theatrical prologues, the piece contains some rather portentous blasts of nationalist rhetoric; in this case, however, Burns was worried that he had overstepped the political mark. He sent a copy in advance to the Provost of Dumfries, acknowledging that 'there is a dark stroke of Politics in the belly of the piece' (*Letters*, II, 18), and jocularly asking whether it ought to see the light. In the event, the prologue was duly delivered, and most modern commentators have seen little reason for Burns's anxiety – Kinsley, for instance, calls the prologue 'a merely patriotic poem'.[7]

The prologue's theme is the need for a native Scottish drama, based on the formative episodes in Scotland's turbulent history. It opens with a tirade against fashionable imports from the London stage:

> WHAT needs this din about the town o' Lon'on?
> How this new Play, and that new Sang is comin?
> Why is outlandish stuff sae meikle courted?
> Does Nonsense mend, like Brandy, when imported –
> Is there nae Poet, burning keen for Fame,
> Will bauldly try to gie us Plays at hame?   (ll. 1–6)

This sentiment may indeed be relatively uncontentious, as Kinsley suggests. It is certainly not daringly original, drawing as it does on the prologue to Addison's *Cato*:

> Our Scene precariously subsists too long
> On *French* Translation, and *Italian* Song.
> Dare to have Sense your selves; Assert the Stage,
> Be justly warm'd with your own Native Rage.
> Such Plays alone should please a *British* Ear,
> As *Cato*'s self had not disdain'd to hear.[8]

Still, it is worth noting that, in what is essentially a piece of epideictic rhetoric, an oration designed to bring an audience together and emphasise its coherent identity,

7 Kinsley, III, 1341.
8 *Cato*, p. v.

Burns appeals, not to a common British patriotism (as Addison does), but to a Scottishness defined *against* England. It may be, too, that a poem urging Scots to shift for themselves and not rest content with 'Nonsense' from London would strike a political chord, and that the 'new Sang' in line 2 would raise thoughts of the regrettable 'end of ane auld sang' in 1707. Certainly, Burns has no compunction in pointing out the dramatic potential of Scotland's historic struggle against England:

> There's themes enow in Caledonian story,
> Wad shew the Tragic Muse in a' her glory.
> Is there no daring Bard will rise and tell
> How glorious Wallace stood, how hapless fell?
> Where are the Muses fled, that should produce
> A *drama* worthy of the name of Bruce?
> How on this spot he first unsheath'd the sword
> 'Gainst mighty England, and her guilty Lord,
> And after many a bloody, deathless doing,
> Wrench'd his dear country from the jaws of Ruin!   (ll. 11–20)

While Burns did not live to fulfil his ambition to write such patriotic dramas, he did celebrate the doings of Wallace and Bruce in some of the political songs and poems he wrote in the course of the next few years.

Still, this allusion to Scotland's former glory is not the most radical passage in the poem. The 'dark stroke of Politics' comes a little later, when Burns delivers a eulogy on the family of Douglas:

> One Douglas lives in Home's immortal page,
> But Douglases were heroes every age:
> And tho' your fathers, prodigal of life,
> A Douglas followed to the martial strife,
> Perhaps, if bowls row right, and Right succeeds,
> Ye yet may follow where a Douglas leads!   (ll. 29–34)

As Noble and Hogg point out, the rather cryptic couplet at the end of this passage apparently refers to Basil William Douglas-Hamilton, Lord Daer.[9] This is the high-born democrat and radical Whig with whom Burns dined at Dugald Stewart's Ayrshire mansion in 1786, and who is celebrated by Burns in the 1786 'Extempore Verses on Dining with Lord Daer' (K, 127):

> The fient a pride, nae pride had he,
> Nor sauce, nor state, that I could see,
>   Mair than an honest Ploughman.   (ll. 40–42)

Widely known for his radicalism and Scottish nationalism, Daer 'had been in Paris at the commencement of the French Revolution, and was an ardent reformer'.[10]

---

9 *The Canongate Burns*, pp. 734–35.
10 Meikle, p. 106.

When the Scottish Society of the Friends of the People was founded in 1792, Daer was one of the movement's leaders; at the first Edinburgh convention he addressed the delegates as 'Fellow Citizens' and commended 'the great principles of liberty and political equality'.[11] In alluding so coolly to this prominent democrat, Burns was signalling his support for radical political reform. In effect, as Noble and Hogg suggest, Burns was touting Lord Daer as a 'potential leader of a reformed Scotland'.[12]

The fact that he was personally acquainted with Daer points to another important – and relatively neglected – aspect of Burns's political profile. Throughout his life – in Ayrshire, Edinburgh and Dumfries – Burns moved in Whiggish circles and cultivated the acquaintance of prominent Whigs and radicals. In Ayrshire, he associated with liberal Freemasons and Whiggish New Light ministers, as well as with prominent reformers like Dugald Stewart – 'that plain, honest, worthy man, the Professor' (*Letters*, I, 60) – and Lord Daer. In Edinburgh in 1787 he wore buff and blue and mixed with a group of leading west-country Whigs, including the Earl of Glencairn, Sir John Whitefoord and James Dalrymple of Orangefield, and attended meetings of the 'boozy, boisterous, in many instances brilliant, radical, reformist club, The Crochallan Fencibles'.[13] Among his 'avowed Patrons' (*Letters*, I, 71) in Edinburgh was Henry Erskine, Whiggish Freemason and leading county reformer. Burns was friendly, too, with Erskine's brothers: David, the radical Earl of Buchan, and Thomas, the liberal lawyer, who would go on to defend Thomas Paine. James Maitland, Earl of Lauderdale, was another Edinburgh acquaintance, whom Burns found 'exceedingly easy, accessible, agreable' (*Letters*, I, 80): a student of John Millar at Glasgow, Maitland travelled to France with Dugald Stewart and John Moore to view the Revolution at first hand, and was one of the leading figures in the Friends of the People.[14] When he returned to the south-west in 1788, Burns's closest friends included Robert Riddell, a Whig polemicist,[15] Maria Riddel, a 'professed republican',[16] and John Syme, one of the 'Sons of Sedition'.[17] He cultivated the acquaintance of Alexander Fergusson of Craigdarroch, hero of 'The Whistle' (K, 272), who had been present at the Fortune's Tavern meeting of reformers in 1792, William Robertson of Lude, 'the father of Scotch County Reform' (*Letters*, II, 264), John Francis Erskine of Mar and Richard Oswald of Auchencruive. Burns

11 Meikle, p. 242.
12 *The Canongate Burns*, p. 640.
13 *The Canongate Burns*, xlii.
14 Meikle, p. 49.
15 A reformist essay, written by Riddell under the pen-name 'Cato', was submitted by Burns to the *Edinburgh Gazetteer*, where it duly appeared. The essay is excerpted in *The Canongate Burns*, p. 747.
16 Carswell, p. 328.
17 So called, along with Burns, William Maxwell, James Mundell and one 'Craken the attorney' in a political squib composed by a Dumfries loyalist club. See the headnote to 'Extempore [on The *Loyal Natives*' Verses]' (K, 450).

was also in correspondence with prominent English radicals like William Roscoe, Mary Wollstonecraft, Helen Maria Williams and Dr Wolcot ('Peter Pindar'), and in contact with United Irish sympathisers like Samuel Thomson and Luke Mullan.[18]

For a man who kept such company, keeping one's counsel was hardly an option. Through his friends and associates, Burns continually advertised his radical Whiggish sympathies. To that extent, his declaration of allegiance in 1789 merely ratified what was already known. Or rather, it confirmed that Burns, as well as being a 'True Whig', was also an adherent of the Whig party. Being, as he acknowledged, 'Bred and educated in revolution principles' (*Letters*, I, 333), he had always been, on an intellectual level, a True Whig. He was, in Kinsley's words, 'naturally Whiggish'[19] – or, in his own description of Robert Riddell, 'A Whig in principle and grain'.[20] He had now decided that the Foxite wing of the Whig party was an adequate repository of genuine Whig principles. The result was that, when the Revolution began to polarise British society towards the end of 1790, when reformist and loyalist groups began to organise in earnest, Burns would be a marked man, a known reformer, one of the dissident and disaffected.

'May Liberty meet wi' success!': The Politics of Optimism

In the spring of 1790, however, Burns's radical principles would have alarmed no one. The rancorous divisions opened up by the Revolution were not yet apparent, and developments in France were still viewed favourably by the propertied elite and the British press. The French, it was felt, had at last caught up with the Glorious Revolution of 1688, whose centenary had so recently been celebrated.[21] The 'October Days' of 1789, when the mob had forced the king to move his residence from Versailles to Paris, had, it is true, unsettled some observers, but most Britons still viewed the Revolution with benign satisfaction. It would not be long, however, before this complacency was shattered. What polarised the British debate over France was partly the increasingly bloody turn of events in France, but perhaps even more significant was the literary intervention of Edmund Burke.

Reflections on the Revolution in France, Burke's impassioned, flamboyant and often superbly written attack on France's political 'experiment', appeared in November 1790. The Revolution, according to Burke, had nothing to do with the moderate and constitutional proceedings of 1688. Nor was it rooted in French constitutional tradition. Rather, it was an infatuated dalliance with visionary schemes and abstract principles which could only issue in catastrophe. The lesson for the British was clear: they should refuse to trust their future to the speculations of 'political

---

18 *The Canongate Burns*, xxi.
19 Kinsley, III, 1313.
20 'A Fragment – On Glenriddel's Fox breaking his chain' (K, 527), l. 18.
21 William Doyle, *The Oxford History of the French Revolution* (Oxford, 1989), p. 161; Devine, *Scottish Nation*, p. 203.

theologians',[22] and must defend the precious inheritance of their organic constitution. Almost as soon as the *Reflections* appeared, reformers rushed to denounce Burke and what they saw as his hysterical libel on the patriots of France. The surge of polemic included two Scottish offerings: Thomas Christie's *Letters on the French Revolution* (1791) and James Mackintosh's *Vindiciae Gallicae* (1791). By universal consent, however, the strongest and most successful of the anti-Burke pamphlets was Thomas Paine's *Rights of Man*, whose first part appeared in February 1791, the second part following a year later. Paine fell with satiric glee on Burke's 'flowery' treatise, ridiculing his 'theatrical' treatment of events in France and mocking the suggestion that contemporary Britons were bound by the decisions of the parliament of 1688, arguing that 'as government is for the living, and not for the dead, it is the living only that has any right in it'.[23]

The Burke-Paine controversy took political debate far beyond the confines of the nation's political elite: 200,000 copies of the *Rights of Man*, and 30,000 of the *Reflections*, had been sold in Britain by 1793.[24] The Paisley poet Alexander Wilson rejoices at the impact of Paine in his 'Address to the Synod of Glasgow and Ayr':

> The 'Rights of Man' is now weel kenned,
>   And red by mony a hunder;
> For Tammy Paine the buik has penned,
>   And lent the Courts a lounder;
> It's like a keeking-glass to see
>   The craft of Kirk and statesmen;
> And wi' a bauld and easy glee,
>   Guid faith the birky beats them
>   Aff hand this day.[25]

Wilson's 'mony a hunder' were devouring newspapers and magazines as well as the works of Paine. There had been eight Scottish newspapers in 1782; by 1790 there were 27.[26] The *Edinburgh Herald* was founded in 1790 to provide detailed coverage and discussion of events in France. A new periodical, *The Bee*, appeared in 1791 and was soon publishing James Thomson Callender's inflammatory and influential articles on 'The Political Progress of Britain', which indicted Britains's 'corrupt' constitution and lamented the impotence and compliance of the Scottish MPs. The growth of the press improved the political competence and confidence of the lower classes as, in towns and villages throughout the Scottish lowlands, in the reading

22 Edmund Burke, *Reflections on the Revolution in France*, ed. by J. G. A. Pocock (Indianapolis, 1987), p. 10.
23 Thomas Paine, *Rights of Man*, ed. by Eric Foner (Harmondsworth, 1984), pp. 45, 49, 59.
24 Doyle, p. 169.
25 *The Poems and Literary Prose of Alexander Wilson*, ed. by Alexander B. Grosart, 2 vols (Paisley, 1876), II, 73.
26 Meikle, p. 86.

societies and debating clubs, working men gathered together to read and reflect on the news.

The new mood of political inquiry did not pass over Ellisland Farm, where Burns shared in the general hunger for news and debate. Burns's dealings with the London press have already been mentioned; the poet was also one of the original subscribers to *The Bee*. Like others of his time, Burns regarded the consumption of news as a social activity, circulating newspapers among his friends. There is an undated letter, probably written from Ellisland around this time, which sees Burns forwarding to his neighbour Robert Riddell a newspaper with 'some foreign . . . news which you may not have seen' (*Letters*, II, 114). In a short poem from the same period, 'To Captain Riddell' (K, 528), Burns acknowledges receipt of another newspaper from Riddell. Burns appears to have read the news assiduously: his lines 'To a Gentleman who had sent him a News-paper' (K, 282), written in 1789 or 1790,[27] reveal, not merely Burns's eagerness for 'intelligence', but his command of European and domestic affairs:

> This mony a day I've grained and gaunted,
> To ken what French mischief was brewin;
> Or what the drumlie Dutch were doin;
> That vile doup-skelper, Emperor Joseph,
> If Venus yet had got his nose off;
> Or how the collieshangie works
> Atween the Russians and the Turks . . .
> Or how our merry lads at hame,
> In Britain's court kept up the game:
> How Royal George, the Lord leuk o'er him!
> Was managing St. Stephen's quorum;
> If sleekit Chatham Will was livin,
> Or glaikit Charlie got his nieve in.   (ll. 4–12, 19–24)

The informal, reductive idiom of the poem nicely suggests the manner in which the modern newspaper reduces the great affairs of Britain and Europe to a manageable compass, and makes the news as accessible and digestible as parish gossip. Something of the enthusiasm with which political news and political ideas were being debated at the time can be seen in 'A Fragment – On Glenriddel's Fox breaking his chain' (K, 527), probably written in 1791.[28] Robert Riddell of Glenriddell was Burns's friend and neighbour, residing at Friar's Carse on the north side of Ellisland. The friendship between the two men was founded on a raft of common interests, including Scottish music, antiquarianism, heavy drinking and – most importantly for our purposes – opposition Whiggism. They also co-

---

27 Kinsley follows Currie in dating the poem to January 1790, but McGuirk places it in April or May 1789. See Kinsley, III, 1326; Robert Burns, *Selected Poems*, ed. by McGuirk, p. 254.

28 Kinsley, III, 1493.

operated in establishing the Monkland Friendly Society, a local book club and circulating library, at whose monthly meetings the latest political developments were doubtless debated.

'On Glenriddel's Fox' takes the form of a facetious attack on Robert Riddell for the crime of keeping a wild fox confined to a 'dirty kennel' (l. 15) on his estate. How, the poem asks, can such a sterling opponent of tyranny, such a determined advocate of natural rights, behave so high-handedly towards this 'free-born creature, / A native denizen of Nature' (ll. 19–20). The rather obvious pun hanging over the poem – that a 'Foxite' Whig should treat a fox so poorly – reinforces the jocular tone:

> The staunchest Whig Glenriddel was,
> Quite frantic in his country's cause;
> And oft was Reynard's prison passing,
> And with his brother Whigs canvassing
> The Rights of Men, the Powers of Women,
> With all the dignity of Freeman. –
>
>   Sir Reynard daily heard debates
> Of Princes' kings' and Nations' fates;
> With many rueful, bloody stories
> Of tyrants, Jacobites and tories:
> From liberty how angels fell,
> That now are galley-slaves in hell;
> How Nimrod first the trade began
> Of binding Slavery's chains on Man . . .
> How Xerxes, that abandon'd tory,
> Thought cutting throats was reaping glory,
> Until the stubborn Whigs of Sparta
> Taught him great Nature's Magna charta;
> How mighty Rome her fiat hurl'd,
> Resistless o'er a bowing world,
> And kinder than they did desire,
> Polish'd mankind with sword and fire:
> With much too tedious to relate,
> Of Antient and of Modern date,
> But ending still how Billy Pit,
> (Unlucky boy!) with wicked wit,
> Has gagg'd old Britain, drain'd her coffer,
> As butcher's bind and bleed a heifer. –
>
>   Thus wily Reynard by degrees,
> In kennel listening at his ease,
> Suck'd in a mighty stock of knowledge,
> As much as some folks at a college. –

> Knew Britain's rights and constitution,
> Her aggrandizement, diminution,
> How fortune wrought us good from evil;
> Let no man then despise the devil,
> As who can say, I ne'er can need him;
> Since we to scoundrels owe our freedom.   (ll. 25–38, 43–66)

A gentle satire on a close friend, the poem is also a telling document of grassroots Scottish radicalism. Three points in particular emerge from this passage. Firstly, the poem testifies to the sheer enthusiasm and vitality of the reform movement: daily debates and open-air seminars, groups of neighbours plunged in disputation – and all this taking place in the wilds of rural Dumfriesshire. Secondly, the poem reveals very clearly the eclectic nature of reformist ideology. The debaters call on a wide range of references, including bibilical figures (Nimrod), classical history (Xerxes, Sparta), the British constitutional tradition (Magna charta), new French ideas ('the Rights of Men'), oral histories of Stuart tyranny and the Covenanting movement ('many rueful, bloody stories / Of tyrants, Jacobites and tories'), and contemporary domestic politics ('Billy Pit' and his assault on 'old Britain'). We should note here, not only the breadth of reference, but the manner in which historical incidents are 'translated' into contemporary discourse, as in the reference to Xerxes as an 'abandon'd tory' (l. 43) or to the 'stubborn Whigs of Sparta' (l. 45). Here, Whig and Tory are not just the labels of contemporary political parties but coherent political philosophies which can be read back into history. There is also the extraordinary reference to 'great Nature's Magna charta' (l. 46), suggesting that the rights asserted in the great charter of English liberty are simply the universal rights of man. There could hardly be a pithier example of the radicals' readiness to combine arguments from natural law and constitutional precedent.

The third point to which the poem attests is the reformist emphasis on political education. In a report on the activities of the Monkland Friendly Society (see *Letters*, II, 108), Burns compares the uneducated peasant to a brute beast. What we see in this poem is a brute beast being schooled in the principles of political liberty. Given Burns's collaboration with Riddell in the Monkland Friendly Society, it is difficult not to perceive this poem as a parable of popular education. It was at clubs like the Monkland society that working men could – like Glenriddell's fox – lay in 'a mighty stock of knowledge' (l. 59), and so become fitted for citizenship, ready to exercise those political rights which were theirs by nature.

'On Glenriddel's Fox' pulses with the intellectual energy released by the French Revolution. By 1792, this energy was turning into political activism, with the appearance of bodies like the London Corresponding Society, founded in January 1792 by a Scottish shoemaker named Thomas Hardy, and the London Friends of the People, founded in April of the same year by Grey, Sheridan, Maitland and others. In July 1792 the Scottish Friends of the People, a sister society to the London organisation, was formed at a Bastille commemoration in Fortune's Tavern, Edinburgh. It spread widely over the coming months, along with groups like the Friends of the Constitution and the Friends of Liberty – indeed, there was 'an explosive growth of reform societies all over Lowland Scotland between October and December 1792'.[29] It appeared, throughout this year, that reform was gaining irresistible momentum. In a Commons speech of 30 April 1792, Charles Grey gave notice that he was preparing a reform motion to bring before the House, and was warmly supported by the Foxite Whigs. Buoyed up by this, and by the staggering successes of the French Revolutionary armies (celebrated by Burns in 'Why should na poor folk mowe'), the reformers felt that their hour was at hand. The *Edinburgh Gazetteer* trumpeted the coming triumph: 'Despotism has now been shook to the centre on the Continent and before the conclusion of next summer the Tree of Liberty will occupy the soil that has long been usurped by merciless tyranny!'.[30] It was towards the end of 1792, at the joyous height of reformist optimism, that Burns wrote a spirited ballad in support of the Whig party leaders.

'Here's a Health to them that's awa' (K, 391) celebrates a group of leading Whig reformers – Thomas Erskine, James Maitland, Norman Macleod and the Earl of Wycombe – in round after round of boisterous toasts. The song is adapted from an old Jacobite ditty, but in this case the toast is not to the king over the water but to the reformers across the border. 'Charlie' is Charles James Fox, and 'our cause' (l. 3) is the cause of reform:

> Here's a health to them that's awa,
> Here's a health to them that's awa;
> Here's a health to Charlie, the chief o' the clan,
> Altho' that his band be sma'.
> May Liberty meet wi' success!
> May Prudence protect her frae evil
> May Tyrants and Tyranny tine i' the mist,
> And wander their way to the devil!   (ll. 9–16)

The tone is festive, even triumphalist. The authorities, it appears, are running scared, taking futile measures to stem the tide of liberty. In the third verse, which toasts Erskine, Burns ridicules the proclamation against seditious writings of May 1792, by which the government tried to ban the *Rights of Man*:

> Here's freedom to him that wad read,
> Here's freedom to him that wad write!
> There's nane ever fear'd that the Truth should be heard,
> But they whom the Truth wad indite.   (ll. 21–24)

Burns had little doubt that Paine's indictment of Old Corruption would stick and that a united British reform movement – 'friends on baith sides o' the Forth, / And friends on baith sides o' the Tweed' (ll. 37–8) – would carry the day. The whole song vibrates with the assurance of victory, and the conviction that those who are not on

---

29 Devine, *Scottish Nation*, p. 206.
30 *Edinburgh Gazetteer*, 7 December 1792.

the reformers' side will shortly regret it. There is in it the kind of complacent certitude displayed by the Dundee Whig Club when, in its 1790 address to the French National Assembly, it hailed the Revolution as 'the triumph of liberty and reason over despotism, ignorance and superstition'.[31] Put in these terms, victory seemed inevitable. Charlie's 'band' might 'be sma'', but they have 'the Truth' (l. 23) on their side, and the Truth will prevail. As it turned out, Burns was entirely wrong. The 'Truth' did not prevail, and his ballad stands as a monument to ill-founded optimism, its cocksure toasts ringing out with a retrospective hollowness. By the close of 1792, the reform movement was already coming apart. The loyalist backlash had begun.

'This unlucky blast': the loyalist backlash and the Excise Board enquiry

It had seemed, in the sanguine days of 1792, that the power of the old regime would dissipate like mist: in fact, what vanished was the reformers' easy optimism, burned off by the ferocious heat of the loyalist reaction. However belatedly, the British elite had woken up to the dangers it faced. It had realised, for one thing, that its interpretation of events across the Channel – the French taking a leaf from the book of English Liberty – was dangerously wide of the mark. When the French king attempted to flee his country, and was dragged back to Paris by a howling mob, 'as hostage, not as king',[32] the elite began to revise its opinion. But what really focused British minds was the 'Second Revolution' of August 10, when a sansculottes uprising forced the suspension of the monarchy. The new order introduced universal suffrage, banished refractory priests and suspended manorial dues. Over a thousand prisoners suspected of counter-revolutionary sympathies were put to death in the 'September Massacres'. Suddenly, too, France's armies were performing with hitherto unsuspected flair. When the invading Prussian forces under the Duke of Brunswick were unexpectedly routed at Valmy, the Revolution was on the march. Leaving the Prussians to retreat, General Dumouriez pushed north to invade the Austrian Netherlands. In the south, Savoy was annexed and French troops took Maine and Frankfurt. In the midst of this expansion – on 22 September – France was declared a republic. Then in November, a bullish National Convention issued the Edict of Fraternity, promising military assistance 'to all peoples who wish to recover their liberty'. What Brissot had been demanding as early as December 1791 – 'a new crusade, a crusade of universal freedom'[33] – now appeared to be taking shape. The Revolution that had promised to curtail France's involvement in European affairs had now produced a republican crusade to threaten every regime in the continent.[34]

---

31 *Caledonian Mercury*, 2 September 1790.
32 Georges Lefebvre, *The French Revolution: From its origins to 1793*, trans. by
   Elizabeth Moss Evanson (1962; repr. London, 2001), p. 203.
33 Lefebvre, p. 211.
34 Lefebvre, pp. 234–5, 238; Doyle, pp. 187–96.

In Scotland, the authorities were further alarmed by outbreaks of domestic unrest. The summer of 1792 saw a spate of disturbances in towns throughout the lowlands. Partly these were 'traditional' responses to economic grievances – corn prices, for instance, had been unusually high – but they also displayed a new political edge. In November, following Dumouriez' victories, another wave of rioting, even more explicitly political in character, tore up the east coast. In Perth, Dundee and Aberdeen, effigies of Dundas were burned and trees of liberty erected. Moderate reformers, among them the leaders of the Friends of the People, were genuinely horrified by the actions of the mob, and rushed to declare their 'abhorrence of riot' and their 'attachment to the constitution', but found it impossible to dissociate themselves from the violence. The authorities blamed the reformers for fomenting plebeian disorder.[35]

The result was a concerted loyalist backlash over the winter of 1792/93 – what Burns described, in April 1793, as 'this unlucky blast which has overturned so many, & many worthy characters who four months ago little dreaded any such thing' (*Letters*, II, 195). The middle classes, according to one observer, were 'now doing everything in their power to check and restrain the Spirit of Sedition they have raised'.[36] Loyalist associations were formed to help distribute conservative propaganda. Pro-government newspapers were subsidised. Radical tradesmen and shopkeepers found themselves blacklisted and boycotted. Professional spies and even unpaid informers rushed to denounce the 'disaffected'. Arrests followed, as leading reformers, among them several acquaintances of Burns, were charged with sedition. James 'Balloon' Tytler was among the first to be arraigned, in January 1793: failing to show at this trial, Burns's friend was duly outlawed. James Anderson, editor of *The Bee* and a correspondent of the poet, was threatened with imprisonment for refusing to divulge the author of 'The Political Progress of Britain': the man in question, James Thomson Callender, promptly fled to America. William Johnston, editor of the *Edinburgh Gazetteer* and another of Burns's correspondents, was charged with contempt of court and later imprisoned.[37]

Burns himself had every reason to be fearful. For a government employee, conscious that politics was 'dangerous ground ... to tread on', Burns had hardly been a model of caution. No enemy of the poet would be tapping his pencil against his teeth when drawing up a political charge sheet. Burns had consorted openly with known radicals and reformers. He had subscribed to a reformist newspaper, encouraging its editor to 'Lay bare, with undaunted heart & steady hand, that horrid mass of corruption called Politics & State-Craft' (*Letters*, II, 158), and his poems had appeared in the same organ. He had been present in Dumfries Theatre, when his

---

35 McFarland, pp. 65–9, 81; John Brims, 'From Reformers to "Jacobins": The Scottish Association of the Friends of the People', in *Conflict and Stability in Scottish Society, 1700–1850*, ed. by T. M. Devine (Edinburgh, 1990), pp. 31–50 (pp. 37–8); Devine, *Scottish Nation*, pp. 204–7; Meikle, pp. 81–2.

36 Home of Wedderburn, quoted in Fraser, p. 14.

37 Fraser, pp. 13–15;

friends had shouted down 'God Save the King', calling for the revolutionary anthem 'Ça ira'. He had been an 'enthusiastic votary' (*Letters*, II, 174) of the French Revolution, reportedly sending four carronades as a gift to the French Assembly. When Dumouriez crushed the Allied armies, he had thrown off a celebratory ballad, 'Why should na poor folk mowe', which he sang in a Dumfries pub. In short, Burns had paraded his progressive political views as he had paraded his heterodox theology as a young man in Tarbolton kirkyard. And with the same result: he 'raised a hue and cry of heresy' against himself. Only this time it was his 'Political heresies' (*Letters*, II, 184) that were at issue, and the punishment he risked was somewhat grimmer than the cutty stool. In late December, Burns's recklessness caught up with him. He was denounced to the authorities as a republican, and the Excise Board launched an enquiry into his political conduct.

The first mention of the affair comes in a rather agitated letter of 31st December. Having got wind of his employers' intention, Burns writes to his friend and patron Robert Graham of Fintry, a Commissioner of the Scottish Board of Excise, protesting his loyalty to the British Constitution. 'Sir', Burns begins:

> I have been surprised, confounded & distracted by Mr Mitchel, the Collector, telling me just now, that he has received an order from your Hon[ora]ble Board to enquire into my political conduct, & blaming me as a person disaffected to Government. – Sir, you are a Husband – & a father – you know what you would feel, to see the much-loved wife of your bosom, & your helpless, prattling little ones, turned adrift into the world, degraded & disgraced from a situation in which they had been respectable & respected, & left . . . almost without the necessary support of a miserable existence. – Alas, Sir! must I think that such, soon, will be my lot! And from the damned, dark insinuations of hellish, groundless Envy too! – I believe, Sir, I may aver it, & in the sight of Omnipotence, that I would not tell a deliberate Falsehood, no, not though even worse horrors, if worse can be, than those I have mentioned, hung over my head; & I say, that the allegation, whatever villain has made it, is a LIE! To the British Constitution, on Revolution principles, next after my God, I am most devoutly attached!   (*Letters*, II, 168–9)

The fear that lay behind the verse epistles – the fear of poverty and destitution – had once more raised its head. In the event, Burns did not lose his job. On 5 January, Graham wrote to reassure him that his position was safe and that no action would be taken against him. He also gave Burns specific details of the allegations that had been made against him. A relieved Burns wrote back at once, making a spirited rebuttal of the charges, and expressing his pleasure that any 'misapprehensions' (*Letters*, II, 175) had been cleared up. The same day he wrote to Mrs Dunlop, declaring that 'the political blast that threatened my welfare is overblown' (*Letters*, II, 171).

The excise enquiry was a sobering experience for Burns, and certainly his letters to Graham of Fintry strive to present his political conduct in the least controversial light. Nevertheless, there is little evidence to suggest, as a number of writers have done, that Burns had somehow renounced his political beliefs. Catherine Carswell's view that Burns had 'abased himself in disingenuous disclaimers and needless apologies' has been echoed by recent commentators. Tom Devine refers to Burns's 'public recantation'. Marilyn Butler writes of Burns being 'forced to apologise and equivocate'. For Ian McIntyre, the first letter to Graham has an 'abject tone' which 'makes painful reading', while Alan Bold describes the second letter as 'an apostatic statement, a diplomatic retreat from principles Burns held dear'.[38] It appears to me, on the contrary, that Burns held his nerve rather coolly throughout the excise enquiry, and so it may be worth looking in some detail at what Burns actually wrote. The opening half of the December 31 letter has already been quoted. Here is how the letter ends:

> Fortune, Sir, has made you powerful, & me impotent; has given you patronage, & me dependance. – I would not for my *single Self* call on your Humanity; were such my insular, unconnected situation, I would despise the tear that now swells in my eye – I could brave Misfortune, I could face Ruin: for at the worst, "Death's thousand doors stand open;" but, Good God! the tender concerns that I have mentioned, . . . how they ennerve Courage, & wither Resolution! To your patronage, as a man of some genius, you have allowed me a claim; & your esteem, as an honest Man, I know is my due: to these, Sir, permit me to appeal; & by these may I adjure you to save me from that misery which threatens to overwhelm me, & which, with my latest breath I will say it, I have not deserved.
> (*Letters*, II, 169)

Far from being 'abject', the tone here is assertive, even prickly. Acknowledging the inequality in their relationship, Burns declares that it is to 'Fortune' – not merit – that Graham owes his superior position. Graham is then informed that, had he no dependants to provide for, Burns would scorn to explain his conduct to anyone. Burns goes on to demand Graham's approval: 'your esteem . . . I know is my due'. He is not asking for a special dispensation or for allowances to be made: he merely seeks his 'due', which Graham is obliged to render him. Nor does he 'beg' or 'implore' Graham to save him from ruin. The verb he uses is 'adjure': he solemnly charges Graham with the duty of saving him from a fate which, Burns reiterates once more, he does not deserve. For a man in Burns's position, facing potential destitution in a climate of mounting political hysteria, this is a letter of some courage, even allowing for the fact that Graham is his ally and friend, albeit one who appears to have been active as a government informer.[39]

The letter of 5 January (*Letters*, II, 172–75) in which Burns rebuts the charges laid against him is a similarly resolute performance. It begins deftly: 'Sir, I am this moment honored with your letter: with what feelings I received this other instance of your goodness, I shall not pretend to describe' – a formulation which neatly does

---

38 Carswell, p. 341; Devine, *Scottish Nation*, p. 215; Butler, 'Burns and Politics', p. 95; McIntyre, p. 319; Bold, p. 104.
39 *The Canongate Burns*, p. 251.

away with the need to actually *express* any gratitude. After this cursory gesture of acknowledgement, Burns turn to the charges against him. Having denied that he belongs to an organised party of Dumfries reformers, Burns responds to the incident in the local theatre:

> I was in the playhouse one night, when Çà ira was called for. – I was in the middle of the pit, & from the Pit the clamour arose. – One or two individuals with whom I occasionally associate were of the party, but I neither knew of the Plot, nor joined in the Plot; nor ever opened my lips to hiss, or huzza, that, or any other Political tune whatever.

Not only is this probably true (it tallies with the account of the same incident given to Mrs Dunlop), but it cleverly returns the ball to the accuser's court by suggesting that 'God Save the King' is as much a party song or 'Political tune' as 'Ça ira'. Burns turns next to his opinion of the king:

> I never uttered any invectives against the king. – His private worth, it is altogether impossible that such a man as I, can appreciate; and in his Public capacity, I always revered, & ever will, with the soundest loyalty, revere, the Monarch of Great-britain, as, to speak in Masonic, the sacred KEYSTONE OF OUR ROYAL ARCH CONSTITUTION.

Again, this is scrupulous stuff. Burns's loyalty is to the *office* of the monarch, as an integral element of the balanced British constitution: he pointedly avoids declaring his attachment to the person of the king.

When he comes to declare his own 'reform opinions', in a passage already quoted in Chapter 3, there are no weasel words, no attempts at subterfuge:

> As to REFORM PRINCIPLES, I look upon the British Constitution, as settled at the Revolution, to be the most glorious Constitution on earth, or that perhaps the wit of man can frame; at the same time, I think, & you know what High and distinguished Characters have for some time thought so, that we have a good deal deviated from the original principles of that Constitution; particularly, that an alarming System of Corruption has pervaded the connection between the Executive Power and the House of Commons. – This is the Truth, the Whole truth, of my Reform opinions . . .

These are hardly the words of one seeking to cover his radical tracks, and indeed this passage was sufficiently robust to draw indignant responses from some of Graham's fellow board-members.

Finally, following a discussion of his doings with the *Edinburgh Gazetteer*, which he describes as a 'manly & independant' newspaper, Burns comes to his opinion of events in France:

> As to France, I was her enthusiastic votary in the beginning of the business. – When she came to shew her old avidity for conquest, in annexing Savoy, &c. to her dominions, & invading the rights of Holland, I altered my sentiments.

It is here, if anywhere, that Burns may be guilty of equivocation, since in a letter to Mrs Dunlop written the same day he refers to the French as 'that gallant people' (*Letters*, II, 172). Nevertheless, Burns's attitude to the French Revolution was not uniformly supportive, as a song like 'The Dumfries Volunteers' (discussed in Chapter 9) makes clear. Nor was uncritical Francophilia a precondition of genuine radicalism. There is no reason why Burns, as a British radical, should feel obliged to defend the annexation of Savoy or for that matter the September Massacres. There is, then, little in the letters to Graham of Fintry to warrant the suggestion that Burns had 'recanted'. As a government employee, Burns acknowledges that he has expressed his political opinions too freely, and he undertakes to be more circumspect in future. But he does not recant. He does not pretend to have abandoned his beliefs. And he does not apologise. Indeed, just how far Burns is from adopting a posture of humble contrition is made apparent in the letter's closing paragraph, in which, with quite astonishing sangfroid, Burns requests promotion to the rank of supervisor.[40]

Nevertheless, there remains one aspect of Burns's conduct during the excise enquiry which particularly perplexes modern critics. This is Burns's declared attachment to the British Constitution. On several occasions, around the winter of 1792/93, Burns voices a strident loyalty to the constitution. He does so in the letters to Graham, and again in the following lines from 'A Toast' (K, 402):

> And here's the grand fabric, our free Constitution,
> As built on the base of the great Revolution.   (ll. 7–8)

Such sentiments appear to be at odds with Burns's strongly held radical views, and critics have been wont to treat them as, in Paul Scott's phrase, 'prudent insincerities'.[41] But are they not rather honest expressions of Burns's radical position, albeit given a maximally uninflammatory spin; if anything, prudent sincerities?

For let us be clear as to what Burns is endorsing. Burns is not declaring his attachment to the constitution as it presently stands, nor to the constitution as an immemorial and organically evolving body of customary practices. Quite unequivocally, Burns's attachment is to the constitution as established on the revolution principles of 1688. The crucial question now becomes: what does Burns understand by 1688? What is the scope of Burns's revolution principles? 'Revolution principles', of course, is a notoriously slippery term, covering a range of positions within eighteenth-century British politics. Essentially, however, there was a 'conservative' and a 'radical' reading of 1688. The conservative reading is perhaps best represented by Burke, for whom 1688 had in fact changed very little: the crown had merely been transferred to another branch of the same royal family; the king

---

40   Burns was appointed Acting Supervisor in late 1794; when he wrote to inform Mrs Dunlop he added: 'My Political sins seem to be forgiven me' (*Letters*, II, 333).

41   The phrase was used by Scott in his paper to the bicentennial Burns Conference at the University of Strathclyde, 12 January 1996.

still ruled by divine sanction, and the duties of passive obedience and non-resistance remained in force. In contrast to Burke, eighteenth-century radicals argued that 1688 had established the constitution on a contractarian basis and confirmed the people's right to resist bad government. For Wilkesite radicals, pro-Americans, and 1790s reformers, 1688 had confirmed 'the natural rights of resistance and popular sovereignty'.[42]

We can gauge which interpretation of 1688 secured Burns's assent by turning to a political letter Burns wrote to the *Edinburgh Evening Courant* on the anniversary of the Glorious Revolution in 1788. In Burns's view, the Revolution was a transforming event; it altered the 'relation between King and subject'; it established the British government on 'covenanted terms', and the king now owed his throne 'to the call of a free people' (*Letters*, I, 334). For Burns, 1688 had established the constitution on a new basis – that of consent and contract. Importantly, in a second letter to the *Courant*, Burns extends the concept of the covenant to comprehend, not merely the relation between ruler and ruled, but also the relation between component territories of a given polity; he refers to the Union of 1707 as having 'solemnly covenanted' (*Letters*, I, 373) the relationship between Scotland and England.

Burns's 'revolution principles' thus comprehend the far-reaching concept of government as a covenant between rulers and ruled. As we have seen, Burns regarded the British constitution as having departed dangerously from its original principles, perverted by a 'System of Corruption'. Whether the constitution had, in Burns's eyes, become sufficiently unbalanced as to jeopardise the welfare of the British people or of one of the component nations (as it had done in the case of America and as it often seemed to be doing in the case of Scotland), remains a moot point. What a poem like 'The Author's Earnest Cry and Prayer' does make clear is that Burns's contractarian view of the British constitution allowed him to envisage circumstances which would justify popular resistance to government and even, perhaps, Scottish rejection of the Union. Far from representing a failure of nerve, then, the conditional attachment to the British constitution which Burns expressed in the winter of 1792/93 is fully in line with the radicalism of the early satires. In early 1793, to declare one's support for the constitution, *on revolution principles*, was a standard gesture of even the most committed British radicals, as the pages of the *Northern Star*, the newspaper of the revolutionary United Irishmen, abundantly witness.[43]

---

42 Kathleen Wilson, 'Inventing Revolution: 1688 and Eighteenth-Century Popular Politics', *Journal of British Studies*, 28 (1989), 349–86 (pp. 362, 386).

43 See, for example, the declaration of the Presbyterian congregation of Drumbo, *Northern Star*, 16–19 January 1793, or the similar declaration by the Randalstown Masonic Lodge, *Northern Star*, 26–30 January 1793.

'Let us DO – or DIE!!!': The Politics of Defiance

The excise enquiry did not lead Burns to recant his 'Political heresies', but it did
bring home to him the dangers that he faced. And what the enquiry – and indeed the
whole bitter winter of 1792/93 – also brought home to the poet was the futility, as
things stood, of constitutional protest. Elaine McFarland has argued that the winter
of 1792/93 marks an important watershed in the development of the Scottish
reform movement. For McFarland, the period 1789–92 is characterised by 'the
politics of optimism', as radicals looked forward to a new age of liberty, trusting that
the power of reason would overthrow the tottering edifices of the old regime. The
ferocious government clampdown of 1792/93 disabused the radicals of this easy
optimism, and the period 1793–94 was marked by 'the politics of defiance', as, losing
faith in the possibility of peaceful reform, the radicals began to consider more
extreme methods, until the movement went 'underground' in the period 1795–97.[44]
There is a sense in which the political poetry of Burns replicates this trajectory.
Burns's own 'politics of optimism', evident throughout 1789–92 and culminating in
the bravado of 'Here's a Health to them that's awa', gives way, from 1793 onwards,
to a darker mood of embattled defiance.

  This altered mood informs 'The Dagger', a longish poem in the Christis Kirk
stanza, which appeared in the *Edinburgh Gazetteer* in May 1793.[45] The occasion of
the poem was a Commons speech by Edmund Burke, delivered on 28 December
1792. Burke was attacking a British subscription scheme which aimed to provide
daggers for the French revolutionary armies in their struggle against Prussia and
Austria. The organiser of the campaign was Dr William Maxwell, a Scot with a
colourful background. Educated by Jesuits in France, Maxwell had been a member
of the French National Guard lining Louis XVI's route to the scaffold: he reputedly
dipped his handkerchief in the dead king's blood. In 1794 he would settle in
Dumfries, becoming the poet's 'most intimate friend'. Burns describes him to Mrs
Dunlop as 'the Dr Maxwell whom Burke mentioned in the House of Commons
about the affair of the daggers' (*Letters*, II, 311).

  In the course of his attack on Maxwell, Burke had theatrically produced a dagger,
waving it around on the floor of the House. For Burns, this is a defining image.
Unwittingly, Burke has embodied the central truth of the new political climate. For
all the solemn flummery of parliamentary debates, what counts now is the naked
force wielded by the state against those it deems its enemies. Parliamentary
eloquence is beside the point:

> For tho' wi' aspect like a Turk,
>   Demosthenes or Tully
> Had tried an argument wi' Burke,
>   An' gi'en him but his gully;

44 McFarland, v.
45 It is reproduced in *The Canongate Burns*, pp. 456–58.

In spite o' a' their eloquence,
    Their rhetoric and logic,
Their Lettres Belle and Common Sense,
    'Twad been a fruitless project,
            For them this day.

For tho' a man can speak wi' grace,
    That matters na a spittle –
Can onie man haud up his face,
    An' argue wi' a whittle?
An Paddy, should the DAGGER fail,
    Before he will knock under,
Can neist apply (to back his tale)
    A twa and forty pounder,
            Wi' birr some day.

But trouth I fear the Parliament
    Its ancient splendour fully,
When chiels man back an argument
    By waving o' a gully:
Yet some there are, wi' honest heart,
    (Whose courage never swaggers)
Will ne'er the public cause desert,
    For cannons or for daggers,
            By night or day.   (ll. 28–54)

The rhetorical armoury of a Cicero or Demosthenes would avail nothing in the British House of Commons. The thrusts of intellect and the parries of wit are powerless against Burke's 'gully'. The irony here is that Burke, the renowned orator, the champion phrase-maker, is shown to rely on the language of violence. He is 'the House o' Commons bully' (l. 13), a description which both degrades and inflates Burke's menace, suggesting as it does that the standards of the schoolyard tyrant or bar-room thug are manipulating the levers of state.

'The Dagger' is a rueful comment on the demise of free debate in a Britain gagged by state intimidation. It is also Burns's recognition of how naïve he had been in a poem like 'Here's a Health to them that's awa', which anticipates the reform movement's triumph in the House of Commons. The notion of reasoned eloquence carrying the day in the British Parliament now appears laughably idealistic. Burns has begun to realise that what confronts the reformers is not a mist of superstition, but the foursquare might of the British State. They face a political elite determined to strain every nerve to hold onto its power and privilege. In this connection, the poem's date is telling. 'The Dagger' appeared on 16 May. Earlier that month, Charles Grey's long-awaited reform motion had been thunderously rejected by a nervous Commons. The dating of the poem implies that the two episodes – the dagger incident and the failure of Grey's motion – are connected: the Commons has shirked its duty, having been cowed by the antics of a loyalist bully. Apart from the few courageous souls who will 'ne'er the public cause desert' (l. 52), the MPs have betrayed the public's trust.

'The Dagger' may be rooted in the events of 1793, but it also points back to an earlier Burns poem in which a knife is brandished at British MPs. In 'The Author's Earnest Cry and Prayer', the Scottish MPs are warned to seek redress of Scotland's grievances or else face the wrath of an insurgent public. If you don't succeed, Burns warns the MPs, then 'auld Scotland' will 'teach you, wi'a reekan whittle, / Anither sang'. The MPs are threatened with popular violence to encourage them to perform their duty. In 'The Dagger', however, the situation is reversed: here the state is threatening force against its own citizens. It is this reversal of natural order that signals the desperate pass to which Britain has come. Peaceful, parliamentary methods have been shown to be useless, and the implication is clear: now is the time for the public at large to trump Burke's gully with their own 'reekan whittle'.

By the summer of 1793, Burns had arrived at the conviction – shared by British reformers generally – that matters had come to a point of crisis. Either liberty would be vindicated by a resurgent populace, or it would be trampled in the dirt by the authorities. The execution of Louis XVI and France's declaration of war on Britain had strengthened the hand of the conservative forces. Two further developments reinforced the reformers' sense of crisis. In July 1793 the Irish parliament placed an outright ban on conventions and seditious assemblies – a draconian measure which, many believed, would shortly be adopted by the British parliament. Then in August came the Scottish sedition trials, and the savage punishments handed down by the coarse and gloating Lord Braxfield. For Thomas Muir's trial, the jury was drawn from members of an Edinburgh loyalist club. Muir got fourteen years' transportation – an unheard-of tariff for the crime of sedition – and William Fysshe Palmer, a Unitarian minister from Dundee, got seven. For many radicals it seemed that the time for action had arrived.[46]

It was at this critical juncture that Burns composed his great war-song, 'Robert Bruce's March to Bannockburn' (K, 425), also known as 'Scots Wha Hae', in which the Wars of Independence provide an implicit commentary on contemporary events. The speaker is Bruce, addressing his troops prior to the battle with the English:

> SCOTS, wha hae wi' WALLACE bled,
> Scots, wham BRUCE has aften led,
> Welcome to your gory bed, –
>   Or to victorie. –
>
> Now's the day, and now's the hour;
> See the front o' battle lour;
> See approach proud EDWARD's power,
>   Chains and Slaverie. –

    (ll. 1–8)

46 Meikle, pp. 131–36.

The Scots troops here are in the position of the Roman senators described in Addison's *Cato* – 'Gods, can a Roman Senate long debate / Which of the two to chuse, Slav'ry or Death!'[47] – or indeed of the French National Assembly as described in Paine's *Rights of Man*: 'Everything now was drawing to a crisis. The event was to be freedom or slavery'.[48] The starkness of the choice facing the Scottish army determines the starkness of the language used by Burns. At this moment of action – 'now's the hour' – words have grown almost irrelevant. Bruce offers no elaborate harangue, but a terse statement of the case. He has little to do but point to the scenes unfolding in front of him ('See the front . . .', 'See approach . . .'), and he scorns to downplay the prospect of carnage: 'Welcome to your gory bed'. When he seeks to rouse the spirit of his troops, Bruce points to the voluntary nature of their service:

> Wha will be a traitor-knave?
> Wha can fill a coward's grave?
> Wha sae base as be a Slave?
> – Let him turn and flie: –
>
> Wha for SCOTLAND's king and law,
> Freedom's sword will strongly draw,
> FREE-MAN stand, or FREE-MAN fa',
> Let him follow me. –   (ll. 9–16)

In true civic humanist style, Burns presents the Bruce's soldiers as a virtuous volunteer militia, defending the nation's liberty against the forces of tyranny. The ideal of the active, arms-bearing citizen – the ideal instilled in Burns by Murdoch and Masson – pervades the song. National liberty is seen to depend less on the provisions of government than on the martial exertions of the populace: 'LIBERTY's in every blow! / Let us DO – or DIE!!!' (ll. 23–4).

As Hogg and Noble observe, that concluding exclamation is the tennis court oath of the French Revolutionaries.[49] Burns's treatment of medieval warfare was evidently meant to bear contemporary resonance. As he wrote to George Thomson, the song was prompted by the recollection of Bannockburn and of 'some other struggles of the same nature, *not quite so ancient*' (*Letters*, II, 236). These italics refer, I take it, not only to the French Revolution, but to the struggles of the Scottish reform movement – Burns sent copies of the song to leading Whigs and reformers, including William Robertson of Lude, Patrick Miller and the Earl of Buchan. 'Scots Wha Hae' was written at the onset of the sedition trials of 1793, when Scottish reformism was being forced underground and had begun to move from a constitutionalist to a revolutionary strategy. At a time when insurrection was being mooted, 'Scots Wha Hae' looks back to a prior instance of violent resistance, in which an army of the people vindicated the nation's liberties.

47 *Cato*, p. 18.
48 Paine, p. 54.
49 *The Canongate Burns*, p. 467.

As we now know, thanks to the researches of Patrick Scott Hogg, 'Scots Wha Hae' was not the only poem on a Brucian theme written by Burns at this period. Two further poems, both entitled 'The Ghost of Bruce', were retrieved by Scott Hogg from the *Edinburgh Gazetteer* of 16 July and 24 September 1793.[50] The scenario in each poem is the same. A troubled patriot, walking at night through Bannockburn field, is visited by the ghost of Bruce, risen from the tomb to guard his nation's threatened liberty. In the first poem, Bruce appears in almost god-like guise – 'A Form Divine illumin'd round with fire' (l. 3) – to threaten vengeance on his country's enemies:

> Go tell my Country that the Shade of Bruce
> Is risen to protect her injur'd Rights; –
> To reinstate in splendour, as before,
> Her Liberty near lost – bid her not fear –
> The time approaches fast when Brucian fire
> Shall slash destruction on her perjur'd foes.   (ll. 17–22)

In the second poem, Bruce once again arises to console the patriot speaker and to prophesy that freedom will be saved:

> I WHO erwhile the Ghost of far-fam'd Bruce
> Bade aft the dread and eke the joy to see,
> Alone went wandering through his laurel'd field
> The other night, revolving all the ills,
> Our country has endur'd from P[it]t, D[unda]s,
> And all their Pension'd Slaves – Curse of our Isle.
> O'erwhelm'd with grief, and bursting into tears,
> I cried, Indignant, 'Oh! dear Native land!'
> 'My country!' 'Is there not some chosen curse.
> Some hidden thunder in the stores of Heaven,
> Red with uncommon wrath to blast the men
> Who owe their greatness to their Country's ruin!'
> Scarce had I spoke, when, thick, involv'd in mist,
> More awful and more grand than former fire,
> The Chief of Men, great minded Bruce appear'd.
> 'Cheer up your heart, my Son; why grieve you so:
> Your Country in her breast still carries Bruce,
> And ne'er shall be enslav'd . . . '   (ll. 1–18)

As Hogg and Noble point out,[51] the speaker's anguished cry is adapted from a passage in the opening scene of Addison's *Cato*:

---

50 *The Canongate Burns*, pp. 464, 469.
51 *The Canongate Burns*, p. 470.

> Oh *Portious*, is there not some chosen Curse,
> Some hidden Thunder in the Stores of Heav'n,
> Red with uncommon Wrath, to blast the Man
> Who owes his Greatness to his Country's Ruin?[52]

We might add that the scenario of the 'Ghost of Bruce' poems recalls another Whiggish drama, Thomson's *Alfred*, and the scene in which a hermit, walking alone in nocturnal meditation, receives a vision of Britain's future glory, 'when th' impatient arm / Of liberty, invincible, shall scourge / The tyrants of mankind'.[53] In alluding so pointedly to Addison and Thomson, Burns is setting up a chain of echoes in which Scotland's contemporary political struggle is connected, not merely to the Wars of Independence, but to republican Rome and the British Real Whigs. Again, we see the radical penchant for parallel and analogy, the tendency to view one struggle for liberty through the optic of another.

What is most telling about the two 'Ghost of Bruce' poems, however, is the extent to which, far from amplifying the sentiments of 'Scots Wha Hae', they sound a rueful counterpoint. The poems are gloomier, less bluffly sanguine than 'Scots Wha Hae'. The change in setting, from the medieval to the contemporary period, and from daytime to midnight, suggests a contrast between ancient virtue and modern degeneracy. Where 'Scots Wha Hae' is an exhortation to action, the speaker of the Bruce poems laments his compatriots' lethargy. His appeal to Heavenly vengeance is a confession of human impotence. No longer aiming to 'DO – OR DIE!!!', the Scots wait passively for deliverance. The figure of Bruce, an inspirational example in 'Scots Wha Hae', has become a godlike redeemer, a deus ex machina. Behind this device lies a dismal admission: the reform movement is broken and can only be saved by divine intervention.

With the middle classes running for cover, or 'Abjuring their democrat doings', as Burns puts it in a late ballad,[54] with the nation at war with the French and with radicalism everywhere under attack, the moment for action had passed. By the end of 1793, in the words of John Brims, 'Reform was dead, and the radicals knew it'.[55] Burns knew it too. Couched in the language of prayers and curses, his letters at this period are full of the impotent anger of the frustrated reformer. Nowhere is this more evident than in his letter of April 1793 to a reform-minded acquaintance, Deborah Duff Davies:

> Good God, why this disparity between our wishes & our powers! . . . Why, amid my generous enthusiasm, must I find myself a poor, powerless devil, incapable of wiping one tear from the eye of Misery, or of adding one comfort to the Friend I love! – Out upon the world! say I; that its affairs are administered

---

52 *Cato*, p. 2.
53 Thomson, *Works*, IV, 223.
54 'The Election: A New Song' (K, 492), l. 27.
55 Brims, 'From Reformers to "Jacobins" ', p. 47.

so ill! – They talk of REFORM – My God! What a reform would *I* make
among the Sons, & even the Daughters of men!

  DOWN, immediately, should go FOOLS from the high places where
misbegotten CHANCE has perked them up . . . (*Letters*, II, 202)

Reform has now become a matter of imaginative projection – a topic for wishful
thinking – rather than a programme to be pursued with any prospect of success.

  In the meantime, the government clampdown continued. In April 1793, Burns
writes to Peter Hill, his genial Edinburgh bookseller, praying that the current
troubles might leave his friend untouched. In June he informs George Thomson
that one of his close friends has not been so lucky: 'a friend of mine in whom I am
much interested has fallen a sacrifice to these accursed times' (*Letters*, II, 218).
'These accursed times' – the phrase sounds a doleful refrain through Burns's letters
of 1793 and 1794.[56] The 'damned Star' (*Letters*, I, 34) dogging Burns's own affairs
had broadened its influence to the nation at large. Burns's sense of futility, his
despair at the prospect of domestic reform movements, is given rather schematic
expression in the 1794 'Ode [For General Washington's Birthday]' (K, 451). Here,
transatlantic liberty and civic vigour confront the political degeneracy of Scotland
and England, as America is hailed as the paradigm of the progressive society:

> But come, ye sons of Liberty,
>   Columbia's offspring, brave as free,
> In danger's hour still flaming in the van:
>   Ye know, and dare maintain, The Royalty of Man.   (ll. 25–28)

But if America remains the land of liberty, there is little to commend either England
or Scotland. The third stanza depicts King Alfred in heaven, surrounded by his
patriot bards, looking down in horror as England sullies her name by joining the
crusade against France:

> Dare injured nations form the great design,
>   To make detested tyrants bleed?
> Thy England execrates the glorious deed!
>   Beneath her hostile banners waving,
>   Every pang of honor braving,
> England in thunders calls – 'The Tyrant's cause is mine!'
>
>   (ll. 34–39)

England has betrayed the glorious heritage of Alfred. As in 'The Tree of Liberty'
(K, 625), where the fruit of freedom 'can not be found, / 'Twixt London and the
Tweed, man' (ll. 63–4), England has turned her back on the good old cause. But if
England is no longer the home of liberty, Scotland has fallen equally far short of her
own libertarian past:

---

56 See *Letters*, II, 233, 278, 280, 337.

Thee Caledonia, thy wild heaths among,
Famed for the martial deed, the heaven-taught song,
   To thee, I turn with swimming eyes. –
   Where is that soul of Freedom fled?
   Immingled with the mighty Dead!
Beneath that hallowed turf where WALLACE lies!
Hear it not, Wallace, in thy bed of death!
   Ye babbling winds in silence sweep;
   Disturb not ye the hero's sleep,
   Nor give the coward secret breath. –
Is this the ancient Caledonian form,
Firm as her rock, resistless as her storm?
Shew me that eye which shot immortal hate,
   Blasting the Despot's proudest bearing:
Shew me that arm which, nerved with thundering fate,
   Braved usurpation's boldest daring!
   Dark-quenched as yonder sinking star,
   No more that glance lightens afar;
That palsied arm no more whirls on the waste of war.   (ll. 44–62)

For England and Scotland, all hope is lost. The shades of their patriot heroes no longer return to their former terrain, as Scotland's king did in the 'Ghost of Bruce' poems. Alfred looks down in disgust, disowning the Englishmen who have tarnished his legacy. Wallace is not even roused from his tomb: his spirit slumbers on, oblivious to his nation's apostasy. The contrast between British decadence and American virtue is reinforced by the title of the poem: whereas Britain's radical icons are half-remembered figures from a distant past, America's patriot hero is a living man. The poem's counsel, then, is one of despair. Like 'Such a parcel of rogues in a nation', it depicts a Scotland whose glory is past and whose future holds nothing but shame and regret: 'Heroic Scotland is dead and gone and with Wallace in the grave'.[57]

Burns sent a copy of the Washington 'Ode' to Mrs Dunlop at the end of June 1794. Within a few days his gloom was deepened when a fresh controversy over his political principles raised once again the prospect of ruin. A certain Captain Dods had taken exception to a drunken Burnsian toast: 'May our success in the present war be equal to the justice of our cause'. Some sort of heated altercation followed. The next morning, a sober and sick-hearted Burns was attempting to repair the damage. He wrote to Samuel Clarke, a local lawyer who had been present at the squabble, begging him to call on every other gentleman in attendance and assure them that Burns meant no disloyalty by his ambiguous toast. The tone is anxious: 'you know that the report of certain Political opinions being mine, has already . . . brought me to the brink of destruction. – I dread lest last night's business may be

57 *The Canongate Burns*, p. 819.

misrepresented in the same way' (*Letters*, II, 301). Clearly Burns felt that if his principles were again to be questioned, his excise superiors might not be so lenient. A poem written around this time, 'Fragment – Epistle from Esopus to Maria' (K, 486), gives an insight into the poet's cowed demeanour, his nervous dread of being denounced to the authorities:

> The shrinking Bard adown an alley skulks,
> And dreads a meeting worse than Woolwich hulks –
> Tho' there his heresies in Church and State
> Might well award him Muir and Palmer's fate.   (ll. 39–42)

As a man and poet for whom 'speaking evil of dignities!' (*Letters*, I, 403) was a cherished sport, who loved to vent his spleen in daring salvoes of satire, Burns chafed and fretted under the restrictions of the times. The coercive loyalist atmosphere, in which every criticism of government was viewed as sedition, in which a man might not pass a remark in the pub without fear of denunciation, wore the poet down. In a letter of late 1794 to Mrs Dunlop, Burns looks forward to the time 'when a man may freely blame Billy Pit, without being called an enemy to his Country' (*Letters*, II, 334). The rather painful irony here is that this is the letter which features the off-hand allusion to the French king and queen that so implacably offended Mrs Dunlop. In describing the murdered royals as 'a perjured Blockhead & an unprincipled Prostitute', Burns may well have been letting off steam, airing his 'Political heresies' in one of the few forums still open to him. Nevertheless, Mrs Dunlop, who not only had four soldier sons but two daughters married to émigré Frenchmen, was appalled. She broke off her correspondence with the poet, only relenting as he lay on his deathbed.

The rupture with his intimate friend and most loyal correspondent was hard for Burns to take. The realisation that not even in his private letters could he express his politics freely without incurring reprisals – this must have wounded Burns deeply. Mrs Dunlop had been his political confidante – 'I have set, henceforth a seal on my lips, as to these unlucky politics; but to you, I must breathe my sentiments' (*Letters*, II, 170) – and yet even she had recoiled from his rebarbative opinions. With the Dunlop estrangement, Burns was nearing the bitter dregs in a cup of disillusion. Already his local reputation was ebbing: middle-class Dumfriesians would cut him in the street, finding a 'Jacobin' gauger beneath their notice.[58] Nor were his Whig patrons faring much better. From Edinburgh came news that Henry Erskine, Burns's 'honored Patron' (*Letters*, I, 77) in 1787, had lost his post as Dean of the Faculty of Advocates to Robert Dundas, having been ousted for chairing a meeting in protest at the 1795 Sedition Bill. Though Burns threw off a mordant ballad on the subject,[59] the incident sapped even further his already depleted morale. In the poetry of his final months, Burns has abandoned all hope of an imminent reformist

58 Carswell, pp. 349, 355; McIntyre, pp. 364–5.
59 'The Dean of Faculty - A new Ballad' (K, 515).

triumph. His political hopes are now focused on an indefinitely deferred future. His best-known political song, 'Is there for honest Poverty' (K, 482), written in 1795, is less a poem than a prayer – it is, in Allan Cunningham's telling phrase, 'a spell against slavery'.[60] Radicalism has become a profession of faith, the millenarian belief in a brotherhood of peace and equality that, *in spite of* everything – 'for a' that' – will come to pass:

> Then let us pray that come it may,
>   As come it will for a' that,
> That Sense and Worth, o'er a' the earth
>   Shall bear the gree, and a' that.
>   For a' that, and a' that,
>   It's comin yet for a' that,
>   That Man to Man the warld o'er,
>   Shall brothers be for a' that.`   (ll. 33–40)

60 *The Works of Robert Burns with his Life*, ed. by Cunningham (1834), in *The Critical Heritage*, p. 412.

CHAPTER NINE

'On Irish Ground': Burns and the Ulster-Scots Radical Poets

The Scotch and Irish, han in han,
Will by each other firmly stan',
Justice then they will demand,
When they speak wi' ane voice in the morning.[1]

As readers and critics, one of our commonest methods of coming to terms with Robert Burns is as a 'political poet'. In the two centuries since his death, writers, scholars and political activists of various persuasions have constructed their own versions of the political Burns. The present book constructs another. Given the accretion of comment over the past two hundred years, it may be worth turning, in this concluding chapter, to the contemporary perspective, to ask how far – and in what ways – Burns figured in his own time as a political poet. In Scotland, where his often locally grounded satire struck home with most immediacy and force, and where his habits, his circle of acquaintance and his political 'indiscretions' were widely known and discussed, Burns could hardly avoid being received as a political poet. In England, too, politics shaped his early reception. Shortly after the appearance of the Kilmarnock edition, Mrs Dunlop was warning Burns that his London readers bridled at his treatment of the king.[2] We know from Lucyle Werkmeister's work on the London press that the Whig opposition in England 'had attempted to adopt Burns as the Party poet',[3] and it is clear that the attraction of Burns for English Romantic poets and critics was partly political.[4] But perhaps the most intense and instructive contemporary engagement with Burns's politics took place in Ireland – and particularly in Ulster. It was in Ireland, of all the nations and regions of the British archipelago, that radicalism possessed the greatest force and momentum. In Scotland and England, the reform movement was effectively

---

1 Anonymous, 'Friendship; or, Wallace's Last Wish', in *The Literary Remains of the United Irishmen*, ed. by R. R. Madden (Dublin, 1887), p. 170.
2 *Robert Burns and Mrs Dunlop*, ed. by William Wallace (London, 1898), p. 113.
3 Werkmeister, 'Robert Burns and the London Daily Press', p. 331.
4 Andrew Noble, 'Wordsworth and Burns: The Anxiety of Being under the Influence', in *Critical Essays on Robert Burns*, ed. by Carol McGuirk (New York: G. K. Hall, 1998), pp. 49–62; *The Canongate Burns*, pp. 203–206.

hamstrung by government intimidation: in Ireland it struggled on to the great conflagration of 1798 and the abortive United Irish Rebellion. The role played by Burns's poetry in the cultural and political life of Ireland during this turbulent period is both significant and unwarrantably neglected. In Ulster, Burns was the inspiration and figurehead for a whole school of radical poets (often writing in vernacular Scots) who attached themselves to the United Irish movement and to its party newspaper, the Belfast *Northern Star*. As Chaucer was to the medieval Scottish makars, so Burns was to the United Irish bards. He was, in many respects, the tutelary poet of radical Ulster.

Burns and Bardic Nationalism

In his recent essay on 'Republicanism and radical memory', Luke Gibbons discusses the 'cult of the bard' in Scotland and Ireland in the later eighteenth century. For Gibbons, the use of bardic personae and imagery in the literature and culture of Scotland and Ireland provides a striking measure of the divergence between the two countries at this period. Essentially, he reads the difference between Scottish and Irish bardicism as the difference between nostalgia and radicalism. In Scotland, an elegiac, backward-looking bardic cult, centred on the figure of Ossian, mourns a Gaelic world which is irredeemably lost – whether that be the third-century world of 'Ossian' himself, or the Gaelic world of James Macpherson, swept away in 1746. In Ireland, by contrast, the bardic vogue is optimistic, forward-looking, politically active. It centres on the relatively recent figure of Turlough O' Carolan, and it underwrites a vigorous nationalist movement:

> While [Scottish] Celticism languished in remote antiquity under the spell of Ossian, the cult of the bard in Ireland shifted from the ancient to the more turbulent recent past, as Turlough O' Carolan (1670–1738), a figure within living memory, became the focus of national sentiment.[5]

Where the Ossianic cult evaporates in Celtic mist, Irish bardic culture condenses into a dynamic political movement, motivating important nationalist projects like the Belfast Harp Festival of 1792, a celebration of Ireland's national music patronised by the United Irishmen. The difference between Scottish and Irish bardicism is the difference between 'the old Celtic notes of melancholia' and the 'new radical chords of memory'.[6]

Now, what is most notable about Gibbons's discussion of 'the cult of the bard' is what it leaves out. On the one hand we have an elegiac Scottish cult of Ossian; on the other the militant Irish cult of O' Carolan. But there was another 'bardic' poet, more recent even than O' Carolan – indeed still alive for most of the 1790s – and

5 Luke Gibbons, 'Republicanism and radical memory: the O'Conors, O'Carolan and the United Irishmen', in *Revolution, Counter-revolution and Union: Ireland in the 1790s*, ed. by Jim Smyth (Cambridge, 2000), pp. 211–37 (p. 225).
6 Gibbons, p. 237.

much more politically relevant that Ossian, who played a significant part in the literary politics of Scotland and Ireland in the 1790s. Robert Burns is an often forgotten influence on 'bardic nationalism' in the late eighteenth century: Katie Trumpener, in her book of that name, barely mentions him. But Burns, as much as Thomas Gray or James Macpherson, shaped literary perceptions of the 'bard'. This chapter considers Burns's impact on a group of Ulster-Scots vernacular poets, but it is worth noting that Burns's Irish influence extends beyond this northern Presbyterian constituency. We can see it, for instance, in Sydney Owenson's classic novel of 1806, *The Wild Irish Girl: A National Tale*. At one point in the novel, Horatio, the young English nobleman who is the book's epistolary narrator, is being tutored in Irish poetry by Glorvina, the accomplished daughter of a Milesian king. Writing to an English friend, Horatio encloses a translation of Irish verse, and introduces the poem as follows:

> Here then is a specimen of Irish poetry, which is almost always the effusion of some blind itinerant bard, or some rustic minstrel, into whose breast the genius of his country has breathed inspiration, as he patiently drove the plough, or laboriously worked in the bog.[7]

It is difficult to read this without the figure of Burns – Henry Mackenzie's 'Heaven-taught ploughman' – hoving into view, and indeed Owenson is echoing Burns's Dedication in the 1787 Edinburgh edition of his *Poems*: 'The Poetic Genius of my Country found me as the prophetic bard Elijah did Elisha – at the *plough*; and threw her inspiring *mantle* over me'.[8] In other words, Sydney Owenson, a writer who shows profound disdain for lowland Presbyterian Scotland and the 'Scottish' parts of Ulster, nevertheless uses Robert Burns as a model for her portrait of the Irish bard.[9]

That Burns was an exemplary 'bardic' figure in this period is not surprising. Unlike Gray and Macpherson, whose bardic poems were exercises in literary ventriloquism, Burns could plausibly claim to *be* a genuine bard, the custodian and exponent of a national vernacular tradition in poetry and song. Despite the fact that, as we have seen, he gained a fairly extensive education, Burns repeatedly emphasises his poetry's debt to an oral culture of Scottish folksong and popular legend, and his commitment to vernacular Scots language. In many of his poems he records national customs and folkways; he writes his poems using the three great national stanza forms of the Scots vernacular tradition; and he works as a collector and adaptor of Scots song. He also, quite explicitly, adopts the bardic role of national political spokesman, speaking out against his nation's wrongs. In a number of early

7 Sydney Owenson, Lady Morgan, *The Wild Irish Girl: A National Tale*, ed. by Kathryn Kirkpatrick (Oxford, 1999), p. 89.
8 Dedication 'To the *Noblemen* and *Gentlemen* of the Caledonian Hunt', from *Poems, Chiefly in the Scottish Dialect* (Edinburgh, 1787); reprinted in Kinsley, III, 977.
9 For Owenson's hostility towards lowland Scotland and Presbyterian Ulster, see *The Wild Irish Girl*, pp. 197–99.

poems – 'A Dream', 'The Twa Dogs', 'The Author's Earnest Cry and Prayer, to the Right Honorable and Honorable, the Scotch Representatives in the House of Commons' – Burns expresses national grievances – 'Scotland an' me's in great affliction' – and lambasts what he views as the misgovernment of Scotland by a corrupt and distant regime. Burns is very much part of a politicised cultural nationalism which developed in response to the 1707 Union, and whose literary manifestations include the poetry of Allan Ramsay and Robert Fergusson, vernacular anthologies like James Watson's *Choice Collection of Comic and Serious Scots Poems both Ancient and Modern* (1706–11), Allan Ramsay's *The Ever Green* (1724) and *The Tea-Table Miscellany* (1724–37), and collections of national music and song like James Johnson's *Scots Musical Museum* and George Thomson's *A Select Collection of Original Scottish Airs*, to both of which Burns contributed.

Nowhere in Ireland was Burns's 'bardic' poetry more enthusiastically received and imitated than among the radical poets of Ulster. A tradition of Scottish vernacular poetry, common to lowland Scotland and the Scots-speaking districts of Ulster, began to assume a renewed prominence in Ulster during the final decade of the eighteenth century. Following the spectacular success of Burns's *Poems, Chiefly in the Scottish Dialect* (1786), a new wave of Ulster-Scots poets emerged in the 1790s. Its members included James Orr, Samuel Thomson, Hugh Porter and James Campbell, as well as the many anonymous or pseudonymous poets who contributed verses to radical newspapers like the *Northern Star*. Scots verse had been written in Ulster prior to the 1790s; but it was in that decade that a new florescence of vernacular poetry got underway, and that a significant body of Ulster-Scots poetry began to be produced. The 1790s was the decade of the Ulster-Scots literary revival.

Despite its centrality to the cultural life of Ulster in the late eighteenth-century, this body of Ulster-Scots poetry remains neglected by scholars, both in Ireland and Scotland. Since the publication of John Hewitt's pioneering anthology of eighteenth- and nineteenth-century Ulster verse, *Rhyming Weavers*, in 1974, Ulster-Scots poetry has attracted little notice.[10] A recent revival of interest in Ulster-Scots language (including the foundation of the Ulster-Scots Language Society in 1992 and the publication of Ulster-Scots dictionaries and a grammar)[11] has gone some way towards bringing the Ulster vernacular poets back into view.[12]

---

10 John Hewitt, *Rhyming Weavers and other country poets of Antrim and Down* (Belfast, 1974).

11 *A Concise Ulster Dictionary*, ed. by Caroline Macafee (Oxford, 1996); James Fenton, *The Hamely Tongue: A Personal Record of Ulster-Scots in County Antrim* (Newtonards, 1995); Philip Robinson, *Ulster-Scots: A Grammar of the Traditional Written and Spoken Language* ([n.p.], 1997).

12 See Michael Montgomery, 'The Rediscovery of the Ulster Scots Language', in *Englishes Around the World: Studies in honour of Manfred Görlach*, ed. by Edgar W. Schneider, 2 vols (Amsterdam, 1997), I, 211–26; Linde Lunney, 'The Nature of the Ulster-Scots Language Community', in *Varieties of Scottishness: Exploring the Ulster Scottish Connection*, ed. by John Erskine and Gordon Lucy (Belfast, 1997), pp. 113–27.

Selections from three of the poets – James Orr, Samuel Thomson and Hugh Porter – have been published in popular editions by Pretani Press,[13] and the same three poets feature in Andrew Carpenter's recent anthology of eighteenth-century Irish verse in English.[14] Nevertheless, these developments hardly amount to a rediscovery of the vernacular tradition, and a more significant cultural datum may well be the total exclusion of Ulster-Scots poetry from the *Field Day Anthology of Irish Writing* (1991). There has, moreover, been little critical work on even the best-known Ulster-Scots poets (Orr, Thomson, Porter),[15] while the wider body of Ulster-Scots newspaper poetry remains almost entirely unknown. This neglect of Ulster vernacular poetry is unfortunate, depriving us of an important window onto the cultural life of the period, and hampering our understanding both of Irish-Scottish radical connections and of the contemporary reception of Robert Burns.

Ulster-Scots Poetry and the Influence of Burns

The clamorous public response which greeted the appearance of Robert Burns's *Poems, Chiefly in the Scottish Dialect* (published at Kilmarnock in 1786) has been abundantly documented – in so far, at least, as it affected lowland Scotland.[16] What is less well known is the enthusiastic reception of Burns's poetry in the Northern counties of Ireland. In the wake of the Kilmarnock volume, Burns appears to have been almost as popular in the North of Ireland as in Scotland. The first edition of Burns's poems outside Scotland appeared in Belfast in 1787, and there were 'sixteen editions of his poems locally printed from 1787 to 1826'.[17] If in England Burns was received as something of a literary curiosity, in Ulster he achieved what one historian calls an 'immense and immediate popularity'.[18] Artisans and farm workers

13 *The Country Rhymes of James Orr* (Bangor, 1992); *The Country Rhymes of Hugh Porter* (Bangor, 1992); *The Country Rhymes of Samuel Thomson* (Bangor, 1992). The series is edited by J. R. R. Adams and Philip Robinson.
14 *Verse in English from Eighteenth-Century Ireland*, ed. by Andrew Carpenter (Cork, 1998).
15 The Ulster-Scots poets are almost entirely overlooked in Mary Helen Thuente's *The Harp Re-strung: The United Irishmen and the Rise of Irish Literary Nationalism* (Syracuse, NY, 1994). See, however, Donald Akenson and W. H. Crawford, *Local Poets and Social History: James Orr, Bard of Ballycarry* (Belfast, 1977); Ivan Herbison, 'A sense of place: landscape and locality in the work of the rhyming weavers', in *The Poet's Place: Ulster literature and society: Essays in honour of John Hewitt, 1907–1987* (Belfast, 1991), pp. 63–75; Herbison, '"The Rest is Silence": Some Remarks on the Disappearance of Ulster-Scots Poetry', in *Varieties of Scottishness*, pp. 129–45.
16 The classic account is Robert Heron, *A Memoir of the Life of the Late Robert Burns* (Edinburgh, 1797), reproduced in Hans Hecht, *Robert Burns: The Man and His Work*, trans. by Jane Lymburn (1936; repr. Ayr, 1986), pp. 257–82.
17 John Hewitt, 'The Course of Writing in Ulster', in *Ancestral Voices: The Selected Prose of John Hewitt*, ed. by Tom Clyde (Belfast, 1987), p. 66.
18 J. R. R. Adams, *The Printed Word and the Common Man: Popular Culture in Ulster 1700–1900* (Belfast, 1987), p. 73.

purchased his poems. Local newspapers featured his work regularly, and even into the early nineteenth century Ulster periodicals such as *The Belfast Monthly Magazine*, *The Strabane Magazine*, and *The Ulster Register* retailed a steady supply of anecdotes and stories relating to Burns.[19] There also grew up a body of tales and anecdotes – probably apocryphal – concerning supposed visits of Burns to Ulster.[20] In the Scots areas of Ulster, as Linde Lunney observes, Burns's poetry 'quickly became almost as much part of the local culture as the Bible or the metrical psalms'.[21] Burns was, in Gramsci's term, a 'national popular' poet in the northern parts of Ireland as well as in Scotland.

That Burns should achieve this success in Ulster is not surprising. The literary verse tradition in Ulster had been 'firmly Scottish in tone' from the beginning of the eighteenth century.[22] In *The Printed Word and the Common Man*, J. R. R. Adams finds that the popular poetry books in eighteenth-century Ulster were the Scottish vernacular classics. Poetry books on booksellers' and chapmen's lists in Ulster were 'exclusively Scottish', and included: Blind Harry's *Wallace* (of which there were Belfast editions in 1728 and 1758); the works of David Lindsay (Belfast edition in 1714); and Montgomerie's *The Cherrie and the Slae* (Belfast editions in 1700 and 1771). For much of the century Allan Ramsay was the most popular author among Ulster-Scots readers, until eclipsed by Burns.[23]

Importantly, Scots verse was being written as well as read in Ulster. As early as 1724, a Strabane broadsheet featured vernacular verses 'by a Northern Bard'.[24] The province's first anthology, *The Ulster Miscellany* of 1753, contained a number of 'Scotch Poems', including the accomplished 'Pastoral Elegy on the Death of Jonathan Swift', a rare instance of densely vernacular idiom being employed in a serious – as opposed to a comic – elegy.[25] At least one of the Ulster-Scots bards, Francis Boyle, had been writing – though not publishing – Scots verses long before the appearance of Burns's Kilmarnock volume.[26] The effect of Burns's success was to galvanise the local Ulster verse tradition. Burns gave this tradition a new credibility, inspiring a new wave of Ulster poets and prompting them to publish their own volumes. For many Ulster poets and readers, then, Burns appeared not as an important foreign poet, but as a

---

19 See, for instance, *The Belfast Monthly Magazine*, 2.10 (31 May 1809), pp. 341–5, 3.12 (31 July 1809), pp. 25–6, 51; *The Strabane Magazine*, September 1800, pp. 413–19, October 1800, pp. 433–36; *The Ulster Register: A Political and Literary Magazine*, 1 (1816), p. 269.

20 A lively debate as to whether or not Burns ever visited Antrim and Down took place in the *Ulster Journal of Archaeology*, 2nd series, 1 (1894–5), pp. 77, 149–50, 231–2, 301.

21 Linde Lunney, 'Ulster Attitudes to Scottishness', in *Scotland and Ulster*, ed. by Ian S. Wood (Edinburgh, 1994), pp. 56–70 (p. 64).

22 Adams, *Printed Word*, p. 73.

23 Adams, *Printed Word*, pp. 72–3.

24 Hewitt, *Rhyming Weavers*, p. 2; 'The Course of Writing in Ulster', p. 66.

25 *The Ulster Miscellany* ([n. p.], 1753), pp. 381–86.

26 Hewitt, *Rhyming Weavers*, p. 6.

great exponent of the shared vernacular tradition: 'Burns, Our Bard', as one Belfast writer described him.[27]

The Ulster-Scots poets influenced by Burns began to publish their own volumes of verse in the 1790s. Samuel Thomson's *Poems, on different subjects, partly in the Scottish dialect* appeared in 1793; James Orr's *Poems, on Various Subjects* in 1804. However, these small volumes of verse, usually published by subscription, are not the only source for the work of the Ulster-Scots poets.[28] Throughout the 1790s, Orr, Thomson and other Ulster poets wrote verses for newspapers, particularly the *Belfast News-letter* and the *Northern Star*. Published under pseudonyms or anonymously, this newspaper poetry was often more politically outspoken than the work published in book-form.

Of the group of Ulster vernacular poets whom Burns directly inspired, the majority came from the Scots-speaking districts of Antrim, Down and Derry, and worked mainly as handloom weavers in the domestic linen industry, or as local schoolmasters. In 'The Course of Writing in Ulster', John Hewitt gives a profile of the Ulster vernacular poets, which reveals how closely their milieu resembles that of Burns: 'The bards, particularly the "Rhyming Weavers", were Freemasons, members of book clubs or reading societies, and often radical and democratic in their politics and liberal in their Presbyterianism'.[29]

From the perspective of Burns scholars, however, the most conspicuous feature of the Ulster poets is their unrestrained bardolatry, which shows just how quickly Burns had become a mythologised, iconic figure. As early as 1791, Samuel Thomson sent Burns a rapturous fan-letter in the form of a verse epistle ('Epistle to Mr. Robert Burns', later published in the *Northern Star*) with a headnote boasting of Burns's delighted response:

> The author of the following Poem, sent a copy of it to MR. BURNS some time ago, who was not only pleased with the compliments it contains, but expressed his admiration of his talents and genius, and requested Mr. THOMSON to accept a present of Books, as a token of esteem from his Scotch friend.[30]

In 1794 Thomson made a pilgrimage to visit Burns. Thomson's friend, the poet Luke Mullan, visited Burns in Dumfries in 1796.[31] Alexander Kemp (who wrote under the pen-name 'Albert of Coleraine') boasted of having 'had the honor of

---

27 'Ode: On the Birth of Burns', by 'J. S.', *The Ulster Register: A Political and Literary Magazine*, 1 (1816), 269.

28 Many of these volumes are listed in J. R. R. Adams, 'A preliminary checklist of works containing Ulster dialect 1700–1900', *Linen Hall Review* (Winter 1989), 10–12.

29 Hewitt, 'The Course of Writing in Ulster', p. 67.

30 *Northern Star*, 18–21 April 1792.

31 Mullan's letters to Thomson discussing this visit to Burns are preserved in the Thomson correspondence held by Trinity College, Dublin, TCD MS 7257. I am grateful to Dr Ian Campbell Ross of Trinity College for alerting me to this correspondence.

[Burns's] intimate acquaintance'.[32] All the Ulster poets, to one degree or another, wrote in the style of Burns, adapting his poems as Burns had adapted those of Ramsay and Fergusson. Burns's nationalist strategies – such as his celebration of native Scottish fare – were transposed into an Irish context, so that Burns's 'To a Haggis' becomes James Orr's 'To the Potatoe', or Burns's 'Scotch Drink' becomes Orr's 'Address to Beer'. The Ulster bards even copied the layout of Burns's texts; a newspaper advert for Samuel Thomson's *Poems* (1793) stated that the volume is 'Printed so as to match BURNS'S POEMS'.[33] When Thomson's 'The Simmer Fair' appeared in the *Northern Star* it was subtitled, 'In the manner of Burns',[34] a phrase which describes much of the Ulster-Scots poetry of the period. Even in the prefaces to their published collections, the Ulster-Scots poets tended to follow the model of Burns's Kilmarnock preface.[35]

In their poetic tributes, the Ulster poets hailed Burns not just as a distinguished practitioner of vernacular verse, but as the paragon of all poets, past and present. Samuel Thomson typifies this hyperbolic praise, when in his 'Epistle to Mr. Robert Burns' he lists Homer, Virgil, Horace, Milton, Young, Gay, Thomson, Shenstone, Goldsmith and Gray as among the poets whom the Ayrshire Bard effortlessly eclipses. In the 'Elegiac Verses' which Thomson composed within a month of Burns's death, he cites the Scots poet as his 'Patron', and again lays claim to a personal friendship:

> Thy hand too, in friendship was given,
> Familiar, my pride and my boast; –
> Now gone, while I murmur to heaven,
> My Poet, my Patron lost![36]

Given their almost religious reverence for Burns, the temptation is to dismiss the weaver poets as a parcel of inept imitators, the kind of poetasters to whom Burns was referring when he wrote: 'my success has encouraged such a shoal of ill-spawned monsters to crawl into public notice under the title of Scots Poets, that the very term, Scots Poetry, borders on the burlesque' (*Letters*, I, 382). But the best of the Ulster poets – Orr, Thomson, Porter – have an intimate understanding not merely of Burns's work but of the whole Scots vernacular verse tradition, and are fully conversant with its genres and metres. Indeed, they often employ the vernacular modes in strikingly original ways. In 'Donegore Hill', for instance, James Orr skilfully exploits the festive connotations of the Christis Kirk stanza – its association with depictions of popular revelry – to suggest the farcically incompetent pre-

---

32 *Belfast News-letter*, 11 September 1797.
33 *Northern Star*, 30 January–3 February 1794.
34 *Northern Star*, 1–5 September 1792.
35 This is true, for instance, of Hugh Porter in his *Poetical Attempts* (Belfast, 1813) and of Andrew Mackenzie, in his *Poems and Songs on Different Subjects* (Belfast, 1810).
36 'Elegiac Verses, On reading the News Papers Account of the Death of the justly celebrated Mr. Burns', by 'S. T.', *Northern Star*, 26–29 August 1796.

parations of the rebel forces for the Battle of Antrim.[37] The result is a work of compelling black humour:

> Now *Leaders*, laith to lea the rigs
> Whase leash they fear'd was broken,
> An' *Privates*, cursin' purse-proud prigs,
> Wha brought 'em balls to sloken;
> Repentant Painites at their pray'rs,
> An' dastards crousely craikin',
> Move on, heroic, to the wars
> They meant na to partake in,
>   By night, or day.

Orr and Thomson, then, are no clumsy poetasters; they are significant, if undoubtedly minor, poets. Their neglect, it seems, has less to do with purported artistic shortcomings than with the tendency to organise the study of poetry along rigidly national lines. And so, the Irish domicile of these poets has put them beyond the attention of Scottish scholars, while their use of Scottish vernacular idiom has encouraged Irish scholars to class them as Scottish. Admittedly, uncertainty over their nationality is shared by the poets themselves; Samuel Thomson, for instance, presents himself as both an Irish and a Scottish patriot:

> I love my native land, no doubt,
>   Attach'd to her thro' thick and thin;
> Yet tho' I'm Irish all without,
>   I'm every item Scotch within.[38]

What needs to be borne in mind is the extent to which the verse tradition we are dealing with is *transnational* (or, in Katie Trumpener's suggestive phrase, 'transperipheral'),[39] a point which a brief consideration of the Ulster poets' subscription lists will help to establish. It is the *Scottishness* of these subscription lists that often proves their most striking feature. Even those Ulster poets who made sparing use of vernacular Scots in their verses (Hugh Tynan, for instance, or Andrew Mackenzie) could count on a large number of lowland Scottish subscribers. Among the subscribers to Hugh Tynan's posthumous *Poems* (Belfast, 1803), almost all those not domiciled in the North of Ireland are Scottish (including, from Edinburgh, one 'Walter Scott, Advocate').[40] The same is true of Andrew Mackenzie's *Poems and Songs on Different Subjects* (Belfast, 1810). Mackenzie's subscription list is in two

37 James Orr, *Poems, on Various Subjects* (Belfast, 1804), pp. 13–17.
38 Samuel Thomson, 'To Captain M'Dougall, Castle-Upton', quoted in Ivan Herbison, 'Oor Ain Native Tung', in *Talking Scots*, a supplement published with *Fortnight: An Independent Review of Politics and the Arts*, 318 (June 1993).
39 Katie Trumpener, *Bardic Nationalism: The Romantic Novel and the British Empire* (Princeton, 1997), p. 17.
40 Hugh Tynan, *Poems* (Belfast, 1803), xv–xxix.

sections. There is a general section, which includes a high preponderance of local Ulster subscribers together with a handful from the rest of Ireland and one or two from London. This is followed by a separate list of Scottish subscribers which, though much smaller than the general list (2 pages to the general list's 23) still runs to almost 150 names, and covers a good range of lowland towns.[41] To the extent that these poets reached a non-Irish audience, that audience was Scottish.

In Ulster as in Burns's Scotland, vernacular poetry was an eclectic cultural form, drawing simultaneously on the resources of a localised folk culture and on contemporary Enlightenment philosophy. On one level, as John Hewitt has emphasised, the vernacular poets were regional writers; their immediate context was the local fraternity of vernacular bards, sustained by the sociable interchange of rhyming epistles. As the young Burns exchanged verse epistles with local Ayrshire poets like David Sillar or John Lapraik, so Thomson, Orr and Porter cultivated a 'sense of craft-brotherhood'[42] through the same medium. Theirs was a poetry rooted in the social life of their locality, dealing with the communal events, the pastimes and customs of their region: the mason-meetings, bull-baitings and wakes in Orr's work; the country dances, Hallowe'en festivals and local fairs in Thomson. A similar concern with locality informs those 'manners-painting' poems of Burns – 'Halloween', 'The Holy Fair', 'The Cotter's Saturday Night' – which concentrate with an almost ethnographic relish on customs, festivals and superstitions of Ayrshire.

This immersion in folk culture, however, did not insulate the vernacular poets from the intellectual currents of the Scottish Enlightenment. For all its folksy 'manners-painting', Burns's *Poems, Chiefly in the Scottish Dialect* is saturated in the idiom of Enlightenment moral philosophy, and is palpably influenced by the concept of 'sympathy' expounded by Adam Smith in *The Theory of Moral Sentiments*.[43] A similar conjunction between the world of the Enlightenment and the world of folk poetry is evident in the work of the Ulster poets. Although he was educated at home by his father, James Orr demonstrates a broad knowledge of contemporary Scottish Enlightenment literature. Orr's *Poems, on Various Subjects* (1804) includes an 'Elegy on the Death of Hugh Blair, D.D.', which adeptly surveys the Edinburgh Professor's religious and aesthetic writings. At one point in this poem, the grieving speaker is visited by the shade of Blair, who voices his hopes for his various writings, reflecting as follows on his *Lectures on Rhetoric and Belles Lettres*:

> "Perhaps my lectures may some genius teach
> "To judge aright of beauty and defect,
> "And, steep sublimity! thy summit reach,
> "Wild, as e'en OSSIAN, though as POPE correct.[44]

41 Andrew Mackenzie, *Poems and Songs on Different Subjects* (Belfast, 1810), pp. 11–36.
42 'The Course of Writing in Ulster', p. 66.
43 Donald Wesling, 'Moral Sentiment from Adam Smith to Robert Burns', *Studies in Scottish Literature*, 30 (1998), 147–55.
44 *Poems, on Various Subjects*, p. 94.

An uneasy yoking of 'wildness' and 'correctness' is indeed a notable feature of much Ulster vernacular poetry. Another of Orr's poems, 'The Thunder Storm', draws heavily on Blair's discussion of sublimity in the *Lectures*. Blair is only one of several Scottish literati to whom allusion is made in Orr's poetry: 'The Vision, an Elegy', was, its subtitle informs us, 'Occasioned by reading Robertson's *History of Scotland*', while Orr's 'Pastoral Elegy' has an epigraph from Home's *Douglas*. These allusions point to the culture of autodidacticism and self-improvement which animated many of the Ulster-Scots poets, a culture reflected in Orr's poem 'The Reading Society', and in Hugh Porter's epistle to his local book club, where we see the local farmers discussing Gibbon and Hume, mulling over current affairs and conducting formal debates. This culture of popular enlightenment recalls Burns's experiences in the Tarbolton Bachelors' Club and his position as treasurer and librarian of the Monkland Friendly Society. Although the *persona* of the untutored rustic was a favourite device in vernacular poetry, then, the poets themselves were no backwoodsmen cut off from the mainstream of Enlightenment thought.

Poetry and Radicalism

The area of Enlightenment culture which most fully engaged the Ulster-Scots poets was the libertarian political philosophy expounded by such key Enlightenment writers as Francis Hutcheson. In A *System of Moral Philosophy* (1755), as we saw in Chapter 1, Hutcheson appeals to the familiar Presbyterian notion of government as a contract or covenant between ruler and ruled. For Hutcheson, government involves: 'a mutual agreement or contract between the governors . . . and the people, the former obliging themselves to a faithful administration of the powers vested in them for the common interest, and the latter obliging themselves to obedience'. When the governors fail to fulfil their side of the bargain, then the people have undoubted 'rights of resistance'.[45] Hutcheson's legacy was taken up by a later Ulsterman, William Steel Dickson. Author of *Scripture Politics* (1793), a manifesto of New Light radicalism which was reputedly more popular than Paine's *Rights of Man* among the radicals of Ulster, Dickson preached that it was 'the duty of teachers to expose . . . the corruption of governments . . . [and] the duty of the people to call for and enforce reform'.[46] For Steel Dickson and the Presbyterian radicals, resistance to tyranny was not just a right but a sacred obligation. A 'Song, in Commemoration of the French Revolution', published in the *Northern Star* in 1792, argues that:

> To be free is a duty man owes the All-wise,
> And he sins, who is tamely a Slave.[47]

The late eighteenth-century reform movements, then, were part of a long-standing

45 *System*, II, 227, 279.
46 *Scripture Politics: Selections from the Writings of William Steel Dickson*, ed. by
    Brendan Clifford (Belfast, 1991), pp. 80–81.
47 *Northern Star*, 27–30 June 1792.

culture of denominational radicalism common to Ulster and Scotland. The common vogue for Burns's poems is itself a symptom of this shared political culture. Burns's egalitarian and democratic sentiments, his outspoken pro-Americanism, his anticlericalism and his depiction of the Westminster government as a 'System of Corruption' (*Letters*, II, 173): all this endeared him to an Ulster Presbyterian audience and to poets like Orr and Campbell who were to participate in the 1798 Rising. So too did Burns's epigram on the Irish Whig renegade Burke, from which I take the title of this chapter:

> OFT I have wonder'd that on Irish ground
> No poisonous Reptile ever has been found:
> Revealed the secret stands of great Nature's work:
> She preserved her poison to create a Burke![48]

The anonymous 'Elegy on the Lately Deceased Mr. Robert Burns, the Celebrated Scottish Bard', which appeared in the *Belfast News-letter* of 8–12 August 1796, praises Burns above all as independent patriot and champion of liberty:

> But still a glorious independent turn
>   Inspir'd by Nature, taught him to abhor
> Mean slav'ry, from his cradle to his urn;
>   Fair Freedom priz'd he more than mines of ore,
>   Until he breath'd his last! alas! and is no more.

James Orr, in his own elegy for Burns, made similar play of the Scottish poet's patriotism and political integrity (as well as his Freemasonic enthusiasm):

> Nane felt the love o' country mair,
> Nor wiss't the BRETHREN'S peace an' health;
> For Independence, firm, an' fair,
> He strave as much as fools for wealth.[49]

That the appeal of Burns in Ulster was at least partly political is suggested also by the regular appearance of his poems in the liberal Belfast newspapers. The *Belfast News-letter* was, as it boasted, 'the first in Ireland to introduce the poetical productions of the celebrated ROBERT BURNS to public notice'.[50] More importantly, however, poems by Burns were regularly featured in the 'Muses' Retreat' column of the *Northern Star*, the official newspaper of the United Irishmen. (One of the founders of the *Northern Star* was the Belfast publisher of Burns's *Poems, Chiefly in the Scottish Dialect*, William Magee.)

48 'On Mr. Burke by an opponent and a friend to Mr. Hastings' (K, 478).
49 'Elegy on the Death of Mr Robert Burns, the Ayrshire Poet', *Poems, on Various Subjects*, pp. 9–12.
50 *Belfast News-letter*, 22 August 1800. The *News-letter*'s editor, Henry Joy, seems to have been a Burns enthusiast; among the Burns materials held in the Linen Hall Library in Belfast is a copy of the 1787 Edinburgh edition of *Poems, Chiefly in the Scottish Dialect*, whose title page is inscribed 'Henry Joy, Junior, Belfast'.

Of the two Belfast papers, the *Northern Star* showed greater interest in promoting Burns's explicitly *political* work, a fact which bears witness to that paper's radical agenda.[51] The longer-established *News-letter* was a reformist paper, but one which advocated a decidedly cautious, constitutionalist approach, and whose popularity was strongest in 'areas of Church of Ireland dominance'.[52] Between 1787 and 1800, the *News-letter* printed at least thirteen poems and songs by Burns, including 'The Vision', 'To a Louse' and 'Tam o' Shanter'. Throughout the 1790s, however, the *News-letter* fought shy of printing Burns's more inflammatory political works (although in 1800 it did print two of Burns's most vehemently radical pieces, 'As I stood by yon roofless tower' and 'Kind Sir, I've read your paper through').[53] The *Northern Star*, a more outspokenly radical paper which drew its support mainly from the Presbyterian community, printed fewer Burns pieces than the *News-letter*; only five in all, between 1792 and 1795. Crucially, however, these included two of Burns's most influential political songs: 'Bruce's Address to his Troops at Bannockburn' (*Northern Star*, 21–24 October 1794) and 'Is there for honest Poverty' (*Northern Star*, 19–22 October 1795). With such appearances in the *Northern Star*, and through his general popularity in Ulster, Burns helped to foster the development of an indigenous Ulster-Scots political poetry. From the mid-1790s the *Northern Star* began to feature political satires in the Burns manner: 'An Address to Mr P—tt, in Guid Braid Scotch', for instance, or 'The Gowden Geordie' (both appearing in the issue of 27–30 October 1794). Tellingly, the contributor of these two poems took as his pseudonym 'PADDY BURNS'.

Political Verse in the Northern Star

In the 'Address to Mr P—tt, in Guid Braid Scotch', a lower-class speaker upbraids the British Prime Minister for his vindictive determination to pick a quarrel with Revolutionary France. Though he has cajoled and bribed the monarchs of Europe into going to war with the French, Pitt has achieved nothing but the spilling of blood:

> Ye fleecht or faught your neebers a',
> To rise at ance, an' smash them down:
> To gather them baith great an' sma'
> Ye pait the piper round an' soun.

51 On Belfast newspapers in the 1790s, see A. Albert Campbell, *Belfast Newspapers Past and Present* (Belfast, 1921), pp. 1–5; John Gray, 'A Tale of Two Newspapers: The Contest Between the *Belfast News-letter* and the *Northern Star* in the 1790s', in *An Uncommon Bookman: Essays in Memory of J. R. R. Adams*, ed. by John Gray and Wesley McCann (Belfast, 1996), pp. 175–98; and Kevin Whelan, *The Tree of Liberty: Radicalism, Catholicism and the Construction of Irish Identity 1760–1830* (Cork, 1996), pp. 65–71.
52 Gray, p. 182; Whelan, pp. 67–8.
53 *Belfast News-letter*, 22 and 26 August 1800.

In lanes, an' subsidies an' gifts,
  Ye've sperslet siller fast awa:
Ye tint your skill; for a' your shifts,
  Ye nathing hae but blood to shaw,
        On ony day.

Celebrating France's success against the warmongering 'Bullies', the speaker then reminds Pitt that he will have to answer to God for his tyrannical actions, and should mend his ways while he still has time:

That Sov'reign Pow'r has fixt a day,
  Tho' nane maun ken how late or soon,
Whan a' your actions he'll display,
  An' bring them out as clear as the noon,
        Tremendous day!

Praud Nimrad, *than*, an' Philip's sin,
  O' tyrants a' the bloody gang;
An' ye, an' a' your titled kin,
  Shall mix amang the vulgar thrang.
Think o' the ghasts o' myriads slain:
  Think how the cries o' guiltless blood
Maun rive the murd'rer's heart wi' pain:
O think o' this, an' yet be guid,
        While ye hae day!

This use of a religious idiom to chastise the powerful and recall them to duty is entirely typical of the Presbyterian radicals. What is also significant here is the manner in which Scots vernacular speech functions as an earnest of political integrity. As in Burns's satires, the speaker's independence from courtly standards of speech signals his freedom from courtly corruption.

Again, as in Burns's political satires, several of the *Northern Star* poems are burlesques, in which the poet satirically adopts the viewpoint of his opponent. Perhaps the best of these is a long poem in the Standard Habbie stanza entitled 'A Prayer at the Consecration of a Military Standard', which appeared in the *Northern Star* of 15–19 October 1795. In this poem, a wheedling loyalist churchman prays to the God of War to lead the British troops to triumph over French foes and domestic reformers:

May they defend us frae Night Cats,
An' gar Conventions rin like rats.
May shoals o' graceless democrats
      Swing on a tree;
Their fa' while Scotland celebrates
      Wi' mirth an' glee.

Like Burns's Holy Willie, the speaker mingles rancour and piety as he calls down God's vengeance on the British State's enemies.

A similar burlesque poem, the anonymous 'Proclamation in Guid Scotch Verse', appeared in the *Northern Star* of 1–5 October 1795. Written, like Burns's 'Address of Beelzebub', in octosyllabic couplets, it addresses the Corsicans, condemning them for their support of the French revolutionaries. The speaker praises the benign influence of George III, who 'keeps a fleet to guard your touns / Frae wicked atheistic louns', and indignantly demands to know why the Corsicans now aspire to freedom:

> What ails you now, ungrateful brats,
> To join het headed democrats?

Unless they 'truckle an' be tame', the Corsicans may find themselves tasting another side of British justice; 'Muir's an' Palmer's fate ye'll share'.

The trial of Muir and Palmer was a *cause célèbre* among British reformers of the period, but by 1796 the Ulster radicals had their own political martyrs. In late 1796, in a move partly instigated by the conservative magnate the Marquis of Downshire, the authorities arrested the *Northern Star*'s editor Samuel Neilson, Thomas Russell and other prominent Northern radicals. The arrests prompted a flurry of poetic responses. 'Ye Reptiles a', baith far an' near', which appeared in the *Northern Star* in October 1796, is a heavily Burnsian piece of 'Ironic Satire' against the Marquis of Downshire, which makes extensive use of the vernacular's reductive power, describing Downshire as 'ane big Chiel', 'That Winle Stra o' Newton-airds, / That's ranked now, forsooth, wi' Lairds'.[54] Another piece written in response to the arrests was John Corry's 'The Tears of Liberty! An Ode', published in the *Northern Star* in late 1796, in which the goddess of Liberty vows vengeance on those who would incarcerate her votaries:

> "Now, TYRANNY, my mortal foe,
> 		Presumes my children to oppress;
> I'll lay the fell destroyer low,
> 		And ev'ry Nation's wrongs redress.[55]

The words of 'Liberty' here recall the injunction to 'lay the proud usurper low!' in Burns's 'Robert Bruce's March to Bannockburn' (published in the *Northern Star* of 21–24 October 1794). The direct echoes of Burns here and in other political pieces of the period – in Thomas Russell's 'Erin's Address to Caledonia', for instance, or Paddy Pindar's 'The Contrast' – reinforce the Scottish poet's status as a pervasive poetic influence in 1790s Ulster.

It would be wrong to suggest that the Burnsian or Scots vernacular mode was the dominant one for the political poets of the *Northern Star*. The *Star*'s 'Muses' Retreat' column contained work from an eclectic range of literary traditions –

54 *Northern Star*, 10–14 October, 1796.
55 *Northern Star*, 31 October–4 November, 1796.

English, Anglo-Irish, Gaelic (in translation), and Scottish – and in a variety of modes ranging from ode to verse fable to ballad.[56] Nor was the verse in the *Northern Star* exclusively political; pastorals, love lyrics and temperance songs were also featured, though to a lesser degree than the political material. However, it is worth pointing out that several of the writers who contributed neoclassical English items to the *Star* (including Luke Mullan and Samuel Thomson) also submitted vernacular verses. Moreover, several of the standard English poems – most notably James Glass's 'The Irish Bard' – were written in a 'bardic' mode which owed quite as much to Burns as to Thomas Gray or James Macpherson. Even the 'English' verse in the *Star*, then, confirms Burns's position as a central influence on Ulster's radical poets

And it was precisely because Burns was such an important figurehead to the Ulster political poets, that their disillusion was great when, following the Excise Board enquiry into his political conduct in the winter of 1792/93, Burns appeared to have weakened his commitment to the radical cause. Something of the bitterness which the young Romantic poets felt towards Wordsworth can be discerned in the response, particularly, to Burns's anti-French ballad, 'The Dumfries Volunteers' (K, 484), published in the *Edinburgh Courant* on 4 May, the *Dumfries Journal* on 5 May and the *Caledonian Mercury* on 7 May 1795.

The 'Dumfries Volunteers' Controversy

'The Dumfries Volunteers' was written as an anthem for the local volunteer militia to which Burns belonged, and which had been raised in 1795 amid fears of French invasion. Burns was proud of the song: he arranged for James Johnson to print up copies which were presumably then distributed to members of the corps. Set to the blustering, breezy tune of 'Push about the jorum', the song voices a swaggering defiance of 'haughty Gaul' (l. 1). Burns calls upon patriotic Britons to defend the constitution, however imperfect it may be, and to unite in resisting the 'Foreign Foe' (l. 7):

> DOES haughty Gaul invasion threat,
>   Then let the louns bewaure, Sir,
> There's WOODEN WALLS upon our seas,
>   And VOLUNTEERS on shore, Sir:
> The *Nith* shall run to *Corsincon*,
>   And *Criffell* sink in *Solway*,
> E'er we permit a Foreign Foe
>   On British ground to rally.
>
> O, let us not, like snarling tykes,
>   In wrangling be divided,

---

56 See Thuente, pp. 89–106, for a discussion of the generic and stylistic range of poetry and song printed in the *Northern Star*.

Till, slap! come in an *unco loun*,
  And wi' a rung decide it!
Be BRITAIN still to BRITAIN true,
  Amang oursels united;
For never but by British hands
  Must British wrongs be righted.

The *kettle* o' the Kirk and State,
  Perhaps a clout may fail in 't;
But deil a foreign tinkler-loun
  Shall ever ca' a nail in 't:
Our FATHERS' BLUDE the *kettle* bought,
  And wha wad dare to spoil it,
By Heavens, the sacreligious dog
  Shall fuel be to boil it!

The wretch that would a *Tyrant* own,
  And the wretch, his true-sworn brother,
Who'd set the *Mob* above the *Throne*,
  May they be damn'd together!
Who will not sing, GOD SAVE THE KING,
  Shall hang as high's the steeple:
But while we sing, GOD SAVE THE KING,
  We'll ne'er forget THE PEOPLE!
Fal de ral &c.

There are sentiments here which sit uneasily with some of Burns's previous works –
with the anti-monarchical satire of 'A Dream', for instance, or the gleeful
Francophilia of 'Why should na poor folk mowe' – and it seemed to many observers
that Burns had recanted his earlier radicalism. Certainly, the note of coercive
loyalism – 'Who will not sing, GOD SAVE THE KING, / Shall hang as high's the
steeple' – is unwonted, and perhaps even hypocritical, if it is true that Burns himself
once sat through that political hymn in behatted silence at the Dumfries theatre.[57]

Nevertheless, the song's central theme of resistance to putative French invaders is
not in itself inconsistent with Burns's radical politics. The prospect of being
'liberated' by foreign arms is not one which anyone imbued with civic humanist
principles could relish. From a civic perspective, liberation by foreign arms is a
contradiction in terms. Liberty is maintained by active exertion in the cause of one's
country; it cannot be secured by proxy. To permit a foreign army to rally on one's
native soil would be a reversal of natural order, as the river imagery in verse one
indicates. This does not mean that Burns now happily supports the Allied war
against France. His scorn for 'these glorious Crusaders, the Allies' who wish to 'set
our modern Orpheus at liberty from the savage thraldom of Democratic Discords'

57 McIntyre, p. 323.

(*Letters*, II, 302) is complete, as several anti-war songs demonstrate.[58] Still, if it is a mistake to imagine that the Allies can force France to be free, then the reverse proposition is equally flawed. The armies of the republic cannot do the work of the Scottish and English reformers. It is only Britons who can legitimately remedy the acknowledged defects of their constitution: 'For never but by British hands / Must British wrongs be righted' (ll. 15–16).

'The Dumfries Volunteers', then, is completely consistent with the Real Whig ethos of British radicalism, a point Burns makes rather neatly through some pointed echoes of Joseph Addison. Not only is the phrase 'haughty Gaul' (l. 1), as noted in Chapter 2, lifted from Addison's 'The Campaign', but the reference to the 'wretch that would a *Tyrant* own' (l. 25) is derived from a passage in Addison's *Cato*, when the hero spurns submission to Caesar:

> Would *Lucius* have me live to Swell the Number
> Of *Caesar*'s Slaves, or by a base Submission
> Give up the Cause of *Rome*, and own a Tyrant?[59]

In echoing the great British Whig writer in his own critique of France, Burns is reminding his readers that liberty was not invented by Mirabeau and Danton, that there are indigenous traditions of radicalism that Britons still ought to admire.

'The Dumfries Volunteers', I would argue, has been poorly served by critics of Burns, its 'patriotic but still radical mood'[60] too often misread as vulgar loyalism. Partly this is a question of careless reading, but it also has to do with misguided notions of the organisation itself. It is often wrongly assumed that Volunteering was the preserve of fanatical church-and-king loyalists and that the Royal Dumfries Volunteers was to all intents and purposes the paramilitary wing of the Dumfries Tory party. It was, in fact, nothing of the sort. Local radicals – including Burns, Syme and Mundell – were among the first to join its ranks, and they often attended with greater punctuality and regularity than some of their more conservative brethren.[61] For the 'Sons of Sedition' (as Burns and his Dumfries cronies were dubbed by their political opponents), there was nothing obnoxious in Volunteering. The Volunteer companies were independent citizen militia in the true civic humanist style. They were not controlled by government. They provided their own arms and uniforms and embodied the old ideal of the active, arms-bearing citizen: officers were elected by the members, and each company was regulated by a committee.[62] Indeed, for these reasons, volunteer militia were viewed with some suspicion by government: as recently as the 1780s the British state had been too

---

58 See 'When wild War's deadly Blast was blawn' (K, 406), 'Logan Braes' (K, 409) and 'As I Stood By Yon Roofless Tower' (K, 555).
59 *Cato*, p. 51.
60 Crawford, *Burns*, p. 237.
61 McIntyre, pp. 377, 385.
62 Gavin Sprott, *Robert Burns, Pride and Passion: The Life, Times and Legacy* (Edinburgh, 1996), pp. 106–7.

nervous to countenance the formation of a Scottish militia, a grievance to which Burns gave angry voice in 'The Author's Earnest Cry and Prayer'. Nor were the fears of the authorities wholly unfounded: the experience of Volunteering in 1780s Ireland had shown how companies formed to resist foreign invasion could very easily become a force in domestic politics, using their muscle to wring reforms and concessions from the government.[63]

Be that as it may, there were those among the radicals of Ireland who were less than impressed by Burns's volunteering ballad. In fact, the contrasting treatment of the song by the two Belfast newspapers gives an insight into the divergence between moderate and radical opinion in Ulster, and also points up the distance between the radicals of Ulster and their counterparts in Scotland. In its edition of 16–19 October 1795, the *Belfast News-letter* printed 'The Dumfries Volunteers', with a headnote (probably lifted from the London *Oracle*) declaring that 'The following will do equal honour to [Mr Burns's] genius and his principles'. A fortnight later, the *Northern Star* reprinted Burns's song, and followed it with a stinging reply, entitled simply 'Song':

> O Scotia's Bard! my muse alas!
> For you in private blushes!
>   You've dipt i' th' dish wi' slee D[unda]s
> An' prie'd the Loaves and Fishes!
>   When *bare-foot* owre the Ayr-shire hills,
> A rustic ye ran chanting,
>   Ye wadna took a score o' gills
> To hae deav'd us wi' sic ranting.
>
>   The *kettle* o' your *kirk* and *state*
> For which your dads contended,
>   Has been sae ding'd and spoil'd of late,
> I fear it can't be mended!
>   And if a British Tinkler dare
> But shaw his bag and nails, man;
>   O bid the meddling loun beware
> O' shaving and South-Wales man.
>
>   There Muir and Palmer, tinklers good
> As ever Scotia rear'd, man,
>   Were banish'd owre the foaming flood,
> For daring to repair man.
>   Then sith ye canna mak' it staunch,
> Swith fling it out of doors, man.
>   Ye'll get a new ane frae the F—h
> Ane worth a score o' yours, man.

---

63 On Irish Volunteering, see McBride, *Scripture Politics*, pp. 123–33.

> But tent me, much revered Bob,
> You err, and unco far man,
> For *those*, you Burke-like, call the *mob*,
> The very PEOPLE are man.
> So now I sing, God Save the King,
> And Queen to keep him warm, sir;
> But may he high as Haman hing,
> Who dares oppose – REFORM, sir.[64]

With its metrical fluency, its polemical poise and its cutting modulation from the democratic 'man' to the mock-formal 'sir', this is a much more assured and competent piece of work than the Burns song to which it replies. In its central verses the author picks up on the rather vulnerable image of the constitution as a leaky kettle, deftly developing the conceit to expose its essential absurdity. Clearly, for this Ulster poet at least, bardolatry had its limits.

There are further manifestations of the Ulster poets' disillusion with Burns around this period. In 'The Ayr-shire Rose', published in the *Northern Star* of 25–28 May 1795, Samuel Thomson (writing under the pseudonym 'Thomalin') laments what he perceives as a falling off in Burns's powers, the Ayrshire 'rose' having been 'stolen away' by 'Presumptive Wealth' and 'planted on a soil unblest'. An endnote informs the reader that the poem is an allegorical representation of the 'fate of BURNS, *once* the Ayrshire Poet and Ploughman'. The sense of the Ulster poets' alienation from their erstwhile hero has tended to be overshadowed by the eulogies which many of them penned after his death in 1796. But in 1795 the disillusion was palpable and it was, in essence, a disillusion at Burns's perceived *political* apostasy. In some respects, this disillusion had always been on the cards. For the Robert Burns who wrote satirical verses about Members of Parliament and monarchs, and who celebrated the libertarian ideals of the seventeenth-century Covenanters, the tradition of 'Presbyterian radicalism' remained something of an academic pursuit, despite his brush with the authorities during the Excise Board enquiry. For his followers in Ulster, political radicalism was a question of practical as well as intellectual commitment: some of the Ulster bards, like James Orr and Luke Mullan, actually participated in the 1798 Rebellion. Given this disparity, a process of disenchantment was perhaps inevitable, and it mirrored the general disappointment felt by Irish radicals towards their Scottish counterparts, the sense that, as one Belfast United Irish agent put it, 'the Scotch were not possessed of sufficient energy' in the struggle for reform.[65]

---

64 *Northern Star*, 29 October–2 November 1795. The song is headed simply 'Song', and the author is given as 'Lowrie Nettle. Lyle's-Hill. Oct. 26, 1795'. This address - Lyle's Hill near Templepatrick – would suggest Samuel Thomson as the author; however, the Scottish poet Alexander Wilson is known to have used the similar pseudonym, 'Laurie Nettle'.

65 John Simpson, quoted in McFarland, p. 139.

The Ulster poets were wrong to think that their idol had betrayed them. But what their anger and disappointment reveal is the depth of their engagement with Burns's work. They would not be the last of Burns's admirers to seek in his poetry an endorsement of their own political views, but the Ulster poets were among the most intelligent and committed of the bard's political disciples. Others would follow, and not only in the British Isles. Americans, from Emerson and Whitman to Maya Angelou, would cherish Burns as the heroic singer of individual freedom and the dignity of man. Russians, enthused by Marshak's translations, would celebrate Burns as the working-class embodiment of the Soviet ideal. Domestically, too, Burns would be cited by political parties of every persuasion and invoked at critical junctures of the nation's political life, from Gladstone's Midlothian campaign to the opening of the new Scottish Parliament. For Edwin Muir, Burns was the archetype of the 'popular' poet, an 'object-lesson in what poetic popularity really means – the prime object-lesson in the poetry of the world, perhaps the unique instance'.[66] We might add that, in many parts of the world, Burns has been the prime instance of the political poet. This has had good effects and bad: if Burns's work has often been appropriated in glib and opportunistic ways, it has also had a currency and relevance denied to most other poets. Ultimately, however, we must try to look beyond the accretions of the years, returning to the poems themselves and to their own immediate contexts. This book will have served its purpose if it has suggested a little of the richness and complexity of Burns's political verse, and if it has conveyed something of what these poems meant in Burns's own time and place.

66 Muir, 'The Burns Myth', p. 10.

Bibliography

Adams, J. R. R., 'Reading Societies in Ulster', *Ulster Folklife*, 26 (1980), pp. 55–64

— *The Printed Word and the Common Man: Popular Culture in Ulster 1700–1900* (Belfast: Institute of Irish Studies, 1987)

— 'A preliminary checklist of works containing Ulster dialect 1700–1900', *Linen Hall Review* (Winter 1989), pp. 10–12

Addison, Joseph, *Cato: A Tragedy, As it is Acted at the Theatre Royal in Drury-Lane, By Her Majesty's Servants* (London, 1713)

Akenside, Mark, *Poems*, 2 vols (London, 1776)

Akenson, Donald, and W. H. Crawford, *Local Poets and Social History: James Orr, Bard of Ballycarry* (Belfast: Public Record Office of Northern Ireland, 1977)

Allan, David, *Virtue, Learning and the Scottish Enlightenment: Ideas of Scholarship in Early Modern History* (Edinburgh: Edinburgh University Press, 1993)

Anon., *Vindiciae, Contra Tyrannos: or, concerning the legitimate power of a prince over the people, and of the people over a prince*, ed. and trans. by George Garnett (Cambridge: Cambridge University Press, 1994)

Ashcraft, Richard, and M. M. Goldsmith, 'Locke, Revolution Principles, and the Formation of Whig Ideology', *Historical Journal*, 26 (1983), pp. 773–800

Bakhtin, M. M., *The Dialogic Imagination*, ed. by Michael Holquist, trans. by Caryl Emerson and Michael Holquist (Austin: University of Texas Press, 1981)

— *Rabelais and His World*, trans. by Hélène Iswolsky (Bloomington: Indiana University Press, 1984)

— *Problems of Dostoevsky's Poetics*, ed. and trans. by Caryl Emerson (Minneapolis: University of Minnesota Press, 1984)

— *Speech Genres and Other Late Essays*, ed. by Caryl Emerson and Michael Holquist, trans. by Vern W. McGee (Austin: University of Texas Press, 1986)

Bentman, Raymond, *Robert Burns* (Boston: Twayne, 1987)

Bishop. I. M., 'The Education of Ulster Students at Glasgow University during the Eighteenth Century' (unpublished master's thesis, The Queen's University of Belfast, 1987)

Blake, William, *The Complete Poetry and Prose of William Blake*, ed. by D. V. Erdman (New York: Anchor, 1982)

Bloom, Harold, ed., *Poets of Sensibility and the Sublime* (New York: Chelsea House, 1986)

Bold, Alan, *A Burns Companion* (London: Macmillan, 1991)

Brecht, Bertold, *Poems: Part Two 1929–1938*, ed. by John Willett and Ralph Manheim (London: Eyre Methuen, 1976)

Brims, John D., 'The Scottish Democratic Movement in the Age of the French Revolution' (unpublished doctoral thesis, University of Edinburgh, 1983)

— 'The Covenanting Tradition and Scottish Radicalism in the 1790s', in *Covenant, Charter, and Party: Traditions of Revolt and Protest in Modern Scottish History*, ed. by Terry Brotherstone (Aberdeen: Aberdeen University Press, 1989), pp. 50–62

— 'From Reformers to "Jacobins": The Scottish Association of the Friends of the People', in *Conflict and Stability in Scottish Society 1700–1850*, ed. by T. M. Devine (Edinburgh: John Donald, 1990), pp. 31–50

— 'Scottish Radicalism and the United Irishmen', in *The United Irishmen: Republicanism, Radicalism and Rebellion*, ed. by David Dickson and others (Dublin: Lilliput Press, 1993), pp. 151–66

Brogan, Howard O., 'Satirist Burns and Lord Byron', *Costerus*, 4 (1972), pp. 29–47

Buchanan, George, *The Art and Science of Government among the Scots, Being George Buchanan's 'De Jure Regni Apud Scotos'*, ed. and trans. by Duncan H. MacNeill (Glasgow: Maclellan, 1964)

Burke, Edmund, *Reflections on the Revolution in France*, ed. by J. G. A. Pocock (Indianapolis: Hackett, 1987)

Burleigh, J. H. S., *A Church History of Scotland* (London: Oxford University Press, 1960)

Burns, J. H., and Mark Goldie, eds, *The Cambridge History of Political Thought 1450–1700* (Cambridge: Cambridge University Press, 1991)

Burnes, William, *A Manual of Religious Belief, Composed by William Burnes (The Poet's Father), For the Instruction of His Children* (Kilmarnock: McKie and Drennan, 1875)

Burns, Robert, *The Works of Robert Burns*, ed. by James Currie, 4th edn, 4 vols (London: T. Cadell and W. Davies, 1803)

— *Reliques of Robert Burns: Consisting Chiefly of Original Letters, Poems, and Critical Observations on Scottish Songs*, ed. by R. H. Cromek (London: T. Cadell and W. Davies, 1808)

— *The Life and Works of Robert Burns*, ed. by Robert Chambers, rev. by William Wallace, 4 vols (Edinburgh: Chambers, 1896)

— *The Poetry of Robert Burns*, ed. by W. E. Henley and T. F. Henderson, 4 vols (London: Blackwood, 1896)

— *The Merry Muses of Caledonia*, ed. by James Barke and Sydney Goodsir Smith (London: Allen, 1965)

— *The Merry Muses of Caledonia Collected and in Part Written by Robert Burns*, ed. by G. Legman (New York: University Books, 1965)

— *The Poems and Songs of Robert Burns*, ed. by James Kinsley, 3 vols (Oxford: Clarendon Press, 1968)

— *Robert Burns's Tours of the Highlands and Stirlingshire 1787*, ed. by Raymond Lamont Brown (Ipswich: Boydell Press, 1973)

— *Poems, Chiefly in the Scottish Dialect* (Kilmarnock, 1786; repr. Gartocharn: Famedram, 1977)

— *Landscape Poets: Robert Burns*, ed. by Karl Miller (London: Weidenfeld and Nicolson, 1981)

— *The Letters of Robert Burns*, ed. by J. De Lancey Ferguson, 2nd edn, rev. by G. Ross Roy, 2 vols (Oxford: Clarendon Press, 1985)

— *The Scots Musical Museum 1787–1803*, ed. by Donald Low, 2 vols (Aldershot: Scolar Press, 1991)

— *Robert Burns: Selected Poems*, ed. by Carol McGuirk (Harmondsworth: Penguin, 1993)

— *The Merry Muses of Caledonia: A Collection of Favourite Scots Songs, Ancient and Modern; Selected for the Use of the Crochallan Fencibles* ([n.p.], 1799; repr. Columbia, SC: University of South Carolina Press, 1999)

— *Robert Burns: Poems selected by Don Paterson* (London: Faber and Faber, 2001)

— *The Canongate Burns: The Complete Poems and Songs of Robert Burns*, ed. by Andrew Noble and Patrick Scott Hogg (Edinburgh: Canongate, 2001)

Butler, Marilyn, 'Burns and Politics', in *Robert Burns and Cultural Authority*, ed. by Robert Crawford (Edinburgh: Edinburgh University Press, 1997), pp. 86–112

Calder, Angus, 'Missionary Scotland?', *Cencrastus*, 21 (1985), pp. 35–39

Calvin, John, *Institutes of the Christian Religion*, ed. by John T. McNeill, trans. by Ford Lewis Battles, 2 vols (Philadelphia: Westminster Press, 1960)

Campbell, A. Albert, *Belfast Newspapers Past and Present* (Belfast: W. & G. Baird, 1921)

Campbell, J. R., *Burns the Democrat* (Glasgow: Caledonian Books, 1945)

Carpenter, Andrew, ed., *Verse in English from Eighteenth-Century Ireland* (Cork: Cork University Press, 1998)

Carruthers, Gerard, 'A Note on Poems Newly Attributed to Burns', *Burns Chronicle* (December, 1998), pp. 26–8

— 'Alexander Geddes and the Burns "Lost Poems" Controversy', *Studies in Scottish Literature*, 31 (1999), pp. 81–5

Carswell, Catherine, *The Life of Robert Burns* (1930; repr. Edinburgh: Canongate, 1990)

Clark, Ian D. L., 'From Protest to Reaction: The Moderate Regime in the Church of Scotland, 1752–1805', in *Scotland in the Age of Improvement: Essays in Scottish History in the Eighteenth Century*, ed. by N. T. Phillipson and Rosalind Mitchison (Edinburgh: Edinburgh University Press, 1970), pp. 200–224

Clark, J. C. D., *The Language of Liberty 1660–1832: Political Discourse and Social Dynamics in the Anglo-American World* (Cambridge: Cambridge University Press, 1994)

— *English Society 1660–1832: Religion, Ideology and Politics during the Ancien Regime*, 2nd edn (Cambridge: Cambridge University Press, 2000)

Cockburn, Henry, *Memorials of His Time* (1856; repr. Edinburgh: James Thin, 1988)

Colley, Linda, *Britons: Forging the Nation 1707–1837* (1992; repr. London: Pimlico, 1994)

Craig, David, *Scottish Literature and the Scottish People, 1680–1830* (London: Chatto and Windus, 1961)

Cranstoun, J., ed., *Satirical Poems of the Time of the Reformation*, 2 vols (Edinburgh: Scottish Text Society, 1891–93)

Crawford, Robert, ed., *Robert Burns and Cultural Authority* (Edinburgh: Edinburgh University Press, 1997)

— 'Robert Fergusson's Robert Burns', in *Robert Burns and Cultural Authority*, ed. by Robert Crawford (Edinburgh: Edinburgh University Press, 1997), pp. 1–22

— ed., *The Scottish Invention of English Literature* (Cambridge: Cambridge University Press, 1998)

Crawford, Thomas, *Burns: A Study of the Poems and Songs* (1960; repr. Edinburgh: Canongate Academic, 1994)

— *Boswell, Burns and the French Revolution* (Edinburgh; Saltire Society, 1990)

— *Society and the Lyric: A Study of the Song Culture of Eighteenth-Century Scotland* (Edinburgh: Scottish Academic Press, 1979)

Crockett, Gilbert, and John Monro, *The Scotch Presbyterian Eloquence: or, The Foolishness of their Teaching Discovered from their Books, Sermons and Prayers, And Some Remarks on Mr. Rule's Late Vindication of the Kirk*, 4th edn (London, 1719)

Court, Franklin E., *Institutionalizing English Literature: The Culture and Politics of Literary Study, 1750–1900* (Stanford: Stanford University Press, 1992)

Daiches, David, *Robert Burns*, 2nd edn (London: Andre Deutsch, 1966)

Damrosch, Leopold, Jr., 'Burns, Blake and the Recovery of Lyric', *Studies in Romanticism*, 21 (1982), pp. 637–60

Devine, T. M., *The Scottish Nation 1700–2000* (Harmondsworth: Penguin 1999)

Dickinson, H. T., 'Radicals and Reformers in the Age of Wilkes and Wyvil', in *British Politics and Society from Walpole to Pitt, 1742–1789*, ed. by Jeremy Black (Basingstoke: Macmillan, 1990), pp. 123–46

— *Liberty and Property: Political Ideology in Eighteenth-Century Britain* (London: Weidenfeld and Nicolson, 1977)

Dickson, William Steel, *Scripture Politics: Selections from the Writings of William Steel Dickson*, ed. by Brendan Clifford (Belfast: Athol, 1991)

Dinwiddy, J. R., *Radicalism and Reform in Britain, 1780–1850*, ed. by H. T. Dickinson (London: Hambledon Press, 1992)

Donaldson, Gordon, *Scottish Historical Documents* (Edinburgh: Scottish Academic Press, 1970)

Donaldson, William, 'The Glencairn Connection: Robert Burns and Scottish Politics, 1786–1796', *Studies in Scottish Literature*, 16 (1981), 61–79

Dowden, Edward, *The French Revolution and English Literature* (London: Kegan Paul, 1897)

Doyle, William, *The Oxford History of the French Revolution* (Oxford: Oxford University Press, 1989)

Drennan, William, *Fugitive Pieces in Verse and Prose* (Belfast: F. D. Finlay, 1815)

Drummond, A. L., and J. Bulloch, *The Scottish Church, 1688–1843: The Age of the Moderates* (Edinburgh: St Andrew Press, 1973)

Dwyer, John, 'Enlightened Spectators and Classical Moralists: Sympathetic Relations in Eighteenth-Century Scotland', in *Sociability and Society in Eighteenth-Century Scotland*, ed. by John Dwyer and Richard Sher (Edinburgh: Mercat Press, 1993), pp. 96–118

Elliott, Marianne, *Watchmen in Sion: The Protestant Idea of Liberty* (Derry: Field Day Theatre Company, 1985)

Erskine, David Steuart, Earl of Buchan, *Essays on the Lives and Writings of Fletcher of Saltoun and the Poet Thomson: Biographical, Critical, and Political* (London, 1792)

Fairchild, Hoxie Neale, *Religious Trends in English Poetry*, 6 vols (New York: Columbia University Press, 1939–68)

Fenton, James, *The Hamely Tongue: A Personal Record of Ulster-Scots in County Antrim* (Newtonards: Ulster-Scots Academic Press, 1995)

Ferguson, Adam, *An Essay on the History of Civil Society 1767*, ed. by Duncan Forbes (Edinburgh: Edinburgh University Press, 1966)

Ferguson, J. De Lancey, *Pride and Passion: Robert Burns 1759–1796* (New York: Oxford University Press, 1939)

Fielding, Henry, *Joseph Andrews and Shamela*, ed. by Martin C. Battestin (London: Methuen, 1965)

Finlay, Richard J., 'The Burns Cult and Scottish Identity in the Nineteenth and Twentieth Centuries', in *Love and Liberty: Robert Burns, A Bicentenary Celebration*, ed. by Kenneth Simpson (East Linton: Tuckwell Press, 1997), pp. 69–78

Fletcher, Andrew, of Saltoun, *Selected Political Writings and Speeches*, ed. by David Daiches (Edinburgh: Scottish Academic Press, 1979)

Fowler, Richard Hindle, *Robert Burns* (London: Routledge, 1988)

Fraser, W. Hamish, *Scottish Popular Politics: From Radicalism to Labour* (Edinburgh: Edinburgh University Press, 2000)

Frye, Northrop, 'Towards Defining an Age of Sensibility', in *Poets of Sensibility and the Sublime*, ed. by Harold Bloom (New York: Chelsea House, 1986), pp. 11–18

Gibbons, Luke, 'Republicanism and radical memory: the O' Conors, O' Carolan and the United Irishmen', in *Revolution, Counter-revolution and Union: Ireland in the 1790s*, ed. by Jim Smyth (Cambridge: Cambridge University Press, 2000), pp. 211–37

Goldie, John, *Essays on Various Important Subjects, Moral and Divine: Being an Attempt to Distinguish True from False Religion* (Glasgow, 1779)

Goldie, Mark, 'The Roots of True Whiggism 1688–1694', *History of Political Thought*, I (1980), pp. 195–236

— 'The civil religion of James Harrington', in *The Languages of Political Theory in Early-Modern Europe*, ed. by Anthony Pagden (Cambridge: Cambridge University Press, 1987), pp. 197–222

— 'Priestcraft and the birth of Whiggism', in *Political Discourse in Early Modern Britain*, ed. by Nicholas Phillipson and Quentin Skinner (Cambridge: Cambridge University Press, 1993), pp. 209–31

Goldsmith, M. M., 'Liberty, luxury and the pursuit of happiness', in *The Languages of Political Theory in Early-Modern Europe*, ed. by Anthony Pagden (Cambridge: Cambridge University Press, 1987), pp. 225–51

Graham, Henry Grey, *The Social Life of Scotland in the Eighteenth Century*, 2nd edn, 2 vols (London: Adam and Charles Black, 1900)

Gray, Alasdair, 'On Neglect of Burns by Schools and His Disparagement by Moralists and Whitewashers With Some Critical Remarks', *Studies in Scottish Literature*, 30 (1998), pp. 175–80

Gray, John, 'A Tale of Two Newspapers: The Contest Between the *Belfast News-letter* and the *Northern Star* in the 1790s', in *An Uncommon Bookman: Essays in Memory of J. R. R. Adams*, ed. by John Gray and Wesley McCann (Belfast: Linen Hall Library, 1996), pp. 175–98

Hamilton, Henry, *An Economic History of Scotland in the Eighteenth Century* (Oxford: Clarendon Press, 1963)

Harvie, Christopher, 'The Covenanting tradition', in *Sermons and Battle Hymns: Protestant Popular Culture in Modern Scotland*, ed. by Graham Walker and Tom Gallagher (Edinburgh: Edinburgh University Press, 1990), pp. 8–23

Hecht, Hans, *Robert Burns: The Man and His Work*, trans. by Jane Lymburn (1936; repr. Ayr: Alloway, 1986)

Herbison, Ivan, 'A sense of place: landscape and locality in the work of the rhyming weavers', in *The Poet's Place: Ulster Literature and Society: Essays in Honour of John Hewitt, 1907–1987* (Belfast: Institute of Irish Studies, 1991), pp. 63–75

— 'Oor Ain Native Tung', in *Talking Scots*, supplement published with *Fortnight: An Independent Review of Politics and the Arts*, 318 (June 1993)

— '"The Rest is Silence": Some Remarks on the Disappearance of Ulster-Scots Poetry', in *Varieties of Scottishness: Exploring the Ulster-Scottish Connection*, ed. by John Erskine and Gordon Lucy (Belfast: Institute of Irish Studies, 1997), pp. 129–45

Hewitt, John, *Rhyming Weavers and other country poets of Antrim and Down* (Belfast: Blackstaff Press, 1974)

— *Ancestral Voices: The Selected Prose of John Hewitt*, ed. by Tom Clyde (Belfast: Blackstaff Press, 1987)

Hill, Draper, ed., *The Satirical Etchings of James Gillray* (New York: Dover, 1976)

Holmes, R. F. G., *Our Irish Presbyterian Heritage* (Belfast: W. & G. Baird, 1985)

Hutcheson, Francis, *An Inquiry into the Original of our Ideas of Beauty and Virtue* (London, 1725)

— *A System of Moral Philosophy*, 2 vols (London, 1755)

— *Philosophical Writings*, ed. by R. S. Downie (London: Dent, 1994)

Jack, R. D. S., 'Burns and Bawdy', in *The Art of Robert Burns*, ed. by R. D. S. Jack and Andrew Noble (London: Vision, 1982), pp. 98–126

— and Andrew Noble, eds, *The Art of Robert Burns* (London: Vision, 1982)

Jamieson, A. B., *Burns and Religion* (Cambridge: Heffer, 1931)

Johnson, Samuel, *The Lives of the Most Eminent English Poets; with Critical Observations on their Works*, 4 vols (London, 1781)

'Junius', *The Letters of Junius*, 2 vols (London: J. Wright, 1806)

Keith, Christina, *The Russet Coat: A Critical Study of Burns' Poetry and of its Background* (London: Robert Hale, 1956)

Ker, W. P., *Collected Essays of W. P. Ker*, ed. by Charles Whibley, 2 vols (London: Macmillan, 1925)

Kidd, Colin, *Subverting Scotland's Past: Scottish Whig Historians and the Creation of an Anglo-British Identity, 1689–c.1830* (Cambridge: Cambridge University Press, 1993)

Kinsley, James, 'Burns and the *Merry Muses*', *Renaissance and Modern Studies*, 9 (1965), pp. 5–21

Kirkton, James, *A History of the Church of Scotland 1660–1679*, ed. by Ralph Stewart (Lampeter: E. Mellen, 1992)

Lamont, William M., 'The Puritan revolution: a historiographical essay', in *The Varieties of British Political Thought, 1500–1800*, ed. by J. G. A. Pocock and others (Cambridge: Cambridge University Press, 1993), pp. 119–43

Laroque, François, *Shakespeare's Festive World: Elizabethan Seasonal Entertainment and the Professional Stage*, trans. by Janet Lloyd (Cambridge: Cambridge University Press, 1991)

Law, Alexander, *Education in Edinburgh in the Eighteenth Century* (London: University of London Press, 1965)

— 'Scottish Schoolbooks of the Eighteenth and Nineteenth Centuries', *Studies in Scottish Literature*, 18 (1983), pp. 1–32

Lefebvre, Georges, *The French Revolution: From its origins to 1793*, trans. by Elizabeth Moss Evanson (1962; repr. London: Routledge, 2001)

Lehmann, William C., *John Millar of Glasgow 1735–1801: His Life and Thought and his Contributions to Sociological Analysis* (Cambridge: Cambridge University Press, 1960)

Lindsay, Maurice, *The Burns Encyclopedia*, 3rd edn (London: Robert Hale, 1980)

Lonsdale, Roger, ed., *The Complete Poems of Thomas Gray, William Collins and Oliver Goldsmith* (London: Longman, 1969)

Low, Donald A., ed., *Robert Burns: The Critical Heritage* (London: Routledge and Kegan Paul, 1974)

— ed., *Critical Essays on Robert Burns* (London: Routledge and Kegan Paul, 1975)

— *Robert Burns* (Edinburgh: Scottish Academic Press, 1986)

Lunney, Linde, 'Ulster Attitudes to Scottishness', in *Scotland and Ulster*, ed. by Ian S. Wood (Edinburgh: Mercat Press, 1994), pp. 56–70

— 'The Nature of the Ulster-Scots Language Community', in *Varieties of Scottishness: Exploring the Ulster-Scottish Connection*, ed. by John Erskine and Gordon Lucy (Belfast: Institute of Irish Studies, 1997), pp. 113–27

Lynch, Michael, *Scotland: A New History*, 2nd edn (London: Pimlico, 1992)

Macafee, Caroline, *A Concise Ulster Dictionary* (Oxford : Oxford University Press, 1996)

McBride, Ian, 'The school of virtue: Francis Hutcheson, Irish Presbyterians and the Scottish Enlightenment', in *Political Thought in Ireland Since the Seventeenth Century*, ed. by D. George Boyce and others (London: Routledge, 1993), pp. 73–99

— *Scripture Politics: Ulster Presbyterians and Irish Radicalism in the Late Eighteenth Century* (Oxford: Clarendon Press, 1998)

McFarland, E. W., *Ireland and Scotland in the Age of Revolution: Planting the Green Bough* (Edinburgh: Edinburgh University Press, 1994)

McGill, William, *A Practical Essay on the Death of Jesus Christ, in Two Parts: Containing, I. The History, II. The Doctrine, of his Death* (Edinburgh, 1786)

McGinty, Joseph Walter, 'Literary, Philosophical and Theological Influences on Robert Burns', 2 vols (unpublished doctoral thesis, University of Strathclyde, 1995)

McGuirk, Carol, *Robert Burns and the Sentimental Era* (Athens: University of Georgia Press, 1985)

— ed., *Critical Essays on Robert Burns* (New York: G. K. Hall, 1998)

McIlvanney, Liam, 'Robert Burns and the Calvinist Radical Tradition', *History Workshop Journal*, 40 (1995), pp. 133–49

— '"Why should na poor folk mowe?": An Example of Folk Humour in Burns', *Scottish Literary Journal*, 23 (1996), pp. 43–53

— ' "Sacred Freedom': Presbyterian Radicalism and the Politics of Robert Burns', in *Love and Liberty: Robert Burns, A Bicentenary Celebration*, ed. by Kenneth Simpson (East Linton: Tuckwell Press, 1997), pp. 168–82

— 'Robert Burns and the Ulster-Scots Literary Revival of the 1790s', *Bullán: An Irish Studies Journal*, 4.2 (Winter 1999 / Spring 2000), pp. 125–43

Mackintosh, James, *The Miscellaneous Works of Sir James Mackintosh*, 3 vols (London: Longman, 1846)

McIntyre, Ian, *Dirt & Deity: A Life of Robert Burns* (London: HarperCollins, 1995)

Mackay, James, *Burns: A Biography of Robert Burns* (Edinburgh: Mainstream, 1992)

McKenna, Steven R., 'Spontaneity and the Strategy of Transcendence in Burns's Kilmarnock Verse-Epistles', *Studies in Scottish Literature*, 22 (1987), pp. 78–90

Mackenzie, Andrew, *Poems and Songs on Different Subjects* (Belfast: Alexander MacKay, 1810)

MacLaine, Allan H., 'The Christis Kirk Tradition: Its Evolution in Scots Poetry to Burns', *Studies In Scottish Literature*, II (1964–65), pp. 3–18, 111–124, 163–182, 234–250

— ed., *The Christis Kirk Tradition: Scots Poems of Folk Festivity* (Glasgow: Association for Scottish Literary Studies, 1996)

Macpherson, Hector, *A Century of Intellectual Development* (Edinburgh: Blackwood, 1907)

Madden, R. R., ed., *The Literary Remains of the United Irishmen* (Dublin: James Duffy, 1887)

Masson, Arthur, *A Collection of English Prose and Verse, For the Use of Schools*, 4th edn (Edinburgh, 1764)

Mathieson, William Law, *The Awakening of Scotland: A History from 1747 to 1797* (Glasgow: James Maclehose, 1910)

Mee, Jon, 'Is there an Antinomian in the House? William Blake and the After-Life of a Heresy', in *Historicizing Blake*, ed. by Steve Clark and David Worrall (London: Macmillan, 1994), pp. 43–58

Meikle, Henry W., *Scotland and the French Revolution* (Glasgow: James Maclehose, 1912)

Millar, John, *Letters of Crito, on the Causes, Objects and Consequences, of the Present War* (Edinburgh, 1796)

Miller, Thomas P., *The Formation of College English: Rhetoric and Belles Lettres in the British Cultural Provinces* (Pittsburgh: University of Pittsburgh Press, 1997)

Mitchison, R., and L. Leneman, *Sexuality and Social Control: Scotland 1660–1780* (Oxford: Blackwell, 1989)

Montgomery, Michael, 'The Rediscovery of the Ulster Scots Language', in *Englishes Around the World: Studies in honour of Manfred Görlach*, ed. by Edgar W. Schneider, 2 vols (Amsterdam: John Benjamins, 1997), I, pp. 211–26

Moore, John, *Zeluco: Various Views of Human Nature Taken From Life and Manners, Foreign and Domestic*, 2 vols (London, 1789)

Muir, Edwin, 'The Burns Myth', in *New Judgements: Robert Burns: Essays by Six Contemporary Writers*, ed. by William Montgomerie (Glasgow: William Maclellan, 1947), pp. 5–12

Murray, W. J., 'Poetry and Politics: Burns and Revolution', in *Studies in the Eighteenth Century IV: Papers presented at the Fourth David Nichol Smith Memorial Seminar, Canberra 1979*, ed. by R. F. Brissenden and J. C. Eade (Canberra: Australian National University Press, 1979), pp. 57–82

Musgrave, Richard, *Memoirs of the Different Rebellions in Ireland* (Dublin, 1801)

Nash, Andrew, 'The Cotter's Kailyard', in *Robert Burns and Cultural Authority*, ed. by Robert Crawford (Edinburgh: Edinburgh University Press, 1997), pp. 180–197

Nenner, Howard, 'The later Stuart age', in *The Varieties of British Political Thought, 1500–1800*, ed. by J. G. A. Pocock and others (Cambridge: Cambridge University Press, 1993), pp. 180–208

Noble, Andrew, ed., *Edwin Muir: Uncollected Scottish Criticism* (London: Vision, 1982)

— 'Burns, Blake and Romantic Revolt', in *The Art of Robert Burns*, ed. by R. D. S. Jack and Andrew Noble (London: Vision, 1982), pp. 191–214

— 'Burns and Scottish Nationalism', in *Burns Now*, ed. by Kenneth Simpson (Edinburgh: Canongate Academic, 1994), pp. 167–92

— 'Wordsworth and Burns: The Anxiety of Being under the Influence', in *Critical Essays on Robert Burns*, ed. by Carol McGuirk (New York: G. K. Hall, 1998), pp. 49–62

Norbrook, David, '*Macbeth* and the Politics of Historiography', in *Politics of Discourse: The Literature and History of Seventeenth-Century England*, ed. by Kevin Sharpe and Steven N. Zwicker (Berkeley: University of California Press, 1987), pp. 78–116

— *Writing the English Republic: Poetry, Rhetoric and Politics, 1627–1660* (Cambridge: Cambridge University Press, 1999)

O' Toole, Fintan, *A Traitor's Kiss: The Life of Richard Brinsley Sheridan* (London: Granta, 1997)

Orr, James, *Poems, on Various Subjects* (Belfast: Smyth & Lyons, 1804)

— *The Country Rhymes of James Orr: The Bard of Ballycarry*, ed. by J. R. R. Adams amd P. S. Robinson (Bangor: Pretani Press, 1992)

Owenson, Sydney, Lady Morgan, *The Wild Irish Girl: A National Tale*, ed. by Kathryn Kirkpatrick (Oxford: Oxford University Press, 1999)

Ozment, Steven, *Protestants: The Birth of a Revolution* (1992; repr. London: Fontana, 1993)

Paine, Thomas, *Rights of Man*, ed. by Eric Foner (Harmondsworth: Penguin, 1984)

Paulin, Tom, *Writing to the Moment: Selected Critical Essays 1980–1996* (London: Faber and Faber, 1996)

— *The Day-Star of Liberty: William Hazlitt's Radical Style* (London: Faber and Faber, 1998)

Pocock, J. G. A., *Politics, Language and Time: Essays on Political Thought and History* (London: Methuen, 1972)

— *The Machiavellian Moment: Florentine Political Thought and the Atlantic Republican Tradition* (Princeton: Princeton University Press, 1975)

— 'Historical Introduction', *The Political Works of James Harrington*, ed. by J. G. A. Pocock (Cambridge: Cambridge University Press, 1977), pp. 1–152

— 'Cambridge paradigms and Scotch philosophers: a study of the relations between the civic humanist and the civil jurisprudential interpretation of eighteenth-century social thought', in *Wealth and Virtue: The Shaping of Political Economy in the Scottish Enlightenment*, ed. by Istvan Hont and Michael Ignatieff (Cambridge: Cambridge University Press, 1983), pp. 235–52

— *Virtue, Commerce and History: Essays on Political Thought and History, Chiefly in the Eighteenth Century* (Cambridge: Cambridge University Press, 1985)

— 'The concept of a language and the *métier d'historien*: some considerations on practice', in *The Languages of Political Theory in Early-Modern Europe*, ed. by Anthony Pagden (Cambridge: Cambridge University Press, 1987), pp. 19–38

— 'Two kingdoms and three histories? Political thought in British contexts', in *Scots and Britons: Scottish Political Thought and the Union of 1603*, ed. by Roger A. Mason (Cambridge: Cambridge University Press, 1994), pp. 293–312

Pope, Alexander, *The Poems of Alexander Pope: A One-Volume Edition of the Twicken-ham Text with Selected Annotations*, ed. by John Butt (London: Routledge, 1963)

Porter, Hugh, *Poetical Attempts* (Belfast: Simms and McIntyre, 1813)

— *The Country Rhymes of Hugh Porter: The Bard of Moneyslane*, ed. by J. R. R. Adams and P. S. Robinson (Bangor: Pretani Press, 1992)

Ramsay, John, of Ochtertyre, *Scotland and Scotsmen in the Eighteenth Century*, ed. by Alexander Allardyce, 2 vols (Edinburgh: Blackwood, 1888)

Renwick, W. L., *Burns As Others Saw Him* (Edinburgh: Saltire Society, 1959)

Richardson, Samuel, *Clarissa: Or, The History of a Young Lady*, ed. by Angus Ross (Harmondsworth: Penguin, 1985)

— *The History of Sir Charles Grandison*, ed. by Jocelyn Harris, 3 vols (London: Oxford University Press, 1972)

Robbins, Caroline, *The Eighteenth-Century Commonwealthman: Studies in the Transmission, Development and Circumstance of English Liberal Thought from the Restoration of Charles II until the War with the Thirteen Colonies* (Cambridge, MA: Harvard University Press, 1959)

Robertson, John, 'The Scottish Enlightenment at the limits of the civic tradition', in *Wealth and Virtue: The Shaping of Political Economy in the Scottish Enlightenment*, ed. by Istvan Hont and Michael Ignatieff (Cambridge: Cambridge University Press, 1983), pp. 137–78

— *The Scottish Enlightenment and the Militia Issue* (Edinburgh: John Donald, 1985)

Robinson, Philip, *Ulster-Scots: A Grammar of the Traditional Written and Spoken Language* ([n.p.]: Ullans Press, 1997)

Robotham, John S., 'The Reading of Robert Burns', *Bulletin of the New York Public Library*, 74 (1970), pp. 561–76

Roe, Nicholas, *John Keats and the Culture of Dissent* (Oxford: Clarendon Press, 1997)

Roy, G. Ross, *Robert Burns and The Merry Muses* (Columbia, SC: University of South Carolina Press, 1999)

Rutherford, Samuel, *Lex Rex: The Law and the Prince* (London, 1644)

Schwoerer, Lois G., 'The right to resist: Whig resistance theory, 1688 to 1694', in *Political Discourse in Early Modern Britain*, ed. by Nicholas Phillipson and Quentin Skinner (Cambridge: Cambridge University Press, 1993), pp. 232–52

Scott, Mary Jane, 'James Thomson and the Anglo-Scots', in *The History of Scottish Literature*, 4 vols, ed. by Cairns Craig and others (Aberdeen: Aberdeen University Press, 1987), II, pp. 81–99

Scott, William Robert, *Francis Hutcheson: His Life, Teaching and Position in the History of Philosophy* (Cambridge: Cambridge University Press, 1900)

Scott Hogg, Patrick, *Robert Burns: The Lost Poems* (Glasgow: Clydeside Press, 1997)

Sefton, Henry, '"Neu-lights and preachers Legall": some observations on the beginnings of Moderatism in the Church of Scotland', in *Church, Politics and Society: Scotland 1408–1929*, ed. by Norman MacDougall (Edinburgh: John Donald, 1983), pp. 186–96

Sher, Richard B., *Church and University in the Scottish Enlightenment: The Moderate Literati of Edinburgh* (Edinburgh: Edinburgh University Press, 1985)

— and Alexander Murdoch, 'Patronage and Party in the Church of Scotland, 1750–1800', in *Church, Politics and Society: Scotland 1408–1929*, ed. by Norman Macdougall (Edinburgh: John Donald, 1983), pp. 197–220

— and Jeffrey Smitten, eds, *Scotland and America in The Age of the Enlightenment*, (Edinburgh: Edinburgh University Press, 1990)

Shields, Alexander, *A Hind Let Loose: Or, an Historical Representation of the Testimonies of the Church of Scotland* ([n.p.], 1687)

Simpson, Kenneth, ed., *Burns Now* (Edinburgh: Canongate Academic, 1994)

— ed., *Love and Liberty: Robert Burns, A Bicentenary Celebration* (East Linton: Tuckwell Press, 1997)

Skinner, Quentin, *The Foundations of Modern Political Thought*, 2 vols (Cambridge: Cambridge University Press, 1978)

Skoblow, Jeffrey, *Dooble Tongue: Scots, Burns, Contradiction* (Newark, NJ: University of Delaware Press, 2001)

Smith, Adam, *The Theory of Moral Sentiments*, ed. by D. D. Raphael and A. L. Macfie (Oxford: Oxford University Press, 1976)

— *An Inquiry into the Nature and Causes of the Wealth of Nations*, ed. by R. H. Campbell and A. S. Skinner, 2 vols (Oxford: Oxford University Press, 1976)

— *Lectures on Rhetoric and Belles Lettres*, ed. by J. G. Bryce (Oxford: Oxford University Press, 1983)

Smith, Sydney Goodsir, 'Robert Burns and *The Merry Muses of Caledonia*', *Hudson Review*, 7 (1954), pp. 327–49

Smollett, Tobias, *The Expedition of Humphry Clinker*, ed. by Peter Miles (London: Dent, 1993)

Smout, T. C., *A History of the Scottish People 1560–1830* (1969; repr. London: Fontana, 1972)

Snyder, Franklyn Bliss, *The Life of Robert Burns* (New York: Macmillan, 1932)

Sprott, Gavin, *Robert Burns, Pride and Passion: The Life, Times and Legacy* (Edinburgh: HMSO, 1996)

Sterne, Laurence, *The Life and Opinions of Tristram Shandy, Gentleman*, ed. by Graham Petrie (Harmondsworth: Penguin, 1967)

Stewart, A. T. Q., *The Narrow Ground: Aspects of Ulster, 1609–1969* (London: Faber and Faber, 1977)

— *A Deeper Silence: The Hidden Origins of the United Irishmen* (London: Faber and Faber, 1993)

Stewart, Dugald, *The Works of Dugald Stewart*, 7 vols (Cambridge: Hilliard and Brown, 1829)

Stewart-Robertson, J. C., '*Sancte Socrates*: Scottish Reflections on Obedience and Resistance', in *Man and Nature: Proceedings of the Canadian Society for Eighteenth-Century Studies*, ed. by Roger L. Emerson and others (London, Ontario: The Faculty of Education, University of Western Ontario, 1982), pp. 65–79

Stones, Graeme, and John Strachan, eds, *Parodies of the Romantic Age: The Poetry of the Anti-Jacobin and Other Parodic Writings*, 5 vols (London: Pickering & Chatto, 1999)

Strauss, Dietrich, *Die erotische Dichtung von Robert Burns* (Frankfurt am Main: Peter Lang, 1981)

Strawhorn John, ed., *Ayrshire at the Time of Burns* (Kilmarnock: Ayrshire Archaeological and Natural History Society, 1959)

— *The Scotland of Robert Burns* (Darvel: Alloway, 1995)

Swift, Jonathan, *Poetical Works*, ed. by Herbert Davis (Oxford: Oxford University Press, 1967)

Thompson, E. P., *Witness Against the Beast: William Blake and the Moral Law* (Cambridge: Cambridge University Press, 1993)

Thomson, James, *The Works of James Thomson*, 4 vols (London, 1757)

— *The Seasons and The Castle of Indolence*, ed. by James Sambrook (Oxford: Clarendon Press, 1972)

Thomson, Samuel, *Poems, on different subjects, partly in the Scottish dialect* (Belfast, 1793)

— *The Country Rhymes of Samuel Thomson: The Bard of Carngranny*, ed. by J. R. R. Adams and P. S. Robinson (Bangor: Pretani Press, 1992)

Thuente, Mary Helen, *The Harp Re-strung: The United Irishmen and the Rise of Irish Literary Nationalism* (Syracuse, NY: Syracuse University Press, 1994)

Todorov, Tzvetan, *Mikhail Bakhtin: The Dialogical Principle*, trans. by Wlad Godzich (Minneapolis: University of Minnesota Press, 1984)

Trumpener, Katie: *Bardic Nationalism: The Romantic Novel and the British Empire* (Princeton: Princeton University Press, 1997)

Turner, Michael J., *British Politics in an Age of Reform* (Manchester: Manchester University Press, 1999)

Tynan, Hugh, *Poems* (Belfast: J. Smyth, D. and S. Lyons, 1803)

Wagner, Peter, *Eros Revived: Erotica of the Enlightenment in England and America* (London: Secker and Warburg, 1988)

Walker, Graham, *Intimate Strangers: Political and Cultural Interaction Between Scotland and Ulster in Modern Times* (Edinburgh: John Donald, 1995)

Wallace, William, ed., *Robert Burns and Mrs Dunlop* (London: Hodder and Stoughton, 1898)

Warton, Thomas, and Joseph Warton, *The Poems of T. Warton and J. Warton* (Chiswick: Whittingham, 1822)

Weber, Max, *The Protestant Ethic and the Spirit of Capitalism*, trans. by Talcott Parsons (1930; repr. London: Routledge, 1992)

Werkmeister, Lucyle, 'Some Account of Robert Burns and the London Newspapers, with special reference to the Spurious *Star* (1789)', *Bulletin of the New York Public Library*, 65 (1961), 483–504

— 'Robert Burns and the London Daily Press', *Modern Philology*, 63 (1966), pp. 322–35

Wesling, Donald, 'Moral Sentiment from Adam Smith to Robert Burns', *Studies in Scottish Literature*, 30 (1998), 147–55

Weston, John C., 'Robert Burns's Use of the Scots Verse-Epistle Form', *Philological Quarterly*, 49 (1970), 188–210

— 'Robert Burns's Satire', in *The Art of Robert Burns*, ed by R. D. S. Jack and Andrew Noble (London: Vision, 1982), pp. 36–58

Whatley, Christopher A., 'Burns: Work, Kirk and Community in Later Eighteenth-Century Scotland', in *Burns Now*, ed. by Kenneth Simpson (Edinburgh: Canongate Academic, 1994), pp. 92–116

Whelan, Kevin, *The Tree of Liberty: Radicalism, Catholicism and the Construction of Irish Identity 1760–1830* (Cork: Cork University Press, 1996)

Whitman, Walt, *Complete Poetry and Collected Prose*, ed. by Justin Caplan (New York: Library of America, 1982)

Will, William, *John Murdoch: Tutor of Robert Burns* (Glasgow: William Hodge, 1929)

Williams, Raymond, *Keywords: A Vocabulary of Culture and Society*, 2nd edn (London: Fontana, 1983)

Williamson, Arthur, *Scottish National Consciousness in the Age of James VI: The Apocalypse, the Union, and the Shaping of Scotland's Public Culture* (Edinburgh: John Donald, 1979)

Wilson, Alexander, *The Poems and Literary Prose of Alexander Wilson*, ed. by Alexander B. Grosart, 2 vols (Paisley: Alex. Gardner, 1876)

Wilson, Gavin Scott, 'The Verse-Epistles of Robert Burns: A Critical Study', (unpublished doctoral thesis, University of Stirling, 1976)

Wilson, Kathleen, 'Inventing Revolution: 1688 and Eighteenth-Century Popular Politics', *Journal of British Studies*, 28 (1989), pp. 349–86

Witherspoon, John, *The Works of John Witherspoon*, 9 vols (Edinburgh: Ogle and Aikman, 1804–5)

Zwicker, Steven N., 'Lines of Authority: Politics and Literary Culture in the Restoration', in *Politics of Discourse: The Literature and History of Seventeenth-Century England*, ed. by Kevin Sharpe and Steven N. Zwicker (Berkeley: University of California Press, 1987), pp. 230–70

Index